WITHDRAWN

The
Innovation
Journey

The
Innovation
Journey

Andrew H. Van de Ven

Douglas E. Polley

Raghu Garud

Sankaran Venkataraman

OXFORD

UNIVERSITY PRESS

OXFORD
UNIVERSITY PRESS

Oxford University Press, Inc., publishes works that further
Oxford University's objective of excellence
in research, scholarship, and education.

Oxford   New York
Auckland   Cape Town   Dar es Salaam   Hong Kong   Karachi
Kuala Lumpur   Madrid   Melbourne   Mexico City   Nairobi
New Delhi   Shanghai   Taipei   Toronto

With offices in
Argentina   Austria   Brazil   Chile   Czech Republic   France   Greece
Guatemala   Hungary   Italy   Japan   Poland   Portugal   Singapore
South Korea   Switzerland   Thailand   Turkey   Ukraine   Vietnam

Published by Oxford University Press, Inc.
198 Madison Avenue, New York, New York 10016

www.oup.com

First issued as an Oxford University Press paperback 2008

Oxford is a registered trademark of Oxford University Press

Library of Congress Cataloging-in-Publication Data
The innovation journey / Andrew H. Van de Ven . . . [et al.].
      p.   cm.
   Includes bibliographical references and index.
   ISBN 978-0-19-534100-3
   1. Technological innovations—Management.
   2. Industrial management.   I. Van de Ven, Andrew H.
HD45.I5375   1999
658.5' 14—dc21   99-12927

Contents

Foreword

Every day, in our personal and professional lives, we innovate. Nothing matters more to our success and our survival—and yet we struggle with our understanding of the process of innovation. Sometimes it is messy; sometimes it is elegant; usually it is both and more.

Our difficulty in grasping the process of innovation is vexing. Successful innovation brings us joy and confidence and well-being. It generates long-term, sustainable growth. Once we've tasted this wonderful experience, we want to experience it again—but we are frequently confounded. The process is not linear, and it cannot be managed in traditional ways. By following our best practices and instincts, we can generate a Post-it® Note or a valuable new pharmaceutical like imiquimod, or we can hit a dry hole.

At 3M, we experience this frustration every day. We don't like it, but if we did not have our share of failures, we would be concerned that we were thinking and acting too timidly. We embrace thinking that promises to change the basis of competition, and we accept the not-infrequent failures that come with such thinking. This is not to say that we or our competitors are cavalier about failure. To the contrary, we are absolutely certain of our demise if we hit too many dry holes.

Most modern companies now recognize that the best way to increase corporate earnings is through top-line growth, and the best route to top-line growth is through innovation. We understand that innovation can bring growth in good times and bad.

The recognition of the importance of innovation—as a source of growth and of personal satisfaction—has led to an expanding body of literature, much of which only illustrates how ineffable innovation is. This effort by Prof. Van de Ven and his colleagues is something else again; by combining scholarly research with the gritty reality of private- and public-sector innovation, they have made a unique and valuable contribution to this literature of innovation. Their careful descriptions of the unfolding of innovations evoke the emotional highs and lows, as well as the practical steps required to bring something new into the world.

A confession: at 3M, we weren't sure that innovation lent itself to academic analysis. We participated in this effort because we were curious and because we are always eager to add another tool to our box. As one who was actively involved in two of the case studies, I was impressed by the researchers' thoroughness. With the results of their efforts before me, I am delighted to see how accurately they have captured our way of working.

I'm also fascinated by their conceptual model for innovation—the journey along an uncharted river, led by individuals with ill-defined, conflicting, or ambiguous goals, comprising both divergent and convergent behaviors. This description is thoroughly consistent with my experience as one who has pushed and pulled innovation through a large corporate bureaucracy, as a scientist and a manager. And I'm pleased that the authors have chosen to put many of their observations in the context of chaos theory. This will be particularly valuable for those engineers who need a mathematical model to feel comfortable with innovation.

The authors' insightful depiction of the 12 stages of innovation—from gestation through development and implementation—is comprehensive and accurate. I'm certain this breakdown will stimulate thinking among researchers and managers with the restless inclination to innovate. I'm equally certain that it will give them a comforting sense of structure; the river may be uncharted, but much of the process of launching and maintaining an expedition can be known. And the authors provide additional comfort by underscoring that everything can't be known. Planning and preparation take us only so far. If we find ourselves bogged down, banged-up after the rapids, lost—none of this should be surprising. It is all part of the journey that we are taking and that others have taken before us.

All this can only help make the process of innovation more reliable and reproducible in the future. And more enjoyable: the authors' suggestion that we immerse ourselves in the river, trying to maneuver but not control it, is solid wisdom. I'm certain that their efforts will provide guidance and support to those who strike out on their own journeys of innovation, in their professional and personal lives.

April 1999

William E. Coyne
Senior Vice President,
Research and Development, 3M

Preface

The Innovation Journey is a synthesis of our findings and the capstone of a trilogy of books from the Minnesota Innovation Research Program (MIRP). It is a product of seventeen years of research devoted to a basic question, "How and why do innovations develop over time from concept to implementation?" Although numerous papers and books have been written about the management of innovation, this one is different. Most have focused on the antecedents (facilitators/inhibitors) or consequences (outcomes) of innovation. Very few have directly examined how and why innovations actually emerge, develop, grow, or terminate over time. An appreciation of the temporal sequence of events in developing and implementing new ideas is fundamental to managing innovation. Innovation managers and entrepreneurs need to know more than the starting conditions and investments that are required to achieve desired innovation outcomes. They are centrally responsible for directing the innovation process that goes on within the proverbial "black box" between inputs and outcomes. To do this, the innovation manager needs a "road map," a process theory, that explains how and why the innovation journey unfolds and what paths are likely to lead to success or failure.

As we will see, this journey is often highly unpredictable and uncontrollable. As a result, a process theory may never reach the precision to tell managers exactly what to do and how an innovation will turn out. Nevertheless, it may produce some fundamental "laws of innovating" that are useful for explaining a broad class of processes, sequences, and paths that are central to managing the innovation journey. Empirical evidence for such a process theory can make a major contribution to improving the capabilities of managers, entrepreneurs, and policymakers to innovate.

The Minnesota Innovation Research Program began in 1983 with the objective of developing such a process theory. Fourteen research teams, involving more than thirty faculty and doctoral students at the University of Minnesota, conducted longitudinal studies that tracked a variety of new technologies, products, services, and programs as they developed from concept to implementation in their natural field settings. Initial findings were published in *Research on the Management of Innovation: The Minnesota Studies*, edited by Andrew Van de Ven, Harold Angle, and Marshal Scott Poole (Ballinger/Harper & Row, 1989). We reported that "no overarching process theory of innovation has yet emerged from the research program, nor are prospects bright in the near future" (p. 4). However, by documenting the historical and real-time events in the development of a wide variety of innovations, this first MIRP book provided a rich empirical database for subsequent analysis and grounded theory building.

Three reasons may explain why our quest for a process theory was premature when the first MIRP book was published in 1989. First, some of the innovations being studied did not reach their natural conclusions until 1991 (when they were implemented or terminated). Hence, the book was written before we knew the end of the story. Second, we were not sure how to write the story, for we lacked an appreciation of the form and style of process theory (as distinct from variance theory prevailing in the management literature). Third, we also lacked the tools to write a process story, since we were not aware at the time of relatively new methods for analyzing dynamic patterns in the chronological event data that we had collected on innovation development.

As the innovations came to their natural end, our field observations subsided, and we took the opportunity to return to the library (as they say) to more carefully study process theories and methods relevant to our research question. At the time, colleagues often asked, "What is your next new research venture?" They were often surprised by our response: "The same old one." We figured that if it took ten years to collect the data, we deserved at least ten years to analyze and make sense of the data. This included conducting literature reviews, attending conferences, and refining methods for analyzing data on theories and methods for understanding processes of organizational innovation and change.

We explored alternative methods for analyzing our rich qualitative data on the innovation process. We found that while our qualitative data generated many important insights, they were often limited to anecdotes and lacked capabilities to make empirical generalizations and inferences. By search, trial, and error we experimented with various methods that retain some of the sensitivity of the narrative method, yet enabled us to systematically deal with larger and longer event sequence data in order to analyze complex processes and derive testable generalizations. We found it necessary both to extend traditional quantitative methods and to introduce some new approaches for diagnosing nonlinear dynamic patterns in our event sequence data on innovations. While developing these methods we conducted research workshops in 1993, 1995, and 1997 at the University of Minnesota that were attended by fifty to seventy researchers interested in process research methods from universities throughout the United States and Europe. These workshops made us aware of a much larger community of researchers, all of whom were commonly interested in studying processes of organizational change but were searching for methods to do so. Workshop participants encouraged us to document and distribute the process research methods we were developing. This resulted in the second book on MIRP, authored by Marshall Scott Poole, Andrew Van de Ven, Kevin Dooley, and Michael Holmes, *The Study of Organizational Change Processes: Theory and Methods*, published by Oxford University Press in 1999.

While preparing this second MIRP book, we applied the methods in a series of journal-length articles on specific innovation topics. While painful at times, this strategy of preparing journal articles turned out to be very useful for learning from the scrutiny and feedback of peers who served as anonymous journal reviewers of our papers. The papers that emerged from this journal review process laid the basic building blocks for writing this third MIRP book. They provided the discipline of peer reviews to sharpen our thinking and methods for explaining how and why the innovation journey unfolds along several dimensions. These dimensions include process theories of change and development (Van de Ven and Poole, 1995; Dooley and Van de Ven, 1999), learning during the innovation journey (Van de Ven and Polley, 1992; Garud and Van de Ven, 1992; Cheng and Van de Ven, 1996; Polley and Van de Ven, 1996), innovation leadership (Van de Ven and Grazman, 1999), new business startups (Venkataraman and Van de Ven, 1998), the development of interorganizational relationships (Ring and Van de Ven, 1994a; 1994b; Bunderson, Dirks, Garud, and Van de Ven, 1998), and industry-level infrastructures for innovation (Van de Ven and Garud, 1993; Van de Ven, 1993; Van de Ven and Grazman, 1999). Our objective in this third capstone book on MIRP is to synthesize and integrate these reports, speculate about the implications of the collective findings, and advance some wisdom for understanding and managing the innovation journey.

This book is a collective achievement that extends far beyond the authors. It is impossible to recognize our debt and gratitude to many colleagues and organizations that made this work possible. Many organizations and managers of the innovations that were studied by MIRP researchers contributed significantly. Particularly noteworthy are the rich learning opportunities provided by managers of the three cases featured in this book: William Coyne, Robert Oliveria, Keith Wilson, and Paul Rosso of the 3M Cochlear Implant Program; William Coyne, Sheldon Klasky, and Karen Welke of 3M; John Gilmartin and James Bray of Millipore who co-ventured in the Therapeutic Apheresis Program; and John Hake and Robert Schoenecker of Qnetics. They and many others provided unusually intimate access to their innovation activities, not after their completion, but as the innovations were being developed—a degree of access that was essential to observing how the innovation process unfolds in real time. Periodically, innovation managers received feedback on their innovation and participated in workshops on the overall findings that were emerging across all MIRP studies. These workshops offered valuable opportunities to discuss common themes in the innovation journey. As a result, managers and researchers found they share many common experiences and insights they had thought were unique to their situations. The contributions of innovation managers in these feedback sessions and workshops were particularly gratifying, as these innovation managers became research partners rather than passive subjects. Their comments lent numerous insights that pointed to new theoretical directions and served as important "reality tests" of the research findings.

The MIRP studies could not have been undertaken without our fellow research colleagues who conducted the longitudinal studies during the 1980s of the fourteen innovations included in the program. They include the following:

1. Development of 3M cochlear implant program—Raghu Garud, William Roering, and Andrew Van de Ven
2. Development of 3M-Millipore-Sarns joint therapeutic apheresis program—Douglas Polley and Andrew Van de Ven
3. Startup of Qnetics, a new computer company—S. Venkataraman, Roger Hudson, and Andrew Van de Ven
4. Development of Honeywell-Navy torpedo system—Gary Scudder, Roger Schroeder, Gary Seiler, Robert Wiseman, and Andrew Van de Ven
5. Introducing site-based management in public schools—John Mauriel and Karin Lindquist
6. Development of 3M-NASA commercialization of space program—Peter Ring, Gordon Rands, and Andrew Van de Ven
7. Development of safety standards for nuclear power plants—Alfred Marcus and Mark Weber
8. Development of government strategic planning programs—John Bryson and William Roering

9. Development of gallium arsenide integrated circuits—Michael Rappa and Andrew Van de Ven
10. Development of hybrid wheat—Mary Knudson and Vernon Ruttan
11. Dynamics of corporate mergers and acquisitions—David Bastien and Andrew Van de Ven
12. Educational reform in Minnesota—Nancy Roberts and Paula King
13. Innovation in multihospital systems—John Kralewski and Bright Dornblaser
14. Innovations in human resource management—Harold Angle and Marian Lawson.

In addition to conducting their own innovation studies, these MIRP investigators had meetings about each month and worked together from 1983 to 1988 to develop and apply a common research framework and to share their research findings across the wide variety of innovations being studied. We fondly recall the intellectual stimulation and excitement produced by the MIRP team meetings. The MIRP framework and approach to longitudinal data collection are clearly the collective learning experiences of this large interdisciplinary group of scholars.

Many other innovation scholars significantly influenced MIRP's development over the years. In particular, we must recognize the valuable contributions of the late Professor Eric Trist, who was visiting professor at the University of Minnesota in 1983. He participated in the initial critical meetings to establish the research program and continued to be a source of inspiration until his death. We are also indebted to many other colleagues, too numerous to name, for their invaluable feedback on MIRP's methods, research findings, and papers over the years.

Funding to support the research program over the years was provided by grants from the National Science Foundation, Office of Naval Research, Bush Foundation, McKnight Foundation, Sloan Foundation, and University of Minnesota Foundation. In addition, we gratefully recognize research support provided by Allina Health System, 3M, IBM, Honeywell, Control Data, CENEX, Dayton-Hudson, First Bank System, Bemis, Dyco Petroleum, ADC Telecommunications, Farm Credit Services, Hospital Corporation of America, the Federal Reserve Bank of Minneapolis, the Minnesota Agricultural Experiment Station, and the Minnesota Historical Society.

In preparing the book we were ably assisted by the superb professional editing of Laura Young. Her review and copyediting of the entire manuscript improved the clarity and style of presentation tremendously. We feel most fortunate that Herbert Addison and Oxford

University Press has agreed to publish our book. Herb provided us tremendous encouragement, guidance, and support in preparing this work. In his distinguished career as Oxford's executive editor of business books, Herb has made numerous contributions in selecting and publishing major contributions that have advanced the profession of management.

Last, but certainly not least, we are indebted to our families and loved ones. They have shared most in this undertaking and made it an exciting, growing, and enjoyable experience—both personally and professionally.

Minneapolis   A. H. V.
February 1999   D. P.
                                                                                               R. G.
                                                                                               S. V.

The
Innovation
Journey

1

Introduction and Overview

Organizations undertake the innovation journey each time they invent, develop, and implement new products, programs, services, or administrative arrangements. This journey typically includes entrepreneurs who, with support and funding of upper managers or investors, undertake a sequence of events that creates and transforms a new idea into an implemented reality. The events that unfold in this journey from initiation to implementation or termination can vary greatly in number, duration, and complexity. Whatever its scope, the journey is an exploration into the unknown process by which novelty emerges. The process is characterized as inherently uncertain and dynamic, and it seemingly follows a random process (Kanter, 1988; Jelinek and Schoonhoven, 1990; Quinn, 1985). To say that the process is open and dynamic implies that the timing and magnitude of events make the system of actions entrepreneurs take, outcomes they experience, and external context events that occur unpredictable, truly novel, and genuinely a "process of becoming" (Polkinghorne, 1989).

We know relatively little about the emergence of novelty or about the generative process by which innovations develop. Most research, to date, has focused on explaining the implementation and diffusion of already-developed innovations (Rogers, 1995). Management and organizational scholars studying the emergence of novelty are taking two approaches. The first approach views the process as progressing through a series of stages or phases of development. Stage-wise models, such as invention–development–testing–commercialization, are of this nature. The stages are believed to follow each other in a predictable sequential manner, and activities within stages are expected to settle down to an

3

orderly, stable, or cyclical equilibrium. Progress along the journey can be judged by the stage in which the innovation team is. As Gordon and Greenspan (1988) note, "we assume stability because only stable behavior persists; an unstable system in disequilibrium soon explodes and therefore, is only of transient interest" (2).

Stability is achieved through a process of trial-and-error learning (March and Olsen, 1975; Cohen and Sproull, 1991) and sense making (Weick, 1979, 1993; Brunsson, 1982, 1985). That is, people learn by trial and error; they do more of what leads to positive outcomes and less of what produces negative outcomes. These action-outcome relationships can be influenced by the decisions and actions of the innovation team, as well as by external environmental events. This approach is conceptually appealing because it articulates a way in which people can gain intelligence during their innovation journey by reducing uncertainties between actions and outcomes during each stage of the process.

However, most innovation journeys are more complex and uncertain than this model assumes. Starting conditions for an innovation may be uncertain, and events in the development of the innovation may not settle down to a stable or quasi equilibrium. In fact, complex systems theory tells us that all "living systems," including innovative ventures, exist at a far-from-equilibrium state; equilibrium in a living system is death (Dooley, 1997). As a result, attempts to explain and manage the innovation journey with a theory that assumes quasi-stable stages of equilibrium may fail. Our research of a wide variety of innovations has found no support for a stage-wise model of innovation development and no support for a linear (cyclical) model of adaptive trial-and-error learning, particularly during highly ambiguous and uncertain periods of the innovation journey.

The indeterminate nature of the innovation process has led many scholars and managers to adopt a second approach that views innovation as a random process (Cohen, March, and Olsen, 1972; Hannan and Freeman, 1989; Tushman and Anderson, 1986). To say that the process is random is to make one of two assumptions. The first is that the source of innovation is external to the system being examined. As a result, each innovative event represents an independent and equally likely draw from an underlying probability distribution of possible actions. The second assumption is that so many unobservable and/or unidentifiable endogenous factors may affect innovation development that it is impossible to isolate what causes what, leaving statistical and actuarial description the only reliable recourse.

The problem with both of these assumptions is that each leads to an ad hoc explanation of the innovation process that tends to mask important dynamics or assign unwarranted special significance to key exogenous events, particularly when this occurs ex post (Cottrell, 1993).

Furthermore, the randomness assumption provides little intelligence for undertaking the innovation journey. As Koput (1992) argues, if we assume the process is random, then the only way to increase the innovative capacity of an organization is to increase its exposure to a stream of external chance events and "blind" variations (Campbell, 1974). This argument amounts to admitting that the innovation journey is neither predictable nor manageable; "it just happens" (Aldrich, 1979). In other words, turn the organization off to invent and develop innovations, and turn it on to implement and diffuse innovations when they emerge. In this case, our knowledge of management and organization has nothing to contribute to innovation invention and development.

However, the seemingly random process of innovation development may in fact not be random; it may be the result of a nonlinear dynamic system. Advances in dynamic systems theory provide mathematical tools to examine chaos as an alternative explanation of the innovation journey. Dynamic systems theory is a branch of mathematics that can distinguish among five types of temporal patterns that may exist in a time series of innovation development events: fixed (static), periodic (cyclical), chaotic (strange), colored noise (pink, brown, or black), or random chance (white noise) (Morrison, 1991). Innovation scholars have tended to focus on static or cyclical models of behavior and treat other seemingly random patterns as random Gaussian, Poisson, or other forms of "error" distributions that undermine their experiments (Abraham, Abraham, and Shaw, 1990; Tuma and Hannan, 1984).

The way in which nonlinear dynamics may be observed has important implications for understanding the innovation journey. Events along the innovation journey found to reflect nonlinear dynamics call into question some of the most commonly held beliefs about the innovation process and our ability to understand it:

1. Innovation development proceeds in an orderly periodic progression of stages or phases or in a random sequence of chance or "blind" events.
2. Innovative behavior that is unpredictable implies an underlying mechanism of randomness or "many variables."
3. Innovation development processes converge to a common outcome somewhat regardless of their initial condition.
4. The innovation journey occurs in a predictable, cybernetic manner.

Empirically finding that the innovation journey reflects a nonlinear dynamic system forces us to question and reexamine almost all of what we thought we knew about managing innovation. Nonlinear dynamics tells us that the innovation journey is neither stable and predictable nor stochastic and random, that unpredictable behavior does not imply

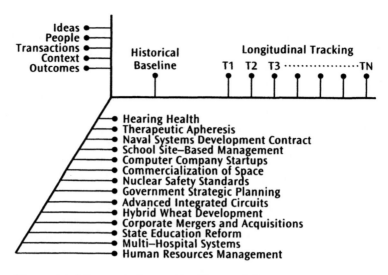

Figure 1.1 Minnesota Innovation Research Program

randomness, that the innovation journey may be extremely sensitive to different initial conditions (path dependence), and that managing the innovation journey may be much more complex than simple cybernetic mechanisms imply. This book explores some of the implications of nonlinear dynamics in the development of the innovation journey.

The Minnesota Innovation Studies

The data on which this book is based come from the Minnesota Innovation Research Program (MIRP), discussed extensively in Van de Ven, Angle, and Poole (1989). This program consisted of longitudinal field studies undertaken during the 1980s by fourteen research teams, involving more than thirty faculty and doctoral students, who tracked the innovations shown in Figure 1.1. They include a wide variety of product, process, and administrative innovations, which MIRP researchers tracked in their natural field settings from concept to implementation or termination.

Although the research teams adopted different methods and time frames that fit the innovations being studied, they used a common framework to compare findings across studies. This framework focuses on five concepts to define the innovation process: ideas, outcomes, people, transactions, and contexts. Specifically, the innovation journey was defined as new *ideas* that are developed and implemented to achieve desired *outcomes* by *people* who engage in *transactions* (relationships) with others in changing institutional and organizational *contexts*. Comparisons of innovations in terms of these five concepts permitted MIRP researchers to identify and generalize overall process patterns across the innovations studied.

Beginning with historical baseline data, these concepts were repeatedly measured using interviews, surveys, site observations, and archival records as the innovations developed over time in their natural field settings. When a change was observed in any one of these five concepts it was defined as an *event*. Recording events as innovations developed was the central task for MIRP researchers. The field studies began in March 1983, as early as access permitted to observe the innovations in their initial conceptual development periods. The studies concluded when the innovations were implemented or terminated. The last field study came to a natural conclusion ten years later, in March 1993, when the innovation was terminated.

We were fortunate to obtain in-depth longitudinal access to different organizations to conduct fine-grained studies of several innovations. In particular, Part II of this book features three detailed studies of innovations in different organizational settings: (1) an internal corporate venture, (2) a joint interorganizational venture, and (3) a new computer software business. Fine-grained studies of these innovations provided opportunities to observe and analyze events as they happened and to apply advanced statistical techniques that revealed patterns not recorded before from field study data of innovation development.

Key Innovation Journey Concepts

Part I of this book develops an empirically grounded model of the innovation journey. As noted, the MIRP studies were undertaken to understand how changes in innovation ideas, outcomes, people, transactions, and contexts unfold over time. Field studies radically altered our initial conceptions of the innovation journey in terms of these five concepts. Table 1.1 compares our initial understanding of the five core concepts when our studies began with what we actually observed. Although the left column may appear naive today, it reflects the mainstream view in the academic and professional literature when our MIRP studies began in 1983.

Conventional wisdom at the time, and often today, treated an innovation idea as a single project that maintained a stable identity during its development. It was assumed that all parties to the innovation share a similar view of the idea. Stakeholders may have differing or opposing viewpoints, but consensus among key members of the innovation team was viewed as necessary. In addition, common views held that the role of innovator was clearly different from other organizational

Table 1.1. Assumptions and observations about core innovation concepts

	Literature implicitly assumes	But we see this
Ideas	One invention, operationalized.	Reinvention, proliferation, reimplementation, discarding, and termination.
People	An entrepreneur with fixed set of full-time people over time.	Many entrepreneurs, distracted fluidly engaging & disengaging over time in a variety of roles.
Transaction	Fixed network of people/firms working out details of an idea.	Expanding, contracting network or partisan stakeholders who converge & diverge on ideas.
Context	Environment provides opportunities and constraints on innovation process.	Innovation process creates and constrained by multiple enacted environments.
Outcomes	Final result orientation; A stable new order comes into being.	Final result indeterminate; Many in-process assessments and spinoffs; Integration of new orders with old.
Process	Simple, cumulative sequence of stages or phases.	From simple to many divergent, parallel & convergent paths; some related, others not.

roles and the people assigned to an innovation team were dedicated to the project as their primary, if not only, responsibility. The network of other stakeholders with whom innovators interacted was also considered fairly stable. The environmental context of the innovation was viewed as a relatively stable source of both resources and constraints during the innovation development period. The innovation process itself was typically seen as unfolding through definable stages (e.g., inception, development, testing, adoption, and diffusion). Progressing through this series of phases or stages resulted in producing an outcome that was clearly interpretable: success or failure.

Our field observations of these concepts disclosed a different reality from these orderly conceptions of the innovation process (Schroeder, Van de Ven, Scudder, and Polley, 1989). As the developmental processes unfolded, we saw innovation ideas proliferate into many ideas. There was not only invention but reinvention; some ideas were discarded as others were reborn. Many people were involved, but most only partially: They were distracted by busy schedules as they performed other unrelated roles. The network of stakeholders involved in transactions was constantly revised. This "fuzzy set" epitomizes the general environment for the innovation, as multiple environments are "enacted" (Weick, 1979) by various parties to the innovation. Rather than a simple, unitary, and progressive path, we recorded multiple tracks and spin-offs, some that were related and coordinated and others that were not. Rather than a single after-the-fact assessment of outcome, we saw multiple, in-process assessments. The discrete identity of the innovation became blurred as the new and the old were integrated.

Thus, early into the research program, we found it necessary to reexamine a number of assumptions that we had held about these core innovation concepts. The field studies led us to adopt the following definitions to conceptualize and study the innovation journey. These concepts provide the general framework for the process model of the innovation journey in Part I of this book.

Innovation Ideas

Whereas invention is the creation of a new idea, *innovation* is more encompassing and includes the process of developing and implementing a new idea. The idea may be a recombination of old ideas, a scheme that challenges the present order, a formula or a unique approach that is perceived as new by the individuals involved (Zaltman, Duncan, and Holbek, 1973; Rogers, 1995). As long as the idea is perceived as new to the people involved, it is an "innovative idea," even though it may appear to others to be an "imitation" of something that exists elsewhere.

Included in this definition are technical innovations (new technologies, products, and services) and administrative innovations (new procedures, policies, and organizational forms). Daft and Becker (1978) and others have suggested keeping technical and administrative innovations distinct. We believe, however, that making such a distinction often results in a fragmented classification of the innovation process. Most innovations involve new technical and administrative components (Leavitt, 1965). For example, Ruttan and Hayami (1984) have shown that many technological innovations in agriculture and elsewhere could not have occurred without concomitant innovations in institutional and organizational arrangements. Moreover, Damanpour and Evan (1984) identified important temporal lags between the rates of adoption of technical and administrative innovations. They found that adopting administrative innovations tends to stimulate adopting technical innovations more readily than the reverse, and that the length of the temporal lag is inversely related to organizational performance. Understanding the close connection between technical and administrative dimensions of innovation ideas is a key part of understanding the management of innovation.

Based on the MIRP studies, and in particular on the detailed case histories of three innovations presented in chapters 8–10, chapter 2 describes the typical sequence of events in which the innovation journey unfolds. The discussion highlights the following dynamics commonly observed during innovation gestation, development, and implementation periods.

1. The innovation journey consists of an accretion of numerous events performed by many people over an extended time. The process does not conform to the Western cultural practice of attributing innovation to the discrete acts of a single entrepreneur on a particular date and at a particular place. In each innovation studied by MIRP, the innovation process began with an extended gestation period that lasted several years, during which a variety of coincidental events set the stage for launching an organizational innovation or change process.
2. Concentrated actions to allocate resources and initiate innovation development are triggered by "shocks," not mere persuasion. These shocks are sufficiently large to trigger the attention and action of organizational participants. When people reach a threshold of sufficient dissatisfaction with existing conditions, they initiate action to resolve their dissatisfaction.
3. When innovation development work begins, the process does not unfold in a simple linear sequence of stages and substages. Instead, it proliferates into complex bundles of innovation ideas and divergent paths of activities by different organizational units. Specifically, after the onset of a simple unitary progression of activity to develop an innovative idea, the process diverges into multiple, parallel, and interdependent paths of activities.
4. Setbacks are frequently encountered during the innovation process because plans go awry or unanticipated environmental events significantly alter the ground assumptions of the innovation. These setbacks signal rejection of the innovation or opportunities for learning through reinvention.
5. Innovation receptiveness, learning, and adoption speed are facilitated when the innovation is initially developed within the user organization and inhibited when end users are provided no opportunities to reinvent, or modify, innovations developed elsewhere. Organizational participants not involved in the development or reinvention of an innovation tend to view it as an external mandate. Regardless of whether an innovation is initially developed inside or outside the organization, the adoption process is facilitated by modifying the innovations to fit the local situations, acquiring extensive top management involvement and commitment to the innovation, and maintaining task completion and momentum throughout the developmental period.

6. Management cannot ensure innovation success but can influence its odds. The odds of success increase with experience and learning from past trials at innovation and decrease with the novelty, size, and temporal duration of an innovation venture. Thus, the odds of success are not only a function of the number of times an organization has undertaken the innovation journey but also the complexity of the journey it has chosen to undertake next.

These observations sketch an overall image of the innovation journey as considerably more complex and fluid than it has been portrayed in the literature by innovation scholars and practitioners.

Innovation Outcomes

Innovation outcomes are conventionally considered to occur after development and implementation of the idea. Kimberly (1981) rightly points out that a positive bias pervades the study of innovation. Innovation is often viewed as a good thing because the new idea must be useful—profitable, constructive, or able to solve a problem. New ideas that are not perceived as useful are not normally called innovations; they are usually called "mistakes." Objectively, the usefulness of an idea can only be determined after the innovation process is completed and implemented. In this sense, it is not possible to determine whether work on new ideas will turn out to be "innovations" or "mistakes" until a summative evaluation occurs after the innovation journey is completed.

Although summative evaluations are of interest to observers, they are not available to the managers and entrepreneurs who are undertaking the innovation journey. These managers and entrepreneurs must rely on interim criteria and subjective assessments to evaluate and guide their progress. MIRP researchers recorded the interim outcome assessments of innovation participants and found that the criteria used by innovation managers and resource controllers shifted over time: They were different in the beginning, converged during the developmental process, and diverged in opposite and conflicting directions as innovation implementation problems arose. Not only did initially nebulous targets crystallize later into more operational criteria, but also the targets themselves were often reconstructed to redirect the innovations. These changes coincided with unanticipated developmental setbacks and problems and shifting organizational priorities, as well as independent environmental events that had "spillover" effects on the innovations.

The fact that outcome criteria shift frequently dramatizes the difficulty of learning along the innovation journey. Most views of adaptive learning begin with the assumption that people act on the basis of their assessments; they do more of what they think leads to success and less of what is perceived to lead to failure. How can learning occur if criteria of success and failure change frequently?

Chapter 3 examines how participants learn while undertaking the innovation journey. Based on quantitative and qualitative longitudinal data across the innovation studies, we found that at different periods of the innovation development process, participants learn by discovery and by testing, and that these different patterns of learning follow different logics: Learning by testing follows a logic of decision rationality, whereas learning by discovery seems to follow a logic of action rationality.

Moreover, in-process assessments of event outcomes are partially a consequence of action and partially a predictor of future actions but often incomplete explanations of actions as innovations develop. These outcome assessments become clear only as developmental progressions stabilize. And even then, although judgments of effectiveness may provide a rational basis for choosing subsequent actions to develop an innovation, unspecified and conflicting priorities or changing frames of reference often produce struggles between innovation managers and resource controllers on the developmental paths of their innovations.

A model of success and failure action loops is proposed in chapter 3 to explain these learning dynamics as innovations develop. Not only does the model explain how innovation outcomes are both a cause and consequence of action, it also acknowledges that outcome attributions can be produced by spurious unknown factors.

One important implication of these findings is that innovation success or failure may be more usefully viewed as "by-products along the journey" than as "bottom-line" results, as they have been viewed in the past. Whereas perceived effectiveness judgments during the innovation process can provide useful rationales for choices of subsequent actions, shifting and conflicting outcome criteria produce compelling opportunities for superstitious learning. Conventional wisdom suggests that one way to avoid these practices is to achieve agreement on goals and criteria among different groups. However, the prevalence of contradictory success criteria found across MIRP studies contradicts this wisdom. It suggests that contradiction and nonlinearity may be inherent in most innovative undertakings.

As a consequence, the central problem in leading the innovation journey may be the management of paradox (Van de Ven and Poole, 1988). As Cameron (1980) found, highly effective organizations were paradoxical because they performed in contradictory ways to satisfy contradictory expectations. This is reminiscent of the way in which ambiguity in official goals is functional for complex organizations (Perrow, 1961), where these goals are kept purposely vague and general (1961) to accommodate the diverse operative goals of various interest groups.

People

Most innovations are too complex for one person to accomplish individually. A group of people needs to be recruited, organized, and directed. As these people associate with the innovation unit, they apply their different skills, energy levels, and frames of reference to the innovation ideas as a result of the backgrounds, experiences, and activities that currently occupy their attention. Mobilizing and directing this innovation team are significantly more complex than molding and directing a single-person venture. Contrary to the view sometimes implicit in the literature that innovation consists of an entrepreneur who works with a fixed set of full-time people to develop a new idea, we observed that many stakeholders fluidly engage and disengage in the innovation process over time as their interests and needs for inclusion dictate.

The focus on people as creators and facilitators of innovation needs to be balanced by equivalent attention to people as inhibitors of innovation. Indeed, much of the folklore and applied literature about innovation management has ignored the research by cognitive psychologists and social psychologists about the limited capacity of human beings to handle complexity and maintain attention. As a consequence, one often gets the impression that inventors or innovators have superhuman creative heuristics or the ability to "walk on water." A more realistic view of innovation should begin with an appreciation of the physiological limitations of human beings, among them a limited ability to handle complexity. They tend to adapt subconsciously and gradually to changing conditions, to overconform to group and organizational norms, and to limit their focus to repetitive activities (Van de Ven, 1986). As a result, the people problem in managing innovation is a leadership challenge of learning what directions to take once the innovation journey has begun. Notwithstanding the best of planning in all the innovations that MIRP studied, we observed the innovation participants to experience numerous setbacks, mixed messages, and unforeseen events that combined to create a highly ambiguous venture that far exceeded human comprehension.

To address this question in the MIRP studies, we focused on key people who were innovation entrepreneurs and top managers or investors. Chapter 4 describes the behaviors and roles of these top managers while their innovations developed from concept to reality. Three common patterns were observed:

1. Many—not one or a few—top managers at different hierarchical levels were actively involved in the development of innovations in their organizations.
2. These top managers performed and often shifted among four roles: sponsor, mentor, critic, and institutional leader. In per-

forming these roles, the managers did not reflect unified and homogeneous perspectives; instead, they held opposing views that served as checks and balances on each other in making innovation investment decisions.
3. They made pragmatic decisions in response to changing innovation conditions and perspectives held by other top managers rather than according to a strategic course of action.

These observed patterns provide the key ingredients for proposing a dynamic view of innovation leadership in chapter 4. This view departs from popular treatments of leadership by arguing that in uncertain and ambiguous situations, organizational learning and adaptability are enhanced by achieving balance between diverse, opposing, and conflicting views among top management decision makers. The common quest —for consensus and support among top managers to a single strategic vision of a leader at the top of the pyramid—may not be effective for dealing with highly ambiguous and uncertain situations. Directing the innovation journey calls for a pluralistic power structure of leadership that incorporates the requisite variety of diverse perspectives necessary to make uncertain and ambiguous innovation decisions.

Although a homogeneous structure of power and leadership is efficient for well-understood tasks, it tends to squelch consideration of diverse and opposing viewpoints that are inherent in ambiguous tasks. Thus, we argue that pluralistic leadership increases the chances for technological foresights and decreases the likelihood of oversights. However, such a pluralistic structure does not ensure intelligent leadership. Instead, it emphasizes that the odds of organizational learning and adaptability increase when a balance is maintained between dialectical leadership roles throughout the innovation journey.

Transactions

As we have just seen, innovation is not the enterprise of a single entrepreneur. Instead, it is a network-building effort that centers on the development of transactions or relationships among people who become sufficiently committed to their ideas to carry them to acceptance and legitimacy. These transactions include a wide variety of relationships:

1. Collegial relationships among peers and hierarchical relationships among superiors and subordinates who engage in developing and managing an innovation.
2. Proposals and commitments to obtain and allocate resources to the innovation and its subcomponents.
3. Quid pro quo arrangements with other individuals, units, and organizations to subcontract, co-venture, or otherwise undertake activities needed to develop an innovation over time.

Chapter 5 examines the sequence of events in which innovation units engage in bilateral relationships with other organizations to develop their innovations. These dyadic relationships evolve in far more complex, interdependent, and dynamic ways than the literature about managing transactions has led us to believe or assume. In chapter 5, we show that these bilateral relationships do not develop in a simple linear sequence of negotiation, commitment, and execution stages. Instead, they develop through periods of high and low activity that spill over on other relationships engaged in by the organizations. The bilateral relationships reach a threshold of interdependencies where the relevant focus for understanding any given relationship becomes the web and not the dyad. Consequently, we argue in chapter 5 that understanding how any one relationship unfolds requires looking beyond that individual relationship to the larger web or network of relationships in which organizational parties become involved to undertake an innovative venture.

Context

Chapter 6 takes a macroscopic view of context to address the emergence of a technological and industrial infrastructure for innovation. In particular, we examine the roles of public- and private-sector actors in creating the economic, political, and market infrastructure that a technological community needs to sustain its members. For most technological innovations, this infrastructure includes institutional norms, basic scientific knowledge, financing mechanisms, a pool of competent human resources, and a market of educated and informed consumers. Some of the infrastructure resources are often initially developed as "public goods" in the public sector. They are then appropriated by proprietary firms which transform them into commercial "private goods." Separate organizations often exist to provide these necessary resources for a given industry. However, these financial, educational, and research organizations are seldom easily accessible to an industry that is emerging to commercialize an innovation. In addition, the infrastructure also requires establishing industry governance structures and procedures to regulate the behavior of competing firms and legitimizing the industry's domain in relation to other industrial, social, and political systems.

This macroview of the innovation journey requires a broader and more complex vision than is normally taken by managers. However, the rewards of taking this broader view are gaining a better understanding of key issues that often blindside managers. In particular, chapter 6 discusses how this macrosystems view draws attention to (1) the role of the public sector in stimulating or inhibiting innovations in the private sector, (2) how and when this infrastructure is organized, (3) what firms cooperate to create this infrastructure, (4) how they bundle their market transactions to establish resource distribution channels (e.g., vendor–supplier–distributor relationships and joint ventures), and (5) what firms emerge as industry competitors as well as cooperators.

Inherent in studying these processes is the paradox of cooperation and competition. Each firm competes to establish its distinctive position in the industry; at the same time, firms must cooperate to establish the infrastructure required for all industry participants to survive collectively. For example, cooperating to set up industry standards clearly benefits all firms. However, in doing so, each firm tries to ensure that standards that suit it best will be institutionalized. Another key paradox is that not only do government policies act to stimulate and retard industry development simultaneously, but they also often change radically and unpredictably, thus creating an investment climate that can inhibit risk taking.

The unfolding of these and other paradoxes lead to the major proposition developed in chapter 6 that firms that run in a pack will be more successful than those that go it alone. This proposition has significant implications for reexamining how private entrepreneurial firms and public agencies learn to cooperate to sustain themselves collectively while competing to perform their unique roles or carve out their distinctive niches in an emerging industry.

Conclusion

We believe that the major contribution of this book is to provide an empirically grounded model of the innovation journey that captures the messy and complex progressions observed in the innovation cases studied by the Minnesota researchers. The next chapters cut a wide swath in describing the innovation journey at different levels and from different perspectives—from a microanalysis of individual creativity to a macrostudy of industry infrastructure for innovation. Many innovation journeys remain uncharted; hence, much further research is necessary to generalize and compare our findings with other innovations. However, among the diverse innovations that were charted by MIRP researchers, we can say that although innovation journeys can follow many different paths and outcomes, the underlying pattern is remarkably alike. *The innovation journey is a nonlinear cycle of divergent and convergent activities that may repeat over time and at different organizational levels if resources are obtained to renew the cycle.*

Chapter 7 elaborates the dynamics of a cyclical model of divergent and convergent activities. Cycles of divergence and convergence appear be the underlying dynamic pattern in developing a corporate culture for launching innovations (chapter 2), learning within the innovation teams (chapter 3), leadership behaviors of top managers or investors (chapter 4), building relationships with other organizations (chapter 5), and developing an industrial infrastructure for innovations (chapter 6). This cyclical model is useful for integrating the major findings presented in this book. It also leads to important theoretical and practical implications for understanding and managing the innovation journey.

Part II of this book presents three case examples of this divergent-convergent cycle model of the innovation journey in three different organizational settings. The three cases compare (1) the cochlear implant program, an internal corporate venture within 3M; (2) the therapeutic apheresis program, a joint inter-organizational venture between 3M, Sarns, and Millipore corporations; and (3) Qnetics, a new company start-up. We examine the different benefits and liabilities to developing innovations in these different structural arrangements. Because these benefits and liabilities often compensate for one another, it is often not clear which organizational arrangement is more appropriate for undertaking the innovation journey. Two major conclusions are drawn from comparisons of the three cases. First, the innovation journey entails many of the same core processes, irrespective of organizational settings. Second, variations on the core process themes can be attributed to the different organizational settings; however, these are variations in degrees, not in substantive characteristics of the innovation journey.

These findings are important because they suggest that the core processes of innovation are fundamentally the same across very different organizational structures and settings. If supported in subsequent studies, the findings call attention to the significant benefits that could be obtained by integrating principles for managing innovation and entrepreneurship from new company start-ups, internal corporate venturing, and interorganizational joint ventures. To date, these areas have been treated as distinct and noncomparable areas of practice. However, in terms of the process of innovation, they may be highly complementary.

PART I

THE PROCESS MODEL

2

Mapping the Innovation Journey

A "road map" of how the innovation journey typically unfolds summarizes common patterns observed during the development of a wide variety of innovations studied by the Minnesota Innovation Research Program (MIRP). Providing an empirically grounded map has eluded innovation scholarship because, to date, few studies have directly examined the innovation process in real time. As a result, few empirically substantiated statements about how the innovation journey unfolds were available. One of MIRP's major objectives was to map empirically how innovations develop from concept to reality. The map is based on what MIRP researchers observed, not on what they thought should have happened.

Such a descriptive map represents a useful first step in maneuvering the innovation journey. It identifies the temporal sequence of events, junctures, and hurdles that innovation teams and managers experience along the innovation journey. Knowing how the innovation process typically unfolds provides useful empirical data for analyzing and then developing prescriptions to undertake the journey.

This journey is as much about discovery as it is about creation. The outcomes of the creative process itself may not be imaginable at the outset, but the processes that underlie these endeavors could be mapped, thereby drawing attention to the generating mechanisms that give rise to innovation processes and outcomes.

But as the saying goes, "To be forearmed is to be forewarned!" The map of the innovation journey crosses a rugged landscape that is a highly ambiguous and often uncontrollable and unique to its travelers. Many journeys remain uncharted. However, from among the innovations that were charted by MIRP researchers, we can say that innovation can be accomplished in a number of different ways and that the journey can unfold along many different routes. Moreover, many important elements of the innovation process were observed to be much alike across the highly diverse set of technological, product, process, and administrative innovations studied by MIRP. These common patterns provide the justification for discussing a generic innovation journey in this chapter.

By "generic" we mean that, for the most part, we will focus on an innovation that (1) consists of a purposeful, concentrated effort to develop and implement a novel idea; (2) is of substantial technical, organizational, and market uncertainty; (3) entails a collective effort of considerable duration; and (4) requires greater resources than are held by the people undertaking the effort. This definition includes the forms of innovation in which most managers and venture capitalists typically invest and hope will produce a useful result—be profitable, be constructive, or solve a problem. This generic definition excludes small, quick, incremental, lone-worker innovations. It also eliminates innovations that emerge primarily by chance, accident, or afterthought, although many of these elements may be contained in our description of how generic innovations develop.

This chapter provides an overview map of the key process characteristics commonly observed in the diverse innovations studied by MIRP. Then we examine the details of each process characteristic and explain their occurrences. We also describe instances in which these process characteristics varied among the fourteen innovations studied by MIRP. We exemplify these process characteristics by featuring the cases of innovation that are presented in Part II, chapters 8, 9, and 10.

1. One innovation, within a large diversified corporation, 3M, is the Cochlear Implant Program (CIP), which was undertaken to create a new business by developing a line of products, including cochlear implants, hearing aids, and otological diagnostics instruments for the hearing health industry.
2. The Therapeutic Apheresis Program (TAP) is a joint interorganizational venture among 3M, Sarns, and Millipore corporations. The TAP was undertaken to create a new biomedical products business and diagnostics instruments to treat a variety of diseases by separating pathogenic substances from blood and returning the beneficial blood components to the patient. Both CIP and TAP represent new-to-the-world technologies and products, and both were major long-term investments and commitments to create new businesses that were expected to generate significant revenues in ten to fifteen years for the corporations involved.
3. In the case of a new company start-up, called Qnetics, founding entrepreneurs pursued a variety of new business crea-

tions during the company's nine-year existence. They include a computer distributor and maintenance business, a
custom-design computer software business, a line of medical
software products for patient and financial records for hospitals and third-party payers, and an electrical load management hardware and software business for the power utilities
industry.

Common Elements in the Innovation Process

Schroeder, Van de Ven, Scudder, and Polley (1986, 1989) and Angle
and Van de Ven (1989) examined the processes of development among
the fourteen different technical and administrative innovations included in the MIRP studies. By comparing longitudinal case histories
on the development of these innovations, they found that none of the
innovations developed in a simple linear sequence or stages or phases
of activities over time. Instead, a much messier and more complex progression of events was observed in the development of each innovation. However, patterns of commonality were found in these developmental progressions. The common elements were empirically derived
and pertain to the initiation, development, and implementation periods of the innovations. Although every process characteristic was not
observed in every innovation case, and although cases varied in the
degrees to which the process occurred, overwhelming support was evident for these process patterns in the majority of cases.

The Initiation Period

1. Innovations are not initiated on the spur of the moment, by a
   single dramatic incident, or by a single entrepreneur. In most
   cases, there was an extended gestation period lasting several
   years in which seemingly coincidental events occurred that
   preceded and set the stage for the initiation of innovations.
2. Concentrated efforts to initiate innovations are triggered by
   "shocks" from sources internal or external to the organization.
3. Plans are developed and submitted to resource controllers to
   obtain the resources needed to launch innovation development. In most cases, the plans served more as "sales vehicles"
   than as realistic scenarios of innovation development.

The Developmental Period

4. When developmental activities begin, the initial innovative
   idea soon proliferates into numerous ideas and activities that
   proceed in divergent, parallel, and convergent paths of development.
5. Setbacks and mistakes are frequently encountered because
   plans go awry or unanticipated environmental events signif-

icantly alter the ground assumptions of the innovation. As setbacks occur, resource and development time lines diverge. Initially, resource and schedule adjustments are made and provide a "grace" period for adapting the innovation. But, with time, unattended problems often "snowball" into vicious cycles.

6. To compound the problems, criteria of success and failure often change, differ between resource controllers and innovation managers, and diverge over time, often triggering power struggles between insiders and outsiders.

7. Innovation personnel participate in highly fluid ways. They tend to be involved on a part-time basis, have high turnover rates, and experience euphoria in the beginning, frustration and pain in the middle period, and closure at the end of the innovation journey. These changing human emotions represent some of the most "gut-wrenching" experiences for innovation participants and managers.

8. Investors and top managers are frequently involved throughout the development process and perform contrasting roles that serve as checks and balances on one another. In no cases were significant innovation development problems solved without intervention by top managers or investors.

9. Innovation development entails developing relationships with other organizations. These relationships lock innovation units into specific courses of action that often result in unintended consequences.

10. Innovation participants are often involved with competitors, trade associations, and government agencies to create an industry or community infrastructure to support the development and implementation of their innovations.

The Implementation/Termination Period

11. Innovation adoption and implementation occurs throughout the developmental period by linking and integrating the "new" with the "old" or by reinventing the innovation to fit the local situation.

12. Innovations stop when implemented or when resources run out. Investors or top managers make attributions about innovation success or failure. These attributions are often misdirected but significantly influence the fate of innovations and the careers of innovation participants.

Figure 2.1 provides an illustration of how these common process characteristics fit together into an emerging process model of innovation. (The figure was initially developed by Schroeder et al. [1986, 1989] and subsequently extended by Angle and Van de Ven [1989]). Imagine ongoing operations of an organization proceeding in the general direction of point A. An innovation is launched that proceeds in

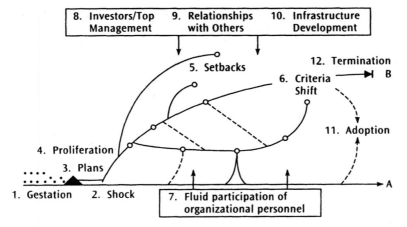

Figure 2.1 Key components of the innovation journey

the new direction of point B. The overall innovation process is partitioned into three temporal periods: (1) an initiation period, in which activities and events occur that set the stage for launching efforts to develop an innovation; (2) a developmental period, in which concentrated efforts are undertaken to transform the innovative idea into a concrete reality; and (3) an implementation or termination period, in which the innovation is adopted and institutionalized as an ongoing program, product, or business or it is terminated and abandoned.

We now discuss the process highlights of this generic innovation journey. Of course, components are not the same in all innovations. As discussed in a later section, the key process elements are expected to be more pronounced for innovations of greater novelty, size, and temporal duration.

Initiation Period

Gestation

What precipitates the initiation of innovation efforts? As innovation historians have found (e.g., Usher, 1954; Layton, 1986), in most of the innovations studied by MIRP, there was an extended gestation period, often lasting three or more years, in which people engaged in a variety of activities that set the stage for innovation (Angle and Van de Ven, 1989). Many initial events during the gestation period were not intentionally directed toward an innovation. Some events triggered recognition of the need for change, for example, deteriorating organizational performance (Cameron, Freeman, and Mishra, 1993) or changing environmental conditions (Huber, Sutcliffe, Miller, and Glick, 1993; Meyer, Goes, and Brooks, 1993). Other events generated awareness of the technological feasibility of an innovation, such as the discovery of cytoplasmic male sterilization that made hybrid wheat possible (Knudson and Ruttan, 1989). "Technology-push" and "demand-pull" events such as these set the stage for launching an innovation. Moreover, none of the innovations studied by MIRP support the proposition that the initiation of efforts to create a new innovation was precipitated by a single dramatic incident or inspiration. Instead, the events that ultimately led to initiating each innovation came from multiple and seemingly coincidental sources, and they had the common cumulative effect of triggering the recognition of a feasible new program or business idea.

The Cochlear Implant Program (CIP) in chapter 8 exemplifies the multiple, quasi-independent, and coincidental events that lead to the launch of an innovation within a complex organization. News from Australia in 1977 about the development of a "bionic ear" intrigued a 3M technical director, who visited a variety of U.S. otological research centers and clinics. The results motivated him to persuade his division manager to explore developing a cochlear implant. The division manager could have rejected the proposal, closing off one of many stimulants for innovation, but he did not and assigned the idea to an "unrelated products" group. To take advantage of a normal career advancement opportunity, the technical director accepted reassignment to a 3M manufacturing subsidiary in California, which happened to have a vendor relationship with the House Ear Institute (HEI). Meanwhile, his successor at 3M established a relationship with the University of California-San Francisco, which developed a cochlear device and implanted it in several patients in 1980, after which it terminated the relationship with 3M. But, with the termination of this one source for the innovation, two others were being cultivated independently. Research on hearing aids was under way in a 3M laboratory, and in another part of the organization, a 3M group was exploring the acquisition of a hearing health company. Although all these parallel events clearly set the stage for initiating the program, few were orchestrated by a central actor and none appeared to be individually sufficient to cause program initiation. It was not until his return from California and promotion that another stimulus occurred when the then 3M division vice president (who was technical director at the beginning of the story) expressed disappointment about the lack of progress in developing a cochlear implant. He combined the independent groups and appointed a manager to initiate the program in the fall of 1980.

A similar extended gestation period of multiple coincidental events occurred before the initiation of the Therapeutic Apheresis Program (TAP) (see chapter 9). 3M labs undertook research on blood treatment systems in 1980 but discontinued it in 1982 because no commercially feasible products were evident from the work. Independently, by 1981 Millipore had developed an apheresis filtration prototype and contacted Sarns as a potential vendor because of its recognized leadership in manufacturing heart blood pumps. But again, for unrelated reasons, negotiations were terminated in 1981 because Sarns had entered into negotiations to be acquired by 3M. In March 1983, Millipore approached 3M about a possible joint venture with its new Sarns subsidiary, when it discovered that 3M itself was also interested in apheresis. Recognition of the complementary competencies of Millipore, 3M, and Sarns precipitated negotiating an informal joint venture and initiating TAP in November 1983.

The third case example presented in chapter 10, Qnetics, includes two independent gestation periods. The first involved the independent parallel events that led two entrepreneurs to leave their employing organizations for different reasons in 1979, start up their own companies, and recognize limitations in making their independent companies commercially viable businesses. The second gestation period began with the coincidental meeting of the two entrepreneurs through a common acquaintance and their subsequent interactions that led them to recognize potential synergies and opportunities to obtain venture capital support by merging their fledgling companies in November 1983.

As these cases exemplify, these gestation events were not planned to initiate a new business in the form that it subsequently unfolded. Instead, it is more reasonable to conclude that the events undertaken by the entrepreneurs and their organizations sent them on courses of action that often by chance intersected with the independent courses of others. These intersections provided occasions for interaction, which led the actors to recognize and access new opportunities and potential resources. And where these occasions were exploited, the actors modified and adapted their independent courses of action into interdependent joint actions and agreements to initiate their new businesses.

Although the gestation processes were more evolutionary and unplanned in almost all cases, it was possible to identify one or more alert entrepreneurs or champions (Kirzner, 1973) who were at the focal points of organizing the subsequent innovation activities. Indeed, these entrepreneurs were the central forces that often coalesced the various seemingly unconnected events, activities, and players into a potential opportunity for their organizations. During opportune moments, these champions offered their organizations an idea or project as the vehicle to solve a crisis or exploit a commercial opportunity. However, as we discuss, in all cases it required a "shock" to actually coalesce the potential opportunity into a formal program of innovation by the rest of the organization.

A comparison of the cases also indicates an important variation in this core gestation process. Different organizational settings vary in the number of potential sources from which stimulants for innovation can arise. The CIP within 3M exhibits the largest number of stimulants for innovation, the Qnetics company start-up the least, and the TAP joint venture an intermediate number of precipitating events. This observation is partially consistent with the initial research finding by Hage and Aiken (1970) that greater structural differentiation enables innovation in organizations. However, the TAP joint venture among 3M, Millipore, and Sarns corporations emerged from the most structurally differentiated organizational arrangement, and yet fewer precipitating events were observed in the gestation of TAP than of CIP. Although it is possible that this empirical finding is idiosyncratic to the cases examined, it is not likely to be due to technology(both CIP and TAP are new-to-the-world biomedical innovations)or industry—(market entry for both CIP and TAP are regulated by the Federal Drug Administration, (FDA).

Boundary-crossing difficulties may explain this empirical finding. The probability of intersecting stimulants for innovation increases with the permeability of organizational boundaries between diverse sources. We observed TAP to experience more difficulties crossing structural boundaries between organizations than CIP experienced crossing departmental and division boundaries within 3M. Organizational boundaries that are permeable through only limited and prescribed modes, such as through TAP's strategic business unit (SBU), limits the probability that ideas for innovation generated within boundaries will transfer across boundaries. This line of reasoning suggests an extension of Hage and Aiken's proposition with an important qualifier: Structural differentiation is positively related to innovativeness if the structural boundaries are permeable.

Although the role of chance has been underemphasized in most managerial perspectives on innovation, these observations emphasize that chance plays a significant role in launching an innovation journey. Increases in the number of initiatives undertaken by a large number of interacting people increases the probability of stimulating innovation. This proposition reinforces the bias-for-action principle of Peters and Waterman (1982). Louis Pasteur's adage, "Chance favors the prepared mind," nicely captures the process that sets the stage for innovation.

"Shocks" Trigger Innovation

Whereas a conducive organizational climate sets the stage for innovation, concrete actions to undertake specific innovations appear to be triggered by "shocks" from sources internal or external to the organization (Schroeder et al., 1989). Many new innovative ideas may be generated but are not acted on in an organization until some form of shock occurs. Shocks served to concentrate attention and focus the efforts of diverse stakeholders in the organizations.

Shocks might include new leadership, product failure, a budget crisis, or an impending loss of market share, although it is evident from the MIRP studies that shocks can occur in many different forms. In a naval systems innovation, a $50 million failure in a product improvement program triggered the organization to expend considerable effort to uncover the underlying human resources problem for the failure and to resolve that it would never happen again. In two cases, a new leader in the organization was the shock that initiated innovation. In a local school district, new leadership combined with a budget crisis caused rethinking about managing schools in a more decentralized manner. The impetus for developing hybrid wheat was a disease called stem rust blight; a hybrid variety of wheat was expected to resist this disease and provide better yields. Shocks do not need to be viewed as negative. In the TAP case, the proposal to engage in a joint venture was seen as the shock necessary to renew an abandoned effort. Thus, Schroeder et al. (1989) note that in all the MIRP cases innovation initiatives could be traced to some kind of shock that stimulated people's action thresholds to pay attention and initiate novel action.

Shocks were important in each case because they allowed the champions of an innovative idea to gain currency with various potential stakeholders within the organization. Even though the entrepreneurs or champions were often convinced about the potential of their ideas, the rest of the organization did not necessarily share this "insight." In the typical scenario, the champions rarely controlled the resources required to develop their insight or ideas. In most of the cases studied, an opportunistic champion could not move the innovation forward. The idiosyncratic vision or insight of the champions was not widely shared in the rest of the organization. Indeed, potential stakeholders had to be convinced to support an idea. Often they were forced to or had to rely on the champions for critical information to make resource allocation decisions but without the benefit of the champions' special "insight" or knowledge about the commercial or technical prospects of the innovative idea. Because of this natural information asymmetry, the incentive and urgency to move from gestation to implementation required an external force. "Shocks" provided this external force to coalesce support around an idea that had the potential to solve a crisis or capitalize on an emerging opportunity. It is interesting to note that in the case of one of the entrepreneurs who went on to form Qnetics, the previous employer of the entrepreneur never experienced the shock required to take the champion's idea seriously. The only way the champion could pursue the idea was to quit the firm and start his own business.

This process observation is consistent with the general belief that necessity, opportunity, and dissatisfaction are the major preconditions that stimulate people to act. March and Simon (1958) set forth the most widely accepted model by arguing that dissatisfaction with existing conditions stimulates people to search for improved conditions, and they will stop searching when a satisfactory result is found. A satisfactory result is a function of a person's aspiration level, which Lewin et al. (1945) indicated is a product of all past successes and failures that people have experienced. This model assumes that when people reach a threshold of dissatisfaction with existing conditions, they will initiate action to resolve their dissatisfaction.

However, even though some people may perceive a given event as a shock that stimulates action; others may not share this perception. This is because individuals have widely varying and manipulable adaptation levels (Helson, 1948, 1964). When exposed over time to a set of stimuli that changes gradually, people do not perceive the changes; they subconsciously adapt to the changing conditions. They may not reach their threshold to tolerate pain, discomfort, or dissatisfaction. As a consequence, they do not recognize opportunities for innovative ideas. Unless the stimulus is of sufficient magnitude to exceed their action thresholds, people do not act to correct their situations, which over time may become deplorable. In general, direct personal confrontations with the sources of problems or opportunities are needed to trigger the threshold of concern and appreciation required to motivate most people to act (Van de Ven, 1986). Shocks serve this function in stimulating innovation.

Resources and Exposure

A common event that signals the end of the initiation period and the start of the developmental period is the development of plans and budgets and their submission to top managers or venture capitalists to launch an innovation. In each case studied by MIRP, financial, personnel, and technological resources to launch innovations came from outside the entrepreneurial unit. In varying degrees, this process event exposed entrepreneurs to two kinds of risks: personal financial exposure and unattainable project performance expectations. Taking on personal risk and providing inflated goals was the typical strategy used to overcome the information asymmetries that existed between the champions and the resource suppliers. To be taken seriously the champions had to commit something dear and personal to them, thus providing the credible commitment necessary to resource suppliers in the face of uncertainty (Williamson, 1985). At the same time, by deflecting attention from the innovation's uncertainty and toward its potential, the champions often inflated the beneficial outcomes of their innovations to resource controllers.

Significant differences exist among MIRP cases in the ways that external resources were obtained to launch the innovations. As an internal corporate venture, CIP obtained its funding from internal 3M corporate capital, personnel with needed competencies were reassigned from other corporate units, and technology came from 3M research and development labs and relationships with university research centers and otological clinics. TAP, a joint interorganizational venture, obtained its funding, technology, part-time professional staff, and research and development from its co-venturing parent firms. Thus, at the outset, significant corporate resources were committed to CIP and TAP for an extended time. Top managers said that although they perceived them to be highly risky, both CIP and TAP were understood to represent major long-term investments and commitments to create new businesses that could position their companies in lucrative new markets in ten to fifteen years.

Unlike CIP and TAP, Qnetics exemplifies the liabilities of the newness and small size of a new company start-up (Aldrich and Auster, 1986). Its founders assumed personal financial risks by making personal investments in their new company. And instead of relying on corporate resources, Qnetics used the market to obtain most of its resources with a private placement arranged by a venture capitalist and by hiring personnel with the needed competencies. In making his sales pitch to potential investors in Qnetics during the winter of 1983, the venture capitalist emphasized that although the investment entailed high risk, it also offered investors a lucrative short-term return when the public placement of Qnetics was to take place in the fall of 1984.

As it turned out, because of a "soft market," the public placement was canceled in October 1984. This event not only pushed Qnetics into its financial crisis but also eliminated any hope of short-term returns that initial private investors were led to expect. Indeed, the value of their combined investment of $465,000 in Qnetics in August 1984 had decreased to near zero six months later. As these events suggest, liabilities in generating external resources for new, small companies influence the fortunes of entrepreneurs and investors alike. Thus, venture capital was found to be more difficult and risky to obtain and had a shorter time horizon than did corporate capital.

A second consequence of the initial investment process is that it created unattainable performance expectations for most innovation projects studied by MIRP. The initial project plans and budgets, colored as they were with optimism, were used more as a vehicle to obtain resource commitments from investors or corporate sponsors than they were to develop realistic alternative scenarios of business creation.

Although all entrepreneurs acknowledged in interviews that parts of their business plans, particularly product development timetables and projected revenues, were overly optimistic, none indicated a will-

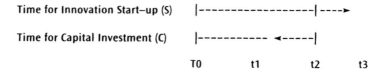

Figure 2.2 Divergent time lines for innovation start-up and capital spending

ingness to document uncertainties in their plans or to propose a more extended timetable for business start-up because that would decrease their chances of obtaining start-up funding. The external investors and corporate sponsors in turn used the targets and schedules specified in the plans to evaluate business creation progress. Those interviewed admitted that they discounted certain projections in the plans "as fluff," and that business creation is an inherently uncertain process that commonly entails setbacks beyond the control of entrepreneurs. However, they steadfastly held to their convictions that the entrepreneurs should be held accountable for achieving the financial and performance targets in their business plans (Van de Ven, Angle, and Poole, 1989).

Thus, because they feared not getting start-up capital, the new business entrepreneurs committed themselves to a course of action and a set of overly optimistic expectations by investors and corporate sponsors. And when they did not achieve expectations for the reasons described later, the confidence of key sponsors and investors was shaken, resulting at first in external interventions that often misdirected business start-up activities and later in decreased commitments to support the entrepreneurial ventures.

Ironically, if the business plans had been a primary vehicle for obtaining start-up capital, it would have been clear that the requested duration of funding for innovation development had been underestimated. As illustrated in figure 2.2, the duration of capital committed to innovation start-up was significantly shorter than the time required for innovation development and implementation. In each of the CIP, TAP, and Qnetics cases, initial time lines for product development and business take-off at t2 were underestimated and slipped to t3, whereas estimates of the length of time that initial capital investments would support innovation development (t2) were overestimated and ran out by t1.

Although Qnetics provides the most dramatic example, both CIP and TAP encountered similar gaps between the durations of capital investment (C) and innovation start-up (S). Early anticipations of this C < S gap were addressed by expecting that revenues from initial product market introductions would support later product development efforts. But in each case, this strategy failed as setbacks and errors developed in commercializing the first products. Subsequent strategies to reduce the expanding C < S gap included differentiation efforts by introducing interim revenue-producing products that would supplement C to reach S (e.g., custom software by Qnetics and hearing diagnostic devices by CIP), but in each case these interim products were insufficient to close the C < S gap. Finally, in each case, frequent appeals were made to obtain additional investment capital, and each of these requests resulted in significant adjustments in the scope and strategy of the new business creation efforts to fit the resources available (e.g., Qnetics and TAP undertook significant budget cuts and program reductions, while CIP redirected its priorities from cochlear implants to hearing aids).

Two reasons are evident for these grossly miscalculated budgets and schedules, one external, the other internal. Consider the external reason first. The entrepreneur, in trying to garner resources, is motivated to make the most attractive case possible for the innovation. Accordingly, cost estimates are usually optimistic, based on best-case scenarios. Entrepreneurs recognize that once committed to a project, funding sources are apt to provide additional funds to "rescue" a project in trouble. Moreover, they recognize that requesting a realistic projection of total required project funding—initial support plus "rescue" funding —may far exceed what funders are willing to accept or provide. Most entrepreneurs are savvy "street psychologists" and recognize the strength of behavioral commitment (cf. Staw and Ross, 1987; Cialdini, 1996). When investors make commitments to a project, they probably will reinvest to "save" their initial outlay.

Self-deception may be a second and more internal reason that initial estimates of innovation costs were understated. Self-deception may be operative, as innovators become personally committed to their innovation ideas and rationalize away many of the disquieting signals that the project may not work out (Aronson, 1973). Part of this process includes looking at cost-benefit analysis through rose-colored glasses (Halpern, 1996). Indeed, this rationalization mechanism may lie at the heart of many of the "low ball" budgets that are presented to resource suppliers early in the innovation process (Bazerman, 1995). However, the entrepreneurs often ignored the price at which future capital is likely to be supplied, especially if the project ran into serious trouble. Because of the uncertain nature of their activities and lacking reliable information to discount such future possibilities, the tendency seemed to be one of self-deception. This observation seems consistent with the considerable research in cognitive psychology, which suggests that there is a tendency to give greater weight to current problems and to treat oneself and one's problems as unique. Thus, uncomfortable statistical truths are often ignored, self-assessed chances of success are not correlated with statistical generalities, and people treat problems as unique and not as statistical patterns or regularities (Kahneman and Lovallo, 1994; Conlisk, 1996).

Of course, the presence or absence of a gap between capital investment and innovation start-up time lines is only a symptom, not a necessary or sufficient condition, of failure or success. Moreover, as the processes described here indicate, it is not at all clear that even if additional resources had been made available, innovation development would have led to greater success. Under conditions of high technological and market uncertainties, additional or excess resources often mask underlying problems and delay subjecting product innovations to "acid" tests of the market (Burgelman and Sayles, 1986).

Developmental Period

Proliferation

In all the innovations studied by MIRP, shortly after developmental activities were launched the process became complex to manage, as the initially simple innovation ideas and activities proliferated into diverse pathways (Schroeder et al., 1989). Specifically, after the onset of a simple activity path to develop an innovative idea, the initial ideas that served to stimulate the innovation efforts branched out into many parallel and interdependent activity paths.

This proliferation of activities over time appears to be a pervasive but little understood characteristic of organizational change and innovation processes. It accounts for much of the apparent complexity of the "fireworks" model illustrated in figure 2.1. A commonly held assumption is that the concept and scope of an innovation remain relatively intact as they are developed and adopted. MIRP findings show that the process is otherwise: After an initial shock that stimulates a simple unitary progression of activities to develop an innovative idea, the innovation process soon proliferates into a multiple divergent progression of developmental activities. Some of the activities in this diverging multiple progression are conjunctive, or related by a division of labor among functions to develop a given alternative, while many activities are unrelated as disjunctive alternative paths pursued by different people or organizational units. As a consequence, after a short "honeymoon" period of launching a relatively simple development effort, the management of innovation soon proliferates into an effort of trying to direct controlled chaos (Quinn, 1985). As one manager said,

"The problem is like trying to grow an oak tree when there are inexorable pressures to grow a bramble bush." Four factors appear to contribute to this proliferation.

1. Innovation is an ambiguous and uncertain process, and it is often impossible to know which path may yield fruit unless plausible alternatives are explored. Some ideas come from and may be sent to the "shelf" for a long time. Others lead to important innovation spin-offs. Still others converge at later times central to making the innovation a reality. For example, in the case of hybrid wheat's development, three alternative paths were followed simultaneously, and it took several years of extensive investments in each path to determine which path was appropriate in developing a hybrid strain of wheat.

Some of this proliferation is produced by the fact that many innovations are components of larger systems and architectures (Clark, 1983; Henderson and Clark, 1990). Development of a particular component depends primarily on advances in a bundle of related innovations (e.g., a new technological procedure requires adopting new administrative procedures, new occupational roles, and new conceptions of suppliers and customers), and each involves a different development and adoption process. Some other organizational activities may appear unrelated to the innovation but often compete for scarce resources thwarting the innovation's development.

2. Most innovations studied did not consist of a single new device, product, or procedure. Instead, families of related new products and procedures were developed to create sufficient critical mass and penetration to become commercially or organizationally viable. This exponentially increases the complexity of managing innovation. For example, in the development of TAP, the initial product idea proliferated into a family of three product ideas. The CIP innovation expanded from initial work on a single-channel device to five new devices using three different technologies. Although these new ideas and products were at different stages of development, work on them tended to occur simultaneously by different and overlapping subgroups within the innovation programs. Each cycle may require linking research and development, prototype development, testing, manufacturing scale-up, and marketing activities for a given product. Subsequent cycles must be simultaneously integrated to create a related family of products yet differentiated enough to permit creation of a unique new product or component.

Even in single-product innovations, proliferation was observed as a result of the division of labor among functions and organizational units (e.g., among research and development and manufacturing and marketing functions or between headquarters and district organization sites) required to develop a given innovation. These specialists, in turn, develop different conceptions of the innovation. As a consequence, the cases show that managing an innovation over time usually involves linking overlapping and parallel cycles of development effort.

3. Proliferation was often produced by diversifying and leveraging risk through multiple pathways. For example, the Qnetics entrepreneurs consistently followed multiple paths as a hedge against the failure of any one product to result in overall company failure. The trade-off for such hedging was divided attention to the various business lines.

4. Another factor of complexity is that different logics or mechanisms govern proliferation. Complicated developmental paths may result from pursuing alternative processes in different parts of the innovation. In particular, Poole and Van de Ven (1989) observe that these diverse innovation activities and paths may be governed by different logics or mechanisms:

    a. Activities governed by institutional rules tend to follow a simple unitary sequence of stages, as prescribed.
    b. Activities governed by goals and plans tend to diverge into multiple interdependent paths and then converge into an overall cumulative sequence, much like a PERT chart.
    c. Ungoverned activities, where institutional rules do not prevail, and where significant conflict exists over innovation goals or means, tend to be divergent, quasi independent, competitive, and not cumulative.

Van de Ven and Poole (1995) note that two or more of these governing mechanisms may operate simultaneously in different parts of an innovation. For example, as the cochlear implant developed, regulatory approval, business creation, and scientific research activities proceeded simultaneously. They were managed by different, though overlapping, managers, and appeared to be governed by different logics. The decision to develop devices for commercial release in the United States implied that each device must go through an institutionally prescribed sequence of hurdles to gain FDA regulatory approval. A functional model appeared to govern the developmental sequence of creating a business out of the cochlear implant technology. To become a self-sustaining business, work began by hiring diverse functional competencies—research and development, manufacturing, marketing, and so on—each performing parallel and interdependent tasks to develop a first product. As these functions completed their work on the first product, they were redeployed to initiate related tasks on the next generation in a family of products that was envisioned to provide a sustainable economic business entity. Finally, an emergent model primarily governed the process of scientific work, except that connected with regulatory approvals of devices. Different researchers pursued alternative technologies—single versus multiple channels—and linked with different technology centers that competed to become the dominant technology. This emergent process was limited only by scarce resources and curtailed by top-management decisions to support only one technological route.

Each of these three processes has its own internal logic, which is easy enough to discover if the process unfolds independently. However, confusion arises when these logics interact. For example, in the cochlear implant case, the regulatory approval process may be interrupted suddenly by a funding cutoff that prevents completing lab work on a key device in the product line. Perhaps scientific evidence emerges indicating the superiority of the discontinued technical route related to the technology chosen for development and on which the whole effort is based. The result of these and other complex interactions is a shifting and tumultuous progression. This picture gets even more complex if we include disruptions from environmental events.

These interactions may explain the apparent complexity of the "fireworks" model illustrated in figure 2.1. What is impressive is that such complexity can be generated by the interaction of a few relatively simple developmental processes. A few substitutions of one simple course of action by another equally simple strategy can create exceedingly complicated and intractable action cycles (Van de Ven and Poole, 1995).

Setbacks Occur Frequently

Another common characteristic of the innovation journey is that setbacks frequently arise because initial plans go awry or unanticipated environmental events occur that significantly alter the ground assumptions and context of the innovation. As Mintzberg, Raisinghani, and Theoret (1976) and Nutt (1984) report in their studies of unstructured decisions, the MIRP innovation studies found that the typical initial response to setbacks was to adjust resources and schedules, which provided a "grace period" for innovation development (Van de Ven, et al.,1989). But there is a path dependency to the setbacks: Over time the problems accumulate into vicious cycles.

Event histories of the CIP, TAP, and Qnetics cases in chapters 8–10 indicate that most activities during the first year or two of innovation proceeded as planned, and failures resulting in slipped schedules, budget overruns, and unsuccessful product launches in the market occurred in only a few critical components. Given the high technological and market uncertainties of innovation development, it is surprising that so few setbacks were initially encountered. Indeed, laws of probability would predict a greater number of errors and setbacks. Yet the few setbacks that did occur were sufficient to produce failures in the entire first product development efforts.

For example, efforts to develop the Phase I product in the TAP case were mostly successful. Prototype filtration modules and equipment were built, clinical trials were successful, the unit was introduced in several foreign countries, and the FDA approved the unit for commercial release in the U.S. market. The only critical problem was manufacturing defects in scale-up production of the unit, which, in turn, resulted in slipped schedules for product market introduction, deferred sales revenues, as well as delayed development of the Phase II device. As a manager said, "TAP has become a complex system, and failures in one or two components derail the entire effort, even though other parts are proceeding effectively."

So also, the major thrust in Qnetics start-up was to design, program, and market medical records software. Design and programming tasks proceeded very well, so well in fact that eight products were developed. But the company was not equally successful in marketing its medical software products, despite multiple trials in building internal marketing competence and in establishing marketing alliances with distributors. These marketing failures, coupled with cancellation of the public offering, drove the company into a financial crisis.

These setbacks and failures in developing the first product or device had important spillover effects on subsequent developmental efforts. Initially, no one recognized these spillover effects, perhaps because logical independence of activities masked their temporal interrelatedness. Business plans appeared to reflect a belief that developmental activities could proceed along parallel, independent streams in developing products and functions. This was reflected in plans made to undertake simultaneously various functional activities to launch a new business, including research and development, manufacturing, marketing, and financial activities. One manager said that these parallel functional activities were undertaken both to increase the speed to market and to build functional competencies needed to run the business "from the ground floor up."

Parallel developments of the innovation continued for a time until setbacks and problems occurred in developing first devices or products. Then it became evident that what were perceived as parallel and independent activities were indeed sequential and highly interdependent activities. For example, with manufacturing defects in the first TAP product, the phases I and II parallel product development paths became sequential, even though there was a clear division of labor among Millipore, Sarns, and 3M. In the CIP case, the HEI and Vienna devices developed in parallel until the second device was announced before the first product had completed its market entry. In the case of Qnetics, domino effects occurred among all product lines as a result of their pooled financial interdependence and the cancellation of the public offering.

Ironically, although multiple parallel development efforts were initiated, management's attention was sequential and focused on one major effort at a time. For example, CIP managers were unable to cut their losses and leave the single-channel HEI device—even when repeatedly told to do so by upper management and corporate sponsors—and move on to other technologies and products. So, also, Qnetics continued to make big investments in developing up to eight medical products, even though none of the products was successfully marketed. Finally, TAP could not get beyond phases I and II products to explore strategic business opportunities in the joint agreement.

Vicious cycles became evident when crises occurred. Masuch (1985) describes a vicious circle as a complex action loop in which a set of activities entail a chain of other activities which, in turn, ultimately recreate and worsen the original situation. The new businesses began with the idea of a family of products, which led to a proliferation of product initiatives and the addition of new differentiated functional activities. When significant problems emerged, cuts were made in program functions leading to program retrenchment, which in turn exacerbated the initial product development problems. In CIP, for example, poor performance led to some program reductions including quality assurance. Subsequently, problems were encountered with the first device, and quality assurance was not available to correct the problem.

As we discuss in chapter 3, many of these setbacks and errors went uncorrected because of four types of learning disabilities:

1. It was difficult to discriminate substantive issues from "noise" in systems overloaded with a combination of positive, negative, and mixed signals about performance over time.
2. Entrepreneurs escalated their commitments to a course of action by ignoring "naysayers" and proceeding "full scale ahead."
3. Some innovation participants became hypervigilant, calling prematurely for changes in a course of action when minor or correctable problems were encountered.
4. In-process criteria of innovation success often shifted over time, as discussed in the next section.

Thus, although errors were frequently detected, few were corrected until they "snowballed" to crisis proportions.

Shifting Innovation Performance Criteria

Dornblaser, Lin, and Van de Ven (1989) reviewed the outcome performance criteria used by entrepreneurs and managers to evaluate their innovations over time. By comparing responses in repeated interviews, the researchers found that criteria of innovation success and failure changed often over time, were different between resource controllers and innovation entrepreneurs, and shifted in opposite directions: They differed at the beginning, converged during the developmental process, and then diverged in opposite and conflicting directions as innovation implementation problems arose.

This pattern is illustrated in Table 2.1, which lists the typical outcome criteria cited by innovation entrepreneurs and resource controllers: venture capitalists or top corporate managers. Although not mutually exclusive, the performance criteria emphasized by resource controllers shifted over time from long-run output goals to process concerns and then to more immediate input criteria. On the other hand, the criteria of innovation entrepreneurs tended to go in the opposite direction over time; that is, from input to process to output criteria.

In the beginning, external resource controllers commonly justified their initial innovation investments and commitments with the guarded optimism that their innovations had the potential of contributing to long-run organizational goals, programs, or business growth. For example, top managers of the CIP and TAP innovations emphasized that although these innovations entailed high risks, (1) such risk taking was an inevitable part of creating the next generation of technologies and businesses necessary to sustain the long-term viability and growth of the corporation, and (2) a long-term, five- to ten-year, corporate commitment to the development of these innovations could achieve this potential. In contrast to these long-run outcome criteria, the initial success criteria of internal innovation entrepreneurs focused much more on short-run hurdles of obtaining resources, recruiting personnel, team building, planning, and mobilizing technical activities that were needed to launch innovation development activities as quickly as possible.

As noted, each innovation encountered unanticipated setbacks and problems as developmental work progressed, causing initially set targets and schedules to slip. These setbacks led innovation entrepreneurs to emphasize meeting process criteria of solving these problems, achieving technical milestones, and meeting deadlines and budgets to maintain credibility for their innovations. Information about these problems was reported to resource controllers during periodic project reviews. In these administrative review sessions, innovation entrepreneurs tended to reconstruct negative information in a positive frame with assurances that they were "on top" of the problems. Because resource controllers were not involved in daily inno-

Table 2.1. Divergent-convergent pattern of outcome criteria held by internal innovation managers and external resource controllers

Period	Resource controllers	Innovation managers
Beginning	*Outcome Criteria* Create a new self-sustaining business/program in 5–10 years.	*Input Criteria* Obtain resources needed to launch innovation.
	Contribute to organization's goals.	Build innovation team.
	Achieve profit objectives.	Develop technical design of innovation idea.
Middle	*Process Criteria* Meet targets and schedules in the plan.	*Process Criteria* Achieve technical milestones.
	Organization of team & implementation of plans.	Debug the system. Meet deadlines and budget.
	Compare progress relative to competing others.	Maintain credibility.
Ending	*Input Criteria* Competency of managers.	*Outcome Criteria* Demonstrate market success and potential ROI.
	Cost & resource drain.	Contribution to organizational goals.
	Effort & commitment of innovation people.	Survival and/or growth.

vation activities, they relied on this indirect and ambiguous information to assess innovation progress. Thus, during this middle period of innovation development, resource controllers tended to mimic the success criteria in the problem areas as had been related to them by the entrepreneurs.

More objective performance information did not become available until a later time—often several years—when innovations were implemented through pilot testing, customer inspections, manufacturing, and market introductions. When these initial "acid tests" were judged successful, the process problems identified earlier were dismissed as unimportant or overcome. However, when innovation implementation efforts went awry, outcome criteria of resource controllers and innovation entrepreneurs diverged. Disappointed with results, the external resource controllers tended to focus on input criteria by expressing concerns about the competency and efforts of innovation managers, the innovation's developmental costs, and its resource "drain" relative to other investment opportunities or priorities that had surfaced during the intervening period. In contrast and in efforts to "salvage" their innovations, entrepreneurs appealed to the long-run potential their projects could achieve if resource controllers looked beyond the immediate "temporary" setbacks and maintained a long-term commitment to their innovations.

Thus, as Ross and Staw (1986) observed, innovation managers interpreted failures less as a symptom that their innovation was incorrect than as an indication that it had not been pursued vigorously enough. As a result, disagreements arose over the meanings of setbacks as resource controllers and innovation entrepreneurs developed quite different stories to interpret the same experience.

Changes in innovation performance goals and criteria triggered innovation managers and entrepreneurs to search and redefine their innovation ideas or strategies. Differences among the cases were observed in (1) search boundaries, (2) search criteria, and (3) good or bad times. These search patterns appear to be associated with organizational settings.

Search by the principals of the new company start-up, Qnetics, appeared to be unbounded by technology or lines of business. Whatever it took to become a financially viable entity appeared to be the open territory as long as it related to the broad area of computer hardware and software systems. CIP and TAP, however, followed a more bounded proliferation of their strategy, perhaps because their domains were more clearly specified by their organizational sponsors.

These search processes appeared to be governed by the relative importance of market, administrative, and consensus criteria in redefining the innovations. Qnetics provided the clearest example of following a sequential trial-and error-process of product developments primarily governed by the "acid test" of the market. A large part of CIP's development, on the other hand, was governed by 3M's administrative hierarchy, and the market test did not govern until a product was introduced into the market. Explorations of new business ideas in TAP required consensus among participants from the co-venturing organizations. However, problems of trust and a divided house, or hung jury, often existed among TAP innovation unit members in selecting new ideas and opportunities for development. As a result, TAP's strategy remained confined mostly to the terms in its initial joint agreement.

Finally, the search processes appeared to differ in good and bad times. When things were going well, search occurred within the innovation's existing strategy. When things went bad, search focused outside the program's business idea. As March (1981) described, disjunctive searches appear to be a way to get a new lease on life. For example, when everything was going well in 1985, TAP's SBU was concerned about retaining its scientists and conducted its slack search to redeploy its assets to TAP-related activities. However, when many technical

a. Relative Power of Internal and External Groups

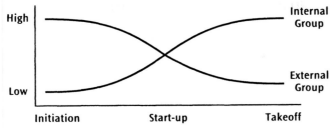

b. Action Loops in Transitions of Power

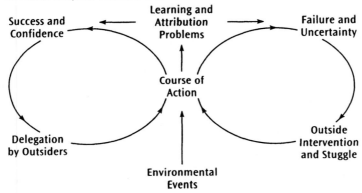

Figure 2.3 Action loops in transitions of power between internal and external groups during the initiation, start-up, and takeoff of an innovation

problems emerged in January 1987, the SBU began looking for other things to do because of problems apparent in what it was doing.

An action cycle produced by shifts in the relative power exerted by entrepreneurs and resource controllers helps explain these dynamics associated with changes in innovation performance criteria and search processes. The action cycle, illustrated in figure 2.3, argues that when the course of action being pursued by an innovation unit is judged successful, external resource controllers' confidence increases and they are more willing to delegate greater control to the entrepreneurial unit, which in turn permits the innovation unit greater discretion to pursue and expand its course of action. However, when failure is perceived, uncertainties arise, and they trigger external resource controllers to intervene and engage in a struggle with innovation managers over the appropriateness of the innovation's present course of action. When this struggle subsides, often by the imposition of a new or modified action plan, the failure loop is completed and recycles in positive or negative directions.

This model shows how innovation outcomes are both a cause and a consequence of action. It also acknowledges that outcome attributions can be produced by spurious unknown factors. In addition to an innovation's course of action, outcome assessments are influenced by environmental events, shifting organizational priorities, and changing personnel. Additional insights to these action loops will be evident as we examine the different activities and roles of innovation personnel and resource controllers during the innovation journey.

Fluid Participation of Innovation Personnel

In almost all the cases studied by MIRP, personnel on the innovation teams only worked part-time, experienced high turnover rates, and, although technically competent, typically lacked experience in developing an innovation (Angle and Van de Ven, 1989). Most of these personnel transfers were a normal part of job mobility and promotion processes. The result for the innovation projects was that most of the participants involved at the beginning of developmental work were no longer involved when it ended. Thus, contrary to the common impression that an innovation team consists of an entrepreneur who works with a fixed set of full-time people to develop an innovative idea, the staffing pattern is much more temporary and fluid. It reflects the organized anarchy discussed by Cohen et al. (1972), where many people fluidly engage and disengage in the innovation process over time as their interests and commitments dictate. Therefore, maintaining continuity and momentum and developing an organizational memory of innovation developmental activities become difficult.

Part-time involvement implies that participants have joint work appointments and must serve multiple masters. Given that work demands of each job typically exceed the time available, part-time participants were often observed to be distracted and stressed and tended to cope by "stealing from Peter to pay Paul." In many cases, the innovation was "Peter" except for relatively infrequent and short intervals of peak innovation experiences or work demands. Thus, the innovation projects were often observed to be the losers from the practice of "skunk working," which Peters and Waterman (1982) heralded as a technique to facilitate innovation. Because they are uncertain and insecure processes, innovations can seldom compete with the security of employment and short-run production demands of performing clearly known routines in most permanent jobs. These structural incentives and demands of noninnovation jobs are partially counterbalanced by the greater intrinsic motivation and satisfaction that people derive from innovative tasks. However, we observed that when "push comes to shove," noninnovation jobs typically command greater allegiance than innovative ones.

Lack of experience implies naive planning and a dearth of fallback positions when unanticipated events arise. Experience provides a foundation for comparing developmental processes and a repertoire of "old friends" (Simon, 1945) to rely on to diagnose and respond to situations.

Personnel turnover serves a number of useful functions (Dalton and Todor, 1979; Staw, 1980). New people contribute fresh perspectives and competencies to an innovation team as needed to address critical problems or challenges as they arise. Appointments and replacements of innovation managers are key levers used by resource controllers and top management to exercise their direction and control of an innovation. Finally, one chief executive officer (CEO) observed that "job demands often outpace the people" as the managerial skills believed necessary to direct innovations from development to business operations often grow more rapidly than many managers can acquire. As a consequence, many entrepreneurs are replaced by professional managers because the former often founder in growing the innovation into a self-sustaining business.

However, high turnover creates significant continuity problems for innovations. Each departing person takes away vital information. Not only are secrets then subject to compromise outside the group, but also vital knowledge that has not been systematically recorded is lost to the group. New people entering the network deflect the attention of others from production to process costs, as the newcomers are "brought up to speed" and new role relationships and norms are negotiated. It is as if the group regresses somewhat in its developmental sequence, as suggested by Tuckman's (1965) stages of forming, storming, norming, and performing. Much of the knowledge possessed by the innovation team is not "coded" in ways that permit easy transfer of information to the newcomers. As Kanter (1988) put it, "Telling about it is not only time-consuming; it is indeed no substitute for having been there" (194).

Angle and Van de Ven (1989) reported that innovation participants experience different human emotions and dynamics during the start-up, middle, and ending periods of the innovation journey. During the start-up period, the dominant dynamics observed are individual recruitment and engagement in an innovation team. It is characterized by emotional euphoria, great expectations, and confidence among participants in the success of the innovative undertaking.

In the middle period, the euphoria wanes, problems surface, and the reality of the difficulty, complexity, and high risk of success becomes apparent. No conclusions or solutions are in sight to provide closure to the innovation effort. It is here where "nit-picking" and lack of trust or confidence in fellow workers and leadership become manifest. Some people desert the effort, creating problems of continuity. New people come on board without an "organizational memory." As a consequence, while the setting should be the most opportune time for learning by trial and error, actual instances of learning are remarkably infrequent.

In the ending period, an "end to the tunnel" comes into sight and group members find closure for their experiences. If the effort was not successful, members concoct reasons why their ordeal was not in vain. Attributions of failure usually point to external "uncontrollable factors." If the effort is a "success," team celebrations emerge. Success attributions are directed to the commitment, talent, and heroic efforts of the team; the leader is personified as superhuman, and a variety of efforts are made to prevent or forestall terminating the group.

Although these periods appear to capture key group transitions of innovation teams over time, individual transitions do not appear to follow this temporal sequence because, as we have seen, individuals with diverse ambitions, frames of reference, and functional expertise often come and go as an innovation develops. As a consequence, individual participants may not be in sync with each other, and the overall innovation unit appears ambivalent or incapable of taking clear courses of action. In these instances, the overall group often gets involved in frustrating periods of "internal navel gazing" and emotionally torn meetings that appear to accomplish little. As discussed in Van de Ven (1985) three contradictory individual-group dynamics may explain this ambivalence:

1. The hung jury, in which individual group members feel strongly about specific but opposing courses of action that should be taken, but they cannot achieve a consensus. On the surface, this phenomenon often appears as a technical difference of opinion among group members. Below the surface, however, group members are pursuing a variety of hidden agendas that are often not clearly understood by the individuals pursuing these agendas. They include ambiguities about willingness to be a member of the innovation unit, the kinds of roles the individual wishes to perform and is capable of performing, and what rewards the individual can receive in return for contributions to the effort.

2. The acquiescent team player, who withholds or does not forcefully argue personal ideas and views to the group for fear that they may upset or derail the collective effort because he or she deeply wants the overall group effort to succeed. The result is a lose-lose situation. The individual who withholds ideas loses because he or she does not achieve personal ownership in the group effort and does not realize the collective effort as a way of achieving personal ambitions. As a result, the individual begins looking elsewhere to achieve personal ambitions. The group also loses the active involvement of a group member and because the person may have withheld

suggestions that might have significantly improved the over-all group product.

3. Tolerance for ambiguity and trust vary among group members. Some members feel quite comfortable with and trust others enough to be able to work productively with the uncertainties of new relationships and the openness of many decisions and issues. Others, often of lower hierarchical status, require and demand more closure and safeguards. In response to the latter, efforts are made to "nail down" decisions and issues, often in writing. But these decisions are sometimes premature, and breaches in social contracts arise when what individuals thought was "nailed down" becomes loose or is "pried open." Further, those who have a greater tolerance for ambiguity or are more secure in their relations with others begin to complain about the "needless bureaucracy" and attempts to substitute "personal trust and norms" for "impersonal contracts."

With the exception of Kanter's work (1983, 1988), adequate recognition or treatment of these social-psychological dynamics of group development have not been found in the innovation literature, although they have been alluded to in the literature on policy implementation (e.g., Pressman and Wildavsky, 1973) and organizational development (Schein, 1969). Kanter (1988) discusses the importance of being sensitive to and orchestrating the transitions human beings go through as innovations develop over time. She emphasizes the need for coalition building, in which power is acquired by selling the project to potential allies. The basis for such "selling" changes over time as the innovation participants move through various emotional stages. Kanter points out more than one currency of exchange on which such selling can take place. Currencies of exchange include information (data, expertise), resources (funding, time), and support (endorsement, approval, legitimacy). Each represents a different sort of "capital" that can be used to motivate people. Their relative appropriateness varies at different stages of an innovation.

Based on these observations, MIRP researchers concluded the type of leadership that is appropriate for an innovation changes over time (Manz, Bastien, Hostager, and Shapiro, 1989). Use of economic and political incentives are often needed to get people to commit to an innovation effort. Those who become involved then need some structure of roles and reciprocal responsibilities. Later, as euphoria turns to reality, and often disappointment, the need for support becomes paramount, as people need support to accomplish their aspirations. Further aspects of these changing leadership styles and roles are related to our next process observation.

Top Management Involvement and Roles

Three common patterns were observed in the behaviors of investors and top managers of their innovations:

1. Many—not one or a few—top managers at different hierarchical levels were actively involved in developing their innovations. Thus, the innovation entrepreneurs did not simply report to a single top manager or investor; they were accountable to a team of top managers or a board of investor/owners.
2. These top managers or investors performed different roles and often shifted among them. For example, in studies of new business innovations, Angle and Van de Ven (1989) noted that investors and corporate top managers were actively involved in their innovations by playing four distinct roles: sponsor, mentor, critic, and institutional leader. So, also, in describing innovation in the public sector, Roberts and King (1989) distinguished between the key roles of policy entrepreneurs, champions, and administrators. However defined, in performing these roles the top managers often did not reflect unified or homogeneous perspectives; instead, they held opposing views that served as checks and balances on each other in making innovation investment decisions.
3. Top managers made pragmatic decisions in response to changing innovation conditions, rather than according to a planned strategic course of action. These decisions significantly influenced the emotions and behaviors of innovation team participants.

These leadership patterns are discussed in greater detail in chapter 4, but we point out here that these patterns varied by different performance conditions and in different organizational settings. The involvement and roles of investors or top managers was most clearly evident when significant setbacks were encountered. As the model in figure 2.3 suggests, vicious cycles were broken by external interventions of business investors or top managers. In none of the innovations studied by MIRP were significant problems solved without the external interventions of top managers or investors. Perhaps this is because of the learning disabilities observed within the innovation teams or because the teams were "locked" into courses of action that required completion before they were open to consider alternatives, which, as Gersick (1988) observed, is a common characteristic of small group development. In such situations, interventions by external groups were necessary to alter the courses of action pursued by the innovation teams.

When these external interventions occurred, they often resulted in seemingly contradictory and abrupt shifts in the developments of the innovations. But, on closer examination, the abrupt shifts represented nothing more than substitutions of one simple developmental sequence or formula for another. For example, the internal TAP group decision to address specific diseases led to a sequence of tasks necessary to obtain FDA approval for this device. However, 3M's external top manager believed that FDA regulatory licensing steps for such a device would be too costly and time-consuming. He proposed instead that the TAP innovation unit market the device as a blood filtration product. This simple market penetration logic overruled the other simple regulatory licensing sequence. Thus, what appeared a complex and chaotic process is one simple sequence supplanting another. Although innovation team members did not often agree initially with the alternative courses of action proposed by external groups, they participated in their formation and implementation and grew to accept them in two to four months after the interventions.

Van de Ven and Grazman (1997) report that very different perceptions of CIP and TAP were found in yearly interviews with managers in the corporate hierarchical levels from the innovation units to the CEO. Top managers, removed one to four levels from the new businesses, were observed to (1) be more knowledgeable and interested in CIP or TAP than the researchers expected, (2) apply different criteria among each other in major decisions about the new businesses, and (3) perform different managerial and institutional roles critical to legitimizing the innovations.

Multiple levels of management involvement appeared to provide a balance of cross-checks between contradictory forces among top managers pushing for expansions and contractions in the scope, resource allocation, time schedules, and performance expectations of the innovations. For example, the ongoing enthusiastic support of CIP's management sponsor, a group vice president, was counterbalanced with "hard-nosed" business skepticism by the sector vice president, while a division vice president, viewed his role as being a "mentor" or "tutor" to the CIP program manager.

In addition, top managers perform the critical functions of institutional support and endorsement, which are viewed as increasingly legitimate the higher the organizational level at which they are performed. Thus, for example, a casual agreement to explore an apheresis joint venture during a golf match between the CEOs of Millipore and 3M, when communicated to lower management levels, brought immediate credibility to the formation of TAP. Also, a brief visit by the 3M CEO to HEI and the election of the 3M group vice president to the board of directors of HEI solidified the 3M-House relationship to develop cochlear implants.

These differing managerial roles and activities were not as clearly evident in Qnetics, the new company start-up. The roles performed by Qnetics's venture capitalist and the board of directors differed in two critical respects from that of CIP and TAP top management. First, the Qnetics board of directors consisted only of the inside owners/ entrepreneurs from 1983 to February 1987, when the board was reconstituted and three outside directors were elected: a physician, a banker, and a professor. Thus, for most of its start-up period, Qnetics's new business entrepreneurs, owners, and board members were talking to themselves. The internal board composition prevented Qnetics's principals from being exposed to the different perspectives and criteria that external board members could have provided, like that of CIP and TAP top managers. Indeed, after February 1987 Qnetics's entrepreneurs reported, and sometimes complained, that they had to spend much more time preparing for board meetings to respond to questions from external board members than previously.

Another important difference is that Qnetics, a new company start-up, did not enjoy the institutional legitimacy provided to CIP and TAP by their established and highly regarded parent corporations. As a consequence, Qnetics could not draw on a corporate infrastructure of functional competencies, resources, and systems available to CIP and TAP. Moreover, Qnetics could not draw on the institutionally derived legitimacy of a parent corporation to launch and conduct its business. These liabilities of newness and small size for Qnetics are clearly illustrated in its repeated failures to secure marketing relationships with other firms and in the highly interdependent and risky set of transactions it developed to conduct its business.

Relationships Frequently Altered

We have seen that as innovations develop over time, more and more players are brought into the game. A complex network of exchange relationships emerges, with individuals and interest groups engaging in a series of transactions necessary to move the innovation forward. As discussed in chapter 5, these relationships, once established, further shape and constrain future interactions. The relationships were often observed to develop into a variety of unintended consequences:

1. Because of resource scarcity, innovations often enter into leveraged sets of highly interdependent and risky transactions (e.g., using a customer contract as collateral to obtain a loan from a bank to hire employees to perform the contract). When any one of these transactions fails, the entire set collapses in domino fashion.
2. Partnerships and joint ventures often produce "hung juries" on the strategic directions of an innovation because of parent organizations' inability to reach agreements on concrete ways to share risks, costs, or potential payoffs of the innovation when they become apparent.

3. Aborted attempts to establish cooperative relationships with other organizations engaged in the development of a similar innovation may turn out a few years later to result in competitive relationships.
4. Close and successful relationships nurtured over the years with other organizations may lead to groupthink.
5. Company acquisitions undertaken to obtain technological or product competence often result in defections of the very people in the acquired organization who possess these desired competencies.

The CIP, TAP, and Qnetics cases exemplify the fragile, interdependent, and unanticipated consequences of engaging in interorganizational transactions, but the Qnetics case is the most dramatic. Qnetics's event history shows that even after numerous attempts, it experienced repeated failures in establishing marketing relationships with distributors or marketing distribution outlets for its medical records software products. When asked, "Why?" Qnetics's principal reported that although the company obtained highly enthusiastic responses, various obstacles prevented it from closing the deals. The two most frequent reasons were that (1) although Qnetics's product might have been technically superior, its capabilities to provide product maintenance and upgrades were not as extensive as its competitors' (e.g., Unisys, Hewlett Packard, and Texas Instruments), and (2) large hospitals or medical software distribution houses have a six- to twelve-month decision-making cycle, but Qnetics's time horizon of financial solvency was measured in weeks.

Qnetics liabilities of newness and small size are also reflected in interdependencies that were structured in its set of seemingly independent transactions. Failures in refinancing the company by the venture capitalist led to problems with the bank, and closing the line of credit by the bank led Prime Computer Co. to terminate Qnetics as one of its distributors, which in turn led to the company's almost losing and then settling for a significantly reduced profit margin on the an equipment sale to a customer. These domino effects, when combined with failures to establish medical product marketing or distribution relationships, accumulated to push Qnetics to the brink of bankruptcy.

While Qnetics was experiencing these liabilities of newness and small size, the TAP joint venture was exposed to the liabilities of double parenting and conflict. Event histories show that the TAP SBU experienced the inflexibilities of a hung jury in exploring new strategic directions for the joint venture. By repeatedly rejecting new business opportunities that came to the unit's attention over time, the basic business strategy for TAP changed very little from its initial joint venture agreement in November 1983.

Finally, CIP exemplifies some of the unanticipated temporal dynamics of interorganizational business relationships over time:

1. After two aborted attempts at establishing relationships with other firms with complementary resources, those firms turned out a few years later to be the major industry competitors of CIP: University of Melbourne subsequently linked with Nucleus, and University of California-San Francisco linked with Symbion.
2. The highly "successful" and close relationship with HEI may have led the CIP into a groupthink (Janis, 1982) about the superiority of the single-channel technology for a cochlear implant. CIP managers repeatedly and unthinkingly rejected claims of the emerging superiority of the multiple-channel technology.

As these cases exemplify, the bilateral relationships that innovations engage in with other organizations tend to develop into far more complex, interdependent, and dynamic ways than the literature on managing business transactions has led us to believe (Ring and Van de Ven, 1994). We show in chapter 5 that these bilateral relationships do not develop in simple sequence of negotiation, commitment, and execution stages over time. Instead, they develop through periods of high and low activity that spill over onto other relationships. The development and institutionalization of interdependencies among these numerous bilateral relationships reach a point of "self-organizing criticality" wherein the relevant focus for understanding any given relationship becomes the web and not the dyad. Consequently, we argue in chapter 5 that understanding how any one relationship unfolds requires looking beyond that individual relationship at the larger web or network of relationships in which organizational parties are spun as they co-venture along the innovation journey.

Industry Team Playing

Not only does the innovation journey involve the micro- and proprietary developments of a particular innovative device or service, it also deals with creating a community or industry infrastructure that is needed to implement or commercialize an innovation. MIRP researchers observed that in varying degrees, innovation entrepreneurs and managers spend large proportions of their working time in collective efforts with other public- and private-sector actors to create an infrastructure that any industrial community needs to sustain its members.

As discussed in chapter 6, this infrastructure includes institutional norms, basic scientific knowledge, financing, and a pool of competent human resources. These infrastructure resources are often initially developed as "public goods" in the public sector and appropriated by proprietary firms that transform them into "private goods" through innovation. Separate organizations often exist to provide these necessary resources for a given industry. However, these financial, educational, and research organizations are seldom easily accessible to a new industry that is emerging to commercialize an innovation. In addition, the infrastructure also requires establishing industry governance structures and procedures to regulate the behavior of competing firms and legitimizing the industry's domain in relation to other industrial, social, and political systems.

Thus, the macromanagement of innovations demands attention to (1) the role of the public sector in stimulating or inhibiting innovations in the private sector, (2) how and when this infrastructure is organized, (3) what firms cooperate to create this infrastructure, (4) how they bundle their market transactions to establish resource distribution channels (e.g., vendor–supplier–distributor relationships and joint ventures), and (5) what firms emerge as industry competitors as well as cooperators.

Inherent in these macroissues is "the paradox of cooperation and competition." Each firm competes to establish its distinctive position in the industry; at the same time, firms must cooperate to establish the infrastructure required for all industry participants to survive collectively. For example, cooperating to set up industry standards clearly benefits all firms. However, in doing so, each firm will try to ensure that standards that suit it best become institutionalized. Another key paradox is that government policies established to stimulate industry development may change radically and unpredictably, thus creating an investment climate that inhibits risk taking. These issues of infrastructure development are discussed in chapter 6.

Implementation/Termination Period

The implementation period begins when activities are undertaken to apply and adopt an innovation. When the innovation is created and developed within the organization, as described in the previous sections, implementation processes include introducing the innovation in the market, transferring it to operating sites, and diffusing it to potential adopters. If the innovation is developed elsewhere, the implementation process centers on the activities undertaken by a host organization to introduce and adopt the innovation.

It is misleading to assume that development of an innovation is completed during the implementation period when much reinvention occurs (Rogers, 1995). Reinvention is a process in which adopters modify an innovation to fit their local implementation setting. Rice and

Rogers (1980) found that reinvention is positively related to the adoption of innovations. They indicate that reinvention facilitates the transition of innovation ownership from developers to implementers. This is true whether the innovation was developed within the organization that uses it or was imported from the outside. In either situation, implementation deals with adopting and tailoring an innovation to the organization's specific needs and constraints.

Following is a discussion of some of the common implementation processes of both "homegrown" and externally developed innovations, as well as the processes observed in terminating innovations.

Linking the New with the Old

In the organizations in which innovations were "homegrown," MIRP researchers found that implementation activities often occurred throughout the developmental period by linking and integrating the "new" with the "old," as opposed to substituting, transforming, or replacing the 'd with the new (Schroeder et al., 1989). The implication of this obs.. va-tion is that because of limited organizational resources, seldom can innovations be simple additions to existing organizational programs. Substituting the old with the new is also often not possible for political reasons. People are reluctant to replace existing organizational programs because of the history of investments and commitments they have made to them. Schroeder et al. (1989) report that innovation implementation proceeded more smoothly in those cases in which the "new" overlapped with and became integrated into existing organizational arrangements.

In terms of the overall developmental sequence, overlapping the new and old was evident in convergent paths of activities that linked the innovation with ongoing organizational arrangements. This convergent process can take several forms, including frequent restructuring of organizational arrangements, joint ventures, personnel responsibilities, use of teams, and altered control systems. Although the importance of integration and coordination mechanisms have long been recognized (e.g., Galbraith, 1973), we were surprised to observe the number, fluidity, and variety of creative mechanisms used in the innovations studied by MIRP. These mechanisms provided incremental ways to make continual transitions between divergent components of the innovations and between the new innovations and existing organizational operations throughout the innovation period. Indeed, as Scudder, Schroeder, Van de Ven, Seiler, and Wiseman (1989) proposed, the earlier and the greater the involvement of interdisciplinary task teams (e.g., swapping of personnel) to deal with problems that cross organizational boundaries, the fewer the problems encountered in developing and implementing complex innovations.

Although these integrating mechanisms serve their purpose of linking homegrown innovations to the operating subsystems of organizations, they do not prevent many problems commonly observed in organizations that adopt innovations developed elsewhere. As we will see, what may be considered a homegrown innovation to one level or division of an organization may be viewed as an externally imposed innovation to another level or division of that organization. Overall, however, we observed homegrown innovations to require less time to implement and institutionalize than externally induced innovations.

However, before we discuss the adoption of externally developed innovation, it is important to address the ending and "letting go" process that innovators must often go through when their innovation is transferred to operating units for implementation and institutionalization. Depending on the nature of the innovation, it may be necessary to make significant changes in organizational structures and systems. There may be problems with loss of ownership and disapproval of compromises made to the original idea in the interest of marketability, cost, or other aspects of feasibility. One is reminded of the lyrics, "Look what they've done to my song." There may be a letdown for the innovation team or, more likely, a time of ambivalence. On the one hand, there is a feeling of relief that the stresses and strains of the intensive innovation process are behind. On the other hand, there may be a depressed realization that there is nothing to fill the void.

The immediate emotional problem for innovation team members is dealing with separation. Sutton (1987) and Albert (1984) discuss the need to structure transition rituals—or "funerals"—to recognize the contributions of innovators and to facilitate the letting-go process. Just as society provides the funeral ritual to mourn the passing of loved ones, organizations need to structure ceremonies at transition times to help people relinquish the past and take on new assignments and ventures. Even though we reported that many people involved in an innovation have only partial inclusion in the project (i.e., they also are doing other things), they often make heavy psychological investments in the projects, and therefore they may need a time of mourning when the project is completed.

MIRP also included studies of the adoption of innovations that were not "homegrown" (i.e., the innovations were selected or imposed from outside the implementing organizational units). These studies included cases of (1) nuclear power plants throughout the United States implementing a safety guide, (2) public school boards or superintendents directing that all schools in the district implement a site-based management process, and (3) local government officials mandating implementation of a management consultant's recommendations. A key finding from these studies is that organizations that appear similar in all important respects may adopt innovations in very different ways. In addition, the process by which innovations are adopted influences implementation success. In particular, innovation adoption is facilitated when (1) the adopting organization modifies and adapts the innovation to its local situation, (2) top management is extensively involved and commits resources to innovation adoption, and (3) process facilitators help people understand and apply the new innovation (Van de Ven, Angle, and Poole, 1989).

For example, Marcus and Weber (1989) describe the organizational effectiveness implications of two different reactions taken by twenty-eight American nuclear power companies in response to a new set of nuclear safety procedures mandated by the U.S. Nuclear Power Commission. They found that the nuclear power plants with relatively poor safety records tended to respond in a rule-bound manner that perpetuated their poor safety performance. Conversely, plants with relatively strong safety records tended to retain their autonomy by adapting the standards to their local situations, a response that reinforced their strong safety performance. They observed that those least ready or willing to adopt the innovation needed it the most.

An important inference can be drawn from the Marcus and Weber (1989) study for managing externally imposed innovations. Be forewarned of the possible consequences of passive acceptance of external dictates by those who strictly follow the letter of the law; they may be doing so in "bad faith" and may not achieve the results intended. Some autonomy is needed for an adopting unit to identify with and internalize an innovation; formal compliance is insufficient for innovation adoption. The disposition of innovation adopters is likely to be negatively affected if they are not granted a sufficient level of autonomy, and their disposition is often critical in assuring successful adoption. This evidence emphasizes the importance of overcoming resistance to change when imposing, or even suggesting, the adoption of innovations that did not originate in the adopting organization. The "not invented here" syndrome is well-known in all sorts of organizations. Adopting agencies or organizations that have not developed any sense of commitment to those innovations may behave "bureaupathically" by simply doing what the "letter of the law" stipulates (Kerr, 1975; Lawler and Rhode, 1976).

In another MIRP study, Lindquist and Mauriel (1989) compared two common alternative strategies for adopting and implementing a site-based management innovation in public schools. One is a "depth" strategy in which the innovation is implemented and "debugged" in a demonstration site before it is generalized to other organizational units. The other is a "breadth" strategy in which the innovation is implemented through successive hierarchical levels across all organizational units simultaneously. Lindquist and Mauriel found that the school district that implemented the site-based management innovation in "breadth"—across all schools in the district—was more successful in implementing and institutionalizing more components of the innovation than was the school district that adopted the "depth" strategy within a school selected as the demonstration site. This finding is contrary to conventional wisdom that successfully implemented innovations start small and spread incrementally with success (Greiner, 1970; Van de Ven, 1980). Lindquist and Mauriel (1989) provide several important generalizable explanations for this finding:

1. When the depth strategy is introduced and heralded by top management, the demonstration project soon loses visible attention and institutional legitimacy from top-level managers, as their agendas become preoccupied with other pressing management problems.
2. With a breadth strategy, top management stays in control of the innovation implementation process, increasing, rather than decreasing, its power. Moreover, slack resources within the control of top management can ensure success better than limited budgets for innovation to a demonstration site.
3. There is a trade-off between implementing a few components of an innovation in breadth versus implementing all components in depth in a particular demonstration site. Fewer hurdles and resistances to change are encountered when a few, presumably easy, components of an innovation are implemented across the board to a few, presumably supportive, stakeholders, than when all, easy and hard, components of a program are implemented in depth with all partisan stakeholders involved.
4. With a depth strategy, it is easier for opposing forces in other parts of the organization to mobilize efforts to sabotage a "favored" demonstration site than it is to produce positive evidence of the merits and generalizability of an innovation.

In another MIRP study, Bryson and Roering (1989) examined the introduction of an administrative innovation—the adoption of new planning systems—in six local governmental agencies. They found that each attempt at implementation was prone to disintegration and cited three reasons:

1. External events and crises frequently occur, distracting participants' attention and priorities and absorbing resources that are available to adopt the innovation.
2. The adoption process itself is partially cumulative: What occurred before was sometimes remembered and had to be accounted for. Even tough past actions and decisions became inconsistent with, or contradicted, subsequent turns of events.
3. Participants get bogged down with information, conflicting

priorities, and divergent issues that fall outside their decision jurisdictions or domains.

Based on these observations, Bryson and Roering (1989) make the following recommendations for managing innovation:

1. Have a powerful innovation sponsor and an effective process facilitator who is committed to continuing with the adoption process, particularly when difficult hurdles and setbacks arise.
2. Structure the process into key junctures—deadlines, conferences, and peak events—because disruptions and setbacks cause delays and interest wanes with time. These structured junctures in the adoption process establish key deadlines to perform planned intermediate tasks and facilitate unplanned intersections of key ideas, people, transactions, and outcomes.
3. Be flexible not only about what constitutes acceptable innovation adoption but also in constructing arguments geared to many different evaluation criteria.

In short, innovation-adoption success, like development success, more often represents a socially constructed reality than an objective reality.

When Innovations Stop

Innovations terminate when they are implemented and institutionalized, as discussed earlier, or when resources run out. Although obvious, this observation is fundamentally important in explaining (1) the tendency, throughout the developmental period, toward "sugar-coated" administrative reviews and impression management by entrepreneurs relative to resource controllers; and (2) the conflict that is structurally inherent in the roles of innovation entrepreneurs and top managers or investors.

Top managers or investors have two somewhat antithetical roles in an innovation: support and coaching on the one hand and resource allocation on the other. If they are primarily viewed as resource controllers, instead of supportive coaches, innovation entrepreneurs have strong motivations to engage in impression management and to sugarcoat information, thus denying upper managers and investors the factual information they need to make sound decisions.

A related issue is the different frames of reference of innovation team members and top managers/investors. The latter do not view the innovation from the "up close and personal" point of view of the innovation team. Whereas the innovation may be the exclusive labor of love for the innovation team, it is but one of a set of interacting, often competing, business considerations for top managers and investors. Thus, as we have seen, the criteria for judging innovation progress may differ considerably from those used at the innovation-team level. This does not necessarily mean that criteria and decision logic are superior at the organizational level, only that they are different. And given these differences, the perspective that most controls the survival of an innovation is that of the resource controllers.

In their oversight capacity, top managers and investors periodically review the progress of their innovations and make attributions about the causes of performance outcomes of their innovations. Angle and Van de Ven (1989) examined these attributions of top managers involved in the MIRP studies and noted that the attributions were often misdirected. But whether correct or incorrect, they significantly influenced the behavior and careers of innovation participants. For example, the unsuccessful first-product take-off in one innovation was attributed to problems of "management implementation." As a consequence, the innovation team manager was replaced. However, the facts in the case indicated that many factors that led to failure were beyond the control of the innovation entrepreneur or participants. The evidence indicated that attributing failure to mismanagement was incorrect and resulted in making entrepreneurs the scapegoats for events beyond their reasonable control. Such attributions reinforced top managers' beliefs that managing innovation is fundamentally a control problem when it should be viewed as one of orchestrating a highly complex, uncertain, and probabilistic process.

Why are attributions for innovation success or failure often misdirected, particularly among managers and evaluators who are closely associated with their innovations? Mitchell, Green, and Wood (1981) proposed an attribution model of the ways supervisors make judgments about the causes of subordinates' poor performance. This model applies well to the innovations studied by MIRP. According to Mitchell and his colleagues, deciding why something went wrong in an organization is a two-stage attribution process. First, the manager must decide whether the deficiency had internal origins (something in the person)or was caused externally (something in the situation). A second attribution is whether the outcome was idiosyncratic or could be expected again under similar circumstances. This is the attribution of stability, or instability, of cause. These attributions and their consequences are illustrated in figure 2.4. As the illustration shows, an innovation failure might occur because of (1) internal-stable, (2) external-stable, (3) internal-unstable, or (4) external-unstable conditions.

In the first instance (internal-stable) the innovation may be judged to have failed because the innovation team and/or its leadership was not competent. The requisite skills and abilities were not present, or per-

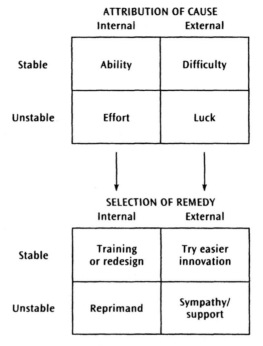

Figure 2.4 Attributions of innovation success or failure. Adapted from Mitchell, Green, and Wood (1981).

haps organization and leadership were inadequate. In this specific attribution, it is assumed that more trained or skilled individuals might have produced a more successful outcome. One conclusion from this attribution is that this particular innovation team was incapable of performing the task.

Alternatively, the innovation effort might have been too daunting or complex. This type of attribution fits our second example (external-stable). In this attributional choice, it is assumed that the innovation team might be successful in other types of innovation efforts, but the one attempted and failed was simply too difficult. It is further assumed that other entrepreneurs or innovation teams would have met the same fate.

In both these situations, the attributions are stable because the same outcomes would be expected over and over, given that (1) the same innovation team was attempting the innovation or (2) the same intractable problems faced the team. They are based on a presumption of a reliable world—one that is essentially the same from trial to trial. In contrast, the other pair of possible attributions assumes a capricious environment—one in which things may not be the same twice.

One such attribution (internal-unstable) is based on the perception that the innovation team, although competent, failed to do all that was needed to bring about success—team members didn't try hard enough, or they failed to pay attention to details. With this lesson learned, the team might do very well on another type of project, because members have the talent.

The fourth possible attribution within this framework (unstable-external) is based on the assumption that failure resulted from one or more bad breaks. In this situation the innovation team is not held culpable. Furthermore, the failure is seen as one that need not have happened; the problem was solvable, but things just did not fall into place. Better luck next time!

These four choices do not occur at random. Rather, there are built-in biases in the judgment process, based on the evaluator's personality and his or her relationship to the members of the innovation team. A more or less universal bias seems to be the tendency to make internal attributions for the failures of others. We seem to be much more even-handed in evaluating our own failures, often attributing them to external causes. With this bias operating, participants associated with failed innovations may find it difficult to escape the stigma of failure. Without compelling evidence to the contrary, upper management may be predisposed to attribute blame to the innovation team. In the case of a successful outcome, the same attribution bias may lead top management to take more credit than is due when things have gone well for the innovation.

This tendency to attribute failure to the innovation team tends to grow if the consequences of the failure are large for the evaluator. Although a rational view of human information processing would treat the cause and severity of outcomes to be independent of each other, much evidence exists to the contrary (Rosen and Jerdee, 1974). If a failed innovation has a particularly damaging effect on senior management, it is more likely that (1) an "internal" attribution of the causes of failure will be made—low effort or lack of ability on the part of the innovation team; and (2) the remedial action is apt to be severe.

Among other factors that bias the attribution process is the empathy in the relationship between top managers and members of the innovation team. Essentially, any factor which makes the leader psychologically closer to the member increases the tendency for the leader to make self-like attributions regarding the member (Mitchell et al., 1981). Conversely, as psychological distance increases, supervisors are more apt to make more severe attributions. One would therefore expect that people filling a mentor role would be biased toward making "external" attributions of the causes of an innovation team's failure because of the personal nature of a mentoring relationship. On the other hand, people filling the "critic" role might make a clear I-they distinction and be inclined toward attributing failure to the team's shortcomings.

Once a cause of failure has been identified, it becomes upper management's job to decide what to do about it. The Mitchell et al. (1981) model suggests that the remedy will follow the specific attribution of cause made by upper management. If it was seen as a case of bad luck, supportive leadership and a chance to try again might be the remedy. However, if the innovation was seen as too difficult, management might be more cautious in the future regarding what is attempted. If failure was deemed to be caused by lack of ability, top management might look for remedies aimed at better staffing or training of innovation participants. Finally, if failure was attributed to a lack of effort or diligence on the part of the innovation team, disciplinary action seems highly likely.

One often hears organizational maxims such as "Here, we let people fail," which indicates an espoused organizational rule that one should not stifle innovation by making people wary that they have only one chance to make it. Yet, the MIRP study findings indicate that this maxim is seldom operative, even in organizations that advocate the failure principle. Among the cases studied by MIRP, in no instances where innovations were judged as failures by top managers or investors were the innovation entrepreneurs offered another opportunity to manage a subsequent innovation. Angle and Van de Ven (1989) note the following: "We have seen instances where innovation team leaders whose projects foundered are stigmatized as 'losers.' We suspect that this label is most often applied where failure was not seen as an anomaly or 'fluke' but was seen as likely to happen again, were a similar innovation to be attempted" (692).

Actually, only one of the four possible attributions (i.e., bad luck) predisposes upper management to give entrepreneurs another chance. All others tend to lead to caution and lead management to "place its next bet on some other horse."

These negative attributions and remedies "spill over" on the innovation entrepreneurs. For example, in the wake of the decision to discontinue further investment in TAP, despite several attempts the TAP program manager was unable to change top managers' pronouncements that he had "failed." Over the course of four years of bimonthly meetings with the researchers, December 1987 was the first time this entrepreneur admitted that his innovation was a "failure," as he was helping TAP participants obtain other jobs in their organizations or elsewhere. In June 1988, the entrepreneur himself assumed a new job as a salesman in another part of his organization at the same salary but at a lower job grade and in a smaller office. A year later, he found employment in another organization.

Variations in Common Process Characteristics

The foregoing sections have identified and explained a dozen common characteristics in the development of a wide variety of innovations that were included in the MIRP studies. They provide an empirically grounded map of the key processes commonly encountered along the innovation journey. Of course, not all innovation journeys are alike. In particular, we expect the twelve process characteristics to be more pronounced for innovations of greater novelty, size, and duration. These contingencies tend to be associated with innovations that are undertaken in different organizational settings.

Radical versus Incremental Innovations

Some innovations change the entire order of things, making obsolete the old ways and perhaps sending entire businesses the way of the slide rule or the buggy whip. Others simply build up what is already present, requiring only modest modifications of the old-world view. In his extensive review of the innovation literature, Rogers (1995) concludes that innovations of different levels of novelty need to be managed differently. Five dimensions of innovation novelty are distinguished in Rogers's model: an innovation's relative advantage, compatibility, complexity, trialability, and observability.

These dimensions of novelty are important not only for predicting an innovation's rate of adoption and diffusion but also for evaluating an organization's capabilities to undertake the development process. Indeed, some organizations may be well suited to one type of innovation but not to another. For example, an organization that values and rewards individualism may have the advantage in radical innovation, whereas a more collectivist system may do better at an incremental one (Angle, 1989). Novelty also influences an innovation's developmental pattern. Pelz (1985) found that the stages of the innovating process were more disorderly for technically complex innovations than for technically simple innovations.

Innovation Stage and Temporal Duration

Transitions from innovation invention to development to implementation often entail shifts from radical to incremental and from divergent to convergent thinking. Cheng and Van de Ven (1996) and Dooley and Van de Ven (1998) found that events in the beginning development periods of CIP and TAP were either random or chaotic, whereas these events settled down to an orderly periodic pattern in the ending development periods of these innovations. As innovations approach the culminating institutionalization step, they become more highly structured and stabilized in their patterns and less differentiated from other organizational arrangements (Zaltman et al., 1973; Lindquist and Mauriel, 1989).

The developmental pattern and eventual success of an innovation is also influenced by its temporal duration. The initiation of an innovation represents an initial stock of assets that provides an innovation unit a "honeymoon" period to perform its work (Fichman and Levinthal, 1988). These assets reduce the risk of terminating the innovation during its honeymoon period when setbacks arise and when initial outcomes are judged unfavorable. The likelihood of replenishing these assets, by obtaining additional funding for innovation development, is highly influenced by how long it takes to complete the change process. Interest and commitment wane with time. Thus, after the honeymoon period, innovations terminate at disproportionately higher rates, in proportion to the time required for their implementation. As Pressman and Wildavsky (1973) say, "The advantages of being new are exactly that: being new. They dissipate quickly over time. The organization ages rapidly. Little by little the regulations that apply to everyone else also apply to it" (130).

Size and Scope of the Innovation

It may be that small organizations have the advantage in starting up an innovation but that larger organizations with more available resources have the advantage in keeping an innovation alive until it is completed. Van de Ven et al. (1989) found that venture capital was more risky, more short term, and more difficult to obtain than was internal corporate venture funding. Larger organizations offer a more fertile ground for sustaining and nurturing spin-off innovations. Also, there may be more places to "hide" in a larger organization until an innovation can stand on its own. Yet, large organizations seem to need bureaucratic systems to manage, which is not particularly conducive to innovation. The message to managers is to keep finding ways to remain flexible, to permit sufficient power to concentrate on innovation, to build access to technical competence, and to listen attentively to the views of those directly responsible for implementation—factors that Burgelman (1983), Kanter (1983), and Nord and Tucker (1987) found were critical success factors for adopting innovations in large organizations.

Conclusion

This road map of how the innovation journey typically unfolds includes a dozen common patterns observed during the initiation, development, and implementation of a wide variety of innovations studied by MIRP. Providing an empirically grounded map represents a useful first step to maneuver the innovation journey. It identifies the temporal sequence of events, junctures, and hurdles that innovation teams and managers experience along the journey. Knowing how the innovation process usually unfolds provides data that are useful for analyzing, planning, and undertaking the journey. In addition, it provides the empirical foundation for subsequent chapters to undertake more in-depth examinations of learning, leadership, and co-venturing processes at innovation and industry levels of the innovation journey.

Of course, the map is far from complete. Many journeys remain uncharted. However, from among the innovations that were charted by MIRP researchers, we can say that the innovation journey can be accomplished in a number of different ways and can unfold along many different routes. Whatever route is taken, the innovation journey crosses a rugged landscape that is highly ambiguous, is often uncontrollable, and involves a good deal of luck.

We therefore conclude by emphasizing that maneuvering each of the twelve common process characteristics will not ensure innovation success. The reason for this caveat rests with a concluding principle that we believe underlies all the key processes along the innovation journey: Entrepreneurs and managers cannot control innovation success, only its odds. This principle implies that a fundamental change is needed in the control philosophy of conventional management practice.

One of the authors uses a case to teach MBA students in which an organization is meeting all its important goals but management is not "in control" because an informal work group is managing itself by "beating the system" and in doing so is meeting management's goals about as well as anyone could hope. The immediate work group supervisor in the case has essentially abdicated a traditional directive role and spends all his time instead providing "enabling conditions." The typical reaction to this scenario is outrage to the students, many of whom have several years of managerial experience. The supervisor is not "doing his job" and top management is "not in control," they say.

We do seem to have a controlling bias in Western managerial society. Even if things are going well, we insist on being in charge. This may raise problems with the management of innovation, because the process may be inherently uncontrollable, at least at levels of intensity that show promise for making a significant contribution.

Professor William McKelvey (1982) tells the story of the 1976 Winter Olympics, where Franz Klammer won the men's downhill skiing competition. When interviewed after the event and asked how he managed such an incredible performance, Klammer said that he chose to "ski out of control" (447–448). He knew that many other top-level skiers were entered against him, several of whom might outpace him on any given day if he were to ski his normal speed—that is, in control. He chose, instead, to ski so fast that he abandoned any sense of control over the course. Although this was clearly not a sufficient condition for victory, he saw it as a necessary condition. Staying "in control" would virtually ensure a loss, whereas skiing "out of control" would make it at least possible to win.

Innovation and change managers may have an important lesson to learn from this vignette. By definition, an innovation is a leap into the unknown. If an innovation is to have a chance to succeed, traditional notions of managerial control may need to be relaxed somewhat. It is not that such letting go will ensure success, merely that it may be a necessary condition.

A number of practical consequences follow if innovation success is recognized to be a probabilistic process. First, innovation success or failure would more often be attributed to factors beyond the control of innovators. This, in turn, will decrease the likelihood that the careers of innovation participants will be stigmatized if their innovation fails and increase the likelihood that they will be given another chance to manage future innovations. After all, one cannot become a master or professional at anything if only one trial is permitted. As we reported, relatively little trial-and-error learning occurred when the journey was initiated for a given innovation. Repeated trials over many innovations are essential for learning to occur and for applying these learning experiences to subsequent innovations. It is primarily through repeated trials and the accumulation of learning experiences across these trials that an organization can build an inventory of competence and progressively increase its odds of innovation success.

For this to happen, Professor Connie Gersick at UCLA suggests that we need to develop ways to let managers practice innovation skills in relatively safe environments. Management educators could act on this idea by developing training programs, possibly with simulation exercises and cases, for managers to take before they embark on the innovation journey. Furthermore, to continue our analogy, managers should have opportunities to hone their skills on "beginner slopes" by launching small and inexpensive innovations before they strike out "on the Alps" by directing major and expensive innovations that are central to the future viability of their organizations.

3

Learning the Innovation Journey

What guides the innovation journey? As described in chapter 2, the development of an innovation is a highly ambiguous uncertain journey in which entrepreneurs, with financial support from investors, undertake a sequence of events over an extended period to transform a novel idea into an implemented reality.

Several years of intensive investment and effort are often required to develop an innovation to the point at which its ultimate results can be determined. As a consequence, a central problem in managing the innovation journey is determining whether and how to continue a developmental effort in the absence of concrete performance information.

Adaptive processes of organizational learning have gained increasing prominence as a way to address this kind of problem (e.g., Levitt and March, 1988; Cohen and Levinthal, 1990; Milliken and Lant, 1991; and *Organization Science*, Vol. 2, No. 1). Other methods for gaining intelligence, such as planning and imitation, do not work well because in highly novel and uncertain situations, precedents and routines do not exist and predictions about future states of events are not reliable (Chakravarthy, 1984; Mintzberg et al., 1976).

Organizational scholars typically describe the process of trial-and-error learning as follows: People undertake a course of action, there is some outcome response from the environment, people interpret and evaluate the response, and then adapt their course of action to increase the propensity of the desired response (March and Olsen, 1976). Numerous simulation and laboratory studies (e.g., Lave and March, 1975; Levinthal and March, 1981; Lant and Mezias, 1990) have examined various forms of this learning. This model has proven quite robust in situations in which preferences are clear, alternative courses of action are specified in advance, and outcomes are unambiguous (March, 1972). But few studies have examined the empirical validity of this model in more ambiguous organizational settings where goals are often vague and shift over time, new courses of action emerge during the developmental process, and outcomes are difficult to assess. To advance our knowledge of organizational learning, it is important to reformulate and test this model of adaptive learning in more ambiguous, real-world organizational settings, such as innovation development.

This chapter examines the adaptive learning process during the development of two biomedical innovations—therapeutic apheresis and cochlear implants—and a software products company. All are described in Part II, chapters 8, 9, and 10. We introduce a model of experiential learning that fits these innovation settings and that proposes how processes of adaptive learning might guide the innovation journey. The analysis focuses on the connections among the goals, actions, and outcomes of an entrepreneurial team as it develops its innovation over time and the influences of resource controllers and environmental events on the learning process.

Conceptual Framework

The model of adaptive learning illustrated in figure 3.1 reflects our existing research knowledge of rational organizational learning. The internal loop between actions and outcomes represents a behavioral model of trial-and-error learning among entrepreneurs or an innovation unit. The top outer loop reflects observations, discussed in the chapter 2, that actions may create new goals or performance criteria may shift to justify action. The bottom outer loop incorporates a key element of organizational learning in which external investors or top management resource controllers may intervene in the assessment process and modify the course of action taken by the entrepreneurial unit. Finally, environmental events may occur independent of the learning loops and may affect outcome assessments and shifts in outcome criteria or trigger intervention by resource controllers. This model is based on four key hypotheses:

1. Focusing on the internal loop between actions and outcomes and following March's (1972) assumption that people are adaptively rational, we hypothesize that trial-and-error learning occurs when actions and outcomes are related, as follows:

   To develop an innovation, entrepreneurs initially choose a course of action, say, course A, with the intention of achieving a positive outcome. If a positive outcome is

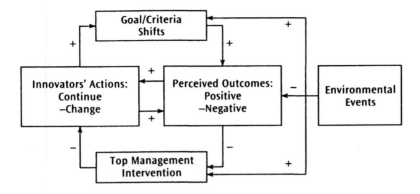

Figure 3.1 Learning model to guide the innovation journey

experienced after action course A, the entrepreneurs
will continue with A, and if a negative outcome is experienced, they will change to a new course of action,
say, course B. Subsequently, if positive outcomes are experienced with action course B, the entrepreneurs will
continue with B, but if negative outcomes are experienced, they will change again to another course of action, C, which may appear the next best alternative course
at that time.

This process of negative outcomes leading to changes in the prior
course of action continues until positive outcomes are experienced,
which in turn, serve as the incentive for continuing with the prior
course of action. Although we assume that people are purposeful and
continue or change their actions intending positive outcomes, in ambiguous situations negative feedback is less valuable than positive
feedback. From positive feedback people learn that if they do again
what they did the last time, they are likely to be successful. But people do not learn what to do to be successful from negative information;
they only learn what not to do. People may change their actions to
avoid the negative outcomes experienced with the prior course of action, but that does not tell them whether a change in action will lead to
positive outcomes. Following the logic of a learning curve, as one persists in a course of action, one learns how to perform it better and better. However, changing a course resets the learning clock back to zero.
Similarly, following the organizational inertia arguments of Hannan
and Freeman (1989), a supporting social structure tends to evolve
around reliable repetitive behavior, which increases the chances of
success, whereas change engenders costs of upsetting this reinforcing
structure. Thus, we expect that the likelihood of obtaining positive

outcomes increases by continuing with a course of action and decreases by changing the action course.

> 2. Negative outcomes will trigger interventions from external resource controllers, and these interventions may subsequently lead to changes in the course of action being pursued by the innovation team.

This hypothesis of when external interventions influence the trial-and-error learning process is based on the double-loop model of success and failure discussed in chapter 2, illustrated in figure 2.2. This model predicts that positive outcomes increase the confidence of top managers or investors in the innovation's course of action, which increases their willingness to delegate greater control to the entrepreneurial unit. In turn, this willingness to delegate provides the innovation unit greater discretion to continue its internal learning process. In this "positive outcomes" loop, development activities tend to proceed smoothly, and relationships between the innovation team and top management resource controllers are uneventful because the latter are satisfied with progress and have little reason to intervene and pose differing views on the innovation unit. In this case, the lower outside intervention loop in figure 3.1 is not triggered.

However, when significant failures are perceived in a course of action, uncertainties arise about the appropriateness of the course of action taken by the innovation unit. This uncertainty stimulates top management resource controllers to intervene and remedy the situation by exploring alternative action courses with the innovation unit. In these instances, power struggles often erupt between the innovation entrepreneurs and resource controllers, with the latter, typically more powerful group, imposing a preferred course of action on the former. When this struggle subsides, often by the imposition of a new or modified action plan, the external intervention loop is completed and recycles in either internal or external directions.

The top outer loop of relationships in figure 3.1 illustrates how prior courses of action may create new goals or new outcome criteria to justify the course of action by an entrepreneurial unit. Performance goals are assumed to remain constant in rational models of choice, but in chapter 2 we saw that performance criteria often change during the innovation journey. March (1972) questioned "how something as conspicuous as the fluidity and ambiguity of objectives can plausibly be ignored in a theory that is offered as a guide to organizational behavior" (72). March (1972) suggested that "we treat action as a way of creating interesting goals at the same time as we treat goals as a way of justifying action. It is an intuitively plausible and simple idea, but one that is not immediately within the domain of standard normative theories of intelligent choice" (72).

Continued persistence in a given course of action implies an increasingly complex and differentiated progression of specialized innovation development activities. Many of these activities will be justified as elaborations of a general goal into many functional subgoals, and some will inevitably drift in divergent directions that in retrospect imply either substantively new goals or new criteria for justifying the actions taken. Such experiments with goals should be especially pronounced when pursuing an ambiguous course of innovation development. Elaborations of an overall goal into multiple subgoals or related goals may increase the likelihood of positive outcome judgments because the latter goals presumably represent more concrete and less ambiguous mileposts to achieving the more ambiguous superordinate goal. Shifting goals also provides ways to preserve and enhance the sense of success. People learn to like what they do well. As March, Sproull, and Tamuz (1991) argue, "this transformation of wants through experience can be conservative in the sense of tending to increase the likelihood of success" (4).

3. Continuing with a course of action over time, as opposed to changing it, stimulates creating new subgoals or outcome criteria, which, in turn, increases the likelihood of positive outcome assessments.

In the long run, the ultimate success of an innovation's development is a product of the probabilities of achieving a series of conjunctive subgoals. Mathematically, this implies that stringing the number of goals or subgoals during innovation development increases the risk of ultimate failure. As Pressman and Wildavsky (1973) indicated, stringing together relatively safe bets—50-50 or even 80-20—can quickly lead to situations in which overall success is very unlikely. Thus, ironically, whereas the elaboration of convergent subgoals should lead to more positive in-process outcome assessments during innovation development, they may decrease the mathematical odds of ultimate success during innovation implementation.

4. External context events (e.g., shifting priorities by external groups, new information about competitors, or other environmental events) disrupt the trial-and-error learning process by an innovation team.

Context events may have three kinds of significant disruptive effects on an innovation's development:

a. External context events may trigger recognition of the need to attain new goals or success criteria if the venture is to "win" in the market with the new technology.

     b. When these environmental events are of substantial im-
       portance, they often trigger direct interventions by top
       management or external resource controllers.
     c. Events can directly influence relative standards of suc-
       cess, according to Kelly and Thibaut's (1959) social com-
       parison theory.

Information about technological advances or progress of competitors typically decreases the attractiveness of the present commitment,
particularly after the current venture experiences some inevitable setbacks. External context events are structurally biased toward producing disappointing results because they counteract the tendency to in-
flate expectations of success (Harrison and March, 1984). These biases
include the tendency of people to attribute success to internal factors
within their control and to blame failures on uncontrollable environmental forces (Nisbett and Ross, 1980; Salancik and Meindl, 1984;
Staw, McKenchnie, and Puffer, 1983).

As the model in figure 3.1 illustrates, whatever the direct effects of
contextual events, they all produce the same consequences: external
intervention; struggle between entrepreneurs and resource controllers;
and often confusing, contradictory, or abrupt shifts in innovation development. To the extent that they arise, innovation start-up may reflect times of discontinuous shifts or terminations in courses of action.

MIRP Studies of Adaptive Learning Model

Van de Ven and Polley (1992), in a study of the development of therapeutic apheresis, and Garud and Van de Ven (1992), in a study of the development of cochlear implants, empirically examined the model in figure 3.1. As discussed in chapter 8, the cochlear implant program (CIP)
was undertaken from 1977 to 1989 as an internal venture within a large
corporation to create an implanted device that permits hearing for profoundly deaf people. The therapeutic apheresis program (TAP), described in chapter 9, was undertaken from 1981 to 1988 as a joint venture by three corporations to create a biomedical technology to treat
autoimmune diseases by removal of pathogenic blood components.

The third study, described in chapter 10, Qnetics, has also been examined using the event history method described later. Qnetics began
in 1983 with the merger of two independent companies and continued
through 1988. Although the learning model expressed in figure 3.1 has
not been rigorously tested using Qnetics data, the Qnetics case provides interesting parallels and contrasts to the model we develop.

A review of the methods used in these studies is needed to understand how learning processes were measured and analyzed. As de-

scribed in Part II of this book, the studies tracked events in the development of the innovations as they unfolded from the time funding and efforts began to develop the innovation ideas until the innovations were implemented and introduced into the market. The researchers collected the event data by attending and recording the proceedings of monthly or bimonthly meetings of the innovation teams and periodic administrative reviews by top managers, by conducting semiannual interviews with all innovation managers and questionnaire surveys of all innovation personnel, and by obtaining documents from company records and industry trade publications throughout the developmental periods of the innovations.

Events were defined as instances in which changes occurred in the innovation idea, innovation team personnel and roles, the activities and relationships in which they engaged with others, the external context beyond the control of the innovation team, and judgments of positive or negative outcomes associated with these events. These events were entered into a qualitative computer data base (Rbase), which recorded each event in terms of its date, the action that occurred, the actors involved, the outcomes of the action, if available, and the data source. Chronological event listings were shared with innovation managers to verify their completeness and accuracy.

These events were then coded according to the conceptual categories in the learning model:

1. *Continue or change in action course.* The direction of actions that occurred in each event was coded according to whether the action represented (a) a continuation or expansion (addition, elaboration, or reinforcement) of the course of action under way or (b) a contraction (subtraction, reduction, or deemphasis) or modification (revision , shift, or correction).
2. *Positive or negative outcomes.* When events provided evidence of results, they were coded as (a) positive (good news or successful accomplishment), (b) negative (bad news or instances of mistakes or failures), (c) mixed (neutral, ambivalent, or ambiguous news of results), or (d) null (events provided no information about outcomes). To minimize classification error, events coded as "mixed" or "null" were not included in the analysis reported here.
3. *Context events.* This category includes external environmental incidents that occurred beyond the control of the innovation participants but were reported as relevant to the innovation.
4. *Interventions by resource controllers.* When investors or top corporate managers were directly involved in an innovation development event, it was coded as such.
5. *Goal criteria shift.* When an innovation manager reported a change in innovation goals or criteria for evaluating the innovation's performance, it was coded as such.

Two researchers independently coded these events. Garud and Van de Ven (1992) agreed on 93% of all codes of CIP events, whereas Van de Ven and Polley (1992) agreed on 91% of all event codes for TAP. The researchers resolved all differences through mutual consent. To apply regular time series methods for analyzing the learning model, the researchers aggregated the event data into monthly frequency counts.

Results

Graphs A through E in figures 3.2 through 3.4 show the monthly number of coded events observed throughout the development of CIP, TAP, and Qnetics innovations, respectively. The CIP and TAP graphs are similar, but those for Qnetics appear very different. Upon closer examination, however, we will show that the Qnetics developmental pattern is similar to that of CIP and TAP. In fact, in chapter 7 we discuss how CIP and TAP represent special cases of a more general developmental sequence than Qnetics reflects.

The CIP and TAP innovations show two temporal periods reflecting very different patterns of relationships between actions and outcomes:

1. There is an initial premarket development period of mostly expanding activities undertaken when decisions were made to launch the innovation efforts with corporate venture capital support.
2. This is followed by an ending market-entry development period of mostly contracting activities that concluded with decisions to terminate TAP and CIP for different reasons.

The initial development period began when the entrepreneurial teams were formed and funded to explore an innovative idea. It was an ambiguous period in which it was not clear which of several possible technical designs should be developed. During this initial ambiguous period, external environmental events—not the actions of entrepreneurs—had a significant negative effect on outcomes. When negative outcomes occurred, they subsequently led the entrepreneurs to continue with, and not change, their prior course of action. These actions, in turn, had no effect on subsequent outcomes in positive or negative directions. These findings suggest a faulty learning process of persistent action despite the occurrence of negative outcomes during the beginning development period.

Major problems of market entry punctuated the beginning and ending development periods of the two innovations: TAP experienced manufacturing scale-up problems, whereas product failures necessitated a product recall for CIP. The ending period dealt primarily with

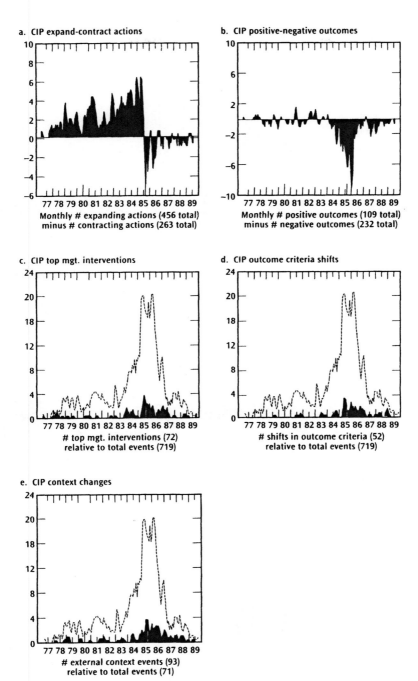

Figure 3.2 Frequencies of coded events in the development of the
Cochlear Implant Program (plots are three-month moving averages)

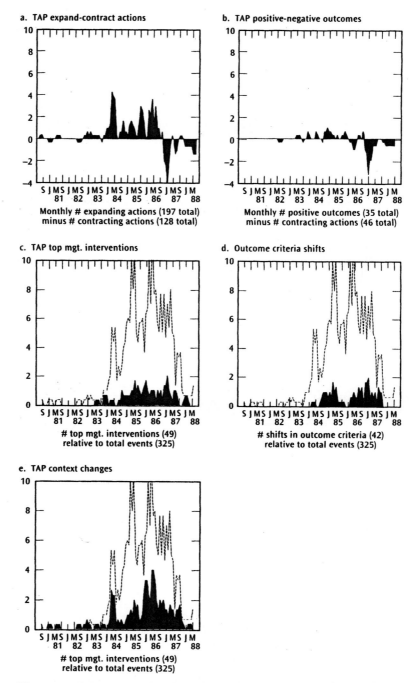

Figure 3.3 Frequencies of coded events in the development of the *therapeutic* apheresis innovation (plots are three-month moving averages)

a. **Expand-contract action**

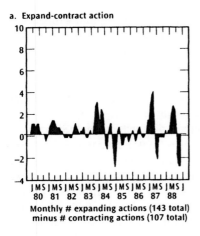

Monthly # expanding actions (143 total)
minus # contracting actions (107 total)

b. **Positive-negative outcomes**

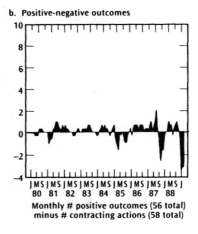

Monthly # positive outcomes (56 total)
minus # contracting actions (58 total)

c. **Investor interventions**

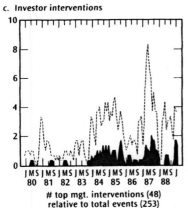

top mgt. interventions (48)
relative to total events (253)

d. **Outcome criteria shifts**

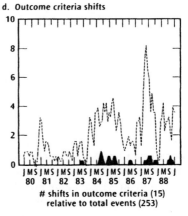

shifts in outcome criteria (15)
relative to total events (253)

e. **Context changes**

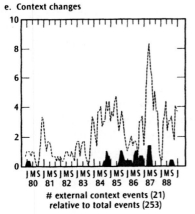

external context events (21)
relative to total events (253)

Figure 3.4 Frequencies of coded events in the development of Qnetics, a new company (plots are three-month moving averages)

uncertain but less ambiguous problems of scale-up manufacturing and market entry of the technical designs that were chosen in the earlier period. During this later period, strong evidence for the learning model was found for both CIP and TAP. Adaptive learning was evident in the positive reciprocal relationships between actions and outcomes.

In explaining these results, Van de Ven and Polley (1992) concluded that the process of learning seems random and unpredictable during the initial period of development but not during the concluding period of development. Garud and Van de Ven (1992) speculated that trial-and-error learning seems to guide innovation development under conditions of uncertainty (i.e., when it is not clear how to achieve known ends) and resource paucity, but persistent action appears to occur when the developmental process exhibits ambiguity (i.e., when it is not clear what specific ends are worth pursuing) and resource munificence.

Another plausible explanation for these results is that the process of learning was not modeled correctly. The linear time series regression techniques that were used cannot distinguish between chaotic behavior that results from an underlying nonlinear system and that which is the result of complex random shocks and stochastic processes. Traditional linear statistical techniques, such as time series regression, assume that a system can produce irregular behavior only when subjected to random inputs. Researchers have treated the error term, reflecting the seemingly random component of the model, as non-meaningful noise when estimating the learning model. Nonlinear dynamic theory provides methods to determine whether the random component of behavior might arise endogenously. For example, the chaotic property of sensitivity to initial conditions precludes using least-squares or maximum-likelihood techniques (Morrison, 1991). As Hibbert and Wilkinson (1994) point out, the parameters of the system set the pattern (i.e., fixed point, periodic, or chaotic), and the initial starting values determine the particular values in the time series.

Cheng and Van de Ven (1996) and Dooley and Van de Ven (1997) re-examined the event data to explore the possibility that the learning processes in the CIP and TAP innovation journeys began in chaos and ended in order. To do this, they examined whether the event time series shown in figures 3.2 and 3.3 A through C reflect periodic, chaotic, colored noise, or random white noise patterns. They applied diagnostics for detecting nonlinear dynamics— such as the correlation dimension, Lyapunov exponent, and Hurst exponent—in the actions, outcomes, and context event time series for CIP and TAP. They reported the following findings:

1. The action event time series during the beginning period of development for CIP and TAP were potentially chaotic, while

they reflected a periodic pattern during the ending market-entry period of development for CIP. There were too few data points during TAP's ending period to make an empirical diagnosis (Cheng and Van de Ven, 1996).

2. The outcome event time series during the beginning period of TAP development were potentially chaotic, while they reflected a random pattern for CIP's initial development period. Outcome events during the ending development periods for both CIP and TAP were periodic (Dooley and Van de Ven, 1997).

3. The context event time series for the beginning development periods of both CIP and TAP were random, as they were for CIP's ending development period. There were too few data points to make an empirical diagnosis of context events during TAP's ending development period (Cheng and Van de Ven, 1996).

The Qnetics innovation event data were also examined by Dooley and Van de Ven (1998). Qnetics exhibits at least two cycles similar to those of TAP and CIP. During its initial period, from the time of the merger in late 1980 until late 1984, Qnetics proliferated in developing many new software products that it could not market successfully, which culminated in the near failure of the new business when financial backers became wary. The withdrawal of a public offering and problems associated with lenders resulted in a period in which Qnetics suffered a major decline. In contrast to TAP and CIP, the Qnetics effort did not end in failure as a result of this decline. The business was subsequently reenergized during 1986. During this resurgence, new projects were started and a new period of elaboration began. This second cycle again came to a close with the final decline of the innovation in 1987 and 1988. Unfortunately, the event time series of expansion and contraction during each of Qnetics's cycles were too short to permit meaningful statistical analysis of actions and outcomes as described for TAP and CIP.

Implications of Findings for Innovation and Learning

Organizational learning is commonly defined as an experiential process of acquiring knowledge about action-outcome relationships and the effects of environmental events on these relationships (Duncan and Weiss, 1979). In her literature review, Barnett (1994) shows that this definition is shared by behavioral and cognitive learning theorists, although they place somewhat different emphasis on actions or outcomes to measure learning. Behavioral learning theorists (e.g., Lave and March, 1975; March and Olsen, 1975; Cohen and Sproull, 1991) tend to emphasize notions of decision rationality and to focus on trial-and-error learning, measured as the propensity of individuals to change their actions to achieve a given set of outcome preferences or goals. Cognitive theorists (e.g., Weick, 1979, 1993; Brunsson, 1982, 1985) tend to adopt notions of action rationality and to focus on sense-making processes by examining how individuals' cognitive maps and preferences change as they undertake a course of action. The key points in either definition are that learning increases when actions and outcomes become tightly linked and random environmental events occur with insufficient frequency or magnitude to provide a context that is stable enough to permit identifying relationships between actions and outcomes.

Our research indicates that learning, according to this definition, did not occur during the beginning period of innovation development when both action and outcome events followed a chaotic pattern, but that learning did occur after the action and outcome time series changed from chaotic to periodic patterns during the ending period (see also Van de Ven and Polley, 1992; Garud and Van de Ven, 1992). The conclusion, then, is that the innovation units either learned nothing during their first four to six years of developmental efforts or that they engaged in some other type of knowledge acquisition not included in the definition of learning. It also begs questions about the prerequisites for learning and how it originates.

Learning presumes some a priori knowledge about the task to be learned. In particular, the definition of learning presumes that learners have some a priori knowledge about (1) alternative courses of action, (2) what outcome preferences or goals are desired, and (3) the institutional rules, resources, and settings in which the task is undertaken. Our efforts thus focus on identifying how this prerequisite knowledge is created.

Our findings also call into question the two most commonly used explanations in the literature of the innovation process. The two explanations are that organizational innovations emerge (1) in an orderly periodic progression of stages or phases or (2) in a random sequence of chance or "blind" events. Neither of these two explanations is valid where chaos or nonlinear dynamics are found. Chaos tells us that the process consists of a nonlinear dynamic system, which is neither stable and predictable nor stochastic and random. Evidence of nonlinear dynamics reduces and sharpens the range of plausible explanations by identifying when and what dimensions of the innovation process are orderly, random, and chaotic. When we know this, we have a better idea of what models to apply to understand the dynamics. As Morrison (1991) discusses, we can (1) use stochastic models and statistics to explain random processes, (2) use stable linear and nonlinear models to explain periodic cycles or equilibria, and (3) use nonlinear dynamic models to explain chaotic processes.

The findings that action events were potentially chaotic in the beginning and shifted to a periodic pattern in the ending period of innovation development provides important clues for reconceptualizing processes of learning during the innovation journey. Low-dimensional nonlinear dynamics typically consist of a relatively simple system of only a few variables. Because learning is our substantive focus, the core variables in our system will most likely include the actions entrepreneurs take, the judgments they make about outcome preferences or goals, and the contextual events they experience as they travel the innovation journey. This system incorporates the key concepts in existing theories of behavioral and cognitive learning.

A nonlinear dynamic model of learning calls for an expanded definition of learning that examines not only how action-outcome relationships develop but also how prerequisite knowledge of alternative actions, outcomes, and contexts emerge. This expanded definition distinguishes learning by *discovery* from learning by *testing.* In particular, our research findings suggest that learning by discovery in chaotic conditions is an expanding and diverging process of discovering possible action alternatives, outcome preferences, and contextual settings. Learning by testing during more stable periodic conditions is a narrowing and converging process of testing which actions are related to what outcomes. Moreover, because learning by discovery is a precondition for learning by testing, we must examine how transitions occur between chaotic and orderly learning patterns.

In a chaotic system, we know that the temporal development of variables is dynamic, nonlinear, and sensitive to initial conditions. Dynamic means that the values that a variable takes at a given time are a function, at least in part, of the values of that same variable at an earlier time. Nonlinearity implies that the dynamic feedback loops vary in strength (loose or tight coupling) and direction (positive or negative) over time. Sensitivity to initial conditions means that small initial differences or fluctuations in variables will grow over time into large differences. The pathways that are taken in this divergent progression cannot be predicted, but we suggest later that they can be viewed as the storehouse of experiences from which learning originates.

One important implication of sensitivity to initial conditions is that the origins of experience and knowledge are important. If the innovation journey is to be explained as a learning process, the origination of true novelty should begin with profound ignorance not only with respect to what actions people initially take but also with respect to what outcomes they desire and the institutional context in which they begin to operate. The characteristics just discussed lead to the following new propositions about learning during the innovation journey:

1. *During the early highly ambiguous period of innovation de-velopment, broad macro goals galvanize action and promote learning by discovery.*

This action permits the development and elaboration of detailed plans and schedules that become successively more detailed as choices are made and discoveries are encountered. The actions generate knowl-edge of possibilities that allow formation of more detailed plans and preferences. Before the construction and discovery of these prefer-ences and alternatives, trial-and-error learning is not possible.

The CIP and TAP cases represent efforts to develop and commer-cialize new-to-the-world biomedical innovations. Each case began with a set of seemingly coincidental events (e.g., news of a "bionic ear" in Australia or advances in basic apheresis research) that captured the attention of certain bioscientists and managers and motivated them to develop a plan and request funding to launch developmental efforts. The initial plans contained vague but optimistic proposals to develop and commercialize new biomedical devices for new markets based on new technologies that were believed to have the potential to sustain the organizations' businesses in the next generation (Van de Ven, Ven-kataraman, Polley, and Garud, 1989). The plans indicated that the start-ing conditions were highly ambiguous; they focused on possibilities and opportunities, not on specific project goals, objectives, or outcome criteria. The action plans were also highly uncertain; they emphasized exploratory research and discovery, not testing or evaluation, because the innovations represented novel undertakings for the organizations. Reflecting a general appreciation of the organizational and institu-tional context, the action steps and targets in the initial plans were anchored in the regulatory review requirements for commercializing biomedical devices by the FDA and in corporate routines for adminis-trative review and budgeting cycles of projects.

Qnetics brought together two independent operations that rapidly identified a mission targeting medical products. This mission gener-ated efforts toward developing six different products. Other efforts from the premerger period were also continued. The contract software efforts and computer sales inherited from the premerger firms were continued as a means to generate funds for the medical product efforts. After a variety of financial and product problems, Qnetics focused its second round of expansion efforts as a "product development com-pany" not "restricted to (the) medical industry." This change in mis-sion allowed the company to refocus on new opportunities in utility-load management.

The selection of diseases to treat with a TAP device provides a more detailed illustration of the need for action in the absence of clear pref-erences. Market considerations required detailed knowledge of filtration capabilities to suggest which diseases could be most profitably treated. Developers, however, wanted to know what they should try to filter out to develop the most effective filtration product. This catch-22 situation could not be fully resolved by rational analysis and ultimately required a commitment to action. Two diseases were finally chosen, and the innovators agreed to move forward with these choices.

Although the choices narrowed the attention to these diseases, they also opened an entirely new set of issues that required resolution. The developers had to design and test filtration units targeted at these diseases. Animal models that mimicked the human diseases had to be identified, and developers discovered that new diagnostic tests would be needed to observe whether therapy was effective. As noted, the development of these diagnostics would themselves become a legitimate business opportunity. The choice of actions thus narrows the focus of attention at the same time that it opens new questions and defines further requirements. This process of elaboration was quite typical of this early TAP activity.

In addition to developing a biomedical device, both CIP and TAP innovation teams had to complete and test their devices and achieve Food and Drug Administration (FDA) approval for commercial release. Each of these steps required additional investigations. What clinics or patients would be the best test sites? How should the devices be introduced to the market place? Efforts to address these questions proceeded in parallel with the design and testing of each device. Subsequent devices depended critically on the capabilities of the first device to accomplish its intended technical performance characteristics.

The emergence of detailed plans took time, and the discovery of unexpected surprises led to revisions. Thus, schedules frequently slipped. Problems were expected and were generally resolved by the teams that encountered them at the most detailed level. This isolation of problems at the lowest level led to persistence as well as success and accommodation.

The activities during this early period also fit within the framework of knowledge acquisition through searching and noticing rather than through experiential learning as discussed by Huber (1991). The establishment of advisory groups is evidence of environmental scanning. Many of the choices (e.g., diseases and animal models) suggest more focused search. As Cyert and March (1963) suggest, much of the searching related to "problems" occurred in the vicinity of problem symptoms. However, contrary to Huber's conjecture, more proactive searching was lacking at the higher managerial levels of the overall program. At the program level, we observed a recurring pattern of action persistence that seemed to rely on a logic of action and commitment (Brunsson, 1982) rather than a logic of rational decision making where negative feedback results in searches for alternative courses of action.

2. *Through learning by discovery, innovation teams identify and transform tacit understandings into explicit understandings of alternative conditions in which to pursue possible actions and outcomes in the development of their innovations.*

In other words, the elaboration and discovery of possible dimensions and categories of innovation development also generate specific technological artifacts in the form of prototypes, products, and specific tests. These represent a transformation from tacit to explicit knowledge, which is required to establish a tangible and stable test setting needed for trial-and-error learning.

Polyani (1966) described the importance of tacit knowledge. The innovators certainly had the background and concepts related to the technology used in the TAP innovation. They were confident of their own abilities yet did not have the product or detailed plans for the therapeutic device. Their early actions led first to concrete schedules and test units. Then, discoveries led to new problems and unexpected changes in direction and in the product. As Nonaka (1994) suggests, this is a process of converting tacit knowledge of what might be into explicit knowledge of concrete actions and performances.

The creation of artifacts in the form of prototypes and concrete schedules was not enough to generate trial-and-error learning in the early innovation period. In some cases, like the opportunity to skip an intermediate product step, events were almost lost in the urge to move toward the final goal. When the tangible outcomes were negative, such as the anticoagulant problem and pump motor difficulties, persistence limited the willingness to change overall direction. Nevertheless, the artifacts did influence the innovation success. Eventually the innovators were held to schedules and construction of one technology—filtration—and foreclosed developing other technologies—adsorption. The construction was one step at a time, using past artifacts to shape the action alternatives and discovered preferences influencing further creation of tangible artifacts.

Qnetics exemplifies this constructive process even more clearly than the more focused operations of CIP and TAP. In Qnetics, the ventures brought specific artifacts to the merger in the form of products, medical software products, under development and in the form of business ventures, Prime Computer distribution, among others, that had already been started. Qnetics managers found that many of the products were not viable but that the potential for some products was sufficient to retain medical products and broaden the focus when the venture was reorganized in 1986. Thus, developed projects were carried forward into new rounds of expansion. Also, during the first cycle of Qnetics development, difficulties discovered with financing affected the arrangements needed for the Prime Computer franchise, which led to modifiying and terminating this line of business. The

Prime Computer franchise was itself a carryover from QCS. Thus, Qnetics managers show evidence of continuing to carry forward tangible artifacts at the same time they learned "survival skills."

3. *Under conditions of ambiguity, innovation discoveries generate information about the social relationships and dependencies among developers and resource providers as well as information about the environment.*

Just as the innovation process involves constructing tangible technological artifacts, it also entails discovery and creation of social relationships among the involved actors and organizations. The CIP, TAP, and Qnetics innovation team members learned that partners sometimes make abrupt changes that look like failures of trust. The effort at strategic redirection by 3M was viewed as a "budget cut" by TAP developers. So, also, the attempt to pursue the multichannel technology by the 3M CIP program was resisted by 3M's partner as a shift in allegiance to the clinical research efforts. Some of the problems in the early development were seen as human failures rather than technical failures. Problems were "assigned" to specific organizations, and when they were not accepted or resolved, the co-venturing parties attributed this to a failure of will as well as to the technical difficulties.

The TAP strategic business unit (SBU) also learned that some issues and decisions are not open for full debate among the team. For example, the innovators revisited the business of diagnostics on repeated occasions. Key individuals outside the SBU initially made the decision not to pursue development of the diagnostics business. Other decisions about funding the TAP innovation unit and other potential business opportunities were also negotiated outside the SBU. This established process precedents that circumscribed the range and discretion of the SBU. Although the SBU professed to be a "board of directors," the precedents set by a few initial decisions prevented the TAP SBU from getting into subsequent debates about key strategic issues.

Thus, in situations of high ambiguity, both physical discovery and social construction proceed together. While tilling the garden, the discovery of a huge stone that requires extensive excavation may lead us to wonder about the wisdom of the partner who wanted the garden in this spot as easily as it leads us to speculate about the vagaries of nature.

4. *Nonlinear dynamic processes facilitate learning by discovery.*

The foregoing observations complement the framework proposed by Garud and Rappa (1994). They note that new technologies emerge through an interaction of technological beliefs, artifacts, and evaluation routines. We suggest that the interrelations described by Garud and Rappa emerge through different temporal patterns that begin with learning by discovery during a chaotic and seemingly random period and end with learning by testing, trial and error, during a more orderly period. Technological innovation begins in a setting where not only interrelations among beliefs, artifacts, and routines are ambiguous but also where there is profound ignorance about what beliefs, artifacts, and routines exist and are possible to relate. Learning how concepts are related through trial and error presupposes discovering what concepts are available to relate.

We suggested several ways in which this knowledge is discovered. The first is with a broad vision that motivates actions needed to gain experiences with (a) alternative ways to think or believe about a technology, (b) various artifact components and architectures that are possible, and (c) different testing or evaluation procedures that might be applied. In addition to this elaboration process of a repertoire of experiences, there is an articulation process of moving from tacit to explicit knowledge as suggested by proposition 2. Finally, there is a testing process of linking explicit beliefs, artifacts, and evaluation routines through trial-and-error learning. As Cheng and Van de Ven (1996) show, this overall cycle in the social construction of a technological innovation tends to begin in seemingly random chaos and end in an orderly pattern.

These observations of the TAP and CIP innovations suggest that the innovators did learn from their initial actions about categories of possible actions, desired outcomes, and contextual settings in which the actions and outcomes are possible. Feldman (1986) suggests a distinction that seems relevant to early innovation development. He notes the distinction between learning categories, correlations between stimuli, and learning schema, rules of causes, and effects. Using the arguments of Siegler (1983), Feldman notes that learning from experience occurs when inaccuracy in prediction is made salient and the resultant feedback is encoded into new rules. Learning from experience most likely occurs when a substantial knowledge about the phenomenon already exists.

With a profound lack of knowledge, the innovators first had to undergo a period of elaboration and exploration to develop knowledge of (a) the alternative courses of action; (b) the outcomes, beliefs, and criteria preferred; and (c) the social and technical context in which the learning was to occur. The elaboration proceeded on many fronts and encountered a variety of positive and negative information. Yet all this information was localized to the immediate area and used to energize or modify the local discovery effort rather than to generate major changes in direction or withdrawal. Although some might suggest that this resulted in unreasonable persistence, we should acknowledge that this persistent elaboration and exploration is necessary before the effort can emerge into the still confusing but better defined period of trial-and-error learning (Harrison and March, 1984).

In chapter 6 we note that persistence also needs to be evaluated in conjunction with the patterns that develop at a macrolevel. Although innovators are developing their own innovations, the world around them is also developing in ways that may support or encumber the particular innovation they are developing. We discuss these infrastructure issues in detail in chapter 6, but it is important to note that the infrastructure may develop in ways that are not conducive to the innovation. For example, TAP innovators discovered that Japanese firms were pursuing apheresis but were using a different technology. This discovery encouraged TAP innovators because their general idea of apheresis was supported, but it also led to profound reexamination of the TAP technology, which was, at that time, undergoing problems. Thus researchers are often placed in a paradoxical situation in which, on the one hand, they need to "create and believe in their own realities to make progress in their chosen paths and convince others. On the other hand, researchers must also be ready to disbelieve their realities and be willing to embrace the emerging shared reality even if it does not match their own" (Garud and Rappa, 1994: 359).

Van de Ven, Venkataraman, Polley, and Garud (1989) describe how the developmental processes in TAP, CIP, and Qnetics proliferated from a simple unitary process into expanding, divergent, and parallel progressions of ideas and activities. Some of these activities were related through a division of labor among functions and interdependent paths of activities, but many appeared to be unrelated in any noticeable form of functional interdependence. Many ideas and action paths perceived as being interdependent at one time were often reframed, reinvented, or discarded at another time as the innovation idea or circumstances changed and as different people fluidly engaged and disengaged in the developmental process. Setbacks, problems, and mistakes frequently occurred along these developmental paths, but they seldom triggered corrective actions; instead, they were treated as unforeseen challenges to surmount. So, also, innovation goals and outcome criteria shifted many times along the way and appeared to reflect the most recent and pressing concerns capturing the attention of entrepreneurs and resource allocators at the time in the innovation journey.

The following visual image of a rugged landscape captures key elements of the initial developmental process:

. We want to cross the dark valley to reach the peak on the other side. A broad goal galvanizes us to action. To reach the other side we must explore the valley at the same time we are constructing a path to the other side. We use our collective and individual skills by dividing up and sending scouts to pick specific paths from among the visible details of the valley (i.e., game paths, open versus thickly wooded areas, caves and canyons, etc.). Some are detoured in the maze of a cave, some get chased up a tree by

wild beasts, others become preoccupied with cataloguing the
vegetation along the trails, while others discover that the peak
on the other side consists of a mountain range with many peaks.
As we move forward and exert efforts in clearing our paths we
discover more about the terrain as well as ourselves. We become
good at trail blazing, at learning what we like and dislike, but
not necessarily at knowing where we will end up. If we get too
tired, we stumble. Thus we learn to eat and rest periodically.
This is certainly trial and error learning, but it is unlikely that it
will manifest itself as major changes in the direction of the innovation. (Polley and Van de Ven, 1995: 14)

Figure 3.5, which provides three-dimensional plots of the action and
outcome events over time in CIP and TAP's development, demonstrates evidence for this image of the rugged terrain along the innovation journey. If we envision the net positive outcomes as a measure of
the current fitness of the innovation effort, we may make a direct analogy to the current research on models of rugged fitness landscapes
(Kauffman, 1989; Bruderer and Singh, 1995; Levinthal, 1997). Although
our picture collapses the myriad innovative alternatives, it does evoke
the "ruggedness" of the innovative situation.

The absence of a relationship found between action and outcome
events during the initial period of innovation development permits a
variety of experiences with alternative courses of action and a variety
of trials with performance goals or possibilities. Building such repertoires of action experiences, outcome preferences, and contextual
practices increase the likelihood of making creative connections between means and ends when actions and outcomes are related.[1] At the
opposite extreme, if learners have experience with only one course of
action and one outcome preference, there is little opportunity for
learning or creativity because the task is reduced to a computational
exercise of linking the only known means with only one agreed-on
end (Thompson and Tuden, 1959). As Simon (1991) discusses, knowledge and expertise come from gaining experience with a wide variety
of cues and stimuli in a domain. Similarly, Weick (1989) argues that

1. This chaotic branching process disconnects actions and outcomes,
much like the garbage can model of choice (Cohen et al., 1972) disconnects
preferences from solutions and problems. It differs, however, in one fundamental respect. The garbage can model does not describe the evolution of solutions and problems; they simply exist in the garbage can waiting to be matched.
The chaotic model being sketched here for learning would deal centrally with
the dynamic sequence of events by which courses of action and outcome preferences originate and develop over time.

Therapeutic Apheresis Program Events

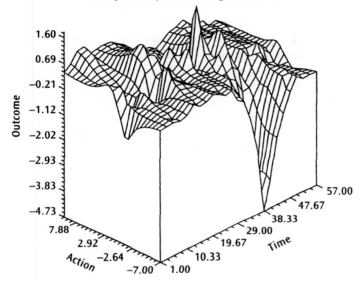

Cochlear Implant Program Events

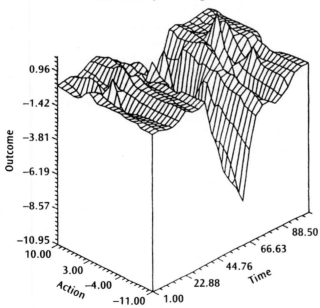

Figure 3.5 Actions and outcomes during the innovation journey. Actions = the number of events in which innovators continued minus changed their course of action; outcomes = the number of positive minus negative outcomes from events

one can improve the quality of one's theory or knowledge by increasing the number of independent thought trials at theory building.

By uncoupling actions and outcomes, a chaotic process facilitates the construction of repertoires of action experiences, outcome beliefs, and contextual practices. These repertoires increase an organization's capacity for creative learning. The coupling of actions and outcomes narrows the repertoires to those that satisfy the linear combination of feasible actions and desired outcomes. Efforts to tie actions and outcomes more closely together increase the efficiency of learning either by testing which action alternatives optimize a chosen outcome goal or by justifying outcome preferences that might emerge from persistence with a given course of action. This narrowing process signals the transition from chaotic to orderly development in dissipative systems.

> 5. *Transitions from chaotic nonlinear dynamics to more orderly periodic patterns in the innovation journey are triggered by the external institutional constraints and by self-organizing processes of learning what desired action-outcome possibilities to pursue.*

The transitions observed in the innovations from chaotic to more stable periods of development might be explained by the fact that these dynamic systems are dissipative structures; the innovation unit must import energy and resources from its environment to undertake a developmental effort. External resources, institutional rules, and macroorganizational directives influence the system by enabling (expanding) or constraining (narrowing) the branching and freedom of movement along the pathways. For example, resource investments by top managers provided the CIP and TAP innovation units slack time for temporary periods to engage in chaotic developmental activities. However, the top managers increasingly demanded achieving performance outcomes as conditions for subsequent yearly investments. Conversely, FDA institutional regulations locked the innovation teams into a prescribed sequence of repetitive actions and hundreds of clinical trials of their biomedical devices before commercial market release was permitted. Although these protocols provided the necessary information for FDA review panels to learn about the safety and efficacy of a medical device, they limited the flexibility of the innovation teams to change the devices during the clinical trials. Thus, while FDA institutional regulations locked the innovation teams into a prescribed sequence of actions, yearly investments contingent on management reviews increasingly narrowed their attention to achieving performance outcomes.

External events act as constraints and opportunities. At least part of this effect is a result of the endogenous self-organizing character of a dynamic human system. "Self-organizing processes are poised on their 'starting marks' to take over from random developments, if proper conditions become established, and to accelerate or make possible in the first place the emergence of complex order. Human systems are pragmatic; they interpret and take advantage of exogenous events or constraints to accomplish their purposes of self-renewal by creating novel structures" (Jantsch, 1980: 8). However, this self-organizing character of chaotic systems does not override cognitive and physiological human limitations to deal with ambiguity and complexity.

A key source of ambiguity in the innovation journey is often the long temporal lag, sometimes lasting years, between developmental activities and implementation performance feedback. During the developmental period, intensive investments and efforts are required to transform a vague inventive idea into a concrete reality without having any objective information that is useful for narrowing developmental activities toward specific outcomes. Concrete performance information cannot be obtained until after the innovation is implemented in the market or the adopting organization. This may explain why the CIP and TAP innovation units did not lock in on clear-cut outcome goals and engage in a process of trial-and-error learning until the ending market-entry period of development.

During the earlier premarket development period, the innovation units had no recourse but to rely on subjectively constructed targets or goals to evaluate the outcomes of their actions and to repeatedly modify both their courses of action and outcome criteria based on experience. In such ambiguous situations Garud and Van de Ven (1992) argued that action persistence is the predicted strategy for narrowing the expanding complexity of developmental efforts to manageable proportions. The ambiguity of exploring broadly defined goals for a new venture, coupled with demands for performance accountability by resource controllers, triggers entrepreneurs to act as charismatic leaders by enacting a solution based on their interpretation of the ambiguous cues. As Weber pointed out (in Gerth and Mills, 1946), the charismatic leader is thought by his or her followers to have solutions or at least the wisdom to find them. As a charismatic leader, the entrepreneur offers a new set of ideas and articulates enough imagination to create a new vision that narrows attention and rallies unity out of diversity.

Weick (1993) provides a social-psychological explanation for this action persistence in ambiguous situations. He argued that when a decision is made, action is more effective when probabilistic information is treated as if it were deterministic and beliefs that are only relatively true are treated as if they were absolutely true. "Commitment marshals forces that destroy the plausibility of alternatives and remove their ability to inhibit action. These forces are nonrational, though their use is functional. . . . We may choose our actions in the first place on a rational basis . . . [but once made] we drive them, energize them, and justify them on the nonrational basis of our motivational commitment to them" (Brinkman, 1987: 54). Thus, enacting a solution results in persistence with a course of action that entrepreneurs believe will succeed in the long run, although they might experience immediate negative outcomes (Garud and Van de Ven, 1992). The logic of action is "damn the torpedoes, proceed full scale ahead." Such action persistence is justified by an entrepreneurial logic of surmounting organizational "naysayers" and inertia (Brunsson, 1982). It can lead to escalating commitments to failing courses of action, as observed by Argyris and Schon (1978) and Ross and Staw (1986). Such risk-seeking behavior manifests itself in the single-minded pursuit of a course of action as entrepreneurs try to recoup past investments. If the venture is successful, action persistence creates heroes; if unsuccessful, it creates tragedies and scapegoats (Sitkin, 1992).

The resource constraints related to Qnetics provide a contrasting situation in which the constraints by outside stakeholders were even more severe than in the CIP and TAP cases. External resource providers precipitated both decline periods, leading to an intricate relationship of internal and external supporters. During times when the Qnetics effort was going well, innovators were able to obtain outside stakeholder support. When problems arose with the innovations, external stakeholders were less supportive and the innovators needed to rely on internal stakeholder support. Having long-term, stable external stakeholders helped TAP and CIP persist in ways that were not available to Qnetics. Qnetics's experience, however, suggests that this is a mixed blessing because the constraints were so severe that the innovation was not able to experience enough of a more stable learning process to become successful in the long run.

The foregoing discussion suggests that the timing of transitions in action and outcome events from chaotic to periodic patterns determines whether a knowledge acquisition process exhibits the decision rationality of trial-and-error learning as behavioral learning theorists discussed or the action rationality of persistent and committed behavior as cognitive learning theorists discuss. If action events change from chaotic to periodic order before outcome events do, an organizational unit will engage in action rationality by persisting with its course of action. Conversely, if outcome events change from chaotic to periodic order before action events do, an organizational unit will engage in decision rationality by engaging in a process of trial-and-error learning. Hence, the difference between behavioral learning theorists and cognitive learning theorists may be just a matter of time.

Conclusion

Our research suggests that much further appreciation and study of learning by discovery is warranted. If the innovation journey is to be explained as a learning process, the origination of true novelty should begin with profound ignorance not only with respect to what actions people take but also with respect to what outcomes they desire and the institutional context in which they will operate. The idea that preferences are not in existence a priori should motivate further study about how preferences are created in situations of high ambiguity. Actions taken without clearly understanding the range of possible outcomes is likely to be critical to the early development of truly innovative ideas. We cannot know whether we will like a new flavor of ice cream until we have tried it. To discover we do not like it can hardly be called an "error," especially when such experimentation leads to discovery of even better new flavors. Similarly, the discovery of a new favorite flavor may lead to even more experimentation and the discovery of other new flavors and foods.

Study of the relationship between social attributions and technological possibilities also should be undertaken. Under conditions of ambiguity, an action rationality is often based on a "belief" that success is possible. Ambiguity means we should expect frequent surprises. These surprises are opportunities to discover both technological and social reality, and it is not clear how these interrelated facets will evolve.

Innovation developers will recognize the complex difficulties of trying to manage ambiguous development processes. The innovators, by adopting an action rationality, likely will be more susceptible to the errors of over persistence. Innovators, often technicians by training, must be aware of the critical role that communication and social attribution play. Although it is necessary and natural to assign responsibility, it is also easy for this responsibility to translate into blame and recrimination. Responsibility is critical to motivation and delegation, but it also may be problematic when clear action outcome links have not been developed. Persistence in problem resolution is a natural result of the elaboration and evolution of the development. This persistence is necessary to make progress in uncharted and often difficult terrain. Nevertheless, persistence is also a source of catastrophic failure. Thus the innovators must manage the tension created between these two possibilities.

Leading the Innovation Journey

The previous chapter raises more questions than it answers: Why did the top managers or venture capitalists who invested in the innovations not intervene and provide order to the seemingly random behaviors during the start-up of their innovation teams? Why did they not engage their innovation teams in adaptive learning to alter their action persistence during the later period of innovation development?

In addition to the uncertainties of learning by discovery and testing confronting the innovation teams, we argue that the problem confronting top managers and investors was one of equivocality as they made yearly investment decisions in their selected innovations. *Equivocality* means that a given event can be interpreted to have several plausible meanings (Weick, 1979). As Weick (1993) explains, this counterintuitive outcome occurs because the top managers are faced with multiple, conflicting meanings of their investment decisions when confronted with information about the developmental progress of their innovations. This information becomes available to top managers during occasional meetings with entrepreneurs and in periodic administrative reviews of innovation progress. It includes information about the extent to which anticipated milestones, schedules, and budgets are achieved, as well as unanticipated setbacks and accomplishments since the last administrative review. This progress information can be interpreted in numerous ways depending on one's perspective. "When the decision means many different conflicting things, the problem is one of too many meanings, not too few, and the problem shifts from one of uncertainty to one of equivocality" (Daft and MacIntosh, 1981: 207).

Equivocality is less a function of ambiguous information about innovation progress and more a result of diverse interpretations of the information. Top managers who periodically evaluate their innovation projects concurrently spend most of their time directing other business operations and ventures. Each is bombarded with information about diverse business priorities and problems, new investment opportunities, and opportunity costs of repeated investments in their innovations. Moreover, these top managers and venture capitalists work together and trade off responsibilities in managing a portfolio of twenty to forty-five other innovation projects and ventures, each with its own set of stakes and interests. As a consequence, top managers bring to bear different and changing perspectives when they repeatedly evaluate and make commitments to multiyear innovation projects.

For some, information about an innovation event may be interpreted as a shift in the meaning or significance of former innovation goals or values. For others, it may mean that some former goals are unattainable with the means available. And for others, the information may mean a discovery of new goals or new courses of action that could minimize the likelihood of making matters worse or increase the probability of obtaining a better return on investments.

This equivocality is a product of the collective and pluralistic settings in which top managers participate. In particular, researchers for the Minnesota Innovation Research Program (MIRP) observed the following three patterns in top managers' behaviors:

1. Many—not one or a few—top managers or resource controllers at different hierarchical levels were actively involved in developing innovations within their organizations.
2. The managers typically did not reflect unified and homogeneous perspectives; instead, they held opposing views and performed roles that often served as checks and balances on each other in making innovation investment decisions.
3. When the top managers met periodically to review an innovation's progress, they followed a process of decision making by objection (Anderson, 1983) in which goals and actions were interpreted through argumentation and debate in settings where justification and legitimacy of decisions were highly visible.

These observations suggest that the top managers, like their innovation teams, were groping for inspiration to interpret and make sense of their innovation journeys. However, unlike the innovation units, which rallied behind the charismatic vision and persistence of their entrepreneurs, the top managers adopted an alternative strategy for inspiration. The collective behavior of top managers reflected a pluralistic structure of conflicting forces and a decision process by objection.

We believe these observations provide the key ingredients for a new perspective on innovation leadership. Combined with the learning perspective discussed in chapter 3 equivocality offers insights into how strategic managers and investors make decisions during the innovation journey. We argue that in uncertain and ambiguous situations, organizational learning and adaptability are enhanced when a balance is achieved between diverse, opposing, and conflicting, views among innovation leaders. The existence of consensus and support among top managers to a single strategic vision appears neither empirically correct nor effective during ambiguous periods of innovation discovery and exploration. We propose that these periods of the innovation journey require a pluralistic structure and process of leadership that incorporates the requisite variety of diverse perspectives necessary to make uncertain and ambiguous innovation decisions. A homogeneous structure of power and leadership may be efficient for exploiting a given course of action, but it tends to squelch consideration of diverse and opposing viewpoints inherent in ambiguous tasks. Thus, pluralistic leadership increases the chances for technological foresights and decreases the likelihood of oversights. However, such a pluralistic structure does not ensure intelligent leadership. Learning to encourage, tolerate, and heedfully accommodate divergent perspectives requires a negotiational style of decision making by objection and constructive conflict resolution processes. Maintaining a balance among pluralistic leadership roles increases the likelihood of organizational learning and adaptability during the innovation journey. We conclude the chapter by offering some speculations for a pluralistic theory of innovation leadership.

Observed Behaviors of Innovation Leaders

Based on the overall patterns identified across the MIRP innovations and detailed study of these patterns in the Cochlear Implant Program (CIP), Therapeutic Apheresis Program (TAP), and Qnetics innovations, we describe the common behaviors of top managers or resource controllers in periodically evaluating and committing resources to their innovation projects.

Active and Collective Leadership

Chapter 2 reported that in a comparison of the innovations studied by MIRP researchers, top managers at several organizational levels exercised active "hands-on" leadership roles. These managerial roles appeared to vary as different problems or opportunities unfolded. Leadership involvement did not appear to diminish over the life of in-

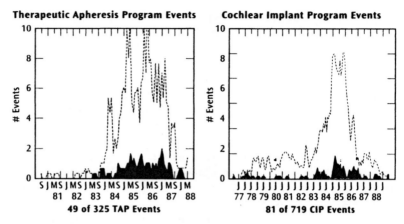

Figure 4.1 Number of events involving top managers during development of TAP and CIP innovations

novation development; it remained relatively constant throughout the innovation development process.

Figure 4.1 shows statistical evidence of the active involvement of leaders in the innovation process. The backgrounds of the graphs plot the total number of events observed in the development of the TAP and CIP innovations. The shaded time series in figure 4.1 indicate the number of times the top management resource controllers were directly involved in the total events: 49 of 325 events in TAP, and 81 of 719 events in CIP. As we see in figures 4.5 and 4.6, these events involved many—not just one or a few—top managers located at different hierarchical levels in the development of TAP and CIP.

Innovation Leadership Roles

Angle and Van de Ven (1989) and Van de Ven and Grazman (1997) examined the qualitative behaviors of top managers or investors in these events. They found that top managers at different levels in the organizational hierarchies did not reflect unified and homogeneous perspectives; instead, they often expressed opposing views and performed roles that served as checks and balances on each other in directing innovation entrepreneurs. As figure 4.2 illustrates, Angle and Van de Ven (1989) identified four different kinds of leadership roles: sponsor, critic, institutional leader, and mentor. Whereas the corporate sponsor or champion role is well known (Schon, 1963), the roles of critic, mentor, and institutional leader are seldom discussed (Howell and Higgens, 1990).

The sponsor or champion role was typically performed by a manager sufficiently high in the organization to command the power and resources to push an innovation idea into good currency. This sponsor

Figure 4.2 Leadership roles in innovation development.
Adapted from Angle and Van de Ven (1989), p. 681.

was an advocate for the innovation and its entrepreneur in corporate and investor circles where investment decisions were made. The sponsor also "ran interference" within the corporation for the innovation. Like all the leadership roles, the sponsor role could be performed by more than one person.

Closely related to the sponsor role was a mentor role, which could be distinguished in some organizations by a division of labor. The sponsor role involved activities of procuring, advocating, representing, and championing an innovation at upper-echelon executive levels; the mentor role entailed coaching, counseling, and advising activities with innovation entrepreneurs on a direct and daily basis. The mentor role was typically performed by an experienced and successful innovator, who assumed responsibility for coaching, and perhaps supervising, the innovation manager or entrepreneur. Mentors served as role models for the innovation team leader and combined with the innovation sponsor to provide encouragement, guidance, and other types of support to the entrepreneur.

In the interest of checks and balances, the role coalition represented by innovation sponsor and mentor was often counterbalanced by a critic role. This role was performed by a "devil's advocate," who applied dispassionate, "hard-nosed" business criteria to the innovation and forced the corporate sponsors and entrepreneurs to reexamine their assumptions and alternative courses of action to develop their innovations. The critic role was evident in administrative review meetings when certain top managers challenged and questioned entrepreneurs about innovation project investments, goals, or progress. Perhaps more than any other role, the critic role was apt to be shared by several people.

Balancing these opposing roles was the role of institutional leader, which was often performed by an executive who was removed from the "battlefield," as it were, and therefore was less subject to the partisan myopia that afflicted people closer to the innovations. The institutional leader maintained a balance of power between the pro-innovation influences of the sponsor-mentor coalition and the reality-testing influences of the critic so that conflicts could be solved based on the merits of the case rather than on power alone. In addition to settling disputes, the institutional leader role was evident when organizational structures and arrangements were established or modified to enable and constrain innovation activities.

In visualizing the power dynamics among these leadership roles, one is drawn to an adaptation of Davis and Lawrence's (1977) analogy of a series of relationships among the general manager, project manager, functional manager, and "two-boss" manager in a matrix organization. As illustrated in figure 4.2, at the base of the triangle is the institutional leader role, performed by a person who is concerned with the innovation as only one of several responsibilities. This psychological distance from the innovation allows a breadth of perspective not easily attained by the more immediate actors. On the opposing ends of the triangle are the two opposing liberal and conservative forces: (1) the sponsor-mentor coalition and (2) the critic. At the bottom is the entrepreneur, or innovation project manager, who is exposed to this dialectical field of forces.

Van de Ven and Grazman (1997) coded the leadership events in the CIP and TAP cases according to the definitions of sponsor, mentor, critic, and institutional leadership roles. Then, as figures 4.3 and 4.4 show, they plotted the number of events in which these leadership roles were exercised during the development of the TAP and CIP innovations respectively.[1]

As might be expected by the extraordinary energy necessary to mobilize resources and support for launching new ventures, figures 4.3 and 4.4 show that in both innovations, the corporate sponsor role was performed almost twice as often as the critic role. In the case of TAP, a joint venture among three organizations, the cumulative occurrence of the institutional leadership role exceeded that of the sponsor role, while in the CIP internal corporate venture, the institutional leader role was as prevalent as the critic role. This may indicate that a joint interorganizational venture requires greater involvement of an institutional leader to create new enabling structures and arrangements between organizational partners for an innovation than is required for an innovation undertaken within an organization.

1. In both figures, the total leadership events are the same as the cumulative numbers of events involving top managers shown in figure 4.2. Two researchers coded these events; they agreed on 93% of the cases, and disagreements were resolved by mutual consent. Figures 4.3 and 4.4 combine mentor events with sponsor events because there were too few mentoring events in the TAP and CIP cases to warrant a separate breakout.

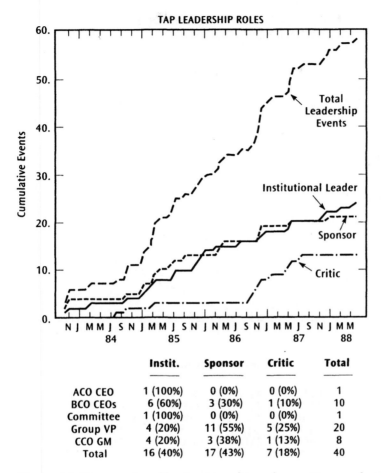

	Instit.	Sponsor	Critic	Total
ACO CEO	1 (100%)	0 (0%)	0 (0%)	1
BCO CEOs	6 (60%)	3 (30%)	1 (10%)	10
Committee	1 (100%)	0 (0%)	0 (0%)	1
Group VP	4 (20%)	11 (55%)	5 (25%)	20
CCO GM	4 (20%)	3 (38%)	1 (13%)	8
Total	16 (40%)	17 (43%)	7 (18%)	40

Figure 4.3 Frequencies of leadership roles and executives performing them in TAP.

The bottom half of figures 4.3 and 4.4 show the number and per-
centage of times that individual executives, identified by the positions they occupied in their organizational hierarchies, performed in
the roles of sponsor, critic, and institutional leadership for the TAP
and CIP innovations, respectively. In the case of TAP, ACO, BCO, and
CCO are the fictitious names of the three organizations involved in
the joint venture, and the most active group vice president is a senior
executive of ACO. In the case of CIP, the executives are listed in hierarchical order. In both cases, the committee , a corporate-level resource allocation board, consists of the executives listed plus other
top managers.

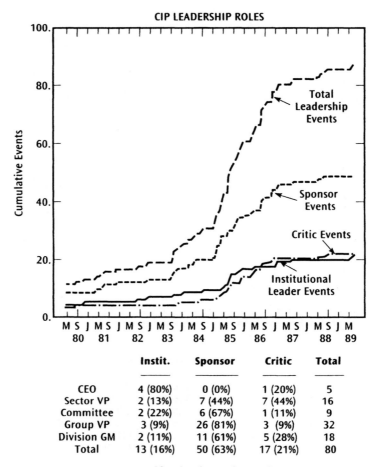

Figure 4.4 Frequencies of leadership roles and executives performing them in CIP

The data in figures 4.3 and 4.4 clearly show that each executive who
was involved in more than one event performed at least two or more of
the leadership roles. Contrary to popular notions that executives are
consistent in their role behaviors (Meindl, Ehrlich, and Dukerich,
1985), the data show a surprising flexibility in which each executive
shifted roles or performed multiple leadership roles over time with respect to the CIP and TAP innovations. These data support the notion of
examining leadership as the performance of specific roles in an organization, rather than as characteristic people in different hierarchical
positions.

Relationships among Leadership Roles

Across the innovations studied by the MIRP researchers, Angle and Van de Ven (1989) observed that innovations encountered significant hurdles in cases in which one or more of the leadership roles were absent. For example, Qnetics, a new company start-up, did not enjoy the umbrella of legitimacy and credibility provided by an institutional leader, nor was the counsel of a mentor available. Both deficits hindered the company's ability to engage in business transactions with large customers and distributors. In addition, the board initially consisted only of inside directors, which limited the exposure of company principals to the kinds of divergent perspectives provided by critics in the corporate settings.

Angle and Van de Ven (1989) note that these leadership roles also serve as checks and balances on each other in guiding innovation development. For example, the innovation sponsor runs interference for the project at corporate levels, while a mentor provides direct supervision, coaching, and counseling to the innovation unit. The counterbalancing role for this coalition is the critic role, which is often expressed by challenging and questioning the reality or wisdom of an innovation's goals, budgets, and schedules in terms of "bottom-line" business criteria and priorities. Without this role, the propensity of innovation sponsors to delude themselves and others by seeing ambiguity through rose-colored glasses might exhaust organizational resources by investing the corporate treasury "down a rat hole." By contrast, if the critic is able to run unchecked, no venture may have a chance to succeed, because innovations are inherently risky undertakings. Thus, the institutional leader's role is that of a power broker, ensuring that supports and restraints for the innovation are reasonably well balanced.

To determine the statistical form of relationships among the leadership roles, we conducted time series regression analyses of the occurrence of the sponsor, critic, and institutional leadership roles in CIP and TAP. Table 4.1 shows the results of three regression equations in which the occurrence of each leadership role was regressed on the other two leadership roles occurring both in the same month and lagged one month. The table shows the statistically significant unstandardized beta coefficients produced after making adjustments for serial correlation, using AR1. The results show that the exercise of each leadership role is significantly predicted by events involving the other two leader roles occurring within the same month or the previous month. These regression results are illustrated in figure 4.5. They indicate that the three leadership roles are reciprocally related.

These reciprocal relationships do not explode; they counterbalance each other over time. Figure 4.5 shows that two self-correcting cycles of relationships exist among the three leadership roles: a clockwise

Table 4.1. Results of time series regression analysis in Figure 4.5 from Van de Ven and Grazman (1997) study of leader roles

Independent variables	Dependent variables at t_o		
	Institutional	Sponsor	Critic
Instit. Events at t_o	—	NS	.28**
at t_{-1}	—	−.36**	.29**
Sponsor Events at t_o	NS	—	.19**
at t_{-1}	NS	—	NS
Critic Events at t_o	.38**	.75**	—
at t_{-1}	.13*	NS	—
Constant	.07	.28**	.05
Rho	−.13	.97	−.51
R^2	.14	.17	.29

N = 150 months
*p < .05
**p < .01

feed-forward loop and a counterclockwise feedback loop. In the clockwise cycle, events involving the sponsor were countered by critic events in the same time period, which then led to institutional leadership interventions in the same or later period. These interventions, in turn, decreased the likelihood of sponsor events in the next time period. The counterclockwise cycle indicates that institutional leadership events had immediate and lagged feedback effects on further critic events, and events by the critic were countered in further sponsor events. However, this counterclockwise feedback loop is short-circuited because sponsor events did not statistically influence further institutional leadership events.

These results lend statistical credibility to our qualitative observations that the leadership roles served as checks and balances on each

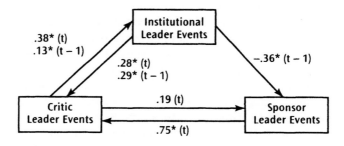

Figure 4.5 Relationships among leader roles. From Van de Ven and Grazman (1997)

other. They also reveal that the patterns of relationships among these dialectical roles consist of two self-correcting cycles of feedforward and feedback effects. A substantive interpretation of these statistical relationships will become clear as we examine the qualitative processes in which the CIP and TAP sponsor, critic, and institutional leaders made decisions by objection.

Decision Making by Objection

When the top managers met periodically to review the developmental progress of the TAP and CIP innovations, they appeared to follow a process that resembles what Anderson (1983) described as decision making by objection. The process of decision making by objection, with its emphasis on sequential evaluation of alternatives, produces binary choices as a default. It does not, however, exclude competing alternatives; competing alternatives appear when (1) there are objections to the initial course of action, and (2) there is a shared recognition that some action is required. Decision making by objection is group decision making via argumentation and debate, and goal discovery occurs as a consequence of the interaction of advocates of opposing views. An alternative with a high probability of making matters worse will simultaneously produce objections that lessen the likelihood that it will be chosen and stimulate the discovery of goals (Anderson, 1983).

This process of decision making by objection was not immediately evident in the event sequence data on managerial behaviors because of the numerous issues, distractions, and "noise" managers addressed in real time from one event to the next. It became apparent by reading the event sequence data pertaining to specific substantive issues or debates that unfolded over time.[2] We exemplify this process of decision by objection with a brief examination of an important debate in each of the CIP and TAP cases. Throughout each issue stream, managerial and leadership actions were taken in response to numerous other issues and problems. Thus, the following examples of decision by objection report only events that pertain to a particular substantive issue stream.

2. These issues could only be determined in retrospect. Once a substantive issue was identified, Grazman and Van de Ven (1997) reread the chronological events, selected the events that pertained to the issue, and then coded how interactions between executives performing different leadership roles unfolded on the substantive issue or debate during the CIP or TAP innovation journeys. A caveat is in order. If it was difficult for the researchers—being nonpartisan real-time observers of the proceedings in these events—to detect these decision patterns, we speculate that it is highly unlikely that the process of decision making by objection on the issues reported here were known to the participants involved in these issue streams. In other words, this reconstruction makes the process of decision by objection appear logical and knowable in retrospect, but it was probably neither in its real time of occurrence.

Decision by Objection in CIP Single- versus Multiple-Channel Technology Debate

One strategic issue that repeatedly surfaced during the CIP innovation journey was the question whether to pursue the development and commercialization of a single- or multiple-channel technology for cochlear implants. In lay terms, the issue dealt with whether to implant surgically one or many electrodes deep inside the ears of profoundly deaf people so they could hear. The CIP story begins when a single-channel device was available and clinical trials found it safe. Multichannel devices were not yet available for clinical trials, but otologists were claiming this more sophisticated, but unproved, technology would be safe and provide better hearing. Throughout the course of the CIP program, its managers were engaged in discussions about which technology would be the more prudent, and potentially more profitable. Table 4.2 presents the chronological sequence of events on this issue, coded in terms of the dominant leadership roles exercised in each event and a characterization of content.

During the initial uncertain and ambiguous period of CIP's gestation, the distribution of leadership roles among managers was skewed toward sponsor behaviors, with little influence of either institutional or critic roles. Because top corporate managers each participated in multiple innovation projects simultaneously, those who chose to act as cochlear implant sponsors[3] encountered little criticism for their pursuit, nor was there significant institutional scrutiny of the project for almost three years. This period of high ambiguity and uncertainty about cochlear implants continued until late in 1980, when corporate sponsors began to consolidate related activities by establishing the CIP as a formal innovation unit. By this time, sponsor behaviors had succeeded in developing a number of external relationships with research institutes that were involved in developing single-channel cochlear implants. Beginning in 1981, corporate executives, acting as institutional leaders agreed to these interorganizational relationships and to setting the organizational structures and operating parameters of the CIP. To legitimize these agreements, the chief executive officer (CEO) of the corporation visited a venture process and increased his familiarity with the details of the cochlear implant technology and program.

The critic role surfaced in response to these changes, and activities by people who played the institutional and sponsor roles increased as well. In December 1983, critics prevented a joint-venture agreement

3. References to managers as "sponsor," "critic," and "institutional leader" are references to the exercise of a particular role, not to any particular individual.

Table 4.2. CIP leadership role events pertaining to the single (SC) versus multiple channel (MC) issue stream

Date	Leader code[a]	Activity
03/02/78	S	SC/MC technologies explored with external organizations
03/02/78	S	SC technology explored with external organization
02/02/79	S/I	Commitment made to acquire SC technology
07/31/79	S	Goals communicated internally
08/15/80	C	Doubts expressed about program goals
11/01/80	I	Central group organized to consolidate operations
04/17/81	S	Internal justification of pursuing both SC and MC devices
07/21/81	S	Strategic plan authored for three generations of devices
12/01/81	S	Agreement made to pursue SC technology with external organization
12/02/82	S/I	CEO visits other organization to show commitment
10/21/83	I	Agreement altered to reflect focus on MC
12/06/83	C	Joint venture agreement for MC device rejected
02/24/84	I	Funds allocated internally for SC and MC development
04/20/84	S	Sector Review: Additional funds requested, SC device supported
06/18/84	S	Need for leadership in MC technology recognized
09/04/84	C	Funding levels for SC questioned, MC development encouraged
02/11/85	S	Funding levels for MC placed under scrutiny
05/06/85	S	Sector Review: MC technology favored
10/11/85	S	Clinician writes letter in support of SC pursuit
10/20/85	S	In response to letter, CIP ends letter to clinician emphasizing MC
12/17/85	S	CIP team awaits additional funding for MC
01/16/86	C	SC viability questioned; various concerns expressed
05/11/86	S	Sector Review: General funding levels for CIP lowered
06/20/86	I	Executive Committee approves involvement in hearing aid market
07/15/86	C	Portion of CIP program sold to outside organization
10/21/86	I	Acquisition of small organization
01/22/87	C/S	Pressure increased to shift focus from cochlear implant to hearing aids
03/01/87	S	MC technology receives renewed focus
09/15/87	I/C	SC technology sold off, development on MC postponed
09/14/88	S	Clinician attempts to revive SC efforts of CIP

a. S = sponsor, 20 (55.9%); C = critic, 6 (20.6%); I = Institutional Leadership, 7 (23.5%)

that would have pushed the multiple-channel device as a clear priority. They believed that the technology was not yet clinically proven and were unwilling to support the heavy research and development investment that such a venture would require. Critics called into question the legitimacy of pursuing both single- and multiple-channel cochlear implant technologies. In February 1984, institutional leaders decided to fund the development of both technologies, but in a sector review held in April 1984, sponsors were able to obtain support for accelerating the single-channel program to "neutralize" the threat of multiple-channel devices in the marketplace. By May 1985, the apparent threat had disappeared, and with continued critic involvement countering sponsors' activities, institutional leaders began to question the single-channel device's market potential. After reviewing funding levels for both technologies, the institutional sector review committee decided that developing the multiple-channel device was now the preferred course of action.

During the ensuing year, critics and sponsors were actively involved in debates over which device had the most market potential, which device would be safer in patients, and what funding levels the organization should allocate. An atmosphere of uncertainty characterized the CIP program team as it sought to define conclusively the mission it had set for itself. In May 1986, institutional actors again became involved during the annual sector review. However, instead of settling the debate between sponsors and critics, the review committee reduced overall funding levels for the project and suggested that managers more actively pursue the hearing aid market. Critics seized on this lack of institutional support for the CIP and advocated dismantling the program all together. However, corporate sponsors generated sufficient support in the spring of 1987 to continue the pursuit of a multiple-channel device. But these efforts did not materialize as the corporation divested the CIP by selling its cochlear implant technology, patents, and assets to a former competitor in September 1987.

Decision by Objection in Defining the
TAP Joint Venture Agreement

The TAP innovation venture was the product of an agreement among three organizations to combine their technological, research, and business capabilities to develop a blood filtration device that could separate pathogenic substances from patients' blood to treat a variety of autoimmune diseases. However, even with careful contracting and due diligence, the definition of the joint-venture agreement among the organizations became a source of ongoing confusion and misinterpretation. Table 4.3 provides a list of the chronological events and leadership roles relevant to this debate.

Table 4.3. TAP leadership role events pertaining to the defining of the TAP joint venture agreement issue stream

Date	Leader code[a]	Activity
01/01/81	I	ACO and BCO discuss pheresis cooperation
03/01/83	S	ACO and BCO begin formal joint venture discussions
06/01/83	I	ACO executives intervene to assist joint venture discussions
11/16/83	I	ACO and BCO sign joint venture agreement. SBU formed
03/01/84	S	Confusion expressed concerning responsibilities
10/29/84	S	ACO managers discus expanding scope of ACO/BCO joint venture
03/12/85	S/C	BCO accuses ACO of changing philosophies about the agreement
07/15/85	I/S	ACO manager visits BCO to renegotiate joint venture agreement
11/13/85	I	BCO reorganizes along business lines
03/26/86	S	ACO discusses dropping BCO as venture partner
04/05/86	I	BCO managers, including CEO, killed in plane crash
10/01/86	C	ACO manager suggests looking outside for manufacturing function
12/01/86	I	TAP reorganizes business and marketing teams; CCO becomes subsidiary of ACO
12/10/86	S	Discussions of synergies between TAP and CCO
12/11/86	I/C	BCO manager agrees to forego 50% of next year's royalty income
12/11/86	I/C	BCO funding levels fall due to financial problems
02/09/87	C	BCO management unhappy with TAP delays
06/01/87	I/C/S	ACO discusses imbalance of spending levels and proposes an adjustment
06/25/87	S	Joint ACO/BCO review of TAP; BCO dissatisfied with ACO's commitment
12/29/87	I	ACO terminates agreement with BCO
01/18/88	I/S	ACO and BCO lawyers meet to unravel agreement
03/09/88	I	ACO and BCO lawyers continue to work through legal issues
06/16/88	I	Final agreement on asset distribution by ACO and BCO

a. S = Sponsor, 9 (31.0%); C = Critic, 6 (20.7%); I = Institutional Leadership, 14 (48.3%)

Because TAP was an interorganizational joint venture, the institutional leader role was called on to lay the framework in which the co-venturing organizations would perform their respective portions of the project. Executives acting as project sponsors, primarily interested in sharing and combining technical and business capabilities to develop an apheresis technology, began talks in January 1981. However, no results materialized from these talks until the CEOs of the respective organizations exercised institutional leadership by meeting and informally agreeing to the strategic alliance. This informal agreement legitimized formation of the TAP innovation and authorized entrepreneurs and sponsors to mobilize interest within and among their respective organizations. In November 1983, the agreement was signed, and the institutional actor's role in the definition of the relationship disappeared until July 1985.

In the interim, managers acted as sponsors and critics in propelling the project along. Throughout 1984 and 1985, confusion continued to permeate the relationship. In March 1984, managers of ACO wrote an official memo outlining issues of misunderstanding related to the TAP agreement. Although there was uncertainty about the TAP venture, corporate sponsors indicated in this memo that "the embryonic nature of this program, the investment risk and the need to minimize the effect on our existing business dictate this unique structure." While trying to coordinate the efforts of scientists and engineers involved in developing the blood-filtering device, managers, acting as both sponsors and critics, were still trying to establish the precise form the agreement would take. Sponsors advocated exploring more cooperation among the organizations during October 1984, while critics questioned the levels of commitment of each party. Executives and entrepreneurs from each organization expressed concern in March 1985 that the other parties were "backing off" from the original philosophy of the joint-venture agreement and that goals were being redefined through objection rather than strategic action.

Leadership roles in 1986 remained relatively balanced. After one of the partners reorganized, managers seemed to achieve a bit more clarity about the nature of the relationship. Although other partners were considered for additional funding to the joint venture during the fall of 1986, significant problems arose in the relationship when one partner experienced internal financial problems and expressed discontent with the delays in commercializing the TAP device. With financial difficulties a reality for one of the partners, more emphasis was placed on reducing the probability that any action would make matters worse rather than better.

During 1987, sponsors and critics within and among the co-venturing firms countered one another's proposals on alternative courses of action and budget levels to commit to the program. During an administrative review meeting of the program in late 1987, a senior executive from one of the partners intervened by informing the other parties that his organization would make no further financial investments in TAP beyond December 1987 and that another investor should be found to join the venture. Failing several attempts to negotiate acceptable agreements with potential investors, executives of the sponsoring organizations agreed to terminate the TAP joint venture. For the next eighteen months, the TAP innovation team occupied itself with solving technical design problems at a significantly reduced budget level. With diminishing hope that a new investor would agree to invest in the program, institutional leaders and their lawyers negotiated a conclusion to the legal relationship, distributed assets, and formally terminated TAP in June 1988.

Implications for Leading the Innovation Journey

The foregoing empirical observations of the active involvement and diverse roles of leaders in the innovations remind us of an important distinction made by Baveles (1960) between leadership as a personal quality and leadership as an organizational function. The first continues to be the dominant view of leadership and leads us to look at the qualities, abilities, or behaviors of the individual leader at the top of the organizational pyramid. The latter, which is more congruent with our data, refers to the distribution of decision-making power and influence throughout an organization. It leads us to look at the patterns of influence and power exercised by organizational participants and the specific conditions or situations when they exercise leadership:

> In these terms we come close to the notion of leadership, not as a personal quality but as an organizational function. Under this concept it is not sensible to ask of an organization, "Who is the leader?" Rather, we ask, "How are the leadership functions distributed in this organization?" The distribution may be wide or narrow. It may be so narrow—so many of the leadership functions may be vested in a single person—that he [she] is the leader in the popular sense. But in modern organizations this is becoming more and more rare. (Baveles, 1960: 494–495)

This point of view is consistent with that of Katz and Kahn (1978), who define leadership as acts of influence (beyond mechanical compliance with routine directives) on organizational-relevant matters by any member of the organization. It suggests that almost any individual in an organization may act as a leader and that different persons may contribute in different and diverse ways to the leadership of the organization. Indeed, in their review of leadership research, Katz and Kahn (1978) linked the distribution or sharing of leadership behavior with organizational effectiveness. Because the sharing of influence increases the quality of decisions and the motivation of organizational participants, Katz and Kahn proposed that the more influential (i.e., leadership) acts are widely shared in an organization, the more effective the organization.

What are these leadership acts? Baveles suggested that they consist of influential behaviors that reduce an organization's uncertainty in making decisions and achieving objectives. Because our topic deals with innovation leadership, we can take a more specific view by focusing on the roles that managers and entrepreneurs performed to influence the commitment of organizational resources—money, personnel, and ideas—to the development of innovations. As we have seen, these leader roles influenced the innovation journeys of CIP and TAP in diverse directions.

Leadership Roles

A *role* is an expected set of behaviors of people occupying an organizational position (Graen, 1976). Roles are both socially constructed through interactions and institutionally prescribed by the structure of rules and responsibilities of actors in positions relative to other organizational positions (Stryker and Statham, 1985). When an individual assumes an organizational position, we expect him or her to perform certain behaviors relative to other people. Certain behaviors become extensions of the role itself, influenced by the ongoing interactions with others in the role set. Based on these expectations, we behave differently toward that individual relative to people performing other roles.

An important implication of this view of a role set is that any role is dependent on others in its constellation. *Understanding one role requires knowing its relationship with others.* The literature on leadership has tended to focus on a single role without reference to other interdependent roles (Stryker and Statham 1985). When we look at all the roles in a constellation of interdependent roles, we find that it is incomplete to discuss a leader without a follower, a plaintiff without a defendant, or a proponent without an opponent. So also, it is equally incomplete to examine an innovation champion or sponsor without explicit reference to the other roles it juxtaposes. As Starbuck points out:

> Every force in a social system tends to initiate an opposing force. While constantly changing organizations are filled with polarities, it is natural to ignore the oppositions in a social system and to see only the elements to which we, as observers, are predisposed (Festinger and Carlsmith, 1959; Simon, 1945; Quinn, 1988). The employment of a paradoxical perspective leads us to a much increased awareness of the polarities that exist in organization phenomena. (Quoted in Quinn and Cameron 1988: 290)

Empirically, there may be unbalanced situations in which only one role, such as a champion, is dominant or evident. These situations are unbalanced not because of the exercise of one role but because of the lack of exercise of other roles in the set. In these and other situations, explanations of how and why a champion behaves are usually found in the relative influence and behavior of other roles in the organization. Indeed, the success or failure of an innovation champion may more often be produced by the behaviors of other interdependent role actors, such as the entrepreneur, critic, or institutional leader, than it is by the actions of the champion role actor.

We observed that these opposing leader roles are performed by different individuals as well as by the same individuals at different times during the innovation journey. These observations call attention to the importance of balance and timing in the performance of different leadership roles. Quinn, Dixit, and Faerman (1987) found that effective leaders were described by their subordinates as exhibiting seemingly contradictory behaviors or styles:

> That is, the most effective leaders did not display a single or unitary style, as most of the leadership literature concludes. Rather, they were characterized as possessing paradoxical styles and displayed behaviors that seemingly were contradictory. [They] argue that the presence of contradictory characteristics had not been discovered earlier because existing theoretical frameworks did not allow it. Contradiction is dismissed before the analysis even begins. (Cameron and Quinn, 1988: 12)

Figure 4.6 presents Quinn's (1988) competing-values framework of leadership roles. The framework emerged from a series of studies by Quinn and Rohrbaugh (1983) that identified the criteria of successful organizational leaders. They found that complex and dynamic organizations require managers to fulfill the many competing expectations outlined in figure 4.6. The figure also shows how our four innovation leadership roles map onto Quinn's four competing models: (1) the sponsor role reflects the inventive, risk-taking style of the open systems model; (2) the opposite of that is the critic role, which tends to assume a conservative and cautious internal process style; (3) our institutional leader role is captured nicely by Quinn's directive, rational goal model; and (4) the mentor role reflects the concerned and supportive style of Quinn's human relation model.

Because our four innovation leadership roles appear totally compatible with Quinn's competing values framework, we expect that Quinn's research findings also apply to our four innovation leadership roles. In particular, Quinn (1988) found that ineffective managers have great difficulty balancing competing philosophies and roles. "They become trapped in their biases. Effective managers have a variety of styles. Although they may have one or two roles that are underplayed, their profiles are far more balanced than the profiles of ineffective managers" (xviii). Quinn goes on to argue that organizational effectiveness is the result of leaders maintaining a creative tension between contrasting organizational demands: "The issue seems to be one of bal-

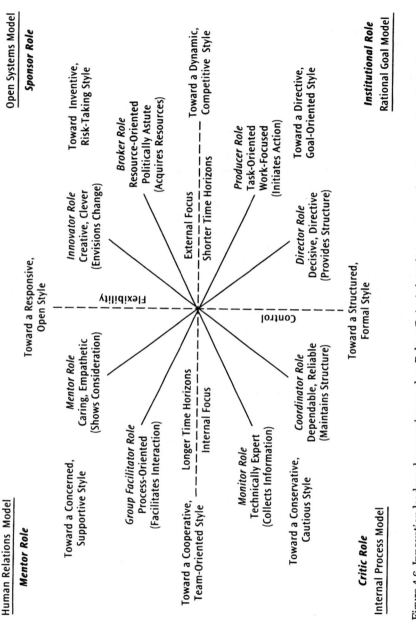

Figure 4.6 Innovation leader roles superimposed on Robert Quinn's (1988) competing values framework of leadership roles. Adapted from Robert E. Quinn, *Beyond Rational Management* (San Francisco: Jossey-Bass, 1988). Used with permission.

ance. For the ineffective groups, the positive scores simply do not counterbalance the negative. . . . When tension is lost, the perception of effectiveness is altered. The roles that are emphasized are seen negatively. A perceptual inversion occurs" (106).

This argument leads to the following proposition on the balance and timing of different leadership roles during the innovation journey: *The likelihood of organizational learning and adaptability increase when the temporal order and degrees of involvement of the leadership roles occur in the manner illustrated in figure 4.7.*

In the CIP and TAP innovations, we observed that the critic role did not emerge with sufficient strength to counter the sponsor role until late in the developmental period and after the entrepreneurial venture had already encountered significant mistakes and setbacks that were, perhaps, avoidable. We believe that the timing of the critic role came too late. The expression of the critic role late in the developmental process tended to surface arguments for terminating, rather than correcting, the innovation venture.

We propose that *the critic role may be most constructive in the early period of innovation development, when ambiguity is high and investments have not accumulated beyond a threshold of "no return."* At this early stage, the critic role can be constructive in forcing sponsors and entrepreneurs to rethink and explore alternative plans and budget requests for launching their innovation. In other words, expression of the critic role early in a developmental process promotes experimentation and learning by discovery. Because resources and momentum toward a given course of action accumulate with time, the constructive influence of the critic role wanes with time. Deferred expression of the critic role until late in the developmental process promotes summative evaluations and terminations rather than corrections to a course of action.

In both CIP and TAP, the roles of innovation sponsor and mentor were observed to be dominant during the first half of the innovation development period but then tended to subside when development problems could not be adequately addressed in response to the questions by critics, who gained strength and legitimacy among top managers. These observations suggest that after the initial support that is needed to make an initial investment decision in an innovation project, *the roles of innovation sponsor and mentor become increasingly important with time during the innovation journey.* This is especially true in the middle of the innovation journey when entrepreneurs most need support and coaching to address inevitable problems as they arise. The sponsor's role continues to increase in importance during the implementation period, when key decisions about structural realignments are often needed to integrate and link the innovation with strategic organizational directions and operations.

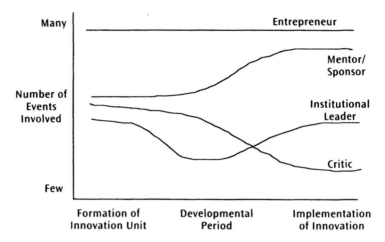

Figure 4.7 Proposition on balance and timing of leader roles

Finally, the institutional leader role serves to balance the opposing views of the critic and sponsor or mentor. Over time, we propose that *the institutional leader's role is most critical at the beginning of an innovation, to legitimize the venture's initial formation and investment, and at the ending implementation period, when institutional arrangements need to be established to implement the innovation.* During the middle period of the innovation journey the institutional leader role is necessary only if irreconcilable conflicts surface between opposing critic and sponsor/mentor coalitions that may create stalemates impeding further innovation development.

Elements of Pluralistic Leadership

The pluralistic structure of leadership roles described here comes close to the strategy initially proposed by Thompson and Tuden (1959) for inspirational decision making. Figure 4.8 illustrates Thompson and Tuden's well-known typology of decision strategies for different levels of uncertainty about means and agreement on ends among decision makers. Thompson and Tuden propose an inspirational strategy of decision making for conditions of uncertainty on means and ambiguity about ends (or goal disagreement). They suggest that inspirational decision making can be accomplished in one of two ways. The first approach is to ignore the uncertainty and ambiguity of the situation by placing faith in a charismatic leader, as discussed in chapter 3 where innovation team members rallied behind the inspirational vision of their entrepreneurial leader. The second approach is to adopt the following process that heedfully accommodates pluralistic perspectives for heuristic decision making:

(1) The individuals or groups must be interdependent and thus have some incentive for collective problem-solving, (2) there must be a multiplicity of preference scales and therefore of factions, with each faction of approximately equal strength, (3) more information must be introduced than can be processed, and it must be routed through multiple communication channels, and (4) each member must have access to the major communication networks, in case [or in the hope that] inspiration strikes. (Thompson and Tuden, 1959: 504)

This pluralistic structure for inspirational decision making represents a significant departure from popular treatments of leadership, which emphasize unity and consensus among the top management team members to a single strategic vision of the leader at the top of the pyramid. A unified homogeneous leadership structure is effective for routine trial-and-error learning by making convergent, incremental improvements in relatively stable and unambiguous situations. However, this kind of learning is a conservative process that maintains and converges organizational routines and relationships toward the existing strategic vision. As Levinthal (1997) discusses, although such learning is viewed as wisdom in stable environments, it produces inflexibility and competency traps in changing worlds.

We have seen that the initial period of innovation development is characterized by high ambiguity (unclear and shifting goals) and uncertainty (unclear courses of actions). In these situations pluralistic leadership encourages expression of the requisite variety of diverse perspectives that are needed for learning by discovery (Polley and Van de Ven, 1995). This type of learning entails mindful alertness to anomalies (Jelinek, 1997), shifting core assumptions and decision-making

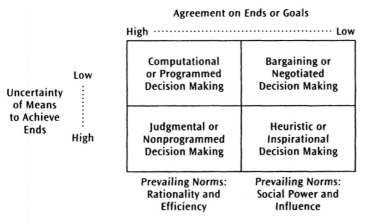

Figure 4.8 Thompson and Tuden typology of decision strategies. Adapted from Thompson and Tuden (1959)

premises, developing new interpretive schemes (Bartunek, 1993), un-learning prior premises and established routines (Virany, Tushman, and Romanelli, 1992), and creating a learning community (Senge, 1998). Whereas routine trial-and-error learning reduces variety by fo-cusing on a singular vision, learning by discovery increases variety and diversity of perspectives from which new understandings and objec-tives can emerge (Hedberg, Nystrom, and Starbuck, 1976). Thus, a plu-ralistic leadership structure increases the chances for technological foresights and decreases the likelihood of oversights.

However, a pluralistic structure does not ensure intelligent leader-ship. Instead, it emphasizes that *the odds of organizational learning and adaptability increase when a balance is maintained among di-alectical leadership roles throughout innovation development.* Such a structure places tremendous strains on the institutional leadership role in preventing the top management team from flying apart into a state of anomie. Selznick (1957) recognized this precarious situation by emphasizing that one of the key functions of institutional leader-ship is to manage internal and external conflict:

> Interest groups form naturally in large-scale organizations, since the total enterprise is in one sense a polity composed of a num-ber of sub-organizations. The struggle among competing inter-ests always has a high claim on the attention of leadership. This is so because the direction of the enterprise as a whole may be se-riously influenced by changes in the internal balance of power. In exercising control, leadership has a dual task. It must win the consent of constituent units, in order to maximize voluntary co-operation, and therefore must permit emergent interest blocs a wide degree of representation. At the same time, in order to hold the helm, it must see that a balance of power appropriate to the fulfillment of key commitments will be maintained. (63-64)

Achieving such internal diversity is difficult to maintain. Perhaps, this is why organizations with executive teams that value contradic-tory perspectives and keep them in balance are seldom observed. However, studies of these exemplars and related literature provide some useful clues for constructive pluralistic leadership. We now offer some speculations about the key ingredients of pluralistic leadership for the innovation journey.

1. Based on his competing values framework, Quinn (1988) empha-sizes the importance of reflective leadership skills in reframing either-or polarities into both-and possibilities: "This requires seeing the strength and weaknesses in each of the polar perspectives. In addition, it requires moving to a metalevel that allows one to see the interpene-tration and the inseparability of the two polarities" (164). He states that accomplishing this requires

seeing past one's own blinders and the blinders imposed by the expectations of others. You begin to do this by obtaining an awareness of your own style, learning what your own strengths and blind spots are. You must then make a conscious effort to appreciate the importance of your weaknesses. What is it that you tend not to see? What skills do you tend to ignore? This kind of thinking is not easy. It involves a certain amount of cognitive complexity and means experimenting with opposing frames of reference. Like a little girl learning to ride a bike, you have to throw yourself into the process and learn by experience. (Quinn, 1988: 24).

2. At the group or executive team level, Bartunek (1993) points out that achieving balanced internal diversity requires strong institutional leadership to tolerate the ambiguity of holding multiple perspectives, to balance the power among managers with different perspectives, and to enable their interaction toward a creative outcome. In the cases in which she observed such balanced internal diversity, institutional leaders used a negotiation approach to issue management, like that described by Ury, Brett, and Goldberg (1988). Bartunek notes that when this negotiation style was used, the eventual resolution of conflicts brought about a more complex and creative understanding than had been present before. The outcomes occurred in part because powerful people were able to have their own perspectives and respect those of others (Bartunek, 1993). Whenever conflicting positions exist, Bartunek (1993) warns that a cooperative, facilitative style that assumes shared interests is more likely to increase the underlying conflict and the possibility of significant oversight, but a negotiation approach that consciously builds on different perspectives is more likely to succeed.

3. The demographic composition, experience, and incentives of top management team members represent a set of human resource practices related to achieving balanced internal diversity. Empirically, Sutcliffe (1994) found that accuracy of environmental perceptions by top management teams is a function of diverse experiences and intense organizational scanning by top managers. In addition, Tushman and Murmann (1997) show that heterogeneity in functional backgrounds of executive teams is related to shorter response times to initiate a strategic reorientation after an environmental jolt.

4. Levinthal (1997) discusses structural mechanisms to maintain diversity within the firm by establishing multiple sources of resources and authority bases that promote multiple communities of practice or learning groups.

5. Finally, a study of fifty-nine minicomputer firms by Virany et al. (1992) discovered two modes of successful organizational adaptation

in this turbulent industry. The most typical mode combined sweeping CEO and executive team turnover and strategic reorientations. A more rare, and over the long-term more effective, adaptation involved strategic reorientations and moderate executive team changes but no CEO turnover. Virany et al. (1992) say that this rare set of extraordinarily successful organizations had relatively stable executive teams that initiated reorientations to stay ahead of turbulent environmental conditions:

> [They] were able to balance relative stability in the senior team along with fundamental organization change. These executive teams initiated second-order learning not through sweeping executive-team and/or CEO change, but through reorientations in the context of executive-team stability. These unique executive teams seem to possess an ability to learn not through executive-team change but through changes in how they work together (March et al., 1991; Eisenhardt, 1989). (89)

The typical mode of organizational reorientations through sweeping top management turnovers indicates an unusually high rate of "bad luck" or a common failure within top management teams to maintain the requisite internal diversity of perspectives and learning processes necessary to deal with environmental ambiguity and change. This typical mode supports Virany et al.'s conclusion (1992) that "executive succession can be a powerful lever for improving organizational performance" (89). However, this lever also represents a major indictment of top management leadership and of the continual search for the hero leaders to drive organizational innovation and change.

Peter Senge (1998) argues that this search for hero leaders may be a critical factor in diverting our attention from building organizations that, by their very nature, continually adapt and reinvent themselves:

> It is extremely easy to think of "leaders" as those few special people who bring about significant institutional change. This leads to an endless search for real *Leaders*, heroic figures who can rescue us from recalcitrant, noncompetitive institutions. But the search for leaders might actually divert our attention from a deeper need—the need to understand why it is that those institutions find it so hard to evolve in the first place. Failing to create institutions that, by their very nature, continually adapt and reinvent themselves keeps us "hooked" on heroic leaders as our only hope for survival. This sets up a reinforcing spiral of crisis and responses in the form of new, still more heroic leaders. The price we pay is incalculable: institutions that lurch from crisis to crisis, continually stress on the members of those institutions . . . the belief that the common people are powerless to change things —only the mythical leaders have such power. (2)

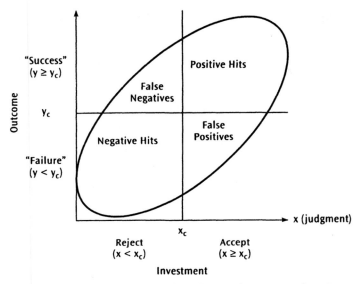

Figure 4.9 Project selection: the relations between a decision and its
possible future outcomes. From Zar Shapira, *Risk Taking: A
Managerial Perspective* (New York: Russell Sage Foundation, 1995).
Used with permission of the Russell Sage Foundation.

Conclusion

Managers of multiyear innovation development projects, such as CIP
and TAP, hope to achieve ultimate project success by making periodic
investments in a learning process that reduces the uncertainty and ambiguity of an innovative idea as it develops into a concrete implemented reality. Shapira (1995) and Garud, Nayyar and Shapira (1997)
provide a useful investment decision model that examines the likelihood of making types I and II errors. Type I errors, or "false positives,"
consist of investing in innovation projects that turn out to be unsuccessful, whereas Type II errors, or "false negatives," are decisions not to
invest in projects that eventually achieve success elsewhere.

Figure 4.9 illustrates Shapira's model for assessing the trade-offs between making types I and II errors when making repeated investments
in the development of an innovation. The likelihood of making Type I
and Type II errors is a function of the (1) the uncertainty or strength of
the relationship between project investment decisions and project outcomes, (2) the ambiguity of knowing what investment decision hurdles
to use and what specific performance targets or outcomes should be
achieved, and (3) the risk aversion of decision makers.

Project uncertainty is illustrated in figure 4.9 by the shape of the el-
lipsoid, which represents a plot of the correlation between the ex ante

investment decision and ex post project success or failure. The shape of this plot can vary from a circle, indicating high uncertainty or total ignorance, to a straight line, indicating no uncertainty, in the relationship between investment decisions and project outcomes. Only by increasing the predictive validity of this relationship can both types of errors be simultaneously minimized. As uncertainty decreases through learning gained from repeated investments (e.g., the correlation between project selection decisions and outcome success increase along the range of $.00 > r_{xy} > 1.00$), the likelihood of Type I and Type II errors decreases, whereas the probability of accepting successful projects and rejecting projects that turn out to be failures increases. Such learning occurs within a project as it unfolds and, equally important, across projects as institutional leaders gain experiences over many years of leading innovation projects.

However, as we found in chapter 3, clearly formed criteria for project selection and performance outcomes are necessary conditions for establishing the predictability of this relationship. Reducing project ambiguity is a precondition for reducing project uncertainty. The ambiguity of knowing what criteria to use for project selection and what desired outcomes to target can only be learned through discovery. This discovery process depends primarily on the repertoire of experiences and perspectives of decision makers. Decision makers who have a broad and diverse base of experience are typically more certain about what decision hurdles and outcome targets to apply to multiyear investment projects. Finally, the risk aversion of decision makers is a key factor because greater returns often come from projects associated with higher levels of ambiguity and uncertainty. This risk orientation reflects the salience of particular rewards and penalties associated with errors of omission or commission. The model reveals this risk orientation in terms of decision makers' relative willingness to commit Type I or Type II errors.

Viewing leadership as a set of interdependent roles for guiding periodic investment decisions in the development of innovations has important implications for understanding the likelihood of Type I and Type II errors. The relative balance and timing of the leadership roles shown in figure 4.5 proposes a leadership structure that is highly pluralistic at the innovation development stage and increasingly unified at the innovation implementation stage. During the initial period of innovation development, we argued that a pluralistic structure encourages multiple and diverse perspectives needed to reduce innovation ambiguity and uncertainty. When this diversity and conflict are kept in balance through institutional leadership, such a pluralistic structure should increase the probability of technological foresights and reduce the likelihood of oversights. As levels of project ambiguity and uncertainty decrease, the likelihood of Type I and Type II errors decrease. In these cases a more traditional homogeneous structure of leadership is appropriate to mobilize a unified and efficient innovation effort.

An imbalance in the sponsor role, however, can cause both Type I and Type II errors. When sponsors are too actively involved early on, perhaps to a level more likely associated with the entrepreneur who enjoys day-to-day involvement in a project, errors of commission (Type I) are likely to occur. Excessively enthusiastic efforts by the sponsor can trigger initial investments that, through a recurrent cycle of sense making and justification (Weick, 1993), can lead to an escalation toward courses of action later determined commercial or technological failures. The opposite situation is not enough involvement or a lack of willingness by any leader to take the role of the sponsor. Low levels of sponsor involvement, especially early in the ambiguous and uncertain formation of the innovation unit, are likely to result in Type II errors because no innovation project is likely to gather enough momentum or guidance to surmount inertial organizational barriers.

Imbalances in the critic role relative to sponsors and institutional leaders are likely to result in both types of errors as well. We proposed that the critic role is essential in the early period of innovation development, when highly ambiguous and uncertain characteristics of an innovative idea are not surfaced or addressed. When the initial phase of an innovation does not include sufficient critic involvement, poor decisions and incorrectly chosen courses of action are likely to go unchallenged, and Type I errors are likely to occur. Too much of the critic's role, however, can cause Type II errors when the critic becomes too aggressive in challenging assumptions and refocusing each debate during the initial stages of an innovation. Unless the critic allows some projects to progress past the formation stages, few investment commitments will continue toward commercialization. Furthermore, if the critic remains excessively active in later periods of innovation implementation, such repeated criticisms likely will prevent any project from successful introduction.

The institutional leader role is important at the earliest stages of an innovation as the innovation team forms and later when an innovation moves from development to implementation and market introduction. As resource controllers and agents of legitimacy, institutional leaders' involvement builds the infrastructure needed for a successful innovation. As with imbalances in sponsor and critic involvement, too much or too little involvement by institutional leaders is dysfunctional to the innovation process through oversights by commission (Type I errors) or omission (Type II errors). When the institutional leadership role is not adequately exercised in the early stages of an innovation, investment decisions that do not enjoy an umbrella of legitimacy with top management or with external actors are likely. Type I errors are likely when institutional leadership is not present to referee debates between the sponsor and critic. Type II errors arise when institutional involvement becomes excessive and sponsors, critics, and entrepreneurs are entangled in a web of bureaucratic and institutional controls and restrictions.

In summary, technological foresights are more likely to occur when a proportional temporal balance of all four leadership roles is exercised during innovation development. Imbalances in any of the leadership roles increase the likelihood of Type I and Type II errors, which in turn may prevent the development of innovations that are the basis for organizational reorientations in response to changing environmental conditions.

This chapter has introduced a pluralistic view of innovation leadership that is based on four key observations of top managers and investors in the innovations studied by MIRP. These observations differ from popular descriptions of innovation leadership in four respects:

1. Instead of viewing leadership as a personal characteristic, we focused on the sharing and distribution of leadership behaviors among decision-making executives, because many—not one or a few—top managers at different hierarchical levels were actively involved in the innovations within their organizations.

2. Diversity and conflict are reflected because, contrary to the common view that top management executives have a unified, homogeneous, and cohesive perspective, these top managers typically expressed opposing views and performed roles that served as checks and balances on each other in directing the innovations.

3. Four counterbalancing roles in an interdependent role set for innovation leadership were examined: corporate sponsor, mentor, critic, and institutional leader. Although the literature has focused almost exclusively on the champion or sponsor role, innovation leadership involves an interdependent set of leadership roles.

4. Top managers made pragmatic decisions in response to changing innovation conditions and perspectives held by other top managers, rather than according to a planned course of action.

We admit that popular treatments of leadership, emphasizing unity and consensus among top managers toward a single strategic vision, may be effective for converging on and exploiting a chosen course of action, as occurs when innovation development ends and implementation begins. But, ambiguous and uncertain situations, as encountered during the beginning of innovation development, require a pluralistic power structure of leadership. Diverse perspectives tend to be squelched in a unitary power structure. Pluralistic leadership increases the chances for technological foresights and decreases the likelihood of oversights. Of course, such a pluralistic structure does not ensure intelligent leadership. However, we expect the odds of organizational learning and adaptability to increase when a balance is maintained among dialectical leadership roles throughout innovation development.

5

Managing Relationships during
the Innovation Journey

As noted in chapter 2, a common characteristic of the innovations studied by Minnesota Innovation Research Program (MIRP) investigators is that they engaged in a variety of relationships with other organizations. None was a self-sustaining, autonomous entity. None possessed all the resources, competencies, and legitimacy necessary to develop and implement their innovations alone. And even if one possessed most of these capabilities, it typically encountered competitors pursuing a similar venture or contended with institutional regulators concerned with the rights and interests of third parties to the venture. As a result, when an organization begins developing a new technology, product, or program, it does so by entering into a web of cooperative, competitive, and regulatory relationships with specific other organizations and players in the venture arena.

For example, to develop the cochlear implant, 3M's Cochlear Implant Program (CIP) innovation entered into several joint research and development relationships with other research institutes to acquire new technology; subscribed to the regulatory regime of the Food and Drug Administration (FDA) to obtain permission to introduce the device in the market; cultivated a variety of cooperative relationships with customers, suppliers, and financiers; and engaged in competitive struggles with rival firms. These rivals were simultaneously developing their own webs of interorganizational relationships (IRs) to make similar or substitute biomedical devices.

The dyadic relationships in these IR webs are interdependent because of their common association with the venture. As the parties in this set of dyadic relationships interact and perform their tasks, they change the technical, institutional, or economic characteristics of the innovation venture. These changes may alter the beliefs of parties about how they stand relative to one another, and in a given dyadic relationship they often spill over to influence other relationships of the focal organization. With time, the parties engaged in dyadic relationships with a focal organization become spun together into a complex web of interdependent and shifting cooperative and competitive behaviors. Lew Platt, chairman and chief executive officer of Hewlett Packard, aptly captures these dynamics: "Once the world was simple, and so were relationships. Your partners were your allies, and your competitors were your foes. Today, people we compete with one day are our partners the next. . . . Alliances are critical. We can't do everything ourselves" (quoted in Sheridan, 1994: 27).

We know very little about how these cooperative, competitive, and regulatory relationships among organizations emerge, shift, and evolve or how they influence each other over time. Very little theory and research have addressed these dynamic process issues. Instead, most of the research has focused on the antecedent conditions for the emergence of IRs (Oliver, 1990; Galaskiewicz, 1985) or on alternative governance structures for market, hierarchical, and network forms of IRs (e.g., Williamson, 1975, 1991; Barney and Ouchi, 1986; Nohria and Eccles, 1992). Although this research is useful to understand the starting conditions, investments, and structures of different kinds of IRs, it does not provide insights about the dynamic sequence of events in which various forms of IRs unfold and change over time.

Understanding these IR dynamics is important for managing innovation, particularly because these IRs constitute a large part of the journey for most new ventures. We argue that how parties construct self identities relative to their standings with others determines their dispositions to work together or alone and for self- or mutual gains. In addition, how parties negotiate with, make commitments to, and execute an IR strongly influence the degrees to which parties judge it equitable and efficient (Ring and Van de Ven, 1992). These processes also influence motivations to continue or terminate an IR (Friedman, 1991). Interactions between parties may cast a positive, neutral, or negative overtone on the relationship and influence the degree to which parties have conflicts and settle disputes arising out of the IR (Lowenstein, Thompson, and Bazerman, 1989; Pruitt and Rubin, 1986).

Given the lack of prior empirical research, MIRP researchers took an inductive approach to examine how IRs develop during the innovation journey. In this chapter, we focus on these dynamics at two levels of analysis, the IR dyad and the IR web. At the dyad level, we examine how an innovation unit enters into and maintains relationships with other parties who are needed to develop the innovation. At the web level, we examine how these dyadic relationships of a focal innovation unit become interdependent and influence each other over time. We examine these issues by tracking how 3M entered into a set of dyadic relationships to develop its cochlear implant innovation and then how these initially independent IRs became a complex web of interdependencies.

We use the metaphor of a web to emphasize the flexible and fragile nature of the links between an interdependent group of organizations as they work out the details of a common venture. An *interorganizational web* is defined as the set of interconnected, dyadic relationships entered into by a focal organization that are related to a specific business venture (e.g., development and commercialization of cochlear implant technology). We view an IR web as an intermediate level of analysis to link dyadic relationships between organizations in contrast to the more macro level of an interorganizational network, as discussed in chapter 6. We therefore define an IR web differently from an interorganizational set. The latter is more inclusive and consists of all the dyadic IRs that a focal organization maintains in all its business activities (Evan, 1966). An IR web is more restrictive than an IR set and includes only the dyadic IRs of a focal organization pertaining to a specific business venture. The concept of an IR web also differs from Aldrich and Whetten's (1981) definition of an action set, also discussed in chapter 6. Although they define an action set as a group of organizations that have formed a temporary alliance for a limited purpose, they do not view this group from the perspective of a focal organization. Our notion of an IR web is perhaps closest to what Powell and Smith-Doerr (1994) refer to as an ego network.

Following a conceptual overview that frames our research perspective, this chapter focuses principally on 3M's twelve-year attempt to develop and commercialize cochlear implant technology. The chapter concludes with the following major findings about the sequences of events in the development of IR dyads and webs:

1. There is an identifiable pattern to the development and maintenance of relationships between pairs (dyads) of organizations, but the pattern is not simple or linear.
2. During the early stages of development, interactions between partners in any given dyad are explained primarily by dynamics within that dyad.
3. As commitments form, any given dyad becomes embedded (Granovetter, 1985) in a larger network of interdependence and, as a result, interactions between dyadic partners are influenced by dynamics in the larger web.
4. Because of these dynamics, change and development in an IR web tends to resemble a punctuated equilibrium process, where terms of relationships are established during relatively short divergent periods followed by longer convergent periods to carry out the agreements made (Tushman and Romanelli, 1985; Gersick, 1988).

Conceptual Framework

Cooperation, competition, regulation (control), and conflict are different forms of behavior between parties regarding how they stand relative to each other on a given issue at a particular time and place.[1] Although the issue can be almost any kind of problem or topic, we focus on the development of an innovation. The relations between parties can be characterized a number of ways. We focus on whether they choose to act together or apart and whether their motivations are toward achieving an inclusive mutual gain or an exclusive self-interested gain with respect to the issue. A classification of behaviors on these two dimensions suggests the following four types of relationships among parties:

1. Parties *cooperate* when they choose to work together by sharing or exchanging resources to achieve a common purpose or inclusive benefit.
2. Parties *compete* when they mutually perceive each other as striving independently to attain scarce resources or an exclusive benefit desired by both parties.
3. Parties *regulate* when one controls or mediates the actions of other parties to achieve an inclusive benefit for all, including third parties.
4. Parties *conflict* when they perceive a party to be acting against the other to inhibit the achievement of the other's self interests.

These four types of relationships are not exhaustive but are sufficient for our purposes. For example, we do not single out the pervasive relationship of *accommodation*, in which parties act to avoid interfering in the achievement of others' self interests when they use a common resource, such as an elevator. Couch (1986) provides the most complete typology of coordinated social action that we have found. In his theory of elementary forms of social acts, Couch proposed eight forms of social interaction: cooperation, competition, autocracy (or regulation), conflict, accommodation, mutuality, social panic, and chase. Bastien (1993) extended Couch's work by examining temporal shifts or progressions among these forms of social interaction. In this chapter, we focus primarily on cooperation, competition, regulation, and conflictual relations between organizations.

1. The definitions provided here attempt to avoid three common problems in the organization and management strategy literature, which tend to (1) treat cooperation and competition as bipolar outcomes, (2) confound competition with conflict, and (3) associate these relationships with the attributes of individual actors. As our definitions indicate, we view cooperation and competition as processes, not outcomes, that are conceptually distinct, but not bipolar, from each other and from conflict and control. Each of these processes is identified by the joint, not individual, standings among the parties.

These different kinds of relationships are temporary and only apply when parties stand in relation to one another at a particular time and place on an issue. This is illustrated with the following example, a modification of Burt's (1992) atavistic driver story:

> You're going with the flow of traffic on a freeway until you come to an open stretch on the road. You speed up to 75 mph in a 65-mph zone. A car behind you also speeds up and drives parallel to you in the next lane. The driver waves to you. How are you to interpret her behavior? Is this a threat, a challenge, a helping hand, or a cop? You slow down, she slows down and stays parallel with you. A few moments later you pass a cop parked along the side of the road. In relief you wave a grateful thanks to the driver who points to the fuzz buster on her dashboard. She waves back with a "come on." You slow down, she slows down. You speed up and so does she. You think, "O.K. I'll take her on." Your tires burn and fly ahead of her. In the mirror, you see her cough in your smoke. A few moments later she pulls up again parallel to you. She scowls at you; you respond in kind. She pulls into your lane, hits the side of your car, and forces you off the road. Coming to a screeching halt in the meridian, you see her wave "bye-bye" as she speeds off. (84)

This story has five episodes, and in each the drivers stand in a different parallel relation to each other, producing processes of accommodation, cooperation, competition, and conflict, respectively, all within the context of a regulated environment. As the parallelism of each relation breaks, the behavior stops and a new one begins. Shifts in the transient cheek-by-jowl relations with respect to the passing environment produce decidedly different episodes of relationships between the same two drivers.

The task of analyzing relationships between organizations is more difficult than this example because only small pieces of the intentions and behaviors of other parties can be observed, and the issue on which relations intersect may itself be ambiguous and vaguely appreciated by the parties involved. Fortunately, as Commons (1950) emphasized, an IR requires joint, not individual, valuation. At a minimum, the process requires that the parties to a relationship be aware of one another. Without this awareness there is no relationship, for there is no one else, except a faceless environment or market, to relate to about an issue. Furthermore, except for simple issues, like our example of the drivers, an IR—be it cooperative, competitive, conflictual, or regulatory—is not a discrete event. A series of interactions are often required between parties to understand the nature of the issue and their possible relations to one another on the issue. As a result, the IR process can be observed as a sequence of events or incidents in which parties come to understand and relate to one another over time.

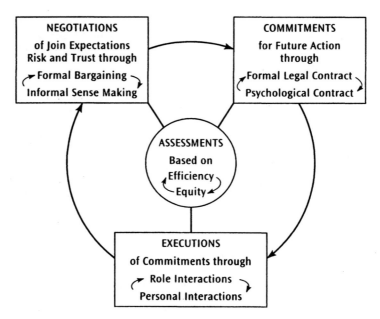

Figure 5.1 Process framework for the development of cooperative inter-organizational relationships. From Ring and Van de Ven (1994, p. 97)

Ring and Van de Ven (1994) propose a useful point of departure to identify process events in the development of an IR. Their process framework is illustrated in figure 5.1. They suggest that the development of a cooperative IR consists of a repetitive sequence of negotiation, commitment, and execution events, on which parties make assessments to judge whether they should proceed, modify, or terminate the relationship. Although Ring and Van de Ven developed these concepts to study cooperative IRs, with small modifications, the ideas can be generalized to apply to processes of competitive and regulatory relationships.

A necessary, but insufficient, condition for an IR, be it a cooperative, competitive, conflictual, or regulatory, is that the parties be jointly aware of each other and their positions on an issue. Parties become aware of positions through negotiations. Negotiations include direct interactions and indirect observations among parties in developing joint, not individual, expectations about each other's motivations, possible roles, and perceived uncertainties about an issue they are exploring to undertake jointly or alone. If the parties directly interact, as is typically required for the onset of cooperation, conflict, or regulation, the focus is on the bargaining processes in which they propose, persuade, argue, and haggle over possible terms and procedures of a potential relationship. If the parties do not engage in direct interactions, as is often the case in competitive IRs, they may rely on indirect information and observations of others to become aware of and make attributions about each other's roles and intentions.

Underlying these direct and indirect negotiation events are social-psychological processes of sense making (Weick, 1994), in which organizational parties come to appreciate ways to relate to others by reshaping or clarifying the identities and roles of their own organizations relative to others regarding the issue. By projecting themselves onto their environment, organizational parties develop a self-referential appreciation of their own identities, which in turn permits them to act in relation to others (Morgan, 1986). Psychologically, sense making derives from the need within individuals to have both a sense of self-identity relative to others and to construct a common external factual order regarding their social relationships (Turner, 1987). Direct communications and indirect observations provide parties the information to produce this shared interpretation, and it often emerges gradually and incrementally.

In commitments, the wills of the parties meet (Commons, 1950) as they make decisions or reach understandings about how they will relate to each other with respect to the issue. At the most basic level, commitments are decisions by parties to work together or alone to achieve a collective inclusive benefit or an exclusive self-interest gain. These commitments designate whether parties choose to engage in a cooperative, competitive, regulatory, or some other form of relationship. If they commit to a cooperative relationship, the parties make additional commitments with regard to the terms and structure for future action together. If it is a regulatory relationship, the governing or controlling party typically sets forth the rules and procedures the other parties must comply with to achieve the inclusive interests of third parties or the law. If it is a competitive or conflictual relationship, the parties tacitly agree to be opponents and engage in rivalry to win an exclusive benefit by the legal means of market behavior.

In execution events, the commitments and rules of action are carried into effect. The parties execute joint or individual behaviors by giving orders to their subordinates, buying materials, paying the amounts agreed on, and otherwise administering whatever is needed to meet the terms of their relationship. Finally, an assessment occurs when one of the parties makes an affective evaluation of the events that are transpiring in the IR.

Some innovation journeys take several years and may require that IRs remain in effect for a long time. With time, misunderstandings, conflicts, and changing expectations among the parties are inevitable, and these factors can motivate the parties to reconsider the terms of their relationships. If these factors do not materially alter the standings and motivations of the parties, they will engage in renegotiations to modify and resolve only the contested issues, but all other terms and commitments of the relationship may remain in effect. In this way, the ongoing relationship is preserved. However, if changing conditions materially shift the standings and motivations of the parties to a business venture, they may terminate the relationship by withdrawing from it or by shifting to a different form of relationship.

Ring and Van de Ven (1994) propose that a simple set of heuristics guide organizational parties through initial and recurrent sequences of negotiations, commitments, and executions:

> If parties can negotiate minimal, congruent expectations of each other in a business venture, they will make commitments to an initial action course of working together or alone for an inclusive or exclusive gain. If exogenous context events or if endogenous assessments reinforce the execution of these commitments, the parties will continue with or expand their relationship. However, if these commitments are not executed in a manner judged acceptable by the parties or if external environmental events materially alter the perceived standings of parties relative to the business venture, they will initiate corrective measures by renegotiating or reducing their commitments to the IR. Thus, we expect IRs to evolve through a recurrent sequence of negotiation, commitment, and execution events that are undertaken to adapt to a changing external context of the business venture and internal assessments of the relationship by the parties involved. (Ring and Van de Ven, 1994: 99)

3M's IRs to Develop Cochlear Implants

Bunderson, Dirks, Garud, and Van de Ven (1998) undertook a detailed study of the relationships in which 3M engaged with other organizations to develop its cochlear implant program. Although this included many organizations, they focused on the following four, which were most important to 3M.

1. 3M engaged in a mostly cooperative relationship from 1977 to 1989 with the House Ear Institute (HEI), in Los Angeles, California, to develop commercially a single-channel cochlear implant device pioneered by Dr. William House, who in 1961 surgically implanted the first one in the United States.
2. 3M also became involved in a second cooperative relationship from 1982 to 1989 with the Hochmairs at the University of Innsbruck in Vienna, Austria, to develop a second generation of cochlear implant devices. As this cooperative relationship with 3M evolved, the relationship between HEI and the Hochmairs developed into a "sibling rivalry."

3. After initial attempts at collaboration failed from 1977 to 1980, Nucleus Corporation in Melbourne, Australia, became 3M's major cochlear implant competitor for most of the 1980s. Nucleus, with the support of the Australian Government, engaged in a cooperative relationship with a scientist at the University of Melbourne to commercialize a multiple-channel cochlear implant technology that he developed. The 3M-HEI single-channel technology was the first cochlear implant device approved for market release by the FDA in 1984, but the Nucleus-Melbourne multiple-channel technology became the dominant cochlear implant design in the market by 1988.

4. Most countries regulate commercial market release of only those biomedical devices proven to be safe and effective. In the United States, the FDA performs this regulatory function. The MIRP study included a detailed tracking of the events that transpired in the regulatory relationship between 3M and the FDA from 1981 to 1989.

Real-time data on the development of the 3M CIP innovation, including these relationships, were collected and described by Garud and Van de Ven (1989a, 1989b). Of the 1,009 events recorded, about one-third (373 events) pertain to developments in 3M's relationships with HEI (129 events), the Hochmairs (77 events), Nucleus (60 events), and the FDA (106 events). Figure 5.2 plots the cumulative occurrence of these events in the development of each relationship.

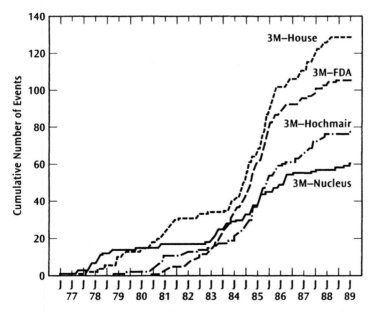

Figure 5.2 Cumulative number of events over time in 3M cochlear implant relationships

Bunderson et al. (1998) coded each of these events using a set of decision rules to operationalize the six process concepts discussed previously: sense making, bargaining, commitment, execution, assessment, and context. Context events include incidents that occurred outside and beyond the control of the parties involved in a relationship. Figure 5.3, A to D, plots the cumulative number of coded bargaining, commitment, execution, assessment, and context events in the temporal development of the four 3M cochlear implant relationships.

These event time series suggest three quantitative findings that provide a useful background to interpret the qualitative findings presented in the next section on the evolution of these IRs. First, figure 5.3, A to D, shows that none of the 3M IRs unfolded in a simple linear progression of bargaining, commitment, and execution stages. This is contrary to much of the literature about transactions cost economics (e.g., Williamson, 1991) and the sociology of interorganizational relationships (e.g., Oliver, 1990), which assume that IRs develop in simple linear sequences in which parties negotiate, make commitments to a relationship, and carry out these commitments for the relationship's duration. The developmental pattern in each of 3M's relationships followed a multiple parallel progression of numerous bargaining, commitment, and execution events throughout the temporal duration of the IR.

More recent work by Poole, Van de Ven, Dooley, and Holmes (1999) suggests some support for Ring and Van de Ven's (1994) hypothesized iterative sequence of bargaining, commitment, and execution when higher levels of aggregation are used to examine the event sequences. Poole et al. found support for two kinds of repetitive cycles of behaviors among parties, which they called experimentation and commitment bargaining. The former is an aggregation of execution events followed by bargaining, sense making, and commitment events. This pattern reflects a process of learning by doing and then bargaining about results. The second pattern was composed of commitment cycles followed by bargaining events. It suggests that people first made commitments to a course of action and then bargained about implementation to fine-tune the commitments. In either pattern, a repetitive cycle consisting of some combination of bargaining, commitment, and execution events was observed throughout the duration of the relationships.

The second major finding was that the frequencies of the occurrence of bargaining, commitment and execution events co-evolve over time within the development of each IR as well as among the four IRs. The graphs show that each IR begins with a relatively brief period of numerous events followed by a longer period of relatively infrequent events until about 1984. This pattern is repeated after 1984 with an active two-year period of events followed by a longer inactive period

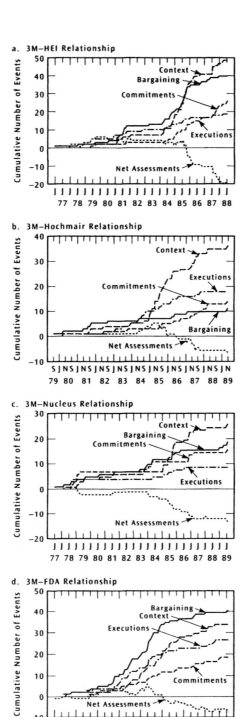

a. 3M–HEI Relationship

b. 3M–Hochmair Relationship

c. 3M–Nucleus Relationship

d. 3M–FDA Relationship

Figure 5.3 Cumulative number of coded events over time in 3M cochlear implant relationships. From Bunduron, Dirks, Garund and Van de Ven (1998)

from 1986 to 1989. As we will see, 1984 represents a qualitatively important transition in 3M's web of IRs. This pattern reflects a punctuated equilibrium process in the development of the IRs over time. This process consists of a repetitive cycle of relatively short divergent periods of rapid change, followed by a longer convergent period of incremental change and adaptation (Gould, 1982; Tushman and Romanelli, 1985). If we assume that this similar pattern in the four dyadic IRs is not circumstantial, there are two possible interpretations: (1) events in one IR affected events in another IR, or (2) events outside of these IRs affected the progression of events in both IR X and IR Y.

Finally, figure 5.3 shows that although external context events occur throughout the duration of each IR, they occur at a disproportionately high rate after 1984. This increase in context events coincided with a shift in assessments by the parties to their IRs from being mostly positive before 1984 to mostly negative thereafter.

To understand these findings about periods of divergent and convergent activities observed in the cumulative event graphs (figure 5.3), we turn to the stories behind the numbers. The next sections provide a qualitative description of divergent and convergent periods in the development of each of the four 3M CIP IRs.

First Divergent Period: "Courtship and Marriage"

3M-Nucleus (11/77 to 7/81)

News of the development of a "bionic ear" by a scientist at the University of Melbourne in 1977 captured the attention of bioscientists and managers at 3M and motivated them to explore the commercial feasibility of cochlear implants. This event precipitated a four-year period of interactions between 3M and the University of Melbourne in which they explored a number of different collaborative options, all of which failed for one reason or another. These collaborative attempts included a joint venture, a manufacturing arrangement, and an acquisition.

3M-HEI (1/79 to 12/81)

The 3M-HEI cochlear implant relationship began as a vendor-supplier relationship in 1977, when 3M's subsidiary company in Santa Barbara, California, manufactured component parts for an experimental "Sigma" cochlear implant device that William House was developing in his research clinic in Los Angeles, California. The dominant interactions between 3M and HEI during this vendor-supplier relationship dealt with the custom manufacturing and supply of the cochlear implant components according to the specifications House required for his research. Most of these interactions were straightforward executions of vendor-supplier contracts.

This vendor-supplier relationship provided the context within which 3M could begin to evaluate HEI as a potential collaborator in its emerging plans to develop and commercialize cochlear implants. 3M and HEI began to explore possible collaborative relationships and even negotiate a few agreements regarding the evaluation of HEI's technology. This continued until August 1980, when HEI began to express dissatisfaction with 3M's delay in committing to a collaborative relationship and stated its intent to look elsewhere. Several people engaged in cochlear implant exploration at 3M argued that the HEI opportunity would be lost if a commitment was not made soon. At the time, 3M was exploring possible collaborative relationships with other cochlear implant research centers throughout the world. These explorations culminated in 3M's development of a strategic plan for cochlear implant development and commercialization in July 1981. As a result of this plan, 3M entered exclusive agreements with HEI and the Hochmairs to develop further, conduct clinical trials, undertake the FDA regulatory review process, and commercialize the prototype devices that were being developed in their centers.

3M-Hochmairs (1/81 to 7/81)

While exploring cochlear implant research institutes in 1979 and 1980, 3M became aware of the Hochmairs, scientists in Vienna, who were conducting research on cochlear implants at the University of Innsbruck. The relationship between 3M and the Hochmairs began with a number of exploratory discussions that resulted in an invitation for the Hochmairs to present their work at 3M. 3M decided the technology was promising and began negotiating licensing and consulting arrangements in 1980. Although these early negotiations were not successful, the Hochmairs' technology played an important role in 3M's strategic plan for cochlear implants that were developed in July 1981. Shortly thereafter, 3M and the Hochmairs entered into an exclusive worldwide licensing and consulting agreement to develop the Vienna device. This event marked the formal beginning of a cooperative relationship.

3M-FDA

Given that products were not being proposed for clinical trials and review during this initial period, there were no significant interactions between 3M and the FDA.

Themes

Interactions between 3M and the other players in its IR web during this first divergent period might best be summarized using the metaphor of courtship and marriage. In courtship, a potential suitor discovers and explores the attractiveness of potential partners until a commitment is made to a specific individual. Similarly, during most of this period, 3M was identifying research groups with expertise in cochlear implant technology, exploring the attractiveness of the technologies these groups offered and considering the feasibility of long-term, collaborative relationships. This divergent process ended when 3M made specific, long-term commitments to pursue collaborative relationships with HEI and the Hochmairs and not Nucleus.

First Convergent Period: "Production"

3M-Nucleus (7/81 to 3/84)

In July 1981, the University of Melbourne entered into a collaborative relationship with Nucleus, and 3M entered into cooperative relationships with HEI and the Hochmairs. These commitments also changed how 3M and Nucleus stood relative to one another, which had two important implications for the relationship between 3M and Nucleus. First, they initiated a two-year period in which very little interaction took place between 3M and Nucleus. During that time, the parties were focused on other activities and other relationships. Second, these outside commitments introduced a competitive element to the 3M-Nucleus relationship as each party tried to execute separate strategies. Consequently, we begin to find competition between 3M and Nucleus emerging for the first time after 1981 as both parties began to execute their manufacturing, clinical trials, and promotion strategies.

3M-HEI (12/81 to 11/84)

The formal agreement between 3M and HEI initiated a fairly long and productive convergent period in the development of their relationship. In fact, one CIP member referred to the relationship during this time as a "marriage." Interactions during 1982 through the beginning of 1984 focused mostly on the product development, testing, and seeking regulatory approval for the adult single-channel device.[2] The crowning achievement from this convergent period of collaboration was the FDA panel approval in June 1984 followed by the FDA approval in November of the 3M-HEI adult single-channel device as the first cochlear implant for commercial market release. The FDA announcement

2. The lack of events during these two years does not signify that no interactions were occurring. Recall that an event was defined as a change in bargaining, commitment, or execution behavior among the parties. The fact that there are few events during this period suggests that there were few changes in the relationship and that the parties were primarily involved in carrying out the tasks at hand.

celebrated the event by indicating that this was the first time in human history that an electronic device replaced one of the five human senses. This event also triggered a March 1986 letter from President Ronald Reagan congratulating 3M and HEI for their contribution to society's health.

3M-Hochmairs (7/81 to 11/84)

After the agreement between 3M and the Hochmairs, a three-year period of convergent behavior ensued as each party focused on carrying out its part of the agreement. Negotiations were straightforward and incremental. For example, to assist in development, the parties modified their agreement so the Hochmairs could add another engineer in October 1983. During this period, both parties reported that things were proceeding better than expected. In late 1983, dates were set for undertaking the approval process and in mid-1984, clinical trials began. This period reached a climax in November 1984 when the Hochmairs reported remarkable performance of their Vienna device on European patients.

3M-FDA (1/81 to 10/83)

In June 1981, when 3M applied to the FDA for an investigational device exemption (IDE) for the world's first cochlear implant device, it found that the FDA's personnel and its scientific review panel members were not knowledgeable enough to evaluate the application. As a result, the panel asked 3M to prepare extensive additional documents and information to educate the FDA about the nature of the cochlear implant technology and the safety of electrical stimulation of the cochlea. Because 3M was determined to be the first company to gain FDA cochlear implant regulatory approvals, the company made significant investments to meet this request (e.g., multiple visits with FDA teams). For its part, the FDA organized open hearings on cochlear implants, which 3M judged extremely favorable because the FDA encouraged speedy cochlear implant work for deaf adults.

Themes

During this second period, interactions between 3M and its dyadic partners were mostly convergent and productive. Work progressed smoothly in each of 3M's collaborative relationships with both HEI and the Hochmairs, as well as in 3M's efforts to educate and influence the FDA. Furthermore, each of these relationships seemed to proceed independently and in relative isolation from the others. Even 3M's emerging competitive relationship with Nucleus did not appear to have significant implications for activities and interactions in the other three dyadic relationships. Interestingly, discussions with 3M managers at the time found that 3M did not wish to compete with Nucleus. Instead, the competitive relationship was a by-product of the dyadic cooperative agreements between Nucleus and the University of Melbourne and between 3M and HEI.

Second Divergent Period: "Turmoil"

3M-Nucleus (3/84 to 5/88)

In March 1984, Nucleus revealed its plans to enter the market with a multiple-channel device that it claimed was more effective in discriminating speech. 3M followed with plans to be the first to market by commercializing the single-channel device, which it claimed to be safer than the multiple-channel technology. These public commitments intensified the competitive relationship between 3M and Nucleus. For the first time, 3M began to view Nucleus as a significant threat. For the next several years, 3M and Nucleus engaged in head-to-head competition for technical performance, FDA approval, and promotion of their respective devices. Few direct interactions occurred between the parties during this time; each party was unilaterally trying to understand the other party and engage in activities that would block the other party. However, even during the heat of this competitive period between 3M and Nucleus, the parties also engaged in a few collaborative activities designed to strengthen and promote the cochlear implant industry.

3M-HEI (11/84 to 1/87)

In November 1984, three weeks after it approved the 3M- HEI single-channel device, the FDA released a press report saying the multiple-channel cochlear implant technology was superior to the single-channel technology. A few weeks later, the Hochmairs, who had been collaborating with 3M, reported remarkable results with their extra-cochlear device. As a result of these events, 3M began to question its single-channel strategy, reduced funding to HEI, and encouraged HEI to test other devices, particularly the Vienna device. HEI responded that it needed to seek support from outside parties and in December began to implant patients with the Nucleus device.

Over the next several years, relations between 3M and HEI became increasingly troubled. 3M continued to move from the HEI device to the Vienna device, and HEI continued to form relationships with other parties (e.g., Nucleus and Siemens) who were competing with 3M in cochlear implants. This divergence of opinion and direction was exacerbated by a product recall of the HEI device in late 1985, which HEI blamed on 3M. In late 1985, a 3M manager reported that the "love affair" between 3M and HEI was ending and by early 1986, 3M CIP members began to view the HEI relationship a failure. In February that year, 3M redirected its resources to the internal development of a multiple-channel "Sprint" device that it hoped would "leap-frog" the Nucleus multiple-channel device.

By late 1986, the cooperative relationship between 3M and HEI had substantially unraveled. 3M had given HEI its freedom, restricted its efforts to develop the 3M children's cochlear implant device, and formally committed resources and energy to the Sprint multiple-channel device and hearing aids. HEI, on the other hand, had increased its contact with Nucleus and other hearing-aid manufacturers such as Siemens. Given that both 3M and HEI had undertaken hearing-aid projects with other parties, their relationship at the end of this period shifted from a cooperative cochlear implant relationship to a competitive hearing-aid relationship.

3M-Hochmairs (11/84 to 6/87)

The FDA press release favoring multiple-channel technology also had implications for 3M's relationship with the Hochmairs. Shortly thereafter, 3M reviewed data showing that the Nucleus device outperformed the Vienna device. This threat caused 3M to promote prematurely the Vienna device at an otolaryngology conference in May 1985. This eventually backfired because 3M was unable to replicate the superior performance previously demonstrated by the Hochmairs. The premature promotion hindered sales of the 3M-HEI device for adults, and the inability to replicate results tarnished the reputation of the Vienna device.

At the same time, a sibling rivalry became apparent between HEI and the Hochmairs. While the HEI and Hochmairs were independently cooperating with 3M to develop cochlear implants, they were competing with each other for 3M's attention and resources. The structure of this triad changed when 3M's relationship with HEI began to deteriorate. Through a series of sense-making events between January and August 1985, 3M compared the performance and the strategic value of the HEI and Vienna devices. Eventually, to counter the competition of Nucleus, 3M decided to decrease its investment in HEI and emphasize the Hochmairs in August 1985. This shift in emphasis among allies, however, was not successful. The Vienna device was far behind schedule in the FDA review process. 3M CIP personnel judged that they had lost their lead over Nucleus and were now three years behind in their strategic plan. As 3M began conceding that the Vienna device would have difficulty catching the Nucleus device, 3M began to deemphasize its efforts in the Hochmairs relationship.

Beginning in 1986, 3M and the Hochmairs made a number of decisions leading to the separation of the parties. In February 1986, 3M switched its research and development efforts from the Vienna single-channel device to its own Sprint multiple-channel device. This switch placed 3M in competition with the Hochmairs because the Hochmairs were also independently developing their own multiple-channel device. Efforts to gain FDA approval for the Vienna device were hindered by device failures in May and July 1986. These device failures, in concert with similarly negative developments in the HEI, FDA, and Nucleus relationships, led 3M to conclude that it had lost the competitive race with Nucleus.

3M-FDA (10/83 to 5/88)

During 1983 and 1984, other cochlear implant firms, such as Nucleus, Richards, Storz, and Symbion, joined 3M in vying for a favored relationship with the FDA to tip regulations in their favor and gain recognized legitimacy for their form of cochlear implant technology. For example, 3M emphasized the safety of its single-channel technology, whereas Nucleus pushed the efficacy (speech discrimination capability) of its multiple-channel technology. In October 1983, when 3M submitted to the FDA its product market application (PMA) for the HEI adult single-channel device, interactions between the parties increased significantly. Fearing early approval of the single-channel device, multiple-channel advocates tried to dissuade the FDA from making a decision, claiming that the 3M-HEI technology was "archaic." 3M countered by claiming that existing multiple-channel technology did not provide a clear enough benefit in speech discrimination to justify the increased possibility of damage to the cochlea. Fortunately for 3M, the FDA ruled that single-channel devices could not be considered inferior until a superior device was actually available. The FDA concluded that it would be wrong to wait for improved cochlear implant technology when an existing technology could offer immediate benefits to patients. The FDA proceeded to approve the PMA in June 1984 and grant approval for the commercial sale of the 3M- HEI adult single-channel device in November 1984. This event represents, perhaps, the "high-water mark" of the 3M-FDA relationship.

However, the FDA sent a mixed signal three weeks later by circulating a report to the press stating the possible superiority of multiple-channel over single-channel technologies. With its statement, the FDA effectively undermined the single-channel technology and the HEI adult single-channel device it had just approved for commercial release. Soon after the FDA's announcement, testimonials appeared in the media promoting the superiority of multiple-channel devices. Although single-channel proponents tried to counter the testimonials, by March 1985 the Nucleus multiple-channel device had, in effect, achieved "FDA-approved" status even though the FDA did not make a ruling to approve the device until July 1985.

Meanwhile, 3M continued to push other devices (e.g., HEI children's device and Vienna device) through the increasingly institutionalized FDA approval process. They also tried to convince the FDA to require a minimum of 100 patients before premarket approval was given for a cochlear implant device, as the FDA had required of 3M for its HEI adult single-channel device. This requirement would have given 3M a chance to realize its objective of being first to market. Nevertheless, the FDA did not agree to these pleas and left patient size flexible.

In mid-1985, several of the FDA-approved HEI devices failed, and 3M voluntarily recalled the device. Although it had agreed with the recall, the FDA was embarrassed because it had approved the device for commercial release a year earlier. The event further tarnished the 3M-FDA relationship. In addition, the product recall reflected negatively on the HEI children's device, which was undergoing a PMA review at the same time.

Themes

During this second divergent period, competition for patients, public and regulatory approval, and technological leadership led 3M and the other players in its web to reevaluate their relationships in the light of marketplace feedback. In the case of 3M, for example, this reevaluation led to a shift of resources and priorities between and within each of its dyadic relationships as they tried to adjust to and anticipate market feedback. But because these relationships were interdependent, changes initiated within any one of 3M's relationships led to counteradjustments in one or more of the other IRs as these other dyads were forced to accommodate the change. In the aggregate, this process led to frequent changes in formal and informal agreements and understandings across all relationships in the web with an associated downward spiral of trust and productivity. By the end of this divergent period, fundamental changes in each of the dyadic relationships had reverberated throughout 3M's web.

Second Convergent Period: "Termination"

3M-Nucleus (5/88 to 8/89)

By 1987, 3M's cochlear implant efforts had been reduced to the Sprint multiple-channel device. By the end of 1987, enthusiasm for the Sprint device had waned at 3M, and it had become evident that FDA approval of 3M's device was contingent upon approval of Nucleus' device. The writing was on the wall: 3M management concluded that its cochlear implant program had lost. In 1989, nine years after the University of Melbourne had offered to sell its cochlear implant technology to 3M, 3M approached Nucleus with an offer to sell its cochlear implant technology. Negotiations continued until August of that year when the sale was made and 3M exited from cochlear implants: "To the victor went the spoils."

3M-HEI (1/87 to 9/88)

Interactions between 3M and HEI during this final period were formal and executional. The two parties continued to work on the children's cochlear implant, according to commitments made in late 1986. This effort eventually culminated in the FDA approval of the HEI children's device in September 1988.

3M-Hochmairs (6/87 to 9/89)

By December 1987, 3M had redirected most of its investments and efforts from cochlear implants to the development of hearing aids. Although 3M extended its relationship with the Hochmairs through 1989, it informed the Hochmairs to proceed alone in mid-1988. When 3M sold its cochlear implant technology to Nucleus, the Hochmairs became aligned with Nucleus given that Nucleus would service Vienna devices in Europe.

3M-FDA (5/88 to 1/89)

With FDA approval for various devices stalled and Nucleus gaining market leadership with its multiple-channel device, 3M was forced to evaluate its cochlear implant product development and regulatory review strategies. Concluding in January 1986 that its strategy of submitting numerous single-channel devices into the FDA review process was wrong, 3M decided to decrease its investments in gaining regulatory approval for its HEI and Hochmairs single-channel devices and focus instead on developing its own Sprint multiple-channel device. However, the FDA circumscribed 3M's strategic flexibility. Accompanying its approval of an IDE for the Sprint multiple-channel device in July 1986, the FDA directed 3M to maintain its field service and support activities for the 3M-House single-channel device.

In October 1986, the FDA issued another status report that stated the superiority of the multiple-channel technology over single-channel technology. By 1987, 3M realized that Nucleus held the favored position with the FDA and that approval of its own Sprint device would be judged in terms of the performance of the Nucleus device. The decisive blow to the 3M-FDA relationship was the May 1988 cochlear implant industry Consensus Conference, at which the participants declared the multiple-channel device the technology of choice. By this time, 3M had substantially redirected its resources to develop hearing aids and maintained a minimal effort to administer the FDA review process on its HEI children's device, for which conditional PMA approval was obtained in September 1988. In January 1989, 3M announced its plans to sell its cochlear implant technology and asked the FDA to withdraw its device from the review process. In response, the FDA informed 3M that it must continue to service and provide warranties for its implanted cochlear implant devices. This responsibility was assumed by Nucleus when it acquired 3M's cochlear implant technology and patents in August 1989.

Themes

The final period might be viewed as the calm after the storm or the cleanup after the battle. Terms of 3M's withdrawal from the cochlear implant market had been established by the end of the third period, and each company conformed to these agreements. Once again, interactions within each dyad were relatively independent from one another. By the end of this period, 3M's withdrawal was complete.

Discussion of IR Developmental Patterns

The foregoing description of the four periods suggests several important patterns about how 3M's CIP web of IRs developed.

1. *The 3M CIP interorganizational relationships developed through two cycles of divergent and convergent activity periods.* All the key terms of the relationships were designed and changed during the relatively brief divergent periods in each cycle. The two divergent periods, one and three, represented frame-breaking periods when new understandings were negotiated and established about the nature of each dyadic relationship among the parties. These periods ended when agreements clearly defined the nature of each relationship within some larger context. The event data indicate that all the defining agreements between IR parties occurred during these divergent periods. They set the stage for periods of convergent execution, periods two and four, in which agreements are carried out within the context of defined understandings.

2. *The divergent and convergent periods of activities in the first cycle were qualitatively different from those in the second cycle.* The first

two periods might be viewed as a cycle of IR dyad development, in which the elements of the web were established by 3M's entering into separate relationships with other organizations and then carrying out these initial commitments through a period of incremental and productive interaction. In the later two periods, however, issues of web dependence became salient as (a) actions in any one IR had significant implications for actions occurring in other IR dyads, and (b) these now-institutionalized relationships acted to constrain and direct responses to competitive demands.

The transition from the quasi-independent dyad cycle to the interdependent web cycle produced unexpected and paradoxical developments. The 3M-HEI relationship, which was a highly productive cooperative "marriage" in 1984 became a cantankerous competitive "failure" by 1986. The 3M-Hochmairs relationship was a better-than-expected cooperative relationship, developing a superior-performing single-channel device in 1985, which turned only a year later into a competitive rivalry to develop multiple-channel devices that could, but never did, match the performance of the Nucleus 22-channel device. After four years of exploring a cooperative relationship from 1977 to 1981, 3M and Nucleus became the dominant competitors in the emerging cochlear implant industry. The competitive race between 3M and Nucleus actually lasted only three years (1983–1986) and by 1989, it ended with a collaborative buyer-seller relationship as 3M sold the "spoils" to the victor and bowed out of cochlear implants. Competitors turned out to be the principal beneficiaries of the institutions that 3M paid the lion's share to create by educating the FDA in cochlear implants and negotiating industry standards for FDA review and approval of the world's first commercially available cochlear implant device. In short, the cooperators became competitors, the competitors became collaborators, and the regulators became the mediators. It turns out these shifts only appear unintended or paradoxical from the viewpoint of the parties engaged in each dyadic IR; from the broader perspective of an IR web, they can be explained and appear almost predictable.

3. *Understanding and explaining how any one relationship unfolded over time requires looking beyond that individual dyadic IR to the larger web of IRs in which the parties are involved.* Figure 5.3 shows that context events increased dramatically after 1984, which was the period of web dependence where actions within a given IR dyad spilled over to affect the development of other IRs. During this period, Bunderson et al. (1998) found a strong negative correlation ($r = -.57$) between these context events and outcome assessments. It turned out that most (69%) of these context events dealt with changes occurring in the other dyadic IRs of 3M's web.

To examine this finding further, Bunderson et al. (1998) conducted regression analysis to determine the relative influence of these context events and outcome assessments on the interactions (a composite measure of negotiation, commitment, and execution events) occurring in each dyadic relationship. They found during the first IR dyad development cycle that context events did not significantly predict interactions among the parties. Instead, outcome evaluations made by the dyadic parties were the most significant predictor of their interaction behavior. In contrast, during the second web dependence cycle, outcome evaluations were *not* significantly related to interactions in the relationships. Instead, context events were the most significant predictors of interactions among the dyadic parties.

Bunderson et al. (1998) concluded that these starkly contrasting results provide statistical support for the existence of two periods in these data: A period in which relationships develop based on the internal logic of the relationship (the dyad cycle) and a period in which the development of IRs is dependent on the larger web of relationships in which they are embedded (the web cycle).

4. *The initially independent dyadic IRs that the parties negotiated, made commitments to, and executed during the first cycle were spun into a spider's web of complex and interdependent network in the second cycle of the process.* The analogy of the spider's web is useful for describing these interdependencies because it consists of an interconnected set of links that revolve around some central point (the focal organization). Because all the links in a spider's web are structurally interconnected, the integrity of the web is a function of the sum of the individual links. Consequently, when one of the links is altered in some way, all of the other links in the web are affected, especially those that are most proximal to the altered link. When one link constricts, the others stretch or break. When one of the links breaks, the others constrict to preserve the integrity of the web.

Conclusion

This chapter took an inductive approach to describe and understand how a web of interorganizational relationships emerges, shifts, and evolves over time. We examined the sequence of events wherein 3M engaged in a web of cooperative, competitive, and regulatory relationships with other organizations from 1977 to 1989 to develop and commercialize cochlear implants. Our analysis suggested a number of conclusions about the development of interorganizational webs.

1. The MIRP study data do not support the argument for a rational, linear progression of bargaining, commitment, and execution events as might be expected given much of the literature on transactions cost economics (e.g., Williamson, 1991) and the sociology IRs (e.g., Oliver, 1990). Instead, the developmental pattern in each of 3M's relationships followed a multiple parallel progression of numerous bargaining, commitment, and execution events throughout the temporal duration of the IR.

2. The findings suggest a punctuated equilibrium process in the development of the IRs over time. This process consists of a repetitive cycle of relatively short divergent periods of rapid change, followed by a longer convergent period of incremental change and adaptation. Divergent periods in these cycles were marked by high activity and instability as parties to relationships negotiated, changed, and agreed to understandings about the nature of their relationship. These periods were followed by longer, more incremental, and stable periods of convergent behavior as the parties carried out their commitments and understandings. We further found that the first divergent and convergent cycle was a period of dyadic IR development in which the structure of the dyadic links in 3M's web were formed and established. The second divergent and convergent cycle was a period of web dependence in which changes in one dyadic IR spilled over to affect the nature of other dyadic relationships.

3. The development and institutionalization of interorganizational relationships reaches a point of "self-organizing criticality" wherein the relevant unit of analysis for the examination of IRs becomes the web and not the dyad. During periods of high web dependence, interactions between any two parties in the web were influenced more by activities occurring in other dyads than by the internal logic of the dyad itself. At this point, changes in any one microrelationship have macroconsequences because of interdependencies and ripple effects. Consequently, efforts to understand interorganizational dynamics that do not include web-level effects will be inadequate.

In conclusion we found that developmental processes in a web of IRs are far more complex, interdependent, and dynamic than the literature has led us to believe or assume. We concentrated on describing these developmental processes. The major tasks ahead are to develop and apply theories that explain the richness of the developmental process that this research has revealed. The application and development of alternative theories that explain the developmental processes observed here constitute an exciting and challenging research agenda.

6

Building an Infrastructure
for the Innovation Journey

Seldom can an individual entrepreneur alone command the competence, resources, and legitimacy to develop and commercialize an innovation. Entrepreneurship is a collective achievement that resides not only within the parent organization of the innovation but also in the construction of an industrial infrastructure that facilitates and constrains innovation. This infrastructure includes (1) institutional arrangements to legitimize, regulate, and standardize a new technology; (2) public-resource endowments of basic scientific knowledge, financing mechanisms, and a pool of competent labor; (3) development of markets, consumer education, and demand; and (4) proprietary research and development, manufacturing, production, and distribution functions by private entrepreneurial firms to commercialize the innovation for profit.

This chapter takes a macroperspective of the innovation journey and focuses on the issues and events involved in developing an industry infrastructure for innovation. In doing so, we make three contributions to managing the innovation journey:

1. We believe that understanding innovation is deficient if it focuses exclusively on the characteristics and behaviors of individual entrepreneurs and if it treats the social, economic, and political infrastructure for innovation as external factors that cannot be influenced. Popular folklore notwithstanding, the innovation journey is a collective achievement that requries key roles from numerous entrepreneurs in both the public and private sectors.

2. Chapter 6 examines how this infrastructure emerges to commercialize technology and product innovations. This infrastructure emerges through the accretion of numerous institutional, resource, and proprietary events that influence each other over an extended period. Moreover, the very institutional arrangements and resource endowments created to facilitate industry emergence can hinder subsequent technological development and adaptation by proprietary firms. This generative process has a dynamic history that is important to study if we are to understand how novel forms of technologies, organizations, and institutions emerge.

3. We emphasize that the innovation journey is not limited to the for-profit sector; numerous entrepreneurial actors in the public and not-for-profit sectors play crucial roles. By studying the roles and how they interact to develop and commercialize a new technology we can understand how the risk, time, and cost to an individual entrepreneur are significantly influenced by developments in the overall industry. This study also explains why the entrepreneurial firms that run in packs are more successful than those that develop their innovations alone.

The practical implications of this perspective emphasize that innovation managers must not only be concerned with microdevelopments of a proprietary technical device or product within their organization but also with the creation of a macroindustrial system that embodies the social, economic, and political infrastructure that any technological community needs to sustain its members. We adopt and extend the social-system framework introduced by Van de Ven and Garud (1989) to understand the components of an industrial infrastructure for innovation. Because new-to-the-world technologies typically transcend the boundaries of many individual firms, industries, and populations (Astley, 1985), the framework adopts the interorganizational field as the unit of analysis and focuses on the infrastructure necessary to develop and commercialize technological innovations. This infrastructure includes a variety of institutional arrangements, resource endowments, and proprietary functions that are necessary to develop and transform basic scientific knowledge into commercially viable products or services.

The first part of the chapter elaborates this social-system framework and links it to several current themes in the organizational and economic literature on technological development. The second part, based on study findings of the Minnesota Innovation Research Program (MIRP), develops a set of propositions that explain how this social system emerges to facilitate and constrain the development of innovations.

Social System for Innovation Development

The proposition that technological and institutional innovations reciprocally produce each other within the system under investigation is a relatively new development in economic and organization theory (Ruttan and Hayami, 1984). This proposition was central to Marx's (1867/1906) analysis of the dialectical relations between the forces of production (i.e., technology or the equipment and labor processes used in production) and the relations of production (i.e., institutions, especially property rights or ownership of production forces) within the superstructure of cultural and resource endowments of a society. However, perhaps because of ambiguities in Marx's own writings about how the forces and relations of production occur, organizational and economics scholars subsequently formed one-sided theories about technical and institutional change (Bottomore, 1983).

Those who advocated a "technological imperative" perspective treated technological innovation as something that happened to the firm but was not determined within it (Abernathy and Clark, 1985). Technological innovation was viewed as an environmental shock to which organizations or economic systems had to adapt if they were to survive (Ruttan, 1978; Freeman, 1986; Tornatzky and Fleischer, 1990). However, the potency of this "technological imperative" view weakened as the definition of technology expanded from a physical concrete device or artifact to include proprietary design knowledge embodied in the physical artifact (Layton, 1986). This knowledge is socially constructed (Pinch and Bijker, 1987), recognized, and protected as a property right through the institutions of patents or royalties (Nelson, 1982) and imprinted with the economic and cultural endowments of a society (Thirtle and Ruttan, 1986).

A second perspective maintained that institutional rather than technical change was the dynamic source of social and economic development. This "institutional determinism" perspective, as Ruttan (1978) labeled it, emphasized that changes in institutional arrangements precede and constrain technical change (North and Thomas, 1973; North, 1990). However, as Commons (1950) emphasized, institutional arrangements not only constrain action, they also liberate and expand the freedom of individuals to undertake a wide variety of actions, including due process provisions, to create and change the institutional arrangements. Institutional arrangements are defined as administrative rules, norms, laws, and conventions that society uses to legitimize, regulate, and coordinate the actions and expectations of individuals, which makes them predictable (Ruttan, 1978; Powell and DiMaggio, 1991).

Hurwicz (1993) importantly points out that institutional rules or laws are typically written by specifying (1) the roles (rights and duties) of various institutional actors and (2) their assignment to actors, be they individuals, firms, trade associations, or state agencies. Individuals and organizations become institutional actors by exercising the institutional roles they assume or are assigned. In this way, institutional arrangements have created roles for "artificial persons," such as firms, unions, trade associations, state agencies, and markets, that enable them to act as though they are individuals. Much of the work on institutionalism in organization theory (Powell and DiMaggio, 1991) and political science (March and Olsen, 1989) focuses on the processes by which these institutional arrangements and actors emerge and how this larger exogenous institutionalized environment enables and constrains entrepreneurs and organizations to develop only certain types of technologies and practices.

A third, and older, tradition emphasized that resource endowments of a society create a supply and demand for both technical and institutional innovations (Ruttan, 1978). As exemplified in Rosenberg and Birdzell's (1986) historical examination of "How the West Grew Rich," this perspective maintains that technical and institutional changes occur as a result of advances in the supply of resource endowments (i.e., knowledge about new social and economic possibilities and the financial capital and human competencies available to develop and apply these possibilities). The demand for technical and institutional change, in turn, is brought about by changes in expectations generated by knowledge of new possibilities, as well as the pressure of population growth against relative factor prices or scarcity of land, labor, and capital (Schultz, 1968; Ruttan, 1978).

Arguments over the relative priority of technical, institutional, and resource endowments are generally unproductive. All three endowments are highly interdependent and therefore must be analyzed within a context of continuing interaction. So, also, Ruttan (1978) argues that demand for and supply of technical and institutional change interact with shifts in resource endowments of new knowledge and relative scarcity of land, labor, and capital. Ruttan and Hayami (1984) proposed an induced theory of innovation that provides a more balanced treatment of the reciprocal relationships between technical and institutional innovations and resource endowments. Although developed independently of Marx, their theory echoes Marx's analysis of the reciprocal relationships among changes in technology, institutions, and resource endowments in an economic sector. Ruttan and Hayami argued that in the study of long-term social and economic change, the relationships among these variables must be treated as endogenous, not as givens within a general equilibrium model. "Failure to analyze historical change in a general equilibrium context tends to result in a unidimensional perspective on the relationships bearing on technical and institutional change" (Ruttan and Haymi, 1984: 216).

Ruttan's model emphasizes the role of history in understanding innovation development; that is, the temporal sequence of events and activities that create and transform basic scientific knowledge into commercially viable products or services delivered to customers. Numerous case histories demonstrate that new technologies are seldom developed by a single firm in the vacuum of an institutionalized environment (see, e.g., Usher, 1954; Jewkes, Sawers, and Stillerman, 1958; Constant, 1980; Nelson, 1982; and Chandler, 1990). Many complementary innovations in technical and organizational arrangements are usually required before a particular technology is suitable for commercial application (Binswanger and Ruttan, 1978; Hughes, 1983; Rosenberg, 1983). Research reviews by Mowery (1985), Thirtle and Ruttan (1986), Freeman (1986), and Dosi (1988) show that the commercial success or failure of a technological innovation is, in great measure, a reflection of the institutional arrangements and available resource endowments that an industrial community needs to sustain its members.

Figure 6.1 sketches a social-system framework that incorporates the various components of an industrial infrastructure for technological innovation. This framework, developed initially from MIRP studies of the development of the cochlear implant technology by Van de Ven and Garud (1989, 1993), was extended in subsequent studies of research and development (R&D) communities by Garud and Rappa (1994); of flat-panel display technologies by Murtha, Spencer, and Lenway (1996) and of the health care provider industry by Van de Ven and Lofstrom (1997).

The framework adopts an augmented view of an industry and focuses on relationships among key components of an industrial infrastructure. The framework examines not only an industry, commonly defined as the set of firms producing similar or substitute products (Porter, 1980), but also many other public- and private-sector actors who perform critical functions to develop and commercialize a new technology. The industrial infrastructure includes (1) institutional arrangements to legitimize, regulate, and standardize a new technology; (2) public-resource endowments of basic scientific knowledge, financing mechanisms, and a pool of competent labor; (3) market mechanisms to educate consumers and stimulate demand for a new technology; and (4) proprietary research and development, manufacturing, marketing, and distribution functions by private entrepreneurial firms to commercialize the innovation for profit.

The relevance of each of these system components to the emergence of innovations follows.

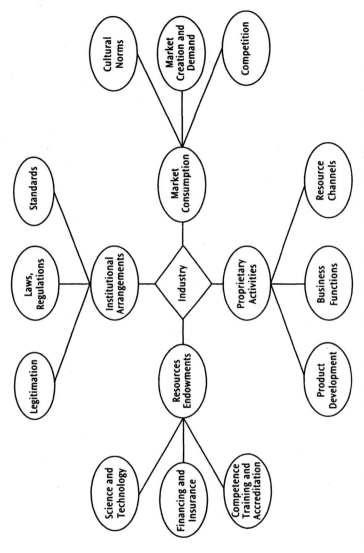

Figure 6.1 An augmented view of an industry. From Van de Ven and Lofstrom (1997)

Proprietary Functions

The proprietary component of the system incorporates the traditional industrial economics definition of an industry (Porter, 1980), which consists of the set of firms commercializing innovations that are close substitutes for each other. Our focus is on the actions of individual entrepreneurs and firms that typically appropriate basic knowledge from the public domain and transform it into proprietary knowledge through applied research and development in areas related to a technological innovation. If they persist in developing the innovation, they subsequently develop a line of products and gain access to the complementary assets (e.g., manufacturing, marketing, and distribution) necessary to establish an economically viable business.

Williamson (1975) and Teece's (1987) transactions costs theory is useful to understand how firms organize to perform these proprietary functions. They emphasize that the boundaries of the firm are an important strategic variable for innovation (Teece, 1987). They propose that if proprietary functions and complementary assets necessary for technological development are difficult to protect from imitators (weak appropriability regimes), require specialized investments, or might be difficult to execute, they should be integrated and performed within the innovating firm. If the functions have strong appropriability regimes, entail nonspecialized investments, and have a number of supply sources, they should be licensed or contracted by firms with outside suppliers and vendors.

From a system perspective, these make-or-buy decisions by individual firms produce the aggregate industry channels of raw materials, manufacturing, marketing, and distribution flows (Stern and El-Ansery, 1982; Hakansson, 1988). Shifts in individual firms' make-or-buy decisions over time also determine changes in industry structure. Stigler (1957) examined this issue in terms of the relationship between product life cycle and vertical integration. He argued that early in the product life cycle, vertical integration of functions within firms (i.e., make decisions) predominate because the market has not yet developed. As Smith (1776/1937) indicated, the division of labor among firms is limited by the extent of the market. When the market expands, many of the tasks and functions grow to sufficient size to make it more profitable to buy them from specialized manufacturers or suppliers, as opposed to making them within vertically integrated firms.

Resource Endowments

Three kinds of resources are critical to developing most technological innovations: (1) basic scientific or technological research, (2) financing mechanisms, and (3) a pool of competent human resources (Mowery and Rosenberg, 1979). Although private entrepreneurs or firms do engage in developing these resources, typically, public organizations, often viewed as external to an industry, play a major role in creating and providing these "common goods."

1. *Basic scientific or technological research* provides the foundation of knowledge that underlies technological innovations and makes the commercial births of most industries possible. This basic knowledge is costly to produce relative to its cost of diffusion and imitation (Mansfield, 1985). In addition, it builds in a cumulative fashion, and its generation is inherently an indivisible activity (Metcalfe and Soete, 1983; Garud and Rappa, 1995). For these reasons, Nelson (1982) and Arrow (1962) argued that the social returns to research investment exceed the private returns to entrepreneurs, a condition leading to underinvestment in research. As a consequence, a variety of studies have shown that firms rely on outside sources of knowledge and technical inventions for the majority of their commercially significant new products (Rosenbloom, 1966; Mueller, 1962; Utterback, 1974; Freeman, 1986; Nelson, 1982; Stobaugh, 1985).

However, the private appropriation of basic scientific knowledge is seldom a simple process of information transfer and diffusion because much of that knowledge may be "sticky," or difficult to disembody from its original source and transfer to an applied problem-solving site (von Hippel, 1990). As a consequence, proprietary firms must often engage in a variety of strategies to acquire this knowledge from basic research sites, ranging from simple communications (Allen, 1977) and personnel transfers (Roberts and Hauptman, 1986) to various licensing arrangements and joint R&D ventures between private firms and basic research centers (Ouchi and Bolton, 1987; Powell, 1990). These strategies appear consistent with von Hippel's (1990) overall proposition that the location of problem-solving activities shifts over time to the sites or locations of that "sticky" data.

2. *Financing mechanisms.* Whereas public institutions (e.g., the National Science Foundation or the National Institutes of Health) tend to play the major role in financing the development of basic scientific or technological knowledge, venture capital, in a corporation, or in the market, tends to be the key financial source that supports private firms in transforming basic knowledge into proprietary and commercial applications. In addition, the commercialization of many technological innovations requires unique industrywide financing arrangements. For example, few biomedical innovations would be commercially viable without the health care insurance industry and the creation of third-party payment reimbursement systems. Without such a financial infrastructure for a broad array of biomedical and health care innova-

tions, most patients would not be able to pay for many biomedical devices and treatments. But because these insurance systems limit coverage to specifically designated medical devices and treatments, the firms competing to commercialize a specific biomedical device must cooperate to educate and influence third-party payers to include the innovation in their payment reimbursement systems.

3. *A pool of competent human resources* is another essential resource necessary for the emergence of a new industry. New technologies often require new ways to perform essential tasks related to research, manufacturing, or marketing. This pool of competence tends to develop in three ways. First, basic research institutes and proprietary firms recruit and train people in specific skills related to the innovation. Over time, job transfers and mobile professionals among institutes and firms diffuse their skills throughout the industry (Rappa, 1989). Second, educational training programs and accredited degrees at colleges and universities help develop this labor market. In addition, industry conferences, technical committees, trade publications, and technical journals provide opportunities for industry participants to share and learn from each other (Nelson, 1982). Finally, the competence pool is created through "collective invention" (Allen, 1983) among "invisible colleges," or networks of practitioners (often scientists and engineers throughout the world), that support further development or problem-solving activities within a new technological paradigm (Hull, 1988; Dosi, 1988; Rappa, 1989; Garud, 1990). For example, von Hippel (1986) observed extensive trading of proprietary know-how among informal networks of process engineers in rival, and nonrival, firms in the U.S. steel minimill industry and elsewhere.

Institutional Arrangements

The ultimate authorities governing and legitimizing collective action are the rules and norms of the society in which organizations function (Galaskiewicz, 1985; Scott, 1987). The political context is the place to institutionalize and legitimize a social system, which permits firms to operate and gain access to the resources they need (Meyer and Rowan, 1977; Pfeffer and Salancik, 1978). The success or failure of a new industry and firms within it depends on their abilities to achieve institutional isomorphism (Dimaggio and Powell, 1983). To achieve this isomorphism, firms may either adapt to institutional requirements or try to build their goals and procedures directly into society as institutional rules (Meyer and Rowan, 1977; Garud and Ahlstrom, 1997a). Thus, firms compete not only in the marketplace but also in this political institutional context. Rival firms often cooperate by collectively manipulating their institutional environment to legitimize and gain access to resources necessary for collective survival (Pfeffer and Salancik, 1978; Hirsch 1975; Meyer and Rowan, 1977).

Governance

It is widely recognized that a variety of governmental regulations and institutional arrangements facilitate and inhibit the emergence of new technologies and industries. Mowery (1985) and Nelson (1982), for example, discuss how government funding, by broadening the industry-wide knowledge base, can encourage new industry entrance and support a more competitive environment. Thus, also, a more permissive antitrust policy permitting certain kinds of joint research ventures among competitors and requirements by the Department of Defense for licensing and second-sourcing new devices speeds the diffusion of innovation and may aid the operation of competitive forces in an industry (Teece, 1987). However as Ouchi and Bolton (1987) discuss, institutional policies encouraging rapid knowledge diffusion, if pursued too eagerly, may undermine the return to the knowledge producer and thus the incentive to invest in information-producing activities. But another institutional mechanism has been devised: The patent system grants monopoly rights to use knowledge for a limited period. Although these institutional arrangements are often highly imperfect, research shows they exert a profound effect on technological and industry development (Nelson, 1982).

Legitimation

Legitimation is critical for the emergence of a new-to-the-world industry. Garud and Rappa (1994) report how the cochlear implant field lacked the necessary legitimacy to attract a critical mass of researchers to commit themselves to developing this device. It was only after an NIH-sponsored effort reporting the potential of cochlear implants that the field gained some legitimacy. Indeed, Garud and Rappa (1995) demonstrated how NIH's report triggered a series of scientific reports that resulted in attracting many researchers to the cochlear implant field.

Trust, or customer certainty about product quality, is fundamental to the efficient operation of the market institution (Aldrich and Fiol, 1994). Under conditions of high-quality uncertainty, inferior products often drive high-quality products out of the market because of the bad reputation they create for other industry products. Consequently, customers require greater assurances to buy a product in the event it is found after the purchase to be a "lemon" (Akerlof, 1970). The potential for product liability suits and other litigation can significantly dampen the commercialization of an innovation. Creating trust represents a particularly significant entry barrier for product innovations that are costly and technologically sophisticated, and whose purchase entails irreversible health or welfare situations for customers. Numerous mechanisms are often established to counteract this quality-uncertainty entry barrier, including guarantees, licensing practices, industry regulations, and endorsements by other trusted institutions.

The costs to create and maintain these industrywide institutional mechanisms are borne by industry members collectively and by individual firms. The mechanisms are both products of and constraints on the legitimacy of individual entrepreneurs or firms to engage in the commercial introduction of a technological innovation. One of the ways in which these firms collectively create and maintain these institutional legitimizing devices is through industry councils, technical committees, and trade associations (Maitland, 1982). These industry associations, in turn, approach, educate, and negotiate with other institutions and governmental units to obtain endorsements and develop regulatory procedures.

Technology Standards

One of the concrete manifestations of industry legitimization is setting technical standards pertaining to component specifications, processes, and performance criteria that new technology designs are expected to achieve (Garud and Rappa, 1994). Such technical standards are powerful institutional mechanisms for selecting dominant designs from among competing technological possibilities and reducing many uncertainties of technological development by channeling the directions of resource investments and technological change. Besen and Saloner (1989), Tushman and Rosenkopf (1990), and Garud and Rappa (1994) describe various ways in which standards develop. In some cases, standards are mandated by governmental regulatory agencies. In others, voluntary standards are established cooperatively, with information exchanged, technologies altered, or side payments made to achieve a consensus among firms in an industry. Finally, setting standards may be left to the market, or de facto standards may be imposed by a dominant producer.

Whatever means are used, the typical process for setting standards is influenced as much by social and political dynamics as it is by technical considerations (David, 1987; Garud and Kumaraswamy, 1994; Garud and Rappa, 1994; Tushman and Rosenkopf, 1990). These sociopolitical dynamics are influenced by the relative benefits to public and private parties for promoting a standard and the extent to which interested parties (producers, consumers, regulators) have different views about the standards chosen (Besen and Saloner, 1989; Garud and Ahlstrom, 1997b), as well as the evaluation complexity of a new technology (Tushman and Rosenkopf, 1990). Inherent in this standard-setting process is the paradox of cooperation and competition (Garud,

1994). Cooperating to set up industry standards clearly benefits all firms, but each firm may try to ensure the standards that suit it best are institutionalized. As Besen and Saloner (1989: 219) state, "standards may be used as tools of competitive strategy as firms promote a standard to gain advantage over rivals." An understanding of this paradox can offer valuable insights about how firms learn to cooperate to sustain themselves collectively while competing to carve out their distinctive positions in an emerging industry.

Markets

The process of translating ideas into commercial products is fraught with difficulties, among them the newness of the products. Debates about the primacy of market pull over technology push notwithstanding, many new-to-the-world innovations have no immediate definable need. New markets have to be created to commercialize many innovations. Potential customers find it difficult, if not impossible, to compare new products because alternatives embody different merits (Garud and Rappa, 1994; Van de Ven and Garud, 1993; Tushman and Rosenkopf, 1990).

To help customers discriminate, institutional environments for evaluation routines and standards become important. Entrepreneurs clearly try to shape emerging institutional environments but at the same time are shaped by them (Garud and Rappa, 1994; Van de Ven and Garud, 1993). On most occasions, entrepreneurs are only partly successful in shaping these institutional environments to their benefit; more often they adapt their own strategies to connect with customers.

This sociopolitical process is complicated by "interpretive flexibility" (Bijker, Hughes, and Pinch, 1987), which alludes to multiple possible interpretations and uses for products that may be different from those originally intended. To benefit from such interpretive flexibility, firms need to harness learning-by-using processes (Garud, 1997). Failure to do so may result in a disastrous mismatch between what a company creates and what customers value.

Firms use publicity and promotion to create needs and shape customer preferences. Often, in their zeal, firms announce their products to set expectations internally and externally. As Garud and Lampel (1997) observed, such announcements backfire when firms are unable to meet expectations they set.

These discussions point out some of the issues salient in thinking about the social-system framework. It is important to remember that, all too often, entrepreneurs, in their zeal, forget that what they create may not be immediately understandable or acceptable to users. Under these conditions, "acts of critical revision," as Usher (1954) suggested, may be as important as "acts of insight."

Table 6.1. A social system framework for understanding innovation development and industry emergence

Components of community infrastructure for innovation	
Proprietary Functions	Technological development functions: R&D, testing, manufacturing, marketing Innovation network/resource channel activities
Resource Endowments	Scientific/technological research Financing and insurance arrangements Human competence pool (training and accreditation)
Institutional Arrangements	Legitimization (creation of trust) Governance (norms, rules, regulations, laws) Technology standards
Market Functions	Vendor-supplier-distributor channels Consumer information and education Market creation and consumer demand

Source: Adapted from A. Van de Ven and R. Garud, "A Framework for Understanding the Emergence of New Industries," in R. Rosenbloom and R. Burgelman (eds.), "Research on Technological Innovation, Management and Policy," Vol. 4, Greenwich, Conn.: JAI Press, 1989, pp. 195–225.

Propositions on the Development of the Infrastructure

The social-system framework illustrated in figure 6.1 and outlined in table 6.1 maps a conceptual territory of the essential components of an innovation infrastructure at the interorganizational-community level. Perhaps more than anything else it helps us understand the key elements of an industrial community. While the framework demands a more encompassing perspective of innovation than has often been used, it integrates an eclectic body of literature that has argued that each of the system components is necessary to foster the development and commercialization of technological innovations. Thus, although many of these components have been studied in varying degrees by people in different disciplines, they have been treated as "externalities" (Porter, 1980) to the system under investigation. If we view them as externalities, we are not likely to examine how the functions are interdependent in time and space. Incorporating these different components within an overall systems framework motivates a more systematic study agenda aimed at understanding how various actors and functions interact over time to create an infrastructure that both facilitates and constrains technological innovation.

For innovation managers, this agenda could be motivated with the following overall proposition: *The odds of success in developing a technological innovation are primarily influenced by the extent to which other components of the infrastructure are established at the industrial-community level.*

Embedded in this overall proposition are a number of macro- and microissues that are central to the framework. From a macropolicy viewpoint, to understand the process of innovation is to know (1) how and when different components in the system emerge and are organized over time, (2) what actors create and perform these components, and (3) what consequences various arrangements of this community infrastructure have on the time and cost that it takes to develop and commercialize various innovations.

Although we propose that this infrastructure is crucial to an individual firm's success at innovation, a single entrepreneurial firm seldom performs all the functions required to create this system. Thus, from the viewpoint of an individual entrepreneurial firm, three key decisions are necessary: (1) What functions will the entrepreneurial firm perform? (2) What other organizations should the firm link to or contract with to perform other functions? (3) Consequently, what organizations will the firm compete with on certain functions and cooperate with on others? As these questions suggest, one way to understand the implications of the systems framework is to examine the process of innovation at two levels of analysis: (1) the system level looking at the community infrastructure as a whole and the interrelations among its components or functions, and (2) the behavior of individual entrepreneurs and firms within the industrial system.

Emergence of the Community System

The industry infrastructure for an innovation system does not emerge and change all at once by the actions of one or even a few key individuals. Instead, a detailed historical study of the development of the cochlear implant technology indicates that the process involved an accretion of 1,009 institutional, resource, market, and proprietary events involving many actors who transcended boundaries of many public- and private-sector organizations. Van de Ven and Garud (1993) provide a graphic breakdown, shown in figure 6.2, by plotting the cumulative number of events observed in the development of specific functions of an industrial system for cochlear implants from 1956 to 1989. They report four qualitatively different periods in the historical development of cochlear implants, as noted on the bottom of figure 6.2:

The first "endowments creation" period began in about 1955 and consisted primarily of advances in basic scientific knowledge of cochlear implants by universities and basic research institutes,

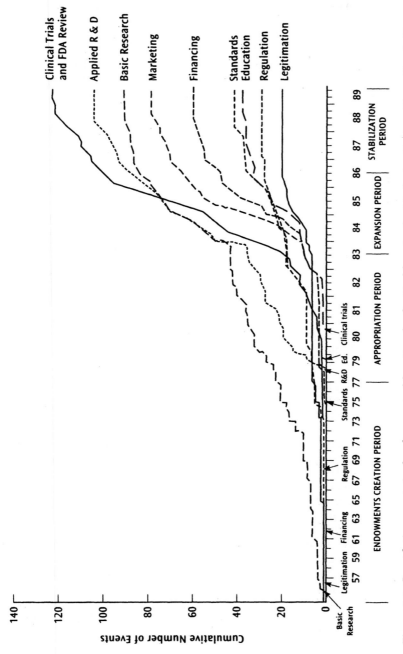

Figure 6.2 Cumulative events in development of function for the Cochlear Implant Industry System. From Van de Ven and Garund (1993)

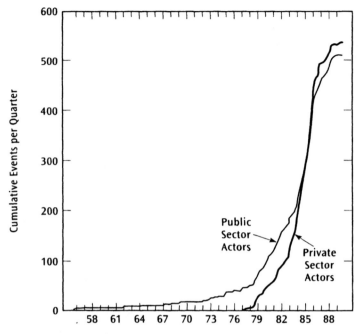

Figure 6.3 Cumulative events involving public- and private-sector actors. From Van de Ven and Garund (1993)

supported by a few events to legitimize and finance this research in the public domain. The second period focused on efforts by private firms beginning in 1977 to appropriate this basic research knowledge for launching proprietary commercial activities by entering into relationships with basic research institutes, and by initiating applied research and development, manufacturing, clinical trials, and marketing functions. When these relationships were established, a third "expansion" period is shown in which a rapid growth occurred from 1983 to 1986 in the number of events to develop each component of the emergent industry system. This expansion period was followed by a period of "stabilization" in all system functions, during which a dominant design for cochlear implants emerged. The very institutional structures that were created in prior periods for industry growth began to constrain subsequent development. (19)

Van de Ven and Garud (1993) also plot the actors involved in these events to develop these system components over time. Figure 6.3 shows that the public sector played the major role during the initial periods of industry emergence beginning in 1955 and that private-sector actors did not become involved in cochlear implant development until twenty-two years later in 1977. However, when private firms became

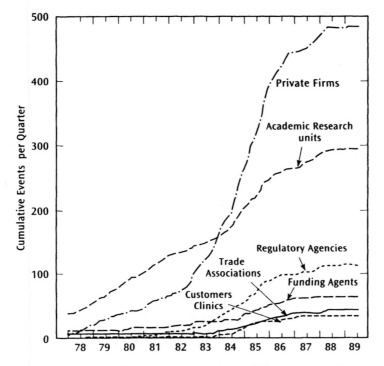

Figure 6.4 Cumulative events involving different types of actors.
From Van de Ven and Garund (1993)

involved, the number of events performed by both private- and public-
sector actors increased dramatically.

A breakout of the public-sector actors in figure 6.4 shows that among
the public-sector actors, academic-research units played the dominant
role, followed by regulatory agencies, particularly the U.S. Food and
Drug Administration, funding agencies, principally the National Institutes of Health, and professional or industry associations. For comparative purposes, figure 6.4 provides a breakdown of the involvement of
private-sector actors, as well as cochlear implant customers, patients,
and otological clinics.

In a parallel set of studies, Garud and Rappa (1994, 1995) and Garud
and Ahlstrom (1997) explored the roles of researchers in shaping the
institutional and technical facets of cochlear implants. As they report,
it is not appropriate to view even researchers as a unitary set of actors
but, rather, as a set of actors performing different roles depending on
their affiliations and motivations. For instance, some researchers create, others regulate, and still others deploy the technology being created. An intense debate among these constituents shapes the rate and
direction of advances in the technology.

These studies are consistent with many other detailed historical studies of technological development. Usher (1954) insisted that the history of mechanical inventions in the nineteenth century is not the history of single inventors or random chance events. Gilfillan (1935) observed a perpetual accretion of little details—having no clear beginnings, completions or definable limits—in the gradual evolution of shipbuilding. Constant (1980) found that advances in aircraft propulsion emerged not from flashes of disembodied inspiration but from many incremental changes and recombinations of existing technology and organizational arrangements, which add up to what might be called a technological revolution.

Moreover, there is a systemic nature to technological advances, as demonstrated in studies by Hughes (1983) of electrical power, Ruttan and Hayami (1984) of agricultural innovations, and Kuhn (1982) and Hull (1988) of science in general. In their study of cochlear implants, Van de Ven and Garud (1993) provide clear statistical evidence that the institutional arrangements, resource endowments, and proprietary events were reciprocally related and coproduced each other over time. Developments in other complementary technologies, institutions, and resource endowments often explain bottlenecks and breakthroughs in the development of a given technology. Thus, as Rosenberg (1983) says, "What is really involved is a process of cumulative accretion of useful knowledge, to which many people make essential contributions, even though the prizes and recognition are usually accorded to the one actor who happens to have been on the stage at a critical moment" (49).

Discontinuities are inherent to the numerous events in developing the institutional arrangements, resource endowments, and proprietary functions, particularly because they require the involvement of many actors from public and private organizations over an extended period. Individual events are often not made known to other actors, and various "acts of insights" pertaining to technical, resource, and institutional capabilities are often required to overcome bottlenecks. These acts or events accumulate probabilistically; they do not proceed deterministically under the stress of necessity or progress (Rosenberg, 1983). They are possible for only a limited number of individuals and organizations which, by virtue of their different roles, competencies, and available resources, become exposed to conditions that bring both awareness of problems and elements of solutions within their frame of reference. Thus, Usher (1954) said "emergent novelty becomes truly significant only through accumulation" (67) of many interrelated events of technical and institutional change.

These historical studies suggest that an explanation of how innovations develop should focus on the numerous microscopic events by which components of the infrastructure emerge over time. This system emerges as a partially cumulative progression of numerous events involving many actors in the public and private sectors who invest resources and perform different roles to develop an innovation.

Specifically, our proposition on the process of innovation emergence follows: *Technological innovations emerge through accretions of many interrelated institutional, resource, and proprietary events involving many actors in the public and private sectors over an extended period of time.*

To determine the relative contributions of various actors in developing each function of the cochlear implant infrastructure, Van de Ven and Garud (1993) report the results (table 6.2) of multiple regressions for each system function, the dependent variables in the rows, on the involvements of six kinds of actors, the independent variables in the columns. The table shows that statistically significant contributions were made by at least two or more different types of actors in the development of each system function of the cochlear implant infrastructure. These results lend clear support for the proposition that numerous public and private actors played key roles in the development of each component of the infrastructure for cochlear implants.

The process by which actors become engaged in the development of an industrial infrastructure can begin any number of ways. It varies with the technology being developed. For example, it can begin with purposeful intentions and inventive ideas of entrepreneurs, who undertake a stream of activities to gain the resources, competence, and endorsements necessary to develop an economically viable enterprise. As they undertake these activities, the paths of independent entrepreneurs, acting out their own diverse intentions and ideas, intersect. These intersections provide occasions for interaction and recognizing areas for establishing cooperative and competitive relationships (Garud, 1994).

Cooperative relationships emerge among the actors who can achieve complementary benefits by integrating their functional specializations. Competitive relationships emerge as alternative technological paths become evident and different entrepreneurs or firms "place their bets on" and pursue alternative paths. We must emphasize that, during this initial period, applied research and development is highly uncertain and often dependent on basic science and technology. Depending on the technological alternative chosen by an entrepreneurial individual or firm, it becomes highly dependent on different clusters of basic research institutions, such as universities, laboratories, and disciplines, that have been producing and directing the accumulation of basic knowledge, techniques, and experience associated with a given technological alternative.

By engaging in cooperative and competitive relationships and by interacting in the same networks, groups of entrepreneurs in the public

Table 6.2. Results of time series regression analysis of the contributions of various actors in developing cochlear implant industry functions

		Independent variables						
Dependent variable	Constant	Professional associations	Regulator agencies	Funding agencies	Academic research	Customer's clinics	Private firms	Adjusted R^2
Institutional functions								
Legitimation	.00	.12	-.11**	-.03	.03	.23**	.03	.48
Regulation/governance	.03	.00	.13**	.05	.04	-.12*	.00	.34
Industry standards	-.01	.35**	.08*	.05*	.04	-.16	.07**	.61
Resource endowments								
Basic research	.07	.30	.01	.09	.21**	.37**	-.03	.61
Financing	-.02	.18*	.12	.81**	-.03	.05	.02	.81
Education and training	-.02	.02	-.10	.27**	.04	.36**	.05*	.58
Proprietary functions								
Applied R&D	.16**	.27	-.24	.22	.22**	-.01	.13*	.49
Clinical tests and reviews	.08	.16	.83**	.24**	-.10**	.03	.05*	.92
Manufacturing	-.01	-.20**	-.04	.05	.01	.09	.36**	.37
Marketing	-.02	.13	-.02	.00	-.01	.11**	.84**	.82

Note: regression coefficients are unstandardized betas.

* = Beta coefficient is at least 1 1/2 its standard error.

** = Beta coefficient is at least 2 its standard error.

and private sectors increasingly isolate themselves from traditional industries by virtue of their interdependencies and growing commitments to and unique knowledge of a new technology. Isolation frees an emerging system from institutional constraints of existing technologies and industries (Astley, 1985) and permits it to develop its own distinctive structural form (Rappa, 1987). Coordination among actors takes place not so much by a central plan, organizational hierarchy, or price mechanism but mostly through interactions (Mattsson, 1987) and partisan mutual adjustments among actors (Astley and Van de Ven, 1983).

As the number of organizational units and actors gains a critical mass, a complex network of cooperative and competitive relationships begins to accumulate. This network itself becomes recognized as a new "industrial sector" and takes the form of a hierarchical, loosely coupled system.[1] We view this emerging system as consisting of the key entrepreneurs and firms that govern, integrate, and perform all the functions required to transform a technological innovation into a commercially viable line of products or services delivered to customers. The structure of this system, when fully developed, consists of the institutional and market arrangements, resource endowments, and proprietary functions illustrated in table 6.1.

Interactions among System Components

It is generally recognized that resource endowments often precede the development of market and institutional system functions because basic research, the search for a fundamental understanding of natural phenomena, provides the foundation of knowledge that makes possible the commercial birth of a technology (Abernathy, 1978; Rosenberg, 1983; Garud and Van de Ven, 1987). What is less well understood is the

1. Of course, hierarchy in an industry system is a matter of degree, and some industry systems may be only minimally, if at all, hierarchical. Hierarchy is often a consequence of institutional constraints imposed by political and governmental regulatory bodies. Hierarchy also emerges in relationships with key linking-pin organizations which either become dominant industry leaders or control access to critical resources (money, competence, technology) needed by other firms in the industry.

Loose coupling promotes both flexibility and stability to the structure of an industry. Links between subsystems are only as rich or tight as is necessary to ensure the survival of the system (Aldrich and Whetten, 1981). Based on Simon's (1962) architecture of complexity, Aldrich and Whetten discuss how a loosely joined system provides short-run independence of subsystems and long-run dependence only in an aggregate way. The overall social system can be fairly stable, due to the absence of strong ties or links between elements and subsystems, but individual subsystems can be free to adapt quickly to local environmental conditions. Thus, in a complex, heterogeneous, and changing environment, a loosely joined system is highly adaptive.

process by which a common pool of basic scientific or technological knowledge is appropriated and transformed by private firms into proprietary innovations that can become commercial monopolies.

Success at creating a monopoly by commercializing a new technology does not rest on a unique command of basic research or on the control of all the competencies and resources relevant to innovation. Instead, as Stobaugh (1985) and Mowery (1985) discuss, it rests on orchestrating a highly uncertain journey by linking with numerous organizations and actors and appropriating the competencies and resources relevant to developing and commercializing the innovation. This journey consists of an interactive search process involving parallel developments in building: basic research, financing mechanism, competence capabilities (the resource endowments), institutional arrangements, market demand, and proprietary commercial activities.

Different search and linking patterns should be expected for innovations in different industrial sectors. As Nelson and Winter (1977) discuss, in many sectors many R&D organizations—some profit-oriented, some governmental, some academic—do different things but interact in synergistic ways. In particular, in medicine, agriculture, and several other sectors, private for-profit organizations do the bulk of R&D that leads to marketing products, but academic institutions play a major role in creating basic knowledge and data used in the more applied work.

Most people understand that R&D is an uncertain business. Uncertainty resides at the level of an entrepreneurial firm, where the "best" way to proceed is seldom apparent and the individuals involved have to be satisfied with finding a potentially promising technological path. Less often understood is that the source of much of this uncertainty confronting individual entrepreneurs and investors resides at the system or community level. As the system framework highlights, if institutional arrangements and resource endowments have not yet emerged for an innovation, proprietary entrepreneurs are exposed to high uncertainties and risks in not knowing what kinds of institutional regulations, technical standards, financing arrangements, and specialized competencies will emerge for the innovation. Uncertainties are reduced as these institutional arrangements and resource endowments become established and embodied in a dominant technological design for the innovation.

This leads to our third proposition about interactions between proprietary, resource, and institutional components of the system framework: *The time, cost, and risk incurred by proprietary firms in developing an innovation are inversely related to the developmental progress of building institutional arrangements and resource endowments for the new technology.*

A concrete example of this proposition emerged from one MIRP study of the development of gallium arsenide integrated circuits in the

United States, Japan, and Western Europe from 1983 to 1987 (Rappa, 1989). Although far more firms and scientists were engaged in the development of this technology in the United States than in Japan, by 1985, Japan was judged to be several years ahead of the United States in commercial developments and applications of the technology. One possible reason for the more rapid advancement of the technology with fewer scientists and engineers is that in Japan, a system infrastructure was already well established through MITI (Japan's Ministry of Trade and Industry), which encouraged firms that were competing on proprietary technical developments to cooperate with one another and many other actors in various industry and trade committees. The Japanese were meeting to develop commercial applications for the technology, to influence industrial governance policies, and to create a competence pool through training programs and informal information sharing. In the United States, no comparable industry infrastructure was in place in 1985. Instead, it appeared that many U.S. firms, while investing heavily in their own proprietary R&D projects, were "sitting on the fence" waiting for others to build the industry infrastructure for collective advancement.

Of course, the degree of system change varies with the novelty of the innovation being developed and commercialized. Some innovations change the entire order of things, making obsolete the old ways and spawning a cycle of creative destruction (Schumpeter, 1942). Most innovations simply build on what is already there, requiring modifications in existing system functions and practices. We expect that innovations of different levels of novelty will require different degrees of change in system functions. For new technologies within established industries, some of the functions, such as governance institutions, may be established and may change in only subtle, nearly invisible ways. That, however, does not deny their importance, but it does explain why radical new-to-the-world innovations are far more difficult to develop and commercialize than incremental innovations within established industries.

Specifically, we propose the following: *More novel innovations require greater change in all system functions and, therefore, greater development time and greater chance of failure.*

Radical or revolutionary innovations not only represent new-to-the-world technologies but also represent vast departures from existing industrial systems. Although development and commercialization of certain radical innovations may require starting from scratch to construct an industry de novo, more often genuinely new industries emerge by relying on metaphors and adapting institutional arrangements that are carried over from other industries. But, as a study by Leblebici, Salancik, Copay, and King (1991) of the institutional evolution of radio broadcasting indicated, the use of more metaphors and arrangements that are borrowed from other industries makes building an integrated infrastructure for institutional scaffolding in the new industry more difficult because the components of an industrial system do not emerge independent of each other; they are highly interdependent. Many convergent and divergent events become bottlenecks that delay the overall development of the system.

For example, in the development and commercialization of cochlear implants, Garud and Van de Ven (1989) identified numerous temporal interdependencies in the creation of different system functions:

> Basic scientific knowledge first had to ensure safety and efficacy of the technology for use in humans before business firms would become involved. The presence of firms wanting to commercialize cochlear implants was necessary as a thrust for the creation of the FDA panel for cochlear devices. The FDA's approval of cochlear devices was necessary for Medicare to extend its coverage for cochlear implants, which in turn is necessary for accessing a wider patient base. (516)

The rate of success for entrepreneurial firms is significantly influenced by the length of time it takes for the system to become established. For an individual entrepreneur, start-up funding for a venture represents an initial stock of assets that provides the entrepreneurial unit a "honeymoon" period to develop and commercialize its innovation (Fichman and Levinthal, 1988; Venkataraman and Van de Ven, 1998). These assets reduce the risk of terminating the innovation during its honeymoon period when setbacks arise and initial outcomes are judged unfavorable. The likelihood of replenishing these assets is highly influenced by the duration of the change process: Interest and commitment wane with time. Thus, after the honeymoon period, proprietary efforts at innovation terminate at disproportionately higher rates, in proportion to the time needed to develop institutional arrangements and resource endowments for the innovation.

Innovation uncertainty decreases over time as system functions that define key technical and institutional parameters for the innovation emerge. In addition, transitions from development to commercialization activities often entail shifts from radical to incremental and from divergent to convergent progressions as system functions develop. Analogous patterns of innovation processes within organizations, which become more highly structured and stabilized in their patterns and less differentiated from other organizational arrangements when innovations are implemented, have been observed (Tornatzky and Fleischer, 1990; Zaltman et al., 1973). Thus, at different periods of technological development, we should expect that different functional arrangements are needed to foster innovation and that different components of the system become the limiting factors that serve as "bottlenecks" to sustained innovation development.

This developmental pattern often culminates in the selection of a dominant design for the technology from among competing alternatives. As Van de Ven and Garud (1993) observed in cochlear implants, this selection process is produced primarily by a convergence in developments of institutional, resource endowments, market, and proprietary system functions that emerged to embody preferences for the dominant design. As this dominant design emerges, there is a leveling off in further developments of system functions. When primarily established, the system infrastructure systematically channels and constrains further technological advances in the direction of the dominant design.

This leads to our proposition on the temporal dynamics of system development: *The very institutional mechanisms and resource endowments that initially develop to facilitate proprietary innovation development become inertial forces that constrain subsequent development in the direction of a chosen dominant design.*

An examination of these propositions on the interactions among system components as they develop over time should lead one to examine whether and how learning occurs between functional events, which could provide guidance as to the next paths taken by actors to develop other parts of the system. By examining the outcomes of alternative paths, one could also identify the feasible sets of paths available in the emergence of an industry. Great interindustry differences should be expected (Mowery, 1985), but only by cumulative longitudinal studies of these developmental progressions between system functions will we come to appreciate how system infrastructures emerge for innovation and entrepreneurship (Dosi, 1982).

Roles of Individual Entrepreneurial Firms

The social-system framework emphasizes that any given entrepreneurial firm is but one actor, able to perform only a limited set of roles, and dependent on many other actors to accomplish all the functions for an industry to emerge and survive. As a consequence, an individual firm must make strategic choices concerning the kinds of proprietary resource endowments and institutional functions in which it will engage and what other actors it will engage to achieve self-interest and collective objectives. These strategic choices make clear that the ways entrepreneurial firms choose to allocate their innovation efforts are variables and that the lines separating the firm from its innovation community are not sharply drawn but are fluid and change frequently over time. These choices and transactions evolve over time, not only as a result of individual firm behavior but, just as important, by the interdependencies that accumulate among firms engaged in numerous components of the emerging industry.

Pragmatically, therefore, firm managers and entrepreneurs should be concerned not only with their own immediate proprietary tasks and transaction modes but also with those of other firms in their resource distribution channel and with the overall social system. Switching involvement among different system functions and proprietary distribution channels is expensive. Influencing one's own existing channel may be more efficient than switching channels or creating new ones. Also, there is an ongoing tension for each industry participant to organize its own proprietary functions and distribution channels as opposed to contributing to the creation of the industry's resources and institutional arrangements. Although the former may advance the firm's position as a first-mover in the short run, the latter provides the infrastructure that ultimately will influence the collective survival of the emerging industry.

There is an important counterintuitive implication in these decisions for individual entrepreneurs, which is captured in the following proposition: *Entrepreneurial firms that run in packs will be more successful than those that develop their innovations alone.*

Conventional wisdom is that entrepreneurs act independently and compete to be the first into the market with their new products or services. There are many technologies and industries in which acting alone may lead to successful monopoly profits. However, acting alone may lead to unsuccessful results when the innovation involves a new technology for a new industry. Running in packs means that entrepreneurs simultaneously cooperate and compete with others as they develop and commercialize their innovations. Running in packs is analogous to bicycle racers who cue their pace to one another and take turns breaking wind resistance until the ending sprint.

The argument for running in packs emphasizes that the interests of entrepreneurial actors with a stake in a technological innovation are both intertwined and divergent (Ben-Ner, 1993). The actors seek to maximize both their total surplus and their respective shares in the surplus. The total surplus amounts to creating an industrial infrastructure that makes it collectively possible to develop and commercialize a new technology for a new market. This draws actors together and drives them to cooperate because no one actor has sufficient resources, competence, or legitimacy to do it alone. The goal of maximizing individual shares propels actors to compete with each other to reap monopoly profits that derive from introducing a dominant technology or product. However, enlightened actors realize that the probability of economic survival from reaping monopoly shares of an orphan technology are much lower than from gaining relatively small shares of a larger and growing new industry. This is why population ecology studies are finding that having more competitors in a new organizational niche increases the survival probability of its members until a threshold level is reached where resource scarcity limits the growth of all members of a population (Hannan and Freeman, 1989). Gaining legitimacy is a key problem in the early emergence of a new industry, and the growth of a critical mass of actors is often a prerequisite for legitimacy.

Three corollary propositions elaborate this overall proposition on the self-interested and collective interdependence or entrepreneurial actors.

Contrary to industrial economists' stress on competitive interfirm relations, the social-system perspective emphasizes that relationships have cooperative and competitive elements (Van de Ven, Emmett, and Koenig, 1974). For example, it is easy to understand that a firm needs to establish cooperative relationships with suppliers, distributors, and customers to make its own activities meaningful. It is also easy to see that other firms that pursue competing technological routes carry out conflicting activities. However, as Mattsson (1987) discusses, there are also important elements of conflict among cooperating firms that have to do with the negotiating and administrating business transactions and adaptation processes. Among proprietary competitors, there are also elements of complementarity, not only when they cooperate to share resources or develop industry institutional functions but also when they are complementary suppliers to the same customers.

Indeed, because firms in an emerging industry are often engaged in multiple issues simultaneously, they create a "multiplexity of ties" (Galaskiewicz, 1985: 296). Thus, Aldrich and Whetten (1981) point out that it is misleading to think of single relations among most firms in an industry. Common forms of multiple links between a given set of firms include exchanging multiple resources, communicating with other firm representatives on industry and trade committees, sharing common pools of knowledge, and acquiring personnel trained and socialized in a common pool of competence, friendship and kinship ties, and overlapping board memberships: *As the number of cooperative and competitive ties among firms increases, the inter-firm relationships become more stable and the overall system becomes more flexible.*

A rupture in one aspect of a relationship does not sever other ties, and continuing ties are often used to correct or smooth over the severed link. From an industry perspective, stability through redundant functions and activities among actors minimizes the negative impact of the loss of services provided by one industry member on the performance of the total system.

Multiple ties among firms emerge over time and often produce unintended consequences. Prior relationships and transactions among firms in the pursuit of an industry subsystem activity are remembered and become the infrastructure on which subsequent relations are based (Van de Ven and Walker, 1984). Galaskiewicz (1985) nicely summarizes some of these temporal dimensions:

> The networks of resource exchange that already existed among organizations are the infrastructure on which political coalitions are built. In all likelihood, these resource networks were created out of competitive struggle for survival by self-seeking and self-centered actors, who were seeking to minimize their dependencies on one another. Now these networks are the infrastructure on which coalitions to achieve collective goals are built. In turn, as political coalitions become institutionalized, they impinge on the struggle for dominance in the resource procurement/ allocation arena. (299)

An appreciation of the temporal dimension of interfirm relationships also provides important insight on how competitors emerge in an industry. Generally, the literature tends to assume that competitors are profit-seeking entrepreneurs who somehow recognize and seize commercial opportunities by entering lucrative markets. Based on their longitudinal study of the emergence of the cochlear implant industry, Van de Ven and Garud (1993) provide quite a different proposition to explain how industrial competitors emerged: *Aborted efforts to establish cooperative relationships may become competitive relationships.*

In studying the development of cochlear implants, Van de Ven and Garud (1993) observed two instances in which the efforts of the first-mover to initiate cooperative relationships or joint ventures with other research clinics failed, leading to the birth of the firm's competitors. Initial negotiations of possible relationships with a foreign university and a domestic university did not materialize. Otological scientists and clinicians in each of these two universities subsequently entered into licensing arrangements with two other firms, one a new company start-up and the other a subsidiary of a large manufacturer, which two years later became the first-mover's major competitors.

The proposition that aborted cooperative relationships lead to competitive relationships applies primarily to conditions in which a small number of organizations, perhaps the size of an oligopoly, exist with the requisite unique competence or assets necessary for innovation development. Such conditions tend to exist during the early emergence of new-to-the-world technologies, where one can often count on one hand the pioneering firms and inventors worldwide who are pursuing the development of a parallel set of basic research ideas or technological designs. These pioneers make themselves known to one another by reporting results of their inventions through patents, professional publications, and association meetings. They thereby come to recognize opportunities to obtain unique competencies or components needed to advance their own work. If efforts to obtain the needed resources go unconsummated because a cooperative relationship could not be established, the negotiating parties will go their separate ways by entering into cooperative relationships with other parties in this limited set of pioneers who possess the unique competencies or resources. As Van de Ven and Ring (1994) discuss, this implies a shift to a competitive orientation between the parties who failed at each other's initial efforts at cooperation.

Through this and related processes, key first-mover organizations emerge that have extensive and overlapping ties to different components of the emerging technological community and play the key role of integrating the system. Because they have ties to more than one subsystem of a community, these first-movers are the nodes through which a network is loosely joined (Aldrich and Whetten, 1981). They serve as communication channels among industry participants and link third parties by transferring resources, information, or specialties within and outside of the industry. By being linked into multiple-subsystem functions in the industry, these first-movers accumulate a broad base of power to ascend to a dominant position in the industry, which permits them to survive at the expense of peripheral participants.

But these first-movers also experience the greatest conflicts of interest in the emerging industry because they tend also to have the greatest amount of visibility, which limits their abilities to capture significant proprietary advantages. This is because their dominance serves as a model that is imitated by others and diffused throughout the industrial community. Thus, the leading firm that chooses to "go it alone" must bear significant first-mover burdens, which permits free riding by other industry participants. In return for these burdens, first-movers are generally believed to have the greatest degrees of freedom to shape industry rules, technology standards, and product perceptions in the directions that benefit them the most (Porter, 1985).

However, these first-mover benefits do not appear to be empirically substantiated for technologies with weak appropriability regimes — that is, those that are easy to imitate, reverse engineer, or substitute (Teece, 1987). Anderson and Tushman (1990) found that the original breakthroughs in cement, glass, and minicomputers almost never became the dominant design except where strong patent protection existed. This research leads to the following caveat: *The technological design of the first-mover often turns out not to become the dominant design that yields the greatest profits.*

While striking out to be the first to introduce a new technology, the first-mover will inevitably make mistakes, and followers who watch can make adjustments in their own technologies. As a result, after the first-mover has introduced the product in the market, the second-, third-, and fourth-movers, who have been carefully following the leader, can often and rapidly introduce a more significant, advanced, and better product or service. These are strong economic motives for first-movers to run in packs, not alone.

Inherent in all the previously discussed relationships among firms engaged in an emerging industry is the paradox of cooperation and competition. Each firm competes to establish its distinctive position in the industry; at the same time, firms must cooperate to establish the industry infrastructure. Olson (1965) summarizes the paradox:

> If the firms in an industry are maximizing profits, the profits for the industry as a whole will be less than they might otherwise be. Almost everyone would agree that this theoretical conclusion fits the facts for markets characterized by pure competition. The important point is that this is true because, although all the firms have a common interest in a higher price for the industry's product, it is in the interest of each firm that the other firms pay the cost, in terms of the necessary reduction in output, needed to obtain a higher price. (10)

Another example that pertains to institutional arrangements is that it clearly benefits all firms to cooperate to set up industry standards. However, in doing so, each firm will try to ensure that the industry standards that suit it best get institutionalized.

One of the major reasons for the origin of industry regulation is that it is an institutional means to address these collective action dilemmas in which individual firms do not voluntarily act in a designated way to achieve benefits for all industry participants (Mitnick, 1980). Institutional ways to guarantee such action must be devised to provide the benefits. Otherwise, individual self-interest may lead some members to free-ride on whatever group benefits may have been obtained by others.

Conclusion

We believe the social-system perspective and its associated propositions make four contributions to understanding the emergence of technological innovations.

1. The social-system framework provides a holistic perspective to examine both the generative process by which a new-to-the-world technology is developed and commercialized and the roles of public- and private-sector actors, which create an infrastructure that supports technological development. By taking the interorganizational community or network as the relevant unit of analysis, the framework provides a more inclusive perspective of a competitive industry. In addition to this proprietary subsystem, the framework examines the industrial infrastructure that supports and constrains innovation. This infrastructure includes resource endowments of basic knowledge; financing mech-

anisms; competent labor; the institutional governance structure that legitimizes, regulates, and standardizes the activities of industry members; and market demand from informed consumers. Although an eclectic body of literature and research substantiates the importance of these component functions of a community infrastructure, they have been treated as "externalities" (Porter, 1980). By incorporating these functions within a conceptual framework, one can undertake a systematic research agenda aimed at understanding how various actors and functions interact to create an infrastructure that both facilitates and constrains innovation.

2. The infrastructure for innovation at the macro community level is grounded in a theory of action at microlevels of individuals and firms. We proposed that the odds of a firm successfully developing an innovation are primarily a function of the extent to which this infrastructure is developed at the industrial-community level. This community infrastructure facilitates and constrains entrepreneurial firms, but it is the actions of individuals and firms that construct and change the community infrastructure. But this infrastructure does not emerge and change all at once by the actions of one or even a few key individuals. Instead, we proposed that this infrastructure emerges through the accretion of numerous institutional, resource, and proprietary events, which coproduce each other through the actions of many public- and private-sector actors over an extended period. This generative process has a dynamic history that itself is important to study systematically if we are to understand how novel forms of technologies, organizations, and institutions emerge.

3. We argued that institutional and market arrangements, resource endowments, and proprietary functions are highly interdependent and coproduce each other over time. The framework allows us to examine the dynamic interplay in the progression of the different system components. Indeed, the very institutional arrangements and resource endowments created to facilitate industry emergence can become inertial forces that hinder subsequent technological development and adaptation by proprietary firms. However, even though various system functions coproduce each other, they are not expected to be completely determined. When tracking a highly uncertain generative process, researchers should consider large unexplained components of chance, noise, or error in the process.

4. The social-system perspective emphasizes that the debate on corporate revitalization through innovation is not limited to the for-profit sector; numerous entrepreneurial actors in the public and not-for-profit sectors play crucial roles that enable a new technology to be developed

and commercialized. This perspective also enables one to examine the different roles and events of these different actors and how their roles affect the roles of other actors, as well as their joint contributions to the emergence of the entire industry. This, in turn, makes it possible to understand how developments in the overall infrastructure for innovation significantly influence the time, cost, and direction of proprietary innovation.

7
Cycling the Innovation Journey

Innovation . . . is anything but orderly. It is sensible, in that our
efforts are all directed at reaching our goals, but the organization
. . . and the process . . . and sometimes the people can be chaotic.
We are managing in chaos, and this is the right way to manage if
you want innovation. It's been said that the competition never
knows what we are going to come up with next. The fact is, neither do we.

> William Coyne, Senior Vice President of
> Research and Development, 3M (1996)

This book has mapped the innovation journey from concept to implementation in a variety of settings observed by the Minnesota Innovation Research Program (MIRP). We defined the innovation journey as
a sequence of events in which new *ideas* are developed and implemented by *people* who engage in *relationships* with others and make
the adjustments needed to achieve desired *outcomes* within an institutional and organizational *context*. As mentioned in chapter 1, our
MIRP field studies radically altered our initial beliefs about the innovation process in terms of these five highlighted concepts.

Adopting the conventional wisdom at the time, and still wide-
spread today, we began by viewing an innovation as a novel idea that
maintains a core identity as it is developed, tested, and implemented
over time. Although different or opposing viewpoints might be expressed by various stakeholders, we assumed that most people involved in the innovation share a similar view of the idea. We thought
that entrepreneurship is clearly different from other organizational
roles and that the people assigned to an innovation team are dedicated
to the project as their primary, if not only, responsibility. We expected
that innovation units would engage in transactions with other vendors

and suppliers and that these relationships would remain fairly stable once established. The environmental context of the innovation was also viewed as relatively stable while the innovative idea transforms from concept to reality. Overall, the innovation process was expected to unfold through definable stages (e.g., invention, development, testing, adoption, and diffusion). By progressing through these phases or stages, we thought that the developmental effort would culminate in a clearly interpretable outcome: success or failure.

Soon after the MIRP field studies began, our observations disclosed a reality different from these orderly conceptions of the innovation process. Chapter 2 mapped this reality by describing how innovations were observed to develop, not as we thought they should develop. From among the fourteen diverse innovations studied by the MIRP researchers, a dozen elements were commonly observed to unfold during the gestation, development, and implementation periods of the innovation journey.

The Initiation Period

1. Innovations are not initiated on the spur of the moment, nor by a single dramatic incident, nor by a single entrepreneur. In most cases there was an extended gestation period lasting several years in which seemingly random events occurred that preceded and set the stage for the initiation of innovations.
2. Concentrated efforts to initiate innovations are triggered by "shocks" from sources internal or external to the organization.
3. Plans are developed and submitted to venture capitalists or top managers to obtain the resources for innovation development. However, when the innovation development begins, repeated efforts at restructuring and refinancing the innovation unit are often necessary to transform innovative ideas into practical realities for adoption and diffusion.

The Developmental Period

4. Soon after developmental activities begin, the initial innovative idea proliferates into numerous ideas and activities that proceed in divergent and parallel paths.
5. Setbacks and mistakes are frequently encountered because plans go awry or unanticipated environmental events significantly alter the ground assumptions of the innovation. As setbacks occur, resource and development timelines diverge. Initially, resource and schedule adjustments are made and provide a "grace" period for adapting the innovation. But with time, unattended problems often "snowball" into vicious cycles.
6. To compound the problems, criteria of success and failure often change, differ between resource controllers and innova-

tion managers, and diverge over time, often triggering power struggles between insiders and outsiders.

7. Innovation personnel participate in highly fluid ways. They tend to be involved on a part-time basis, and high personnel turnover rates occur. During the course of their involvement, personnel tend to experience euphoria in the beginning, frustration and pain in the middle period, and closure at the end of the innovation journey. These changing human emotions represent some of the most gut-wrenching experiences for innovation participants and managers.

8. Investors and top managers are frequently involved throughout the development process and perform contrasting roles that serve as checks and balances on one another. Seldom were major innovation development problems solved without intervention by top managers or investors.

9. Innovation units typically engaged in relational contracts with other organizations to obtain the resources, competencies, or proprietary assets necessary to develop their innovations. These dyadic relationships operated independently of other interorganizational relationships for a while, but with time and changing conditions, they were spun into complex webs of interdependent networks where actions in one dyadic relationship cascaded in a domino effect on other relationships in the web.

10. Entrepreneurs were often involved in activities beyond their immediate innovations by working with competitors, trade associations, and government agencies to create the industry or community infrastructure necessary to gain support and legitimacy for their collective innovation efforts.

The Implementation/Termination Period

11. Innovation adoption and implementation efforts do not wait until innovations were completed; they often occur throughout the developmental period by linking and integrating the "new" with the "old" or by reinventing the innovation to fit the local situation.

12. Innovations stop when they are implemented or when resources run out. Investors or top managers make attributions about innovation success or failure. Although these attributions are often misdirected, they significantly influence the fate of innovations and the careers of innovation participants.

How might we explain these twelve process observations? They document empirically a scenario of the innovation journey that is considerably different from the prevailing view. Perhaps the most widely known model that reflects this prevailing view was developed by Everett Rogers (1995), who portrays the process of innovation as a linear sequence of stages. The process begins with the invention of an idea, which comes from a recognition of needs or problems and basic or applied research; then it advances through development, production, and testing into a concrete device or program; and it culminates in its diffusion and adoption by end users. Cooper (1993) also describes six stages to industrial innovation, progressing through preliminary investigation, detailed investigation, development, testing and validation, full production, and market launch. Such a life-cycle model has been the dominant view in past treatments of the innovation process.

The messy and complex progression observed in the innovation cases studied by MIRP researchers cannot be reduced to a linear model of stages or phases. Instead, if we are to explain the twelve observations, *we propose that the innovation journey is a nonlinear cycle of divergent and convergent activities that may repeat over time and at different organizational levels if resources are obtained to renew the cycle.*

This concluding chapter elaborates the dynamics of this cyclical model of divergent and convergent activities. Figure 7.1 outlines the core elements of this model. They were evident in the foregoing chapters as we examined different aspects and levels of the innovation journey. A divergent-convergent cycle appears to underlie launching an innovation venture (chapter 2), learning within the innovation teams (chapter 3), leadership behaviors of top managers or investors (chapter 4), building relationships with other organizations (chapter 5), and developing an industrial infrastructure for innovations (chapter 6). This cyclical model is useful for integrating the major findings presented in this book. This process model also leads to important theoretical and practical implications for understanding and managing the innovation journey.

A Cyclical Model of Divergent and Convergent Behavior

Dooley and Van de Ven (1999b) propose a cyclical process model for explaining temporal dynamics in a wide variety of organizational change and innovation processes. The cycle consists of two phases in a set sequence of divergent and convergent behavior. Divergent and convergent phases reflect what March (1991) described as exploration and exploitation, respectively. According to the model, iterations of the cycle are enabled by an influx of resources and restructuring of the system and are constrained by external rules and internally chosen directions.

Divergence involves branching behavior that explores and expands in different directions. It is triggered by the infusion of resources into

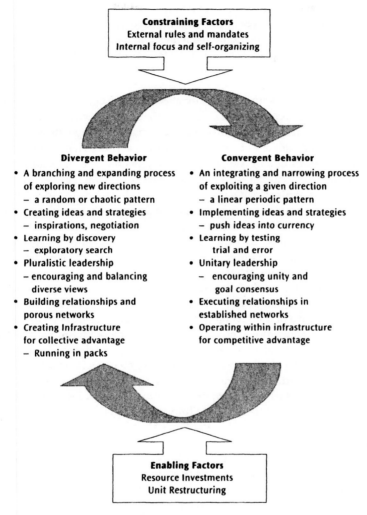

Constraining Factors
External rules and mandates
Internal focus and self-organizing

Divergent Behavior

- A branching and expanding process of exploring new directions
  - a random or chaotic pattern
- Creating ideas and strategies
  - inspirations, negotiation
- Learning by discovery
  - exploratory search
- Pluralistic leadership
  - encouraging and balancing diverse views
- Building relationships and porous networks
- Creating Infrastructure for collective advantage
  - Running in packs

Convergent Behavior

- An integrating and narrowing process of exploiting a given direction
  - a linear periodic pattern
- Implementing ideas and strategies
  - push ideas into currency
- Learning by testing
  trial and error
- Unitary leadership
  - encouraging unity and goal consensus
- Executing relationships in established networks
- Operating within infrastructure for competitive advantage

Enabling Factors
Resource Investments
Unit Restructuring

Figure 7.1 Cycling the innovation journey

a system. Divergence does not occur without the expenditure of attention and time, and such expenditures require additional resources — people, time, ideas, money — above and beyond the system's normal sustenance. As we discuss in the next section, divergent behavior increases the number of dimensions or complexity of a system and tends to follow a random or chaotic process.

Convergent behavior is an integrating and narrowing process that focuses on testing and exploiting a given direction. It reduces the dimensions or complexity of a system and moves it toward a periodic pattern of quasi equilibrium. Convergent behavior is triggered by external and internal dynamics. External constraints include institutional rules and organizational mandates that narrow the boundaries of permissible action. Internal constraints include resource limitations and discovering a possibility that focuses attention and actions in a chosen direction.

From this perspective, the innovation journey consists of a repeatable cycle of divergent and convergent phases of activities that are enabled by resource investments and are constrained by external rules and internal discovery of a chosen course of action. Each cycle begins with the design of an organizational arrangement and the infusion of resources from external sources, followed by a "honeymoon" period of divergent exploratory behaviors that continue until resources are depleted or a solution is found, and concludes with a convergent period of focused behavior to exploit the solution or to embark on a new one. If the latter, the innovation unit restructures itself to satisfy stakeholders' demands and obtain resources to initiate the next cycle of divergent-convergent phases.

This cyclical model of alternating divergent and convergent phases is exceedingly generalizable. Dooley and Van de Ven (1999b) illustrate how divergence and convergence are core processes underlying most theories of organizational change and development, including punctuated equilibrium, teleology, life cycle, dialectics, and evolution. They use it to examine change and development processes in a wide variety of topics and entities that may be nested at different levels of analysis and that may overlap in temporal duration. The cycles may exist at multiple levels of scale and time (individual, group, organization, industry). A single larger cycle can often decompose into several smaller cycles. Thus, the model reflects the property of *self-similarity* (Gleick, 1987). This means that the cycles of divergent and convergent behaviors are evident at multiple levels of scale and time of the system being examined, and if we look within any level or period, we see similar processes of divergence and convergence.

To explore the implications of this cycle model, we first examine and illustrate the technical characteristics of divergent and convergent behaviors. These technical considerations provide a vocabulary that enriches our appreciation of the model and its implications for theory and practice.

Dimensions and Patterns of Divergent and Convergent Events

We noted in the previous section that divergent behavior increases the dimensions of a system and that it follows random or chaotic patterns, whereas convergent behavior reduces the dimensions of a system and

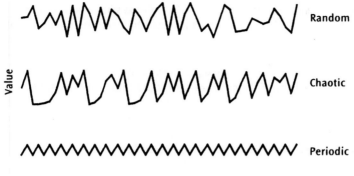

Figure 7.2 Examples of periodic, chaotic, and random event time series. From Poole, van de Ven, Dooley, and Holmes (1999)

reflects a periodic or quasi-equilibrium pattern. These dimensions and patterns of behavior can be distinguished empirically by diagnosing a sequence of events that might be observed in an organizational innovation or change effort.

Poole, Van de Ven, Dooley, and Holmes (1999) introduce figures 7.2 and 7.3 to clarify the dimensions of periodic, chaotic, and random patterns in event time series. Figure 7.2 shows three event time series and figure 7.3 shows their respective return maps. A return map plots the

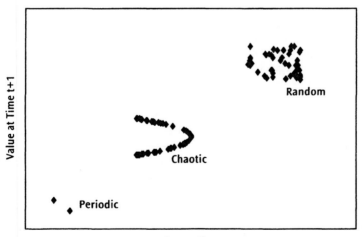

Figure 7.3 Return maps of periodic, chaotic, and random event time series in figure 7.2. From Poole, Van de Ven, Dooley and Holmes (1999)

points $(x(t), x(t+1))$ to see temporally related patterns in the data. The dimensions of these patterns indicate the complexity of the time-series data.

From geometry, we know that a point has a dimension of zero, a line has a dimension of one, a plane has dimension of two, and a cube has a dimension of three. *Dimensionality* refers to the number of dimensions in a geometric space that are required to plot all the points in a return map, or phase space, of a time series. When a time series is periodic, the alternating fixed points in the return map can be plotted on a line in one dimension, as illustrated in figure 7.3. The return map of a chaotic time series is often known as a strange attracter, and plotting all its points may require three to six dimensional spaces. Chaotic time series are low dimensional compared to the nearly infinite number of dimensions required to plot all points of a random time series.

Figure 7.3 illustrates that a phase plot of a random time series fills the two-dimensional space. If these random numbers are plotted against each other in three-dimensional space, $\{x(t), x(t+1), x(t+2)\}$, they will fill the cube. If we continue to plot the random time series in higher and higher dimensions, they will continue to fill the spaces into which they are embedded. As Jayanthi and Sinha (1998) discuss, a major difference between a chaotic process and a truly random process is that although both appear random to the naked eye, a truly random process has high to infinite dimensions, whereas a chaotic process has low dimensions.

Periodic, chaotic, and random time series also differ in terms of a prediction of path versus a prediction of pattern. *Path* is the specific temporal trajectory of a set of data points that a system follows moment by moment. *Pattern* is the distinctive, often visual, temporal shape that emerges when one views the path of points over a long period plotted in a particular manner. Periodic systems are predictable in both path and pattern. For example, both the time-series plot and the return map for the periodic time series shown in figures 7.2 and 7.3 demonstrate order and predictability. Random systems are not predictable in path or pattern. The corresponding plots for the random time series demonstrate a complete lack of order and predictability. Chaotic systems are predictable in pattern but not path. The plot of a chaotic time series in figure 7.2 appears unpredictable, while its return map shown in figure 7.3 demonstrates an obvious pattern of points that are bounded in a relatively small space. As this pattern suggests, chaos has a hidden order that typically consists of a relatively simple nonlinear deterministic system of only a few variables. Thus, unlike random behavior, which is infinitely dimensional, chaotic behavior is low dimensional, typically three to six dimensions, and periodic behavior consists of only one or two dimensions.

In mathematical terms, dimensionality relates to the number of different independent variables that affect the output of a system (Gell-Mann, 1994). If an event time series is high dimensional, many variables are affecting output variation; if it is low dimensional, few variables are affecting output variation. Furthermore, a random pattern implies that the many variables influencing the system are doing so in an independent fashion (Ruhla, 1992).

The discovery of chaos implies low dimensionality in an observed time series. That means there are clear boundaries within which all the activities or events being examined can be plotted and that these boundaries are limited to about three to six dimensions (Brock, Hsieh, and LeBaron, 1989). Thus, a shift from high-dimensional random behavior to low-dimensional chaotic behavior represents a major convergence in behavior.

When an event time series is diagnosed as chaotic, we know that a model explaining this divergent behavior must be dynamic, sensitive to initial conditions, and nonlinear. *Dynamic* means that the values a variable takes at a given time are a function, at least in part, of the values of that same variable at an earlier time. *Sensitive to initial conditions* means that small initial differences or fluctuations in variables may grow over time into large differences. Chaos also depends on the necessary, although not sufficient, condition that *nonlinear* interactions exist between the causal factors that enable or constrain the behavior. These nonlinear interactions typically reflect the presence of positive and negative feedback loops (Koput, 1992), as might be generated by the interaction of enabling and constraining factors on the cycle in figure 7.1.

Periodic behavior also arises from systems that are low dimensional. The key difference between periodic and chaotic behavior is that the causal factors do not interact in a periodic system, or they do so in a simple linear fashion. Although such a system could arise naturally, it is also possible that interactions are linear (or absent) because the system was designed to be so. For example, consider situations in which behavior is calendar driven, such as daily, weekly, monthly, or annual phenomena. The temporal regularity of events will be mirrored in the periodic pattern.

We should note that it is possible to obtain periodic or chaotic behavior by adjusting "order parameters" in many nonlinear systems (e.g., the logistics map). This implies that chaos and periodicity can potentially point toward the same generative mechanism. The fact that causal factors in a periodic system interact not at all, or in a simple linear fashion, has important implications. Simple interaction patterns among causal factors leads to a lack of sensitivity to small changes (unlike chaos, where there is sensitivity to initial conditions) and to some level of predictability in outcomes. One should not be "fooled," however, by these implications: Because chaotic dynamics and periodic dynamics produce outcomes that are far apart does not mean they are far away from one another in terms of causal theories or implied organizational stories. In fact, the butterfly-effect metaphor may be useful: Even though the causal mechanisms generating chaotic and periodic behavior may be nearly identical (small difference in initial conditions), this small difference (the nature of interactions between causal factors) leads to huge differences in observed output.

Dooley and Van de Ven (1999a) point out that these distinctions between random, chaotic, and periodic patterns are very different from the common, vernacular use of the word *chaos*. Managers and organizational writers (e.g., Brown and Eisenhardt, 1998; Peters, 1991) commonly use the word chaos to mean "a state of extreme confusion and disorder" (*Webster's Revised Unabridged Dictionary*, 1913). From a common language standpoint, their use of the word is correct. From a mathematical standpoint, in fact, the opposite is true. *Chaos, in its correct mathematical form, implies a state of bounded order and predictability of pattern, but not path.* The bounded order of chaotic systems is produced by enabling and constraining factors that reduce the system's many degrees of freedom to only a few more dimensions than periodic behavior and far fewer than random behavior. Relative to randomness, chaos greatly reduces confusion because future action is in large part deterministically generated based on the current state.

Knowing what kind of temporal pattern is present in an event time series provides important clues for explaining the dynamics. As Morrison (1991) discusses, one should use (1) stochastic models (e.g., actuarial probabilities) to explain random processes, (2) linear deterministic models (e.g., life-cycle models) to explain periodic cycles or stable equilibria, and (3) nonlinear dynamic models (e.g., the logistics equation) to explain chaotic processes.

When we observe a random pattern of events, the individuals involved are behaving independently and acting in an uncoordinated, uncontrolled fashion. Because a random pattern is path independent, the divergent behavior progresses with no memory of past behavior. In other words, people are not using any cognizance of their current state to guide their next steps, or such information is interpreted uniquely by each individual, leading to independent actions.

We might ask how is it possible to obtain low-dimensional behavior in an innovating system in which individuals have free will, unique interpretive schema and behavioral rules, unique goals, and unique access to relevant information? Dooley and Van de Ven (1999a) argue that if the system in question is large in scope, the decrease in dimensions must be the result of global feedback and/or constraints. For example, in monitoring financial expenditures within the organization, the discovery of low-dimensional behavior may imply that a centralized budget or an authorization entity tightly controls local expenditures. Low-dimensional behavior implies a reduction in freedom or autonomy of individuals, a mechanism that ensures that interpretive schema and behavioral rules are common and provides unified access to relevant information. These mechanisms can be thought of as representing control of individuals and/or cooperation among the individuals. Control and cooperation may be managerial (Simon, 1962), adaptive (March, 1994), institutional (Scott, 1995), or self-induced (Dooley, 1997).

Humans, however, do not tend to develop organizational controls that are nonlinear in nature because they are difficult to design, operate successfully, and understand. In addition, humans typically do not consciously (adaptively) respond in a nonlinear fashion, unless they do so for strategic, competitive reasons. Their reactions tend to be linear in nature where response is proportional to desired change (March, 1994). Therefore in a chaotic system, the nature of control and/or adaptation probably exists beyond the full cognizance of organizational members. For example, if an observed time series of leadership action events were found to be chaotic, an erroneous conclusion would be that the leaders of the organization "lacked order and were in a state of extreme confusion." The correct interpretation instead would be that leaders were exerting decisions that represented a deterministic (albeit nonlinear, and therefore not completely rational) mapping from the past to the present and were being tightly constrained (self-induced, or due to exogenous forces) in their strategy.

Case Illustrations of Divergent and Convergent Cycles

To illustrate divergent and convergent cycles during the innovation journey, let us reexamine the event sequences in the three cases in foregoing chapters: (1) Qnetics, a new company start-up; (2) the Cochlear Implant Program (CIP), an internal corporate venture within 3M; and (3) the Therapeutic Apheresis Program (TAP), an interorganizational joint venture of Millipore, 3M, and Sarns. Chapters 8 to 10 document the sequences of events and the structural adaptations made over time in these innovations.

Figure 7.4 provides a graphical representation of the innovation events and structures over time in the three cases. The figure plots the monthly number of action and outcome events, and the vertical lines indicate when key organizational changes occurred in the three cases. The coded events are based on the model of trial-and-error learning examined in chapter 3 and show how action and outcome events are related. Actions are coded as the net number of monthly events in which the entrepreneurs expanded versus contracted their courses of action from the previous event. Outcomes are coded as the net number

a. Cochlear Implant (CIP) Internal Corporate Venture

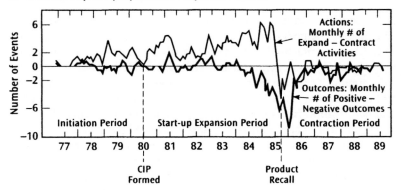

b. Therapeutic Apheresis (TAP) Interorganizational Joint Venture

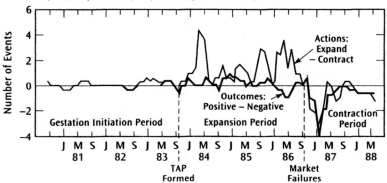

c. New Software Company Start-up (Qnetics)

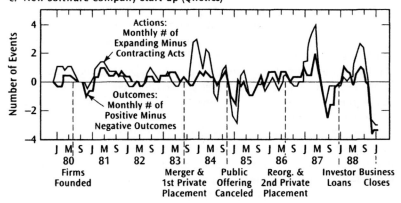

Figure 7.4 Action and outcome events during the development of three innovations. (Plots are three-month moving averages of the number of monthly events in which actions expanded minus contracted and in which outcomes were positive minus negative.) From Van de Ven (1991)

of positive minus negative outcomes that entrepreneurs experienced from the events throughout the development of their innovations. Although numerous organizing events occurred throughout the temporal development of the three cases, the vertical lines indicate times when major changes occurred in the structure and funding sources for the innovations.

The time series of action and outcome events for the CIP and TAP innovations look similar in figure 7.4 a and b, and they appear different from Qnetics in plot c. Upon closer examination, however, we show that the Qnetics developmental pattern is similar to that of CIP and TAP. In fact, CIP and TAP represent special cases of a more general developmental sequence that Qnetics reflects.

Figure 7.4 a and b suggests that after their initial gestation period, CIP and TAP undertook a single overall cycle of divergent and convergent behaviors. The cycle began after the innovation projects were formed and funded and had a divergent period of development where most events expanded in different directions to explore the idea with the resources available. This was followed by a convergent period of mostly contracting activities and negative outcomes associated with market-entry problems. As reported in chapter 3, Cheng and Van de Ven (1996) found that the pattern of action events was potentially chaotic in the divergent period and periodic in the convergent period. Failing successful market entry toward the end of the convergent period, a number of unsuccessful attempts to restructure and refinance the ventures occurred, and the CIP and TAP innovations were terminated. However, the organizational and technical competencies created by the CIP and TAP innovations were redeployed in other business ventures by the parent organizations.

During its life span, Qnetics transformed through three qualitatively different structural and financial arrangements: (1) as two independent new company start-ups, (2) their merger as a computer software company, and remaining financially unsuccessful (3) restructuring once again to develop software for an electric load-management device. Figure 7.4c shows that action events grew rapidly to explore or expand in new directions shortly after the start of each restructuring period and then contracted dramatically toward the end of each period because of the company's repeated failures to generate sufficient revenues from new product sales or venture capitalists to sustain its livelihood. Thus, the history of Qnetics involved three cycles of divergent and convergent development and major restructurings and refinancing arrangements to initiate each cycle.

Unlike CIP and TAP, Qnetics's principals were successful in undertaking the major restructurings and refinancings necessary to initiate each cycle of business development. Like CIP and TAP, each structural arrangement enabled Qnetics to initiate a new cycle of divergent and convergent phases. Within each cycle, divergent exploratory behavior dominated until significant marketing problems arose and resources became scarce, which triggered a shift toward more convergent and focused behaviors. At the end of each cycle, the existing structural arrangement of the fledgling business became a liability that inhibited further resource commitments by investors.

These observations suggest that the structural arrangements used to organize and manage an innovation unit are temporary and change with each cycle. From this we infer the following proposition: *Changes in structural and financial arrangements are necessary, but not sufficient, enabling conditions to renew the divergent and convergent cycle of innovation development.* Qnetics was able to engage in new cycles of development only with major organizational restructurings that generated a willingness of new investors to infuse new resources. CIP and TAP entrepreneurs were unsuccessful in finding investors willing to commit resources to any further plans for organizational restructuring; failing this the innovations were terminated.

Finally, figure 7.5 shows that the divergent and convergent phases in the three cycles varied in degrees of magnitude and duration. Across the peaks and valleys of the three cycles, the arrows indicate an increasingly divergent progression in the history of Qnetics. This divergent progression across the three cycles indicates that Qnetics's developmental journey increased in dimensionality or complexity over time. This overall divergent progression across the three cycles could not sustain Qnetics as a viable economic enterprise. We think that Qnetics might have become a sustainable business if its progression across cycles had converged and settled down to fewer dimensions over time.

Most of the other innovations included in the MIRP studies did not follow Qnetics's divergent overall progression across cycles. In fact, our twelve process observations indicate that it was the reverse. Specifically, we propose that *innovation journeys that eventually reach sustained implementation and operation will follow a convergent progression with a smaller number of dimensions in each successive cycle of development.* Figure 7.6 illustrates this proposition. Observations of the innovations studied by MIRP researchers lend evidence for this proposition.

In the beginning, a gestation period of seemingly random events set the stage for initiating an innovation project. Some of these gestating events were sufficiently large to "shock" the action thresholds of entrepreneurs and converge on a specific plan used to secure funding and organize structural arrangements to launch an innovative venture.

As innovation development began, the process soon proliferated from a simple unitary process into a divergent progression of ideas and activities. During this exploratory period, Cheng and Van de Ven's (1996) findings suggest that divergent action events followed a chaotic, not a random or periodic, pattern. This divergent pattern was con-

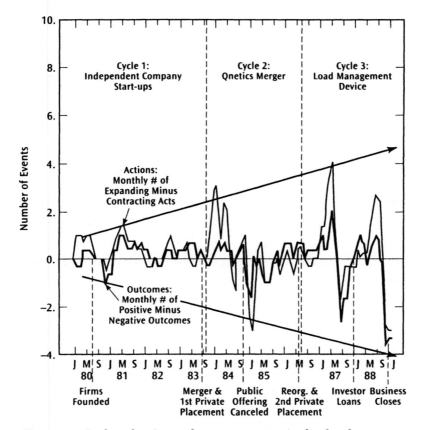

Figure 7.5 Cycles of action and outcome events in the development of Qnetics

strained by institutional regulations (e.g., Food and Drug Administration clinical trials and review procedures), leadership directives (e.g., develop the TAP device to achieve specified filtering capabilities and not the treatment of a disease), and internal persistence to an entrepreneurial vision. This divergent and chaotic process continued until significant and measurable setbacks occurred, such as manufacturing failures for TAP, a product recall for CIP, and withdrawal of a bank's line of credit for Qnetics. These tangible "shocks" shifted the divergent progression into a convergent focus on problem solving through trial-and-error testing. Empirically, Cheng and Van de Ven (1996) found the action events during this convergent period to reflect a unidimensional periodic pattern.

Ideally, innovations stop when they are adopted and implemented. However, in most of the cases studied by MIRP researchers, initial in-

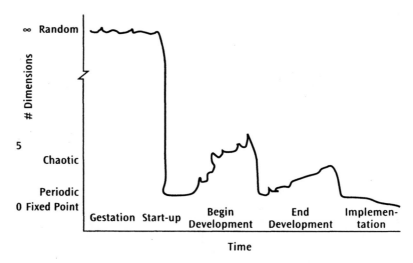

Figure 7.6 Random, chaotic, and periodic dimensions in the innovation journey

vestments were not sufficient to support the complete development of innovation. As a result, innovation development efforts were often terminated when resources were depleted and when investors were unwilling to renew further investments in the innovations. In the case of Qnetics, where new or existing investors were willing to make further investments in the innovations, the divergent and convergent cycle repeated twice but in each cycle with a different structure and leaders for the innovation unit. We noted before that Qnetics's subsequent cycles diverged into higher dimensionality that did not lead to a viable operating business. In other cases, we observed that innovation adoption and implementation occurred by linking and integrating the "new" innovation with the "old" existing operations. For this to happen, the innovation needs to converge to a periodic pattern with that of the existing operating entity at the time of implementation.

Divergent and Convergent Dimensions of the Innovation Journey

Gestation of Innovations

We observed in chapter 2 that innovations are not initiated on the spur of the moment, by a single dramatic incident, or by a single entrepreneur. An extended gestation period, often lasting several years, of seemingly random events occurred before concentrated efforts were launched to develop an innovation. Many of these divergent events were not intentionally directed toward starting an innovation. Some events triggered recognition of the need for change. Other events generated awareness of the technological feasibility of an innovation. Events such as these often "shocked" entrepreneurs on courses of action that, by chance, intersected with independent actions of others. These intersections provided occasions for people to recognize and access new opportunities and potential resources. When these occasions were exploited, people modified and adapted their independent courses of action into convergent interdependent actions to mobilize efforts to initiate an innovation.

These observations emphasize that chance plays a significant role in affecting the decision and subsequent course of innovation adoption. Increases in the number of initiatives undertaken by a large number of interacting people increases the probability of stimulating innovation. This proposition reinforces the bias-for-action principle of Peters and Waterman (1982). Perhaps Louis Pasteur's adage, "Chance favors the prepared mind," best captures the process that sets the stage for innovation.

The important practical question then becomes, "What can organizations do to increase their preparedness to capitalize on the chance of innovation?" The quest of many managers is to make their organizations more innovative. This quest often focuses on a desire to stimulate "revolutionary" innovations that create new markets and alter the basis of competition, as opposed to developing incremental variations on existing product platforms (Coyne, 1996).

This quest can be thought of as an optimization search on an emerging and uncharted landscape. Because discovery entails divergent search, this landscape is likely to be complex and have many dimensions (e.g., many local peaks and valleys emerge), or, in Kauffman's (1995) terms, it may be "rugged." Search in such rugged landscapes becomes very difficult because it is easy to get "stuck" in a suboptimal part of the landscape. Traditional linear (hill-climbing) techniques, while sufficient for simple landscapes, fall apart in such environments (Levinthal and Warglien, 1999). What is required is a search strategy that has less path dependency and more "novelty" as it enacts future actions based on past responses. A completely random search is most likely to find the "best" response to a complex problem. Landscapes, however, even rugged ones, do have some structure. To ignore such structure is to unnecessarily make the search process uneconomical.

Other realities make a high-dimensional random search infeasible. First, institutional pressures require organizational actors to legitimate their actions in a rational way (Scott, 1987). A linear search serves this purpose well, whereas a random search tends to be viewed as irrational and ad hoc. However, unidimensional behavior is not likely to generate sufficient variety to produce novel possibilities or connections. Organizational designs to run efficiently and reliably often have the effect of programming people into cognitive routines or habits that desensitize them to novel events (Starbuck, 1983). This habit-bound perception is particularly prevalent in contexts in which people perform repetitive tasks. "What people do most is often what they think about least" (Van de Ven, 1986: 595).

Second, even if a random search has the highest statistical probability of finding the "best" solution, humans do not possess the cognitive capability to deal effectively with the complexity present in random systems. Therefore, whereas a random search may uncover a better solution, it may be costly, and it may not lead to innovations that build on the organization's distinctive competencies. Thus, a random search might find an answer, but the reasoning behind the answer may be lost to the participants.

A chaotic search process is far less complex than a random process and yet stimulates sufficient variety to yield novel innovative ideas. As noted previously, a random process provides no prediction of path or pattern to behavior, but a chaotic process provides a prediction of pattern but not path. Only linear periodic processes provide predictions of path and pattern. Thus, although chaotic processes are nonlinear, they provide a search mechanism that may be effective, efficient, and able to deal with the complex nature of rugged landscapes (Carley and Svoboda, 1996). These considerations lead to the following proposition: *Organizations that enable and motivate chaotic divergent behaviors are more likely to develop a tradition of innovation than those that promote random or periodic behaviors.*

The 3M company is the best exemplar we have found of this proposition. William Coyne, senior vice president of Technology at 3M, emphasizes that creating an organizational culture for innovation is both possible and necessary for corporate growth and survival. He argues that making innovation a corporate character trait is built over time. A tradition of innovation is a historical product of an accretion of past organizational innovation activities. In his March 1996 United Kingdom Innovation Lecture, Coyne presented six principles that he believes are responsible for creating a tradition of innovation in 3M's ninety-six-year history.

1. *Vision.* Declare the importance of innovation; make it part of the company's self-image.

> Our efforts to encourage and support innovation are proof that we really do intend to achieve our vision of ourselves . . . that we do intend to become what we want to be . . . as a business and as creative individuals.

2. *Foresight.* Find out where technologies and markets are going. Identify articulated and unarticulated needs of customers.

> If you are working on a next-generation medical imaging device, you'll probably talk to radiologists, but you might also sit down with people who enhance images from interplanetary space probes.

3. *Stretch goals.* Set goals that will make you and the organization stretch to make quantum improvements. While many projects are pursued, place your biggest bets on those that change the basis of competition and redefine the industry.

> We have a number of stretch goals at 3M. The first states that we will drive 30% of all sales from products introduced in the past four years. . . . To establish a sense of urgency, we've recently added another goal, which is that we want 10% of our sales to come from products that have been in the market for just one year. . . . Innovation is time sensitive . . . you need to move quickly.

4. *Empowerment.* Hire good people and trust them, delegate responsibilities, provide slack resources, and get out of the way. Be tolerant of initiative and the mistakes that occur because of that initiative.

> William McKnight [a former chairman of 3M] came up with one way to institutionalize a tolerance of individual effort. He said that all technical employees could devote 15% of their time to a project of their own invention. In other words, they could manage themselves for 15% of the time. . . . The number is not so important as the message, which is this: The system has some slack in it. If you have a good idea, and the commitment to squirrel away time to work on it and the raw nerve to skirt your lab manager's expressed desires, then go for it.
>
> Put another way, we want to institutionalize a bit of rebellion in our labs. We can't have all our people off totally on their own . . . we do believe in discipline . . . but at the same time 3M management encourages a healthy disrespect for 3M management. This is not the sort of thing we publicize in our annual report, but the stories we tell—with relish—are frequently about 3Mers who have circumvented their supervisors and succeeded.
>
> We also recognize that when you let people follow their own lead . . . everyone doesn't wind up at the same place. You can't ask people to have unique visions and march in lockstep. Some people are very precise, detail-oriented people . . . and others are fuzzy thinkers and visionaries . . . and this is exactly what we want.

5. *Communications.* Open, extensive exchanges according to ground rules in forums that are present for sharing ideas and where networking is each individual's responsibility. Multiple methods for sharing information are necessary.

> When innovators communicate with each other, you can leverage their discoveries. This is critically important because it allows companies to get the maximum return on their substantial investments in new technologies. It also acts as a stimulus to further innovation. Indeed, we believe that the ability to combine and transfer technologies is as important as the original discovery of a technology.

6. *Rewards and recognition.* Emphasize individual recognition more than monetary rewards through peer recognition and by choice of managerial or technical promotion routes. "Innovation is an intensely human activity."

In his conclusion Coyne (1996) said:

> I've laid out six elements of 3M's corporate culture that contribute to a tradition of innovation: vision, foresight, stretch goals, empowerment, communications and recognition. . . . The list is . . . too orderly. Innovation at 3M is anything but orderly. It is sensible, in that our efforts are directed at reaching our goals, but the organization . . . and the process . . . and sometimes the people can be chaotic. We are managing in chaos, and this is the right way to manage if you want innovation. It's been said that the competition never knows what we are going to come up with next. The fact is, neither do we.

Three points merit reflection on Coyne's remarks. First, it is evident that Coyne does not adopt the common meaning of chaos as "a state of extreme confusion and disorder." Instead, as a scientist himself, he uses the correct mathematical meaning of chaos discussed earlier as a state of bounded order and predictability of pattern, but not path.

Second, Coyne's six principles are directed at creating a low-dimensional corporate culture for innovation. On the one hand, his remarks are clearly directed at relaxing the rigid structures and managerial controls prevalent in most unidimensional organizations. On the other hand, he is not advocating high-dimensional random behavior. Instead, based on his experiential knowledge, we think he provides sound practical suggestions for developing a tradition of innovation by creating a corporate culture that enables and motivates chaotic behavior.

Third, Coyne's six principles are supported with an extensive body of management theory and research. They echo Angle's (1989) conclusion, based on an extensive review of the literature, of the need to struc-

ture the organization's context to *enable* and *motivate* innovative behavior. This context includes the legitimacy, resources, structure, and
culture of the encompassing organization that innovation projects
draw upon to diverge and converge into innovative behaviors. Amabile
(1988), Angle (1989), and Kanter (1988) summarize a large body of research indicating that innovation is facilitated in organizations that
provide a context that enables and motivates innovation; it does not
occur where enabling or motivating conditions are absent.

The immediate context for most innovations is the organization itself, and Coyne's principles are directed at modifying the culture and
practices of this corporate context. Organizations are complex social
systems that provide templates for playing out many distinctive roles
important to innovation. The design of an organization's structure, systems, and practices influences the likelihood that innovation ideas will
be surfaced and that once surfaced they will be developed and nurtured toward realization.

With respect to structure, several features affect the gestation of innovative activities. The more complex and differentiated organization,
with easy-to-cross boundaries, offers potential for a greater number of
sources from which innovative ideas can spring (Hage, 1980). However, as Kanter (1983) discusses, with increasing organizational size
and segmentation come bureaucratic procedures that push organizations in periodic and unidimensional directions. These procedures
often constrain innovation unless special systems are put in place to
motivate and enable innovative behavior.

Key motivating factors include providing a balance of intrinsic and
extrinsic rewards for innovative behaviors (Amabile, 1983). Although
people work for pay to make a living, monetary rewards turn out to be
a relatively weak motivator for innovative behavior; they often serve
as a proxy for recognition. Angle (1989) found that individualized
rewards tend to increase idea generation and radical innovations,
whereas group rewards tend to increase innovation implementation
and incremental innovations.

However, the presence of motivating factors, by themselves, will not
ensure innovative behavior. Angle (1989) emphasizes that enabling
conditions are equally necessary. As Coyne's principles indicate, they
include the following:

1. Slack resources for innovation.
2. Moderate environmental uncertainty and mechanisms for focusing attention on changing conditions.
3. Frequent communications and use of constructive conflict-
   resolution methods with people holding dissimilar viewpoints from other functions, customers, and research communities.
4. Access to innovation role models and mentors.

5. Moderately low personnel turnover.
6. Psychological contracts that legitimize and solicit spontaneous innovative behavior.

Research findings suggest that the importance of open communications and networking for stimulating innovation cannot be overstated. Von Hippel's (1981) research found that ideas for most new product innovations come from customers. Utterback (1971) found that about 75% of the ideas used to develop product innovations came from outside the organization. Not only do direct contacts with customers force organizational participants to acknowledge problems and needs, but also, by being outside the organizational unit, customers are not trapped by its bounded rationality. Outsiders can see ways to approach problems other than the ways organizational participants are used to taking for granted. Placing people in direct personal confrontation with the sources of organizational problems and opportunities is necessary to reach the threshold of concern and appreciation to motivate most people to act (Van de Ven, 1980). Personal exposure increases the likelihood of triggering action thresholds that affect a person's awareness of changing technological, organizational, and environmental needs.

Angle (1989: 165) concludes that "*normal people have the capability and potential to be creative and innovative.*" The actualization of this potential depends on whether management structures the organizational context to motivate and enable individuals to innovate.

Learning in Divergent and Convergent Phases of the Cycle

Cycles of divergent and convergent behaviors were helpful for explaining different patterns of learning that innovation teams followed to guide their innovation developmental journeys. In chapter 3, we reported that during the beginning development period of CIP and TAP, the relationships between action and outcome events were unrelated, but they were strongly positively correlated during their ending development period. In addition, we reported that during the beginning development period, the divergent actions of CIP and TAP innovation teams reflected a nonlinear chaotic pattern, and they reflected a more orderly periodic pattern during the ending development period.

These findings have important implications for understanding how people learn the innovation journey. Organizational learning is typically defined as an experiential process of acquiring knowledge about action-outcome relationships and the effects of environmental context events on these relationships (Barnett, 1994; Duncan and Weiss, 1979). *Our findings call for an expanded definition of learning that examines not only how action-outcome relationships develop but also how pre-*

requisite knowledge of alternative actions, outcome preferences, and contextual settings emerge. This expanded definition distinguishes learning by *discovery* from learning by *testing.* In particular, our research suggests that learning by *discovery* in chaotic conditions is an expanding and diverging process of discovering possible action alternatives, outcome preferences, and contextual settings. Learning by *testing* during the more stable convergent period is a narrowing and converging process of determining which actions are related to what outcomes. Finally, because learning by discovery is a precondition for learning by testing, and vice versa, we must examine how transitions occur between divergent and convergent phases of the cycle.

If we are to explain the innovation journey as a learning process, then *an understanding of how true novelty emerges should begin with profound ignorance with respect to what actions people might take initially, what outcomes they desire, and the nature of the institutional context in which they begin to operate.* Chapter 3 discussed several ways in which this knowledge is created and socially constructed by interactions among people involved in the discovery process. The first is with a broad vision or macrogoal that motivates actions needed to gain experiences with alternative ways to think or believe about a technology, various artifact components and architectures, and different testing or evaluation procedures. In addition to this *elaboration process*, an *articulation process* moves from tacit to explicit knowledge of alternative conditions under which possible actions and outcomes might be pursued. Finally, a *testing process* links explicit actions to selected outcome criteria in given settings through trial-and-error learning.

We proposed that *a nonlinear chaotic process facilitates learning by discovery.* The CIP and TAP cases were new-to-the-world innovative ventures. Beginning with a profound lack of knowledge, the innovators first had to undergo a period of exploration and elaboration to experience and discover what courses of action were possible, what outcome goals and criteria they preferred, and in what kind of environmental context or setting they were to work. The elaboration proceeded on many fronts and encountered a variety of positive and negative information. Yet all this information was localized to the immediate area and used to energize or modify the local discovery effort rather than to generate major changes in direction or withdrawal. Whereas some might suggest, as some investors and top managers did, that this seemingly random chaotic exploration is unproductive, it should be emphasized that this divergent period of discovery is necessary before innovators can converge into the still confusing but better defined period of trial-and-error learning.

Indeed, we argued that *a convergent process of trial-and-error learning is not feasible until after alternative courses of action, outcome preferences, and the contextual setting are discovered.* By uncoupling actions and outcomes, a chaotic process facilitates the construction of repertoires of action experiences, outcome beliefs, and contextual practices. These repertoires increase an organization's capacity for creative learning. The coupling of actions and outcomes narrows the repertoires to those that satisfy the linear combination of feasible actions and desired outcomes. Efforts to couple actions and outcomes tightly increase the efficiency of learning by testing which action alternatives optimize a chosen outcome goal or by justifying outcome preferences that might emerge from persistence with a given course of action. In either case, this narrowing process signals the transition from chaotic to orderly development in dissipative systems.

Convergent behavior also channels subsequent divergent behavior during the innovation journey. Choices to narrow developmental efforts toward a specific technical design or market niche for the innovation open whole new sets of issues that require further exploration. For example, CIP's decision to converge on a multiple- versus a single-channel design opened a host of new issues requiring discovery and exploration. Convergent choice behavior thus narrows the focus of attention at the same time that it opens new questions and defines boundaries for further divergent exploration.

Finally, we proposed that *transitions from chaotic divergent discovery to more orderly convergent testing activities are explained by the fact that innovation units are dissipative structures.* The innovation unit must import energy and resources from its environment to undertake a developmental effort. External resources, institutional rules, and leadership directives influence the system by enabling (expanding) or constraining (narrowing) the branching and freedom of movement along the pathways.

Learning and the internal self-organizing character of innovation units influence transitions. "Self-organizing processes are poised on their 'starting marks' to take over from random developments, if proper conditions become established, and to accelerate or make possible in the first place the emergence of complex order. Human systems are pragmatic; they interpret and take advantage of exogenous events or constraints to accomplish their purposes of self-renewal by creating novel structures" (Jantsch, 1980: 8).

Thus, *a critical function of leadership is to define the boundaries of search behavior as it makes investment decisions to continue the cycle of divergent and convergent innovation development.* The amounts and kinds of investments define the boundaries within which divergent and convergent behaviors can occur. Increasing resource investments and decreasing institutional constraints on an innovation unit increase the boundary dimensions for divergent and convergent behavior.

Leading Divergent and Convergent
Phases of the Cycle

In chapter 4, we found that the *process of leadership* itself entails balancing divergent and convergent forces on the development of an innovation among leaders who hold and shift between pluralistic views about the innovation. The Minnesota researchers observed three patterns in the behaviors of top managers:

1. Many, not one or a few, top managers or resource controllers at different hierarchical levels were actively involved in developing innovations within their organizations.
2. The managers typically did not reflect unified and homogeneous perspectives; instead, they held opposing views and performed roles that often served as checks and balances on each other in making innovation investment decisions.
3. When the top managers met periodically to review an innovation's progress, they followed a process of decision making by objection (Anderson, 1983) in which goals and actions were interpreted through argumentation and debate in settings in which justification and legitimacy of decisions were highly visible.

These observations suggest that the top managers, like their innovation teams, were groping for inspiration to interpret and make sense of their innovation journeys. However, unlike the innovation units, which rallied behind the charismatic vision and persistence of their entrepreneurs, the top managers adopted an alternative strategy for inspiration. The collective behavior of top managers reflected a pluralistic structure of conflicting forces and a decision process by objection.

This pluralistic structure of innovation leadership was reflected in four kinds of leadership roles: sponsor, critic, institutional leader, and mentor. We pointed out that while the corporate sponsor or champion role has been widely recognized, the roles of critic, mentor, and institutional leader have received very little attention.

We found that these opposing leader roles were performed by different individuals and by the same individuals at different times during the innovation journey. These observations call attention to the importance of balance and timing in the performance of different leadership roles. Specifically, we proposed that *the likelihood of organizational learning and adaptability increases when a balance is maintained between the relative involvement of the sponsor, mentor, critic, and institutional leadership roles during the innovation journey.*

We argued that *the critic role may be most constructive in the early period of innovation development when ambiguity is high and investments have not accumulated beyond a threshold of "no return."* At this early stage, the critic role can be constructive in forcing sponsors and entrepreneurs to rethink and explore alternative plans and budget requests for launching their innovation. In other words, expression of the critic role early in a developmental process promotes experimentation and learning by discovery. Because resources and momentum toward a given course of action accumulate with time, the constructive influence of the critic role wanes with time. Deferred expression of the critic role until late in the developmental process promotes summative evaluations and terminations versus corrections for a course of action.

After the initial support that is needed to make an initial investment decision in an innovation project, *the roles of innovation sponsor and mentor become increasingly important with time during the innovation journey.* This is especially true in the middle of the innovation journey, when entrepreneurs most need support and coaching to address inevitable problems as they arise. The sponsor's role continues to increase in importance during the implementation period, when key decisions about structural realignments are often needed to integrate and link the innovation with strategic organizational directions and operations.

Finally, the institutional leader role balances the opposing views of the critic and sponsor or mentor. Over time, we propose that *the institutional leader's role is most critical at the beginning of an innovation to legitimate the venture's initial formation and investment and at the ending implementation period when institutional arrangements need to be established to implement the innovation.* During the middle period of the innovation journey, the institutional leader role is necessary only when irreconcilable conflicts surface between opposing critic and sponsor-mentor coalitions that may create stalemates, impeding further innovation development.

We believe these observations provide the key ingredients for a new theory of innovation leadership. Specifically, we propose that *innovation success increases when the dimensionality of leadership behaviors matches the dimensionality of the tasks undertaken.* This proposition is based on Conant and Ashby's (1970) principle of requisite variety, which argues that the internal capabilities of a social system should match the diverse requirements of its environment. A homogeneous structure of power and leadership appears more appropriate for leading convergent periods of the innovation journey. During convergent periods, innovation activities narrow in dimensionality and tend to focus on exploiting a given course of action. For these kinds of unidimensional tasks, unitary leadership may be most efficient and effective in reaching a clear objective. However, this traditional pattern of unitary leadership is too myopic to manage multidimensional activities.

During divergent periods of innovation discovery and exploration, learning and adaptability are enhanced when leaders reflect the multidimensional perspectives inherent in the activities being undertaken. During divergent periods of innovation development, a quest for consensus among leaders toward a single strategic vision appears neither correct empirically nor necessarily effective. Unidimensional leadership of multidimensional activities tends to squelch consideration of diverse and opposing viewpoints inherent in ambiguous tasks and often results in near-sightedness. Such myopic behavior occurs when leaders become strategically committed to and invest the "corporate treasury" in a course of action that in hindsight turns out to be wrong. As argued in chapter 4, multidimensional leadership behavior increases the chances for technological foresights and decreases the likelihood of oversights.

We noted, however, that pluralistic leadership does not ensure intelligent leadership. Learning to encourage, tolerate, and heedfully accommodate divergent leader roles and perspectives calls for a negotiational style of decision making by objection and constructive conflict resolution. Moreover, switching between multidimensional leadership of divergent activities and unidimensional leadership of convergent activities becomes a central challenge for leading the innovation cycle.

Divergent and Convergent Cycles in Relationships with Other Organizations

In addition to the temporal progressions in learning and leadership, we also observed spatial elaboration of divergent and convergent cycles in the developments of relationships among organizations in chapter 5 and at larger community and industry levels to develop an industrial infrastructure for technological innovation in chapter 6.

In chapter 5, we focused on how 3M engaged in a set of interorganizational relationships (IRs) to develop its cochlear implant innovation. We reported that the 3M CIP interorganizational relationships developed through two cycles of divergent and convergent activity periods. All the key terms of the relationships were designed and changed during the relatively brief divergent periods in each cycle. The divergent periods were times at which new understandings were negotiated and established about the nature of each dyadic relationship between 3M and other parties. These periods ended when agreements were reached that defined the nature of each relationship within some larger context. All the defining agreements between IRs occurred during these divergent periods. They set the stage for periods of convergent execution when agreements were carried out within the context of defined understandings.

The divergent and convergent periods of activities in the first cycle were qualitatively different from those in the second cycle. The first cycle focused on 3M's entering into new dyadic relationships with various organizations that then carried out their commitments through a period of incremental and productive interaction. In the second cycle these separate dyadic relationships became woven together into an interdependent web in which (1) actions in any one IR had significant implications for actions occurring in other IR dyads, and (2) these now-institutionalized relationships acted to constrain and direct responses to competitive demands.

The transition from the quasi-independent dyadic cycle to the interdependent web cycle produced unexpected and paradoxical developments. Cooperators became competitors, the competitors became collaborators, and the regulators became the mediators. Although these shifts were unintended or paradoxical to the parties engaged in each dyadic IR, they appeared mostly predictable when analyzing the dynamics from the broader perspective of an IR web.

Thus, *understanding and explaining how any one relationship unfolded over time required looking beyond that individual dyadic IR to the larger web of IRs in which the parties became involved.* The initially independent dyadic IRs that the parties negotiated, made commitments to, and executed during the first cycle became a spider's web of complex and interdependent network in the second cycle of the process. The analogy of the spider's web aptly captures the dynamic structure of emergent networks. Because all the links in a spider's web are structurally interconnected, the integrity of the web is a function of the sum of the individual links. Consequently, when one of the links is altered in some way, all the other links in the web are affected, especially those that are most proximal to the altered links. When one link constricts, the others stretch or break. When one of the links breaks, the others constrict to preserve the integrity of the web.

Divergent and Convergent Cycles in Building an Infrastructure for Innovation

As these IRs suggest, seldom does or can an individual entrepreneurial unit command the competence, resources, or legitimacy necessary to develop and commercialize its innovation alone. It turns out that the innovation journey will not likely achieve its desired destination if undertaken by a single entrepreneur; it entails a collective migration of numerous entrepreneurs. This collective effort resides not only within the parent organization of the innovation or just in the organization's web of IRs but also in the construction of an industrial infrastructure that both facilitates and constrains innovation.

Chapter 6 presented a social-system framework to define this infrastructure. It includes (1a) institutional arrangements to legitimate, regulate, and standardize a new technology; (2) public-resource endowments of basic scientific knowledge, financing mechanisms, and a pool of competent labor; (3) development of markets, consumer education, and demand; and (4) proprietary research and development, manufacturing, production, and distribution functions by private entrepreneurial firms to commercialize the innovation for profit. This framework requires taking a macroperspective of the innovation journey and focuses on the issues and events involved in the development of an industry infrastructure for innovation.

This social-system framework makes three contributions to understanding the innovation journey. First, an understanding of innovation is deficient if it focuses exclusively on the characteristics and behaviors of individual entrepreneurs and if it treats the social, economic, and political infrastructure for innovation as external factors that cannot be influenced. *Popular folklore notwithstanding, the innovation journey is a collective achievement requiring key roles from numerous entrepreneurs in both the public and private sectors.*

Second, we examined how this infrastructure emerges to commercialize technology and product innovations. This infrastructure does not emerge and change all at once by the actions of one or even a few key entrepreneurs. Instead, it emerges through the accretion of numerous institutional, resource, and proprietary events that influence each other over an extended period. Moreover, this accretion of events progresses through divergent and convergent cycles of development. *The very institutional arrangements and resource endowments created to facilitate industry emergence in the divergent phase tend, in the convergent phase, to become inertial forces that narrow and constrain subsequent technological development and adaptation by proprietary firms.* This generative process of divergent and convergent macroforces has a dynamic history that is important to understanding how novel forms of technologies, organizations, and institutions emerge.

The practical implications of this perspective suggest that *innovation managers must not only be concerned with microdevelopments of a proprietary technical device or product within their organization but also with the creation of a macroindustrial system, which embodies the social, economic, and political infrastructure that any technological community needs to sustain its members.* This leads to important practical questions of what roles each actor chooses to play and how their joint contributions interact to develop and commercialize a new technology. The social-system framework also sheds insights on how the risk, time, and cost to an individual entrepreneur are significantly influenced by developments in the overall industry infrastructure for innovation.

We proposed that the entrepreneurial firms that run in packs will be more successful than those that go it alone to develop their innovations. Conventional wisdom is that entrepreneurs act independently and compete to be the first into the market with their new product or service. There are many technologies and industries in which this may lead to successful monopoly profits. However, this practice may lead to unsuccessful results when the innovation involves a new technology for a new industry. Running in packs means that entrepreneurs coordinate (i.e., simultaneously cooperate and compete) with others as they develop and commercialize their innovation. Running in packs is analogous to bicycle racers who cue their pace to one another and take turns breaking wind resistance until the ending sprint.

The argument for running in packs emphasizes that the interests of entrepreneurial actors with a stake in a technological innovation are both convergent and divergent (Ben-Ner, 1993). The actors seek to maximize their total surplus and their respective shares in the surplus. The total surplus amounts to creating an industrial infrastructure that makes developing and commercializing a new technology for a new market collectively possible. This draws actors together and drives them to cooperate because no one actor has sufficient resources, competence, or legitimacy to do it alone. The goal of maximizing individual shares propels actors to compete with each other to reap monopoly profits that derive from introducing a dominant technology or product. However, enlightened entrepreneurs realize that the probability of economic survival from reaping monopoly shares of an orphan technology are much lower than from gaining relatively small shares of a larger and growing new industry.

Enlightened entrepreneurs may also be aware of the accumulating research evidence that the technological design of the first-mover often turns out *not* to become the dominant design that ultimately yields the greatest profits. This is because while striking out to be the first to introduce a new technology, the first-mover inevitably makes mistakes. And the followers, who are observing the practices of the first-mover, can make adjustments in their own technologies. As a result, after the first-mover has introduced the product in the market, the second-, third-, and fourth-movers, who have been carefully following the leader, can often and rapidly introduce a more significant, advanced, and better product or service. In short, there are strong economic motives for first-movers to run the innovation journey in packs, not alone.

Convergent and Divergent Cycles of Creative Destruction

The major theme that emerges from our analysis is that the innovation journey is a nonlinear cycle of divergent and convergent events that may recur over time and at different levels of organization. Nested cycles of divergent and convergent behaviors were evident in the developments of innovation team learning, organizational leadership, interorganizational relations, and industrial infrastructures. We believe this theme can be extended to apply to an even more macrolevel of economic development because it is directly compatible with Joseph Schumpeter's (1942) seminal ideas about entrepreneurship and discontinuous cycles of creative destruction.

Schumpeter proposed a dynamic evolutionary model of economic development. The model emphasizes that innovations come from within the economic system—not merely from random variations to external changes (Hagedoorn, 1989). He linked macroeconomic dynamics with microentrepreneurial processes. Schumpeter observed that innovations produced by entrepreneurs at the microlevel occur discontinuously and bring about qualitative changes or "revolutions" that fundamentally displace convergent equilibria and create radically divergent macroeconomic conditions (Elliott, 1983). As viewed by Marshallian economists, Schumpeter allowed for economic growth as a continuous stream of small changes adapting to "demographic data" from the economic system (Awan, 1986). But he explicitly distinguished this economic growth from economic development as a difference between convergent equilibrium and divergent revolutions. In his own words:

> Development . . . is entirely foreign to what may be observed in the circular flow or in the tendency towards equilibrium. It is a spontaneous and discontinuous change in the channels of the flow, disturbance of equilibrium, which forever alters and displaces the equilibrium state previously existing. . . . Add successively as many mail coaches as you please, and you will never get a railway thereby. (Schumpeter, 1942: 64)

In striking parallel with Karl Marx, Schumpeter proposed a dialectical theory that explained why economic development proceeds cyclically rather than evenly because innovations appear discontinuously in groups or swarms (Elliott, 1983). Schumpeter's theory reflects cycles of divergent and convergent development, as is represented in a "punctuated equilibrium" model (Gould, 1989; Tushman and Romanelli, 1985) or a model of partial cumulative synthesis, originally proposed by Usher (1954).

This theory is exemplified by entrepreneurs, financed by capitalists who strike out, often in competition with other, like-minded entrepreneurs, to introduce new innovations. If successful, these innovations provide opportunities to reap extraordinary profits for a temporary period. Imitators follow, and an avalanche of consumer goods pours onto the market, which dampen prices, profit margins, and innovation investments. This in turn forces reorganization of production, greater efficiency, lower costs, the elimination of inefficient noninnovating firms, and the replacement of old products and processes with new ones.

This "perennial gale of creative destruction" (Schumpeter, 1942: 85) explains macroeconomic development as cyclical fluctuations produced by discontinuous bursts of microlevel processes of entrepreneurship and innovation investment. Because monopoly profits are temporary, the process of "creative destruction" benefits society through the introduction of new products or processes. In addition, the extraordinary profits realized by the innovative firm will be a source of funds for the next round of innovation in the original industry and elsewhere. However, depressions or recessions are a normal part of this cyclical process and are produced by adaptations to the bunching of innovations during the preceding period of prosperity.

As a theory of economic development, Schumpeter's formulation is an impressive achievement. The *engine* of this theory is innovation, which Schumpeter *uses* to explain how and why economic development evolves cyclically through gales of creative destruction. We believe this engine consists of a nonlinear cycle of divergent and convergent behaviors that are enabled by resource investments and organizational structuring and constrained by external institutional rules and internally chosen directions.

Concluding Observations

Let us imagine that the innovation journey is like an uncharted river:

> Most people are clinging to the bank, afraid to let go and risk being carried along by the current of the river. At a certain point, each person must be willing to simply let go, and trust the river to carry him or her along safely. At this point he learns to "go with the flow" and it feels wonderful.
>
> Once he has gotten used to being in the flow of the river, he can begin to look ahead and guide his own course onward, deciding where the course looks best, steering his way around boulders and snags, and choosing which of the many channels and branches of the river he prefers to follow, all the while still "going with the flow." (Quinn, 1988: 164)

This metaphor is helpful to make three concluding observations.

First, just as it is useful to become familiar with the river before trying to maneuver it, we have focused on mapping the innovation journey before prescribing how to manage it. Unfortunately, popular management writers tend to offer prescriptions for innovation journeys that do not exist or that have little empirical grounding. *We believe our major contribution has been to develop an empirically grounded model of the innovation journey that captures the messy and complex progressions observed in the innovation cases studied by the MIRP researchers.*

Many innovation journeys remain uncharted; hence, further research is necessary to generalize and compare our findings with other innovations. However, among the diverse innovations that were charted by MIRP researchers, we can say that although innovation journeys can follow many different paths and outcomes, the underlying pattern is remarkably alike. We cut a wide swath to examine the innovations—from a microanalysis of individual creativity to a macrostudy of industry infrastructure for innovation. Through it all, we see a repetitive pattern. *The innovation journey is a nonlinear cycle of divergent and convergent behaviors that may repeat itself over time and reflect itself at different organizational levels.* We found the divergent and convergent cycle to be the underlying dynamic pattern in developing a corporate culture for innovation, learning within the innovation teams, leadership behaviors of top managers or investors, building relationships with other organizations, and developing an industrial infrastructure for innovations. Figure 7.1 summarizes the core elements of the innovation journey by indicating the characteristics of divergent (left column) and convergent (right column) behaviors in cycles of learning, leadership, relationships, and infrastructure development.

Second, charting how the innovation journey actually unfolds provides a solid empirical foundation for guiding future research and practice on managing the innovation process. This chapter explored some of the implications of our major empirical finding that the innovation journey consists of a nonlinear cycle of divergent and convergent behaviors. It requires us to question and reexamine much of what we think we know about managing innovation. Finding nonlinear dynamics tells us that the innovation journey, particularly during divergent periods, is neither stable and predictable nor stochastic and random; that unpredictable and ambiguous behavior does not imply randomness; that the innovation journey may be sensitive to different initial conditions (path dependence); and that managing divergent behavior may be much more complex than managing convergent behavior. We believe that our propositions just scratch the surface of potentially important new principles that we and others may develop for managing the innovation journey.

Finally, *our concluding prescription is that innovation managers are to go with the flow—although we can learn to maneuver the innovation journey, we cannot control it.* The journey entails maneuvering through stretches of divergent and convergent waters. In divergent waters the river branches and expands in multiple dimensions and flows in chaotic or random patterns. Maneuvering these stretches entails divergent search, learning by discovery, pluralistic leadership, and running in packs with others to create new relationships and institutions for collective survival. Occasionally the river converges in a particular direction and flows in a more orderly periodic pattern. Many familiar principles of rational management are useful for maneuvering and exploiting these stretches, including implementing strategic goals, trial-and-error learning, unitary leadership, and executing agreements within established institutions for competitive advantage.

Maneuvering transitions between divergent and convergent flows are particularly problematic for two reasons. First, just when people gain some comfort and skill in going with a convergent flow, the innovation river may transition again into a divergent pattern that requires very different managerial skills. As a result, maneuvering the entire innovation journey requires developing ambidextrous management skills. Second, like a river, the paths of these transitions are often unpredictable and beyond the control of those floating down the uncharted river. However, unlike a river, innovation leaders and investors can intervene and place boundaries on divergent and convergent patterns. As figure 7.1 illustrates, resource investments and organizational structuring enable undertaking the innovation journey, while external institutional rules and internal focus constrain the boundaries of cycles in this journey.

PART II

CASES IN DIFFERENT ORGANIZATIONAL SETTINGS

Part II of the book presents the three cases that were used as examples to ground the divergent-convergent cycle model of innovation developed in part I. The three innovation cases reflect efforts to create new businesses in three different organizational settings.

- The first case is an internal venture within a large diversified corporation (3M) to develop the Cochlear Implant Program. CIP was undertaken to create a totally new business by developing a line of new product, including cochlear implants, hearing aid, and otological diagnostic instruments for the hearing health industry.
- The second case, the Therapeutic Apheresis Program, is a joint interorganizational venture between 3M, Sarns, and Millipore Corporations. TAP was undertaken to create a new biomedical products and diagnostics instruments business for treating a variety of diseases by separating pathogenic substances from blood and returning the beneficial blood components to the patient. Both CIP and TAP represent new-to-the-world technologies and products, and both were major long-term investments and commitments to create totally new businesses that were expected to generate significant revenues in ten to fifteen years for the corporations involved.
- The third case examines innovation and new business creation in a new company start-up, called Qnetics, Inc. In efforts to become a financially viable company, Qnetics pursued a variety of new business creation effort during its nine-year existence. They include a computer distributor and maintenance business, a custom-design computer software business, a line of medical software

products on patient and financial records for hospitals and third-party payors, and an electrical load management hardware and software business for the power utilities industry.

We examine the benefits and liabilities to developing innovative businesses in these different structural arrangements. Because these benefits and liabilities often compensate for one another, it is not clear at the onset which organizational arrangement is more appropriate for undertaking the innovation journey.

We draw two major conclusions from comparisons of the three cases. First, the innovation journeys in the three organizational settings follow a similar pattern of divergent and convergent cycles of behavior. Second, the rich detail in the cases also reveal variations in the process model that can be attributed to the different organizational settings. However, we view these as variations in degrees, not in substantive characteristics of the innovation journey.

These comparative findings are important because they suggest that the core processes of innovation are fundamentally the same across very different organizational structures and settings. If supported in subsequent studies, the findings call attention to the significant benefits that could be obtained by integrating principles for managing innovation and entrepreneurship from new company start-ups, internal corporate venturing, and interorganizational joint ventures. To date, these areas have been treated as distinct and noncomparable areas of practice. However, in terms of the process of innovation, they may be highly complementary.

Organizational Structures for Innovative Business Creation

Conventional wisdom attributes a significantly higher rate of innovation per technical employee to the smaller firm than to the larger firm. A study of innovation by the U.S. Department of Commerce (Charpie, 1967) called attention to this disparity. Gellman (1976) confirmed this by examining 635 innovations that reached the marketplace. The study found that small firms (fewer than 500 employees) produce 2.5 times as many innovations as large firms per employee, and that small firms bring their innovations to market 27% more rapidly than large firms. (No study was found that includes interorganizational joint ventures in these comparisons.)

Goldman (1985) notes that the proliferation of successful high technology companies nurtured by an explosive venture capital market widens the disparity between large and small firms in innovation rate. The irony in this trend is that in the early postwar U.S. economy, it was generally assumed that the proclivity to innovate was fed by the industrial R&D establishments that tended to be highly concentrated in large firms.

Why are small firms more innovative than large firms? The common answer is that small firms are more flexible and quicker to adapt to changing environmental opportunities and threats than larger organizations. Large firms experience greater bureaucratic forces of inertia due to their "liabilities of aging and bigness." However, this explanation ignores a corresponding set of "liabilities of newness and small size" that small businesses must surmount in order to survive and be innovative.

Liabilities of newness include both internal and external obstacles that make survival difficult (Stinchcombe, 1965). Aldrich and Auster (1986: 177–179) and Schoonhoven and Eisenhardt (1986) point out that barriers to entry into a new domain are the major external obstacles for new firms, including (1) product differentiation, (2) technological barriers, (3) licensing and regulatory barriers, (4) problems of vertical integration, (5) illegitimate acts of competitors, and (6) lack of experience. New organizations also face internal obstacles, including the creation and clarification of roles and structures consistent with external constraints, along with the ability to attract qualified employees and managerial talent.

In addition to these liabilities of newness, many new organizations also face *liabilities of smallness*, including (1) problems of raising capital, (2) tax laws pertaining to normal income versus capital gains work against the survival of small organizations, (3) government regulations that place a proportionately higher overhead cost on small than on large firms, (4) major disadvantages in competing for labor with larger organizations, and (5) limited abilities to obtain benefits from specialization and economies of scale.

These liabilities of newness and small size may be more difficult to overcome than the liabilities of aging and bigness. As a result, one should expect the success probabilities of new business creation to be lower in new small firms than in larger and more mature firms. Aldrich and Auster (1986) and Singh, Tucker, and House (1986) review the empirical evidence showing that older and larger organizations have a substantial advantage over younger and smaller organizations in terms of not being decimated and replaced. New, small organizations fail at disproportionately higher rates than do older and larger organizations. Moreover, of those that survive and grow old, the vast majority of firms (75% according to Reynolds and West, 1985) remain small "mom and pop shops" throughout their existence.

As suggested, older and larger organizations must deal with a different set of liabilities of aging and bigness, which lead to organizational inertia and make them increasingly less fit for changing environments. Aldrich and Auster (1986: 183) point out that "the obstacles faced by new, small organizations can be easily overcome by larger, more established organizations, whereas the constraints faced by larger, more established organizations can often be easily surmounted by new, small organizations." In a similar vein, Williamson (1975) argues that while new company start-ups may be especially good at developing new innovations, large corporations are better at introducing and marketing new products into the market.

The joint interorganizational venture, being an intermediate form of organization to that of new small and old large firms, may provide a more conducive environment for new business creation. In theory, it can over-come the liabilities of newness, small size, aging, and bigness. The new-ness and small size of a joint venture promotes flexibility and minimizes bureaucratic forces of inertia, while the competence, resource base, and institutional legitimacy of the large mature parent organizations help the joint venture overcome the liabilities of newness and smallness. By this logic, the joint interorganizational venture should be more conducive to innovation and business creation than new company start-ups or internal corporate venturing.

However, this conclusion does not consider the problems endemic to joint interorganizational ventures, which we will label, "the liabilities of double parenting and conflict." The problems in managing joint ventures largely stem from having more than one parent organization, who "often disagree on just about anything: How fast should the joint venture grow? Which products and markets should it encompass? How should it be orga-nized? What constitutes good and bad management?" (Killing, 1982:121). Harrigan (1985: 36) adds to this list the problems of antitrust, sovereign conflicts, losses of autonomy and control, and loss of competitive advan-tage through strategic inflexibility. As a consequence, joint ventures have a high overall failure rate, and many of the failures are very costly for the partner companies.

This brief review suggests that no clear conclusions can or should be drawn about the comparative merits of alternative organizational arrange-ments for innovation and business creation. While each organizational set-ting has its potential benefits, each also is exposed to unique liabilities. The rich and detailed longitudinal studies of CIP, TAP, and Qnetics provide an opportunity to address these arguments about the comparative benefits and liabilities of alternative organizational structural arrangements of in-novation and new business creation.

Unfortunately, the three cases are not ideal for comparison. CIP and TAP are directly comparable because they each represent new-to-the-world biomedical business creation efforts that are subject to the regulated FDA review and approval process. Although also involved in the health care in-dustry, Qnetics business creation efforts were not subject to FDA regula-tions to develop and commercialize its innovative medical records soft-ware business. Hauptman and Roberts (1985) found that regulatory constraints significantly influence the formation and growth of biomedical and pharmaceutical start-ups. Keeping this caveat in mind, it is neverthe-less instructive to systematically compare the business creation processes that unfolded in the three cases.

The Nature of New Business Creation

Creating a new *business* is more encompassing than *product* innovation and more proprietary than *technological* innovation. Creating a business usually entails developing and organizing all the functions necessary to exploit a technological invention into a family of related proprietary products, which, if successful, constitute a self-sustaining, ongoing economic enterprise. Seldom can a business achieve commercial viability with a single product in the marketplace. An ongoing business requires the creation of synergy and economies of scale across functions, which are obtained from developing and applying functional competencies (i.e., R&D, testing, manufacturing, marketing, and service) in creating a family of related products and services over time. Thus, a description of the business creation process entails making statements about (1) how a business idea (or strategy) emerges over time, (2) when and how different functional competencies are created to develop and market the first proprietary product, (3) when and how these functional competencies are redeployed to develop subsequent new products in a family of products that may sustain the business, and (4) how these business development efforts both influence and are constrained by organizational and industry contexts.

Timely orchestration of resources along interdependent functions is needed to develop each product, and redeployment of these functional resources to subsequent generations of products become two key challenges for business managers.

The first challenge is typical of any single product innovation effort. If it is true that functions tend to be established sequentially for the first generation of products, then each preceding functional step becomes a "bottleneck" for succeeding steps in the product development sequence. Errors not detected in preceding steps are passed along to the next functional step. The consequence is that these errors may either compound developmental work for subsequent functions (or at the extreme result in market recalls, if undetected) and may entail costly revisions in all functional steps of the product development cycle.

The new business creation challenge is more complicated because it involves developing a family of product innovations. Here another set of "bottlenecks" arise in redeploying resources and attention from one product to the next generation of products. When a functional step is completed in a preceding product, those specialized resources are freed up and must be redeployed or they remain idle. These specialized resources are usually reassigned to begin similar functional work on the next generation of products.

Each product generation involves its own unique mix of required skills, interdependent processes, and development timetable. However, a business typically does not have that mix of skills required for a new product.

Instead, it has the mix of skills and resources that it learned and used for the last product development effort. Thus, without significant retraining and "retooling," simple redeployment of specialized resources to the next product when the prior one is completed invariably results in replicating the previous product development effort and compromising the design specifications and timetable for the new generation product. Alternatively, the excitement and timetable for a new generation product may result in a "flee" from the predecessor product without adequate completion or market exploitation.

Accumulation Model of New Business Creation

An *accumulation* model of change (as described by Etzioni, 1963) was helpful to study the process of business creation in CIP, TAP, and Qnetics. This model views change as springing from the business ideas and purposeful behavior of entrepreneurs. Over time, these entrepreneurs accumulate the external resources and technology necessary to transform their ideas into a concrete reality by constructing a new business unit that produces outputs (a marketable family of products and services), which, if successful, eventually sustain the business as an ongoing economic enterprise.

Initiation, start-up, and takeoff are key temporal periods in this accumulation process. *Initiation* is the time when entrepreneurs decide to form a business venture (if successfully launched it becomes the birthday of the business) and *takeoff* is the time when the unit can do without the external support of its initiators and continue growing "on its own." The period between initiation and takeoff could be called *start-up*, where the new unit must draw its resources, competencies, and technology from the founding leaders and external sources in order to develop the proprietary products, create a market niche, and meet the institutional standards established to legitimate the new business as an ongoing economic enterprise.

The process of accumulation is like that of an airplane that first starts its engines and begins rolling, still supported by the runway, until it accumulates enough momentum to "take off," and continue in motion "on its own" energy to carry it to higher altitudes and speeds. While relying initially on external support, the necessary conditions for autonomous action are produced through a process of accumulation (Etzioni, 1963).

As applied to business creation, we should expect to observe cycles of initiation, start-up, and takeoff for each of the multiple components and products that may constitute the business. As a consequence, the overall business creation process may be nested with multiple, overlapping, and iterative progressions of initiation, start-up, and takeoff activities of various business components. Some of these components or products that are initiated may not startup, and some start-ups may not takeoff; and takeoffs in one component may facilitate or inhibit the initiation, start-up, or takeoff of other components. Hence, an understanding of overall business takeoff requires study of the interactions among business components and their relationships with external sources of support and resistance.

The accumulation model directs attention to three basic questions that guided study of the business creation process in CIP, TAP, and Qnetics.

1. *Where are the resources and power located that control the business creation process?* From the initiation to start-up to takeoff periods, the relative power (resources and control) shifts from external to internal sources in the accumulation model. For example, whereas outside investors or corporate managers may largely control the resources and set the direction to initiate a new business, the innovation unit entrepreneurs/managers should increasingly gain power and control of the process during the start-up period, culminating at takeoff with all the resources and power necessary for the new business to operate on its own. This implies that both internal and external groups govern the business start-up period and that a central dynamic of this period is the transition in power from external to internal groups. When the business creation process proceeds smoothly and according to plan, this transition may be uneventful. However, since business creation is a highly uncertain process, mistakes and setbacks usually occur, and power struggles often erupt between external and internal groups on the appropriate actions to take to continue the business creation cycle. Resolutions to these struggles may entail confusing, contradictory, and abrupt shifts in business development.

As a consequence, the process of new business start-up often tends to reflect the period of rupture and discontinuous change, as described by a punctuated equilibrium model of change (Tushman and Romanelli, 1985). If the innovation unit surmounts these business start-up hurdles by the takeoff period, activities in the accumulation model begin to reflect the convergent period of continuous change and increasing business refinements in the punctuated equilibrium model.

2. *What is the temporal sequence in the development of various business components and products?* This question examines how and which business ideas, functional competencies, and technological products were developed and introduced first, second, and so on. How did they affect subsequent developments of business components? These questions deal with the progression of paths followed in the development of a new business. Van den Daele (1968, 1974) provides a useful vocabulary for examining whether unitary or multiple paths of divergent, parallel, and convergent progressions were followed, and if these paths of activities were conjunctive (i.e., related), iterative (i.e., repetitive), or structured (i.e., hierarchically nested and overlapping). Examining these paths leads to an appreciation of the timing, momentum, and resource allocation conditions where the takeoff of one component or product may facilitate, preempt, or exhaust the initiation of other new business components and products.

3. *What outcomes are associated with different paths and progressions?* Given that the business creation process is inherently uncertain, we should expect many trials and errors, as witnessed by multiple divergent paths leading to dead ends, stalemates, and terminations over time. Moreover, study of outcomes leads to further investigation of how learning from previous paths might provide guidance in identifying the next paths that are taken to create the business. Timing and momentum in these business development paths are important for examining the success of these paths (Etzioni, 1963: 490). In general, the longer the development of each path and the more dispersed the resources among business development paths during the start-up period, the lower the overall market awareness and interest in the new business venture, and the more difficult it is to mobilize commitments from investors and potential key suppliers and customers. By contrast, if the start-up period for one or more business components is too fast and concentrated, there may be insufficient time during start-up to learn and build requisite competencies, develop quality products, or build the momentum needed for market penetration and new venture takeoff. As the principle of "moderation in all things" would suggest, we hypothesize that the probability of successful business takeoff increases with intermediate amounts of time, momentum, and focus that are invested in business initiation and start-up activities.

These process questions, which guided the development of the CIP, TAP, and Qnetics cases, are related in terms of an input-transformation-output model from systems theory. The first question examines system inputs in terms of the resources and power that a new business draws from its external environment in the initiation period, and how power shifts from external to internal groups during the start-up period. At any given time, the ideas, competencies, and products produced by the new business can be viewed as system outcomes (the third question). Finally, the processes of transforming inputs into outputs are addressed by the second question, in terms of the progressions in which ideas, competencies, and products develop.

The Innovation Journey within an Internal Corporate Structure

The 3M Cochlear Implant Case

This case describes efforts by the Cochlear Implant Program (CIP) at 3M Corporation in St. Paul, Minnesota, to develop a family of cochlear implants and hearing aids. Cochlear implants are surgically implanted electronic devices that provide the profoundly deaf a sensation of sound (see illustration in figure 8.1). Hearing aids facilitate hearing in less severely impaired deaf patients by amplifying sound.

The CIP was part of the Health Care Specialties division, which was a part of the Health Care Specialties group of 3M's Life Science Sector (see organization chart in figure 8.2). Sales revenue of the life Sciences Sector was $1.4 billion in 1985. At its most active stages, the CIP consisted of about fifty full-time people and was managed by a steering committee consisting of nine functional managers and a program director. The steering committee met once a month to review and make strategic decisions.

Minnesota Innovation Research Program (MIRP) researchers began real-time study of the CIP in December 1983. Data collection included observations at monthly meetings of the CIP steering committee, semi-annual interviews with CIP managers, surveys by CIP personnel, annual interviews with 3M top managers, company records, published materials about industry developments and attendance at major ontological trade conferences. From these data, we constructed a chronological list of events that is presented in the appendix to this chapter.

Several generations of program managers and team members led the program over CIP's eleven-year duration from 1978 to 1989. Transitions in program management occurred in 1985 and 1987 because the program repeatedly failed to meet milestones that the managers had set

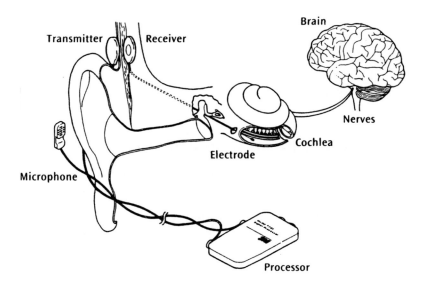

Figure 8.1 The technical components of a cochlear implant device.

for themselves and for the program. Each time a new program manager was appointed, the direction of the program was changed and new milestones were set.

Figure 8.3 summarizes responses of key CIP members to a survey administered six times between February 1985 and October 1987. Program members' perceptions of their own effectiveness was least favorable during a survey conducted in January 1986; interviews uncovered low morale because the program had suffered major setbacks. However, program members also reported demonstrating resilience in their efforts to overcome these setbacks. For the most part, though, members felt that the CIP offered 3M one of the few long-term opportunities. Consequently, an overall sentiment was that 3M would continue funding the CIP despite its setbacks.

Top managers overseeing the CIP, however, offered conflicting opinions about the CIP. In 1985 and again in 1986, one top manager, playing the critic role, expressed reservations about the CIP. This executive felt that the CIP was one of the most risky programs of the thirty-five new ventures he was overseeing. Another top manager, the sponsor of the business idea, expressed strong support for the program. He maintained that, in contrast to venture capitalists, 3M wanted to fund programs that might become self-sustaining division-sized businesses in about ten years. A third member of the top management team, the institutional leader, did not express either of the extreme views expressed by the other two top managers.

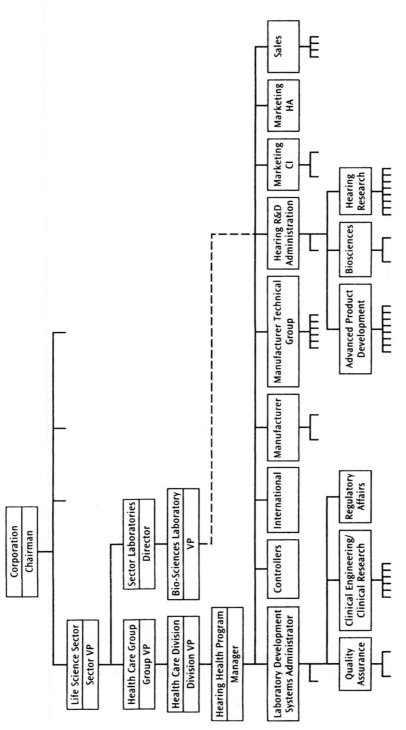

Figure 8.2 CIP organization chart, March 1987

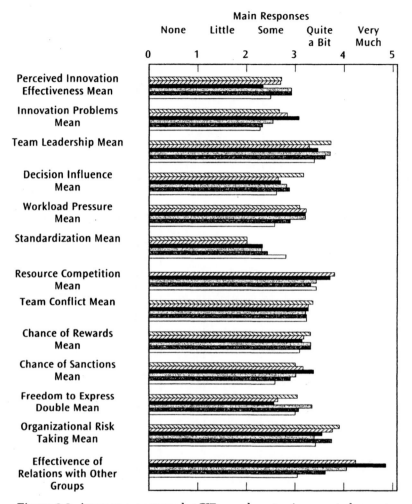

Figure 8.3 Average responses by CIP members to six repeated surveys at times: 1 (2/85, top bars), 2 (6/85), 3 (1/86), 4 (8/86), 5 (2/87), and 6 (9/87, bottom bars)

This case describes the complex innovation journey of the CIP in terms of its development of single-channel and multiple-channel devices, followed by reviews of program strategy. It also explores how the CIP developed a children's device and diversified its business to include hearing aids and diagnostics. The case ends with an analysis of the CIP's development process in terms of (1) temporal progressions, (2) resource acquisition and allocation, and (3) risk, persistence, and learning.

Cochlear Implant Program Initiation

In 1977, the technical director of 3M St. Paul's surgical laboratories was informed that 3M's subsidiary company in Australia had been approached by the University of Melbourne for a possible collaborative relationship to commercially develop a "bionic ear." This electronic device, one that would allow the profoundly deaf a sensation of sound, was an outcome of more than ten years of research conducted by Graeme Clark and his colleagues at the University of Melbourne, Australia. Besides 3M, the University of Melbourne had approached two other business firms to find a suitable industrial partner for the commercial development of the artificial ear.

Preliminary evaluations at 3M St. Paul suggested that the bionic ear project could be very promising; at a price of $1,000 per device, the U.S. market alone could be worth $100 million. The evaluation report also suggested that the first company to commercialize a device could possibly dominate the market, as had been the case in the pacemaker industry. Encouraged by these findings, 3M executives informed the University of Melbourne researchers of their interest to further explore the proposal. At the same time, 3M executives embarked on a systematic search for other research institutes and organizations in the United States engaged in the development of the cochlear implant technology.

By 1978, the idea of an "electronic ear" had gained sufficient credibility to persuade 3M's technical director and his supervisor to commit resources. The idea to explore development of a cochlear implant was assigned to an "unrelated products group" in 3M. About this time, two other groups within 3M were also conducting preliminary work on cochlear implants and related products such as hearing aids. One group was located in the biosciences laboratory. This group hired a full-time scientist in 1979 to start up a research program in hearing and speech in 1979. At first, program members intended to focus on the development of hearing aids. However, considering the level of competition and lacking a strong patent position on hearing aids, program members decided to shift their attention to the development of cochlear implants. The other group involved in hearing health products was an acquisitions group within 3M. In 1979, this group looked into the commercial viability of entering the hearing health care industry by acquiring a firm manufacturing hearing health products.

In their search for organizations conducting cochlear implant–related activities, 3M program members first contacted Audiotronics California Corporation (ACC), a small start-up company engaged in the development of implantable medical prostheses. Two principal shareholders of ACC were Melvin C. Bartz, an engineer who had worked previously with Beckman Instruments, and Robin P. Michelson, professor of otolaryngology at the University of California San Francisco Medical School (UCSF). ACC had been supplying cochlear implant parts to the House Ear Institute (House) and UCSF and had been developing cochlear devices on the basis of designs originating from the Coleman Laboratories at UCSF. Encountering financial difficulties, ACC wanted to sell off its operations.

On the basis of information from ACC, 3M researchers visited House and UCSF laboratories in March 1978. At House, they met with William House, who had implanted twenty-three patients with his single-channel device. House and his colleagues had initiated developmental and clinical research with a multichannel device in 1961 but had switched over to a single-channel device because the results achieved with the multichannel device had not been very encouraging. House felt that a substantial amount of research would first have to be carried out with the single-channel device before multichannel devices could be taken up for commercial development.

At UCSF, 3M researchers met with Michelson and his colleagues. Researchers at UCSF were in the process of implanting their first multichannel device as the single-channel device that they had so far implanted had not demonstrated satisfactory results. Cochlear implant research was carried out at Coleman Laboratories, which was affiliated with the department of otolaryngology at UCSF. Michelson, an auditory physiologist, directed the cochlear implant efforts at Coleman Laboratories.

While 3M initiated its search of cochlear implant technology in the United States, it simultaneously entered into a confidentiality agreement with the University of Melbourne to evaluate its technology. Graeme Clark informed 3M of the encouraging results that researchers at the University of Melbourne had observed with the recently implanted multichannel device and offered 3M circuit diagrams and samples for its evaluation. In the latter part of 1978, 3M and the University of Melbourne researchers exchanged visits.

University of Melbourne researchers were keen to finalize an agreement with 3M as soon as possible. At the same time, they were being persuaded by the Australian Department of Productivity to accept financial support from the department in exchange for an agreement to develop and manufacture the device in Australia. In October 1978, after weighing all the pros and cons, 3M informed University of Melbourne researchers that it would not be willing to underwrite the research and development (R&D) expenses of the Melbourne device. The university had projected an expenditure of 300,000 Australian dollars (A$) to develop the second-generation device based on an expenditure of A$500,000 incurred on the project from its inception. Two factors influenced 3M's decision. First, the Australian proposal did not indicate a strong patent position and was somewhat vague about exclusive rights after investments by 3M. Second, the geographical distance involved between the United States and Australia could potentially create a problem in the commercial development of the device.

Although 3M had decided not to fund the Australian device, it showed an interest in negotiating nonexclusive rights to the Australian device and associated technical information. The University of Melbourne declined 3M's offer. Accepting 3M's offer of partial support would necessitate searching for additional funds for its R&D activities — possibly from the Australian Department of Productivity.

Unable to consummate a mutually acceptable relationship with 3M, the University of Melbourne accepted a grant of A$400,00 from the Australian Department of Productivity in February 1979 to develop a detailed plan to establish joint public–private-sector cooperative manufacturing capabilities in Australia. In September 1980, the Australian government released additional funds for further developmental work and commissioned an Australian company, Nucleus Ltd., to undertake feasibility studies. By July 1981, the University of Melbourne had formally entered into a collaborative agreement with Nucleus Ltd. to develop its cochlear implant. For its part, 3M wrote to the University of Melbourne that its "door would be open" for exploring any future interaction with the Australian team.

In January 1979, a 3M biosciences laboratory scientist visited House, ACC, UCSF, and Stanford to gather more information about single- and multiple-channel cochlear devices. Based on this trip, the scientist came to the conclusion that the UCSF multichannel device was superior to the other two for both present and future applications. UCSF researchers had recorded encouraging results with the multichannel device. They were convinced that patients should not be implanted with the single-channel device as it might be difficult to upgrade. In comparison to the UCSF device, the House design was empirically based and simpler, not founded on a priori scientific knowledge and theory. It appeared that House would not have the capabilities to develop its own multichannel system in the future.

On the basis of this trip, program members at 3M came to the conclusion that the ACC approach to multichannel stimulation appeared to be reasonable as an initial choice for 3M. The overall approach was to buy rights to ACC's cochlear device, retain Bartz and Michelson as consultants, and supply UCSF with cochlear implant parts that had previously been supplied by ACC. By supplying UCSF with electrodes, 3M hoped to gain a better understanding of the most suitable electrode configuration and speech processing system without having to commit to a formal agreement with UCSF. The group at 3M also decided to evaluate the value of 3M getting involved with a single-channel device with House in more depth.

With this objective, 3M drafted a proposal to acquire patent rights owned by Bartz and Michelson and to retain both as consultants for the purpose of bringing 3M up to speed in building electrodes and electronics similar to the ones being supplied to the UCSF. In June 1979, 3M wrote to Merzenich at Coleman Laboratories indicating an interest in building multichannel electrodes for human implantation by Michelson and his group at the otolaryngology department at UCSF. Merzenich had received grants from the National Institutes of Health (NIH) to conduct research on multichannel devices. 3M suggested that Merzenich set aside a portion of the NIH grant money as a subcontract to manufacture the electrodes. 3M stated that it would not be interested in assigning to NIH the rights of patents that could result from developmental work carried out within 3M for Coleman Laboratories.

Soon thereafter, 3M executives visited Coleman Laboratories to discuss details of the offer that they had made. Merzenich wanted Coleman Laboratories to engage in research and 3M to function as a facility for clinical testing, conducting experiments for Coleman Laboratories (and therefore for the NIH). In contrast, 3M wanted to become involved in developmental activities. 3M and the otolaryngology department at UCSF eventually entered into a vendor agreement in June 1979. 3M's subsidiary, McGhan Medical located at Santa Barbara, would supply UCSF with electrodes. At the same time, in December 1979, 3M entered into contractual agreements with Bartz and Michelson for the assignment of all proprietary information owned by ACC. 3M also purchased two cochlear implant patents owned by Beckman and retained Bartz and Michelson as consultants. However, 3M did not retain Merzenich in any capacity.

Though 3M had been successful in entering into a vendor relationship with UCSF, 3M engineers encountered some difficulties in supplying promised UCSF electrodes as their complexity rendered them difficult to fabricate. When electrodes and cochlear implant parts did become available, 3M offered them first to Michelson, thereby upsetting Merzenich. Merzenich felt that 3M had not adequately recognized his talents. Merzenich felt that he had offered key inputs to the development of the new electrode designs and other physiological approaches but had not been included in the consulting agreements into which 3M had entered with Michelson and Bartz. Moreover, Merzenich identified key differences in approaches between Michelson and himself. Merzenich said that he would not be interested in interacting with 3M as long as 3M dealt with Michelson and followed his physiological approaches. Convinced that 3M would not be able to supply him with the contractually promised electrodes, Merzenich established his own electrode manufacturing laboratory with help from Biostim. At the same time, Merzenich denied 3M access to speech testing facilities and new technologies being developed at Coleman Laboratories. Assessing the situation on February 1981, 3M's biosciences laboratory manager stated:

> I am convinced that we have lost the opportunity to work with Coleman Laboratories. By signing only with Bartz and Michelson over a year ago and disregarding the talents of Coleman Laboratories, we did not create an optimal situation for collaboration. The lack of delivery of promised electrodes has led to UCSF developing its own manufacturing facilities—with the help of Biostim. Not only have we lost access to the multi-electrode system at UCSF, but we have lost access to the human evaluation system at UCSF as this had been developed with Coleman Laboratories. It saddens me to realize that we have made less progress than Coleman Laboratories on the development of the multi-electrode system.

Though 3M had lost access to activities at Coleman Laboratories, 3M continued to interact with Michelson and his team and continued to have access to multichannel clinical activities at UCSF's otolaryngology department.

As these events were unfolding between 3M and UCSF, 3M entered into a confidentiality agreement with House to evaluate House's single-channel technology in more depth. Some people within 3M were becoming concerned that 3M's delay in finalizing a deal with House could cost 3M the opportunity to develop House's single-channel technology. One engineer who had spent one year in residence at House stated:

> I am afraid that our delay in developing the single-channel system leaves us very vulnerable to competition. The best experts estimate 3 to 5 years before multichannel systems will be available. Even with the multichannel system, there will be a need for single-channel devices. House needs technical help and has asked 3M. There is a real danger in that while concentrating on electrode and multichannel system development we are passing up a golden opportunity in single-channel systems.

3M's technical director, who had been instrumental in the initiation of the program efforts, too, had misgivings about 3M's interactions with House. In 1978, the technical director had been transferred to California to direct McGhan Medical Products, a 3M subsidiary. McGhan Medical expressed its willingness to supply cochlear implant parts to House to alleviate House's problems in obtaining cochlear implant parts, while 3M decided whether to pursue a more encompassing agreement with House. In June 1979, 3M McGhan Medical received a formal purchase order from House for the supply of 100 sets of cochlear implant stimulators and internal coils.

As with UCSF, 3M encountered difficulties in fulfilling its commitments to House, which included (1) the miniaturization of House's stimulator unit, (2) the development of a magnet system, and (3) tank testing of the basic implant. House therefore began a search for another company that could carry out the engineering developmental changes it desired. House was anxious to expand his clinical study to as many patients as he could through his co-investigators, though he wanted to proceed more slowly in the commercialization of his unit. One member of the innovation team at 3M stated in September 1980: "It seems that a decision is necessary now if we wish to continue to work with House. Follow the present course and we will probably lose them."

Clearly, 3M had to make some choices and commit itself to some group. House wanted to continue refining his single-channel unit and was not particularly interested in exploring other approaches to a better multielectrode device. Michelson, by contrast, felt that animal data had established the superiority of multielectrode cochlear devices over single-channel devices and saw no point in pursuing the latter approach. Moreover, Michelson was disturbed by some of the clinical practices that had been employed at House, and he had counseled 3M not to continue funding House. Michelson also felt that it was unethical to implant patients with a percutaneous plug transmission system, an approach that 3M researchers wanted to pursue in their quest to develop a multichannel device for the future.

3M's technological choices were not restricted to those being pursued by researchers at UCSF and House. There were three other groups with which 3M had initiated discussions. One was a group headed by Donald Eddington, who had developed a multichannel system at the University of Utah. Eddington, retained as a consultant by 3M sometime early 1981, had provided inputs to 3M from time to time. The second was a group at Stanford University headed by Blair Simmons and Robert White. 3M had not pursued this alternative any further after an initial visit to Stanford facilities in October 1978.

A third relationship that 3M pursued vigorously was with the Hochmairs of Vienna, who had developed single- and multiple-channel implants at the University of Innsbruck in Vienna, Austria. 3M researchers had first contacted the Hochmairs in 1979 and had invited them to 3M's St. Paul facilities to make a presentation in June 1979. The Hochmairs' multichannel device had been able to demonstrate "open set speech" with patients. Moreover, the Hochmair device was elegantly simple, and 3M engineers were confident that they would be able to manufacture this device. Finally, the Hochmairs had been able to demonstrate very encouraging results with their single-channel system.

3M's choice of technology was also being directed by an overall strategy emerging within the program. The most important element of this strategy was a move to be the first to obtain regulatory approvals for the commercial sale of the device.[1] Early regulatory approvals would make cochlear implants available to a large number of profoundly deaf patients while providing 3M with a "window of opportunity" within which to recoup investments made in the development of its first product generation. Being first would also allow 3M a unique opportunity to set the "ground rules" in an emerging industry. Among all the cochlear implant technologies available, the House group had been able to accumulate the largest clinical experience with its single-channel device, thereby providing 3M the best opportunity to be the first to obtain regulatory approvals from the Food and Drug Administration (FDA) for commercialization in the market. As the program manager stated: "Although the House product is the least sophisticated of the devices 3M has been evaluating, it has the longest history and therefore the best chance of earliest market entry."

Despite the differences in approach between 3M and UCSF, Michelson and his colleagues wanted to continue joint developmental work with 3M. Michelson informed 3M in May 1981 about the outstanding results that had been achieved with the UCSF multichannel device. However, some 3M researchers and engineers had begun questioning the usefulness of taking up the complex UCSF electrode system for development. One engineer labeled it a "construction nightmare." Another clinician thought that the complex electrode system could increase the potential for damage of the cochlea. 3M researchers and engineers were coming to the conclusion that the complexity of the device was not justified without stronger evidence of its superiority in

---

1. All medical devices in the United States must have approval from the Food and Drug Administration (FDA). The FDA requires a variety of testing to ensure that the devices are safe and that they do what the manufacturers claim. The FDA requires testing with animals before testing with humans can begin. Approval to begin human testing (investigational device exemption, or IDE) allows a limited number of locations to test the safety and effectiveness of the devices. These initial human tests lead to the premarket approval (PMA). With the PMA, devices may be sold in the United States. PMA does not allow the manufacturer to make claims about the therapeutic benefits of the device. Such claims can be made only after additional testing demonstrates the accuracy of these claims. The FDA testing process represents a major commitment of time and money by medical product developers. In this case of the CIP, the approval process took about five years, much longer than 3M managers anticipated and prolonged in part because FDA personnel were unfamiliar with the new technology. 3M program members shared their accumulation of knowledge with the FDA.

comparison to a single-channel device. However, such comparative tests were not yet available.

By July 1981, 3M program members had decided to first undertake commercial development of the House device. This would soon be followed by future generations of cochlear implants. In a presentation made to House in April 1981, 3M's program manager stated:

> Simplicity is a big plus with the House device; more information comes to patients with single-channel stimulation than is predictable on old principle. Multichannel systems are not necessarily a significant improvement over single-channel systems. Needs of the patient will dictate two or more different implant product options. After the introduction of the House device, we will plan to introduce devices based on technology from the Hochmairs. This will be followed by a third generation multielectrode system.

In 1981, 3M entered into contractual relationships with both House and the Hochmairs to develop cochlear implants. A multielectrode system was intended to be a by-product of research work in which 3M had been engaged with UCSF researchers. However, 3M found that resources required to undertake the development of the multichannel device competed directly with the more immediate tasks of developing the House and Hochmair devices and therefore declined Michelson's requests for 3M resources to undertake multichannel developmental work. In December 1982, 3M reevaluated its relationship with Michelson and decided not to renew its contract with him. Later in July 1983, UCSF researchers entered into a contractual relationship with Storz to commercially develop its cochlear implant. The two other research groups that 3M had evaluated also entered into collaborative arrangements with other business firms to commercially develop their devices. The Stanford group entered into a relationship with Biostim in March 1980, and Eddington at the University of Utah entered into a relationship with Symbion in January 1983.

In December 1982, 3M's program manager arranged a visit for the 3M chairman and other top company officials to HEI. According to the program manager, this trip proved important a short time later when additional support was requested for the program in the midst of a "belt-tightening" period at 3M. The request for funds was approved by top management overseeing the cochlear implant program because of their firsthand awareness of the program. In May 1983, to effect an acceleration of the program, the surgical products division was permitted to reduce its profit target to avoid the need for continual justification of a lower-income statement. Obtaining corporate support in May 1983 was significant because it allowed for substantial personnel additions.

Initial Strategy Formulation

With the promotion of 3M's technical director's supervisor to group vice president in the fall of 1980, the technical director returned from California as the division vice president to direct the surgical products division in St. Paul. To accelerate the development of the program, the division vice president asked a 3M employee to direct and integrate four independent 3M activities into a single unit in December 1980. These four activities included (1) a manufacturing relationship between McGhan and House, (2) a developmental relationship with UCSF, (3) an ongoing research effort within 3M's biosciences laboratory, and (4) and a laboratory development effort in 3M's surgical products division.

The newly appointed program manager, though initially skeptical about the value of cochlear implants, decided to seriously examine the idea because of his great respect for his supervisor. Two events motivated the program manager. First, a hearing-impaired 3M colleague strongly encouraged him to invest his energies in building a cochlear implant program for both social and business reasons. Second, the program manager was influenced by an anecdotal story of a profoundly hearing-impaired woman who was intentionally bumped by shoppers with carts in grocery stores when she failed to move after being asked to.

Having committed himself to cochlear implants in early 1981, the program manager began building his team and understanding prior activities in the three areas that were integrated into the program. Team discussions resulted in a preliminary business plan's being prepared in July 1981. In this plan, program members reconfirmed their basic strategy of being the first company to obtain regulatory approvals for commercial sale of a cochlear device. They would achieve this by taking up the House single-channel device for commercial development, even though this device was the least sophisticated of all the devices they had explored.

The simplicity and limited performance potential of the House device required that future generations of more sophisticated devices also be developed. Second-generation cochlear devices would be based on the Hochmair technology. The Hochmair devices, in order of planned introduction would consist of a four-electrode single-channel intracochlear device for adults, an extracochlear implant for children, and a multichannel intracochlear implant. Furthermore, the joint research activities with UCSF scientists would provide the third-generation multichannel device. As stated earlier, during a program review held in 1983, solving the tasks of providing hearing to totally deaf people was best approached by beginning with the simple and uncomplicated

House device before proceeding to more complex devices. As the program manager stated, "You have to crawl, walk, then you can run."

In contrast, competitors had begun work with more complex devices. In particular, Nucleus Corporation had initiated developmental work on the University of Melbourne twenty-two-channel device, which 3M researchers felt was "too sophisticated." 3M executives also felt that Nucleus was "too research oriented." In contrast, the founder of Nucleus Corporation advised 3M not to commercialize too fast.

In developing successive generations of cochlear devices, 3M executives reasoned that future generations would not necessarily render previous generations obsolete, as patients' needs would require several different devices. 3M would offer a "catalogue" of products, each product suitable for a particular segment of the market depending on the extent and nature of deafness. In contrast, 3M competitors had chosen to enter the market with a single product. The preliminary plan also indicates an intent to establish what program members later referred to as "design continuity." It would be possible to use parts designed for one generation with parts designed for a different generation. The overall focus on being the first in the market was linked with "establishing market share." These two related objectives were verbalized in a mission statement articulated in August 1983: "The mission is to be the first multinational corporation to successfully enter and maintain a large dominant market share in cochlear implant products and services for the otologic community."

This "share" strategy was in contrast to traditional 3M "niche" strategies which were based on developing products with unique features that could command high premiums in the market.[2] In a training meeting held for co-investigators in early 1984, the 3M marketing manager explained the rationale for the market share strategy. This was a new industry, explained the marketing manager, in which no one firm occupied a dominant share. The cochlear implant industry had identifiable boundaries with few options or substitutes and formidable entry barriers. These barriers included (1) the complexity of therapy, (2) high technical investments, (3) long-term program investments, and (4) expensive customer linkage. Therefore, establishing market share would lead to a strong competitive position in the industry.

In 1981, CIP personnel realized that they were involved in an enterprise of much bigger magnitude than cochlear implants: they were addressing the broad domain of hearing health. Consistent with this broader vision, program members redefined their strategy to read: "As AT&T is to communication, and IBM is to computers, 3M will be to hearing health."

2. "3M's nichemanship revisited." (1985). In *In vivo: The business and medicine report* (pp. 9–11). New York: Channing Weinberg & Company.

Program members developed a vision of "planting a seed which one day would grow into an oak tree" consisting of a family of hearing health products. The first few branches would consist of diagnostics and rehabilitation. As one founding member explained, it would have been difficult to justify resource commitments for cochlear implants alone; a broader vision of a family of products was needed.

While this overall strategy was being formulated, specific functional strategies that were congruent with the overall strategy of being the first in the market were also being articulated. These functional strategies, initially pertaining to the commercial development of the first-generation House single-channel device are described next.

First-Generation (House) Device

R&D

To reduce the time required to commercially introduce the first-generation cochlear device, program members decided not to undertake any major design changes in the device originally developed by House. Not only would major changes consume valuable developmental time, but, more important, clinical data already collected by House clinicians would no longer be useful to support claims of safety and efficacy for the redesigned product with the FDA. Fresh clinical studies would need to be initiated for such a "new" device, thereby substantially delaying its market entry.

However, several essential developmental activities were initiated to improve "peripheral" aspects of the device while ensuring that the electrical signal delivered to the patient remained unchanged. One set of changes sought to improve the reliability, aesthetic appeal, and other operational aspects of the device. For instance, it was planned to develop a hermetic internal receiver to improve the reliability of the device. Aesthetic appeal would be improved by incorporating a magnetic coupling system and by miniaturizing the device. Miniaturization would also lead to lower power consumption, thereby leading to higher battery life.

Another set of design changes was undertaken to establish the safety of cochlear implants. It was possible that the FDA would raise safety-related questions during the premarket approval (PMA) application process. 3M would be especially vulnerable to such questions as House had not conducted chronic animal studies. Rather than risk significant delays in PMAs for the lack of chronic animal studies, 3M decided in 1981 to initiate animal studies as well as to analyze temporal bones of cadavers who had been implanted with a cochlear device for a long time. Based on the understanding that emerged from these studies, 3M researchers reduced the length of the implanted electrode from 15 mm to 6 mm to minimize internal trauma to the patient's cochlea.

These "peripheral" changes consumed a lot of resources. One 1982 estimate indicated that at least 65% of the program's resources were being employed for short-term developmental efforts, leaving only limited resources for longer-range R&D. Researchers and engineers at 3M projected that the resources allocated for R&D for the first-generation cochlear device would soon decrease as its developmental activities were completed.

But developmental activities for the first device continued for a considerable length of time. Although initial developmental efforts had improved the aesthetic appeal of the device (specifically its processor) and had rendered the device safer and easier to manufacture, reliability issues had yet to be significantly addressed. For instance, in July 1984 the redesign of the electrodes and internal receiver enclosure was identified as the most urgent product improvement objective; a redesign required to eliminate problems encountered in the field.

However, design of a hermetic internal receiver was constrained by internal manpower shortage. Earlier, program members had articulated a key philosophy, especially for bioelectronic components, of exploiting outside resources whenever possible and building in-house only those components that were considered essential. Congruent with this philosophy, program members identified a vendor, Sermed, to help 3M develop and supply hermetic internal receivers with titanium electrodes. Later in June 1985, these developmental efforts enabled 3M to make a swift transition to a hermetic titanium electrode.

Other R&D projects, too, kept the development team busy with the first-generation device for a considerable time. For instance, at the insistence of Dr. House, customized devices were developed to suit the requirements of particular patients. Still another project was undertaken to develop a power booster that could enhance patients' processor signal output to counterbalance the short depth of electrode insertion and overcome certain anatomical constraints, both of which resulted in increased threshold limits. A third effort was undertaken to develop a universal fitting system that could be employed with future generations of cochlear devices.

These projects, and other efforts to speedily introduce the first-generation device into the market, resulted in little progress in the development of the second-generation cochlear device. Noting this lack of progress in commercializing the second-generation device, program members decided in October 1984 that they would avoid any further internal efforts to bring about "incremental improvements" in the House device. Instead they would seek only "quantum jumps" in the House device. For instance, a "behind the ear" (BTE) version and a version for children would be developed. To achieve a quantum jump in processing over the current 3M/House device, they would also focus on the Hochmairs' "full-bodied" analog processing technology. The technical manager also articulated a shift in the design philosophy. Instead of developing a "universal" signal processor that could be employed with multiple generations of cochlear device, the technical manager felt that it would be prudent to design a processor that could handle known aspects of the technology. A universal system was not the wisest design approach, said the technical manager, because it was not possible to predict the future. Moreover, patients with different ear hearing problems might require different devices for different segments.

Clinical and Regulatory Affairs

3M's first task on entering into a collaborative relationship with House was to assume control over the clinical trials that House had so far directed. One plan was to lease computer hardware to clinical investigators. This plan would provide 3M an opportunity to establish a computer-linked network of investigators that would facilitate testing and fitting of patients, simultaneously helping 3M to consolidate its database. To evaluate this and other related clinical and rehabilitation concepts, in early 1985 3M initiated a collaborative venture with a local Minnesota clinic: the Cochlear Implant Services of Minnesota.

Noting the lack of previous animal studies, chronic animal studies were initiated in 1981 to better understand cochlear implant safety issues. While clinical activities were under way at 3M, a potential easing of FDA PMA protocols was reported for bone cement because of its similarity to products that had already been approved by the FDA. 3M regulatory personnel feared that there could be a similar easing of regulatory requirements for subsequent generations of cochlear devices, thereby making it easier for competitors to obtain FDA approvals. The regulatory group at 3M felt it was important to seek clarification from the FDA on this issue and establish a precedent with the large clinical database that had been collected with the House device. When they were contacted by 3M, FDA staff informed the company that regulatory requirements would only be eased for devices that were similar to products already marketed prior to 1976 and that all new products, including future generations of cochlear devices, would need to pass through the same regulatory approval process.

Another important task identified by the regulatory group at 3M was establishing a good relationship with the FDA. With this objective, 3M researchers visited FDA personnel in Washington, D.C., in August 1982 to discuss safety and efficacy issues related to the 3M/House device. During this visit, the FDA staff raised few questions about the efficacy of the device. Rather, discussions centered around device safety. 3M engineers explained to the FDA staff that they had been able to make the House device safer while ensuring that the signal delivered to the patient was kept the same. As one 3M engineer stated: "Generally, the FDA had to be reminded again and again that the device was the simplest one with the least amount of complexity. But the device still provided a clearly demonstrated benefit."

During this visit, 3M personnel also found out that the FDA staff were not well informed about audiological tests usually employed to measure speech-hearing patterns. 3M's clinical group had employed the Monosyllable Trochee Spondee (MTS) and environment sounds tests. The MTS test consisted of a list of twelve individual words varying in number of syllables and stress patterns. The environmental sounds test was a measure of the patient's ability to discriminate sounds of daily life. Although these tests did not represent an ability to discriminate running speech that occurred in real-life conversation, they did allow the patient some ability to discriminate between speech elements. 3M clinicians explained that these tests were appropriate because current and near future markets lay "not in solving deafness but in providing useful, conservative devices to improve lip-reading skills to allow for mainstreaming."

To expedite the transfer of cochlear implant knowledge to FDA staff, 3M invited FDA personnel to its St. Paul laboratories in late 1982 and to House premises in Los Angeles in early 1983. During these visits, 3M learned of several concerns that FDA staff members had about the 3M/House cochlear device. First, FDA staff members were concerned about water absorption and leakage into the epoxy-coated internal receiver. In response, 3M collected and submitted considerable data to the FDA in February 1983 to demonstrate that epoxy-coated internal receiver design employed for the 3M/House device would not be a biological safety hazard to patients. 3M engineers argued that competitors were using titanium hermetic packaging because epoxy-coated internal receivers were not appropriate for multielectrode devices. 3M also made improvements in the electrode copper winding solder joints and the procedures used to clean the internal receiver in order to reduce the possibility of internal receiver failure. As a result of these inputs and changes, the FDA informed 3M in February 1983 that epoxy-coated internal receivers would be acceptable.

A related issue raised by the FDA concerned the life of the epoxy device. In response, 3M and House personnel informed the FDA that the rapid change in technology made it likely that the device would be replaced with an improved version within five years, clearly before the assumed life expectancy of the epoxy devices.

A third issue raised by the FDA staff related to standardized protocols for the selection of patients. 3M agreed with the FDA that such standardized protocols for the selection of candidates would indeed be desirable. Both 3M and House had prescreened patients to find appropriate candidates. However, one difference between the selection protocols adopted by 3M/House and those adopted by Nucleus was that the former was willing to implant a wider array of patients who could benefit from this device, whereas the latter had chosen to implant only patients with the highest potential for speech perception improvements.

While these interactions were proceeding between the FDA and 3M, FDA staff received inputs from other cochlear implant researchers pursuing the multichannel route. These researchers considered the House device to be "archaic." Fortunately for 3M, the head of the FDA ear, nose and throat (ENT) committee believed that a device could not be considered archaic until a superior device was actually available. She stated that it would be wrong to wait for improved cochlear implant versions when the existing device could offer immediate benefits to patients in the market. She was becoming increasingly impatient to see results with the multichannel device. Moreover, she was influenced by arguments presented by 3M and House researchers that multichannel devices did not provide clear benefits in speech discrimination to justify the increased possibility of trauma and decreased reliability.

3M submitted a pre-market approval application (PMAA) on October 1, 1983, on the basis of clinical data gathered with 231 adult patients. Upon receipt of the application, the FDA raised a number of questions pertaining to product failure, design changes, and manufacturing and clinical data. Over the next few months, 3M's regulatory team supplied FDA with detailed answers addressing these questions. Eventually, FDA staff members were satisfied with 3M's responses to the questions raised and agreed to hold a presentation before a panel. The panel meeting was scheduled for February 1984.

At the panel presentation, the FDA statistician while accepting the validity of 3M's statistical results wanted confirmation that the test methods were "clinically relevant." Audiological test methods employed by 3M were critiqued. One panelist stated that speech reading was the key benefit from cochlear implants and questioned why 3M had not conducted controlled tests to demonstrate this. Another important issue raised by panel members and the FDA staff was whether the implantation of single-channel devices could cause damage to the cochlea, thereby precluding implantation of a better device in the future. At the end of two days of questions and answers, panel members were adjourned because of lack of time in which to address all the questions raised. FDA instructed panel members to mail in their questions to FDA, which would then be forwarded to 3M. Before the panel meeting, 3M program members had hoped to obtain a PMA step by

July 1984. 3M lost this opportunity with the adjournment of the FDA panel meeting.

In March 1984, 3M received a letter from the FDA that included more than eighty questions raised by panel members. Some of these questions pertained to (1) the usefulness of substitute products such as vibrotactile devices, (2) the training required of clinicians and audiologist, and (3) the upgradability of the device to keep pace with technological changes. Again 3M prepared a detailed response addressing each question. Issues concerning upgradability were the most troublesome as 3M had maintained that the shallow insertion of its single-channel electrode would reduce trauma, thereby preserving the cochlea for future technological advances. In contrast, the deep insertion multichannel electrodes employed by competitors could cause greater damage. Just at that time, a patient who had originally been implanted with a House device was reimplanted with a Nucleus device. Even though the patient performed better with the reimplanted Nucleus device than he had with the House device, 3M's program manager took this as a sign of upgradability and reported it to the FDA. One consequence of the FDA's questions was that device upgradability and the preservation of the cochlea for future technological advances became important promotional themes in cochlear implant articles written by 3M (Radcliffe, 1984).

While the PMA review was under way, 3M continued implanting patients with the House device. Informed of this, FDA staff asked 3M to stop implanting patients when the PMA was under review, as implanting during the review process could be construed as premature commercialization. 3M clinicians explained that they had continued implanting patients to gain further experience with the redesigned device and to gain further insights into any adverse reactions with the implant. Though it initially accepted this explanation, the FDA asked 3M to stop implanting the device soon thereafter until such time that the PMA had been approved.

At this time, FDA staff members were also involved with the development of a set of overall guidelines for cochlear implant PMAAs and had contacted all cochlear implant manufacturers for their inputs. Having the largest number of implants among all the firms in the industry and being the first firm to have submitted a PMAA, 3M felt it incumbent to provide its input to shape the guidelines. 3M clinicians suggested that a minimum of 100 patients be evaluated for at least twelve months in order to support claims of device safety. This recommendation was congruent with the statistical approach that 3M had adopted (a one-way analysis of variance), where the pooled performance results of patients before implantation were compared with their performance after implantation. In contrast, Nucleus had adopted an approach in which the performance of individual patients had been tracked over time with a speech tracking test, data that Nucleus had been able to gather because of a tightly controlled clinical protocol. 3M clinicians also supported their arguments on the minimum number of patients by providing to the FDA details of research that they had conducted earlier relating to the safety of cochlear devices.

In June 1984 FDA informed 3M that it preferred that 3M base its claims on the redesigned House product alone and cite the data collected with the earlier House version as "historical evidence" relevant to complete safety evaluation. The FDA ENT head stated that the panel members would have to rule on the adequacy of the redesigned House device data by itself. The FDA staff felt that the reduction of electrode length from 15 mm to 6 mm, while presumably making the device safer, had potentially decreased its effectiveness. Because approval was sought for the redesigned product, evidence of effectiveness would only be based on the 163 patients implanted with the redesigned product; the clinical data collected earlier with the remaining 206 patients would not be useful in supporting efficacy claims.

In June 1984, the FDA advisory panel members gave PMA for the House device. Official approval from the FDA was granted five months later in November 1984, thirteen months from the date of submission of the PMAA. Noting the historic nature of this approval, the FDA said: "This is the first time that one of the five human senses has been replaced by an electronic device." Besides gaining permission to claim the detection of environmental sounds, the approval permitted 3M to claim that its cochlear implant could benefit some postlingual adults with the acquisition and improvements of speech-reading ability. This speech-reading claim, not originally envisioned by 3M, had been allowed when 3M had submitted, in June 1984, clinical evidence on seven patients with a speech-reading test called the McConky test. The PMA also stated that "without visual contact and some speech reading ability, the use of the device does not provide speech discrimination and understanding." Inability to provide speech discrimination was reinforced in a status report distributed by the FDA in the same month it granted 3M approval.[3] The status report mentioned:

> The single-channel implant involves the placement of a single electrode within the cochlea. This type of device provides rhythm and intensity information to the patient but it does not provide any perception of pitch and is not effective in speech comprehension. Multichannel implants have an array of several electrodes placed within the cochlea. Preliminary results indi-

3. "Current status of cochlear implants." (1984 Update). Division of OB/GYN, ENT, and Dental Devices, Office of Device Evaluation, Center for Devices and Radiological Health.

cate that by stimulating the proper electrodes in the array in multi electrode devices, the patient can perceive pitch and may be able to comprehend speech more effectively than with a single-channel implant.

Manufacturing

Two considerations directed 3M's overall manufacturing strategy. First, rapid technological changes along with associated uncertainties required that 3M maintain flexible manufacturing operations. Flexibility was also required to facilitate changes in manufacturing operations as different product generations became available. Second, 3M executives planned to minimize capital investments in manufacturing facilities, both because of the uncertainties involved and, more important, because of the low-volume sales projected for several years. 3M executives felt that the price of the device would not be a major concern until 1985. Manufacturing investments would be tied to sales volume and price elasticities.

Low investments in manufacturing facilities and flexibility of operations led to a philosophy of "selective vertical integration," which would minimize capital investments. 3M manufacturing would only entertain those devices for which production capacity was a competitive factor or those cases in which a proprietary process precluded the use of outside vendors. A scale-up group was created at St. Paul to identify and qualify such facilities. This scale-up group was also responsible for the initial stages in the translation of prototypes into marketable products.

This overall manufacturing approach resulted in cochlear implant parts being manufactured at several different sites. Over time, the major sites were located at (1) McGhan Medical, a 3M subsidiary located in Santa Barbara; (2) Sarns, a 3M subsidiary located in Ann Arbor, Michigan; and (3) 3M's corporate facilities at St. Paul, Minnesota.

The flexibility/low investment approach toward manufacturing also influenced design decisions. For instance, in July 1983 the group decided to continue with an epoxy-coated internal receiver design as the group had decided not to purchase a welder costing about $250,000 that would have allowed it to internally manufacture hermetic receivers. The program manager stated: "The development of hermetic implants is vital to maintaining leadership position. To speed up this program, we will purchase outside technical capabilities. It is premature to entertain setting up our own hermetic packaging operations until several different material approaches, especially ceramic, have been evaluated."

In several evaluations of their own strengths and weaknesses, 3M managers considered their manufacturing operations to be a weak point. First, coordination problems always existed between the different manufacturing sites. Second, the dispersion of these sites led to a loss of control for managers at St. Paul. This created problems as reports had to be submitted to the FDA in compliance with "good manufacturing practices." Third, 3M felt that it did not possess the expertise and manufacturing facilities (such as a clean room) that would enable it to reliably manufacture difficult parts of the cochlear implant, including the hermetic receiver and the more complicated multielectrodes.

Marketing, Sales, and Promotion

In a presentation made to 3M's sector management committee in June 1982, the newly appointed marketing manager argued that the first company in the market would have a strong opportunity to shape the distribution system. Being the first in the market would provide 3M with an opportunity "to establish a price benchmark, a distribution base of selected participants, clinical acceptance, regulatory involvement and early definition of market and product mix requirements." It would also provide 3M with an opportunity to develop "kindred markets" in rehabilitation and diagnostics, which would not only generate additional revenues for the program but would also help strengthen 3M's distribution hold. The marketing manager argued that other researchers had not really grasped the large potential of this nascent market and were more focused on achieving dramatic therapeutic discoveries. 3M, by aggressively investing in market development, could "steal a march" over others and thereby establishing early market share, which could be maintained by introducing future generations of products.

Having established market share as a key derivative of the strategy to be first in the market, 3M program members argued that the long, drawn-out regulatory process in the United States compelled them to initiate early action internationally to dominate the cochlear implant market on a global basis. They initiated actions in collaboration with 3M international subsidiaries to develop "centers of excellence" in several countries. The intent was to train and equip one key surgeon and audiologist in each country who would then later train and equip other surgeons and audiologists. By creating such centers of excellence, 3M hoped to counter the upfront computer investments of $15,000 to $20,000 that Nucleus required of its implant centers; 3M found that such investments could "lock" the surgical and rehabilitation teams into an extended period of Nucleus implants.

3M opened seventeen such centers of excellence globally and cochlear implantation was initiated, even in Australia, where Nucleus and the University of Melbourne were located. 3M also initiated actions initiated to appreciate the myriad health care systems around the world and to seek coverage for implants from third-party insurance payers, including the government. The centers-of-excellence concept was clearly successful. The international marketing manager, with obvious satisfaction, stated in an interview held in 1985: "We beat them [Nucleus] in their own backyards."

In the United States, efforts to make the therapy easily accessible to patients had required 3M to select and train a larger number of clinicians across the nation than it had previously selected and trained.

3M initiated other actions that would allow it to interface with a larger number of clinics to make the device accessible to a large number of patients. First, 3M initiated efforts to convince insurance carriers to extend coverage to cochlear devices even before the FDA had granted its approval for commercial sale of the device. These efforts were fruitful when, in early 1983, insurance carriers agreed to extend insurance coverage to the device. 3M also initiated efforts to obtain Medicare coverage. Second, 3M hired salespeople to initiate personal sales calls to the various clinics all over the United States. Congruent with the program's overall strategy of eventually selling a wide variety of associated hearing products, 3M recruited general salespeople rather than audiologists. Third, 3M added professional service people to address the concerns of audiologists in the field.

In crafting its media promotion policy, 3M decided not to make exaggerated claims about its device. For instance, 3M media would promote the performance of its average patients as well as its star performers; in contrast, 3M executives felt that some of its competitors had promoted the performance of only its star patients and had attempted to "overgeneralize" device performance based on experience gained from a handful of implanted patients. 3M had also decided to direct its messages to the professional community (mainly the otologist) and not the public. 3M executives had learned from other firms' experience that people knowledgeable about cochlear implants reacted negatively when they read overstated statements about the "miracle of the bionic ear."

Despite these efforts and the imminence of an FDA PMA, sales of the House device were "sluggish" during the third quarter of 1984. Potential reasons for sluggish sales were provided by clinicians at Baptist Medical Hospital. Profoundly deaf patients were not interested in the implant because of (1) comfort level, (2) peer pressure, and (3) a desire to wait for a better devices. To better understand the reasons for sluggish sales, 3M initiated a "focus" program in three cities: Miami, Kansas City, and Chicago. Preliminary information from the focus program further explained the poor sales of the House device. One implant center stated that it was awaiting the commercial release of the Vienna device, which 3M had promoted as being more effective while being safer than other existing cochlear devices. Two other centers reported that they were switching to implanting children, as adult patients were hard to find for the House device.

Some action was required to create an appreciation of the value of the House technology in the minds of physicians. The next section reviews efforts undertaken by program members to establish this appreciation and provides an update of the overall strategy.

Overall Program-Level Strategy Update

Having accomplished the initial major objective of being the first company with an FDA-approved device in the market, the focus shifted to protecting and exploiting the window of opportunity that had been created. 3M took several steps in this direction.

First, 3M initiated a mass media campaign with the objective of creating an appreciation for the single-channel technology by potential users and implantation decision makers. One unique aspect of the 3M-House device that 3M could promote was its perceived safety. 3M's own research had suggested that the 3M-House device was indeed the safest among all cochlear implants then available.

Articles about the device's safety began to appear in trade journals. The first article appeared in the November 1984 issue of the *Hearing Journal*:

> The 3M-House implant system uses a 6-mm single-channel electrode engineered for minimum trauma and maximum safety. Previous studies have shown that electrodes inserted deep in the cochlea beyond the first turn can damage the cochlear tissue. The 6-mm electrode preserves a maximum number of nerve cells, allowing a patient to benefit immediately from a cochlear implant while preserving nerve cells for future devices that might be able to take fuller advantage of these cells. The device is also designed to accommodate signal processing and other technical improvements as they become available in the future. (Radcliffe, 1984: 9–10)

3M's competitor, Nucleus, had encountered difficulties in implanting certain patients with its deep-insertion cochlear implant system. For such patients, Nucleus had announced plans to develop a short insertion single-channel device of its own. Nucleus's U.S. president had said that downgrading its complex multichannel technology to offer a simpler single-channel device would be easier than for 3M to upgrade its device. At the same time, testimonials began to appear in news media urging customers to wait for the superior multichannel implant. A typical testimonial provided by Daniel Ling, dean of Applied Health Sciences School at the University of Western Ontario, a consultant retained by Nucleus, appeared in the November 30, 1984, issue of the *Wall Street Journal* almost immediately after 3M received its formal FDA approval in November 1984. It read: "Single-channel implants are better than nothing. But that is all they are—better than nothing. Why implant a single-channel today when you know a 22-channel is right round the corner?" In the same article, a 3M technical manager responded, "Multichannel implants are currently too expensive and could harm the cochlea because they need to be embedded deeper."

In March 1985, the Marketing Services Associated Inc. of Pennsylvania completed results of a cochlear implant positioning study, commissioned by 3M. In conducting this study, the market research consultant approached a large number of audiologist, patients, and associations for the hearing impaired and surfaced several potential reasons for the poor sales of the House device. Marketing Services identified two important reasons: (1) a perception that existing technology was inadequate, and (2) a reluctance to undergo surgery to implant existing cochlear devices when a multichannel implant would soon be available. One doctor said: "If it is true that more sophisticated devices will be developed in the future, then it would be wise to postpone the implantation of single-channel units since this will probably cause enough damage of the inner ear so that it cannot later be replaced by me." Similarly, a spokesperson for an association for the hearing impaired said: "We don't want to get involved with a 'Model T' if a Cadillac is coming along."

By March 1985, the Nucleus device had become a major threat to the 3M-House device. Even though the FDA had not yet granted its approval, the Nucleus multichannel device had been able to achieve FDA-approved status in the industry. 3M somehow had to convince practitioners and users that its cochlear implant would provide benefits to the user immediately, while allowing the user benefits from future technological advances. In a widely read issue of the *Hearing Instruments* published in June 1985, the following message appeared:

> 3M has designed its cochlear implants to provide the many benefits of today's devices without compromising the patients ability to benefit from future improvements in technology by preserving the delicate membranes of the cochlea. At this point in the cochlear implant's short history, not enough is known about the long-term effects of implanting an electrode into the cochlea. For this reason, 3M has taken a "prudent" approach to minimizing risk to the cochlea and to preserve remaining functions for the future products and technologies. Several studies have shown that serious, irreversible damage may result from inserting a multielectrode cluster into the cochlea. This damage may be due to presence of multiple electrodes (up to 22 in one device) as well as the lengths of the electrodes (up to 25 mm long).

Based on today's evidence of the neural degeneration from mechanical damage, 3M feels it is irresponsible to take such a risk. Patients who might be able to benefit from deep-penetrating electrodes today may find that in five or 10 years the damage to their cochlea may prevent them from using any cochlear implant. (*Hearing Instruments*, 15)

The quote reflects the escalating media conflict that ensued between cochlear implant firms. A media analysis conducted by 3M's marketing group showed that 3M had achieved 290 media placements and had reached more than 95 million people during the first half of 1985 compared with 28 placements that had reached 6.1 million people in the first half of 1984. In contrast, all the competitors combined had achieved 70 placements during the first half of 1985, which had reached about 7.3 million people.

Reviewing the claims in these media announcements, 3M executives felt competitors had exaggerated the benefits and minimized the risks of their devices. In a cochlear implant review article that appeared in the journal published by the American Speech Hearing Association (ASHA) in May 1985, a 3M spokesman said:[4]

One of 3M's biggest concerns is the issue of realistic expectations. To be sure, the cochlear implant is an exciting medical advance; it is the first device that can substitute for one of the body's five senses. 3M believes that it is the responsibility of everyone in the cochlear-implant field to present a balanced picture of this new technology. We are particularly concerned about the accuracy of some of the stories that have appeared recently in the mass media. We urge hearing health professionals to take an active role in providing accurate, responsible information to their communities. (27–34)

At the same time, 3M asked the FDA to police claims of safety and efficacy made by cochlear implant manufacturers even before they had been able to substantiate their claims before an FDA panel. Competitors, restricted by FDA policies from widely promoting safety and efficacy aspects during the investigational device exemption (IDE) stage, responded by encouraging independent researchers to publish articles in refereed journals that extolled the virtues of the multichannel device. For instance, Loeb of the NIH supported the superiority of the multichannel device over single-channel devices in an article that appeared in the February 1985 issue of the *Scientific American* (Loeb, 1985).

4. Cochlear implant: Five companies respond to ASHA survey. (1985). American Speech & Hearing Association.

For a while, the media advertising strategy seemed to improve sales of the House device. In April 1985, program members reported that sales of the House device had been above forecasts for the first quarter of 1985. Program members used this achievement to request five additional salespeople in the second quarter of 1985 to maximize the sales of the House device and to set an industry standard for full service that competitors would find difficult to duplicate. 3M's project manager said that achieving a "critical mass of 3M cochlear implant distribution within the window of opportunity" was important. To establish this critical mass, 3M salespeople began approaching members in the otological community and offered to equip and train them to implant the 3M cochlear device in return for agreeing to be associated with 3M for a reasonable time. Nucleus salespeople were also trying to "lock up" clinicians by asking them to make significant investments in computers to become a part of the Nucleus program. Furthermore, reports indicated that Nucleus was offering free devices to encourage surgeons to implant.

Besides increasing its sales force, 3M also considered a link with Richards Medical in May 1985. Richards had severed its association with Biostim after the latter's legal problems and was searching for a cochlear implant manufacturer with which to join. 3M marketing personnel felt Richards's distribution strength in the medical products area could help 3M achieve the high-velocity sales it needed. However, 3M executives eventually decided not to join Richards Medical because Richards had a number of distribution layers calling for a corresponding number of margin layers that would reduce 3M's margins. 3M executives stated the industry was not mature enough to support a Richards type of distribution arrangement.

Despite 3M's various efforts, sales of the House device never increased substantially. Salespeople reported that clinicians wanted to implant an extracochlear device, which 3M had promoted as better and safer than current cochlear devices. The Hochmairs in Vienna, Austria, developed the extracochlear device. However, the Vienna extracochlear device was not accessible to all implanters because the FDA had imposed a maximum ceiling of fifty implants during the IDE stage. The FDA would allow further implantation of the Vienna extracochlear device only if warranted after a review of the results of the first fifty patients.

Capturing the dilemma confronting 3M, the marketing manager reported, in August 1985, "The most immediate issues impacting our financial growth are perceptions of obsolescence of the House device, the promise but inaccessibility of the Vienna device, and the common misconceptions that multielectrode devices are inherently more sophisticated."

Convincing audiologists and patients to use the available House device was critical. Program members decided to reinforce their original concept of a "catalogue of products," each product suitable for a different segment of the market depending on the type and extent of hearing impairment. In a newsletter sent in September 1985 to potential users and implanters nationwide, the program manager said:[5]

> Profoundly deaf patients can vary significantly in the amount of nerve survival at the cochlea, in the amount of bone growth, and in their ability to process the sound they receive. For this reason, a range of implant devices is appropriate—with some that can be used in the presence of extensive bone growth, some that are surgically very conservative and easy to adjust in young children, some that are relatively straightforward and cost effective for people who may not be able to benefit from more advanced and expensive technologies, and some that offer very sophisticated features for the people who can fully benefit from them. (3)

In the same month, with the PMA of the Nucleus device imminent, 3M group members acknowledged internally for the first time that 3M was no longer the technological leader in the industry.

Parallel with efforts to increase sales of the House device, a second effort had been initiated to protect the window of opportunity that had been created by ensuring that other cochlear manufacturers also would be subjected to the same rigorous FDA scrutiny that 3M had experienced. When the FDA contacted manufacturers to seek their opinions for crafting guidelines for PMAAs, 3M suggested that any device should be tested for its safety and efficacy on a minimum of 100 patients before it was approved by the FDA. To support these arguments, 3M researchers organized a technical seminar about safety issues for FDA staff members in January 1985 in Washington, D.C. At later meetings, 3M researchers also presented arguments to dispel "misconceptions about the apparent sophistication and superior performance of multielectrode devices."

Nucleus had also been providing its input to the FDA while the PMA guidelines were formed. The number of patients required to support claims of safety and efficacy was important because Nucleus had clinical data on forty-three patients at the time of its PMAA submission to the FDA in June 1984. If the FDA imposed a minimum requirement of 100 patients to demonstrate clinical safety as proposed by 3M, Nucleus's PMAA could be delayed significantly.

Audiologists from Nucleus visited the FDA and argued that the sample size required to demonstrate safety and efficacy should be a function of (1) the actual performance of each device, (2) the claims each manufacturer wanted to make about its device, and (3) the statistical approach adopted to support such claims. In conducting its clin-

---

5. *3M News and Information*, September 1985.

ical evaluation, Nucleus had adopted a within-subjects analysis in which improvements in the speech hearing of each patient had been mapped before and after the implantation of the device over time. That is, each patient had acted as his or her own control.[6]

After some deliberations, FDA staff members agreed with Nucleus's arguments. Draft FDA guidelines circulated in June 1985 said that the FDA would not specify the number of patients required for a PMAA but would leave sample size requirements flexible so a clinical trial sponsor could tailor the study to achieve statistically valid results. Pursuing 3M's line of logic about safety, the FDA also considered setting maximum and minimum limits to the test population size. The maximum limit would protect the number of patients at risk. The manufacturer would be allowed to expand its patient base to clarify the statistical significance of an adverse-reaction rate only if rate increased during clinical trials.[7]

This concern for safety was also reflected in the FDA's recommendation to Nucleus during its PMA panel review. FDA panel members recommended that Nucleus consider a larger sample size for a longer period to demonstrate device safety.[8]

Apart from the House device for adults, 3M had also been talking with the FDA about the House children's and Vienna extracochlear devices. A PMAA had been filed for the House children's device in September 1985, and 3M planned to explore the possibility of filing a PMAA for its Vienna extracochlear device as well. 3M argued that the unique electrode placement of the extracochlear device precluded any trauma to the cochlea and helped patients. However, upon further review, both 3M and the FDA decided that 3M was not yet ready to establish the statistical validity of its claims for the Vienna extracochlear device. 3M, therefore, did not proceed with its PMAA for the Vienna extracochlear device. But FDA staff members, impressed with 3M's arguments about the increased safety and the reduced trauma of the extracochlear device, informed 3M that it would prefer to wait for an extracochlear device developed for children.

A third effort to exploit the window of opportunity was in progress on the R&D front. One project objective was to establish "design upgradability" in laboratory and marketing efforts. This effort was motivated by a need to demonstrate improved performance with the House device in a relatively short time to match claims made by Nucleus in its PMAA. The approach was to use a Vienna processor with the House internal receiver, a hybrid design that could potentially shorten the time to get approval of a device with improved performance. However,

6. Discussions held with Nucleus audiologist, on May 2, 1988.

7. *MDDI Reports*, July 22, 1985, p. 11.

8. *MDDI Reports*, July 22, 1985, p. 11.

such a hybrid design had not as yet been clinically proven. If the design did not work, the program would have wasted valuable resources on a project that did not work instead of developing and testing a true second-generation device. But 3M researchers never got the opportunity to gamble with their resources. Reliability problems encountered during the second quarter of 1985 with the epoxy-coated House device led to an internal audit that one participant described as an inquisition that consumed considerable program resources. This incident was a symptom of growing internal conflict among program members and resulted in increasing upper management dissatisfaction with the progress of the program. In July 1985, 3M's division and group vice presidents intervened. The founding program manager was replaced by another manager transferred from another 3M division.

A second product failure took place in November 1985 when three newly FDA–approved titanium electrodes failed in quick succession. The program members decided voluntarily to recall the device from the market. Redesign efforts to prevent similar failures in the future and to seek reapprovals from the FDA consumed most of the program's resources for the next six months. One salesperson characterized the actual recall of the device as engaging in "negative sales." The recall not only reduced the window of opportunity for the House device but also adversely affected Vienna product-development schedules. In April 1984, program members requested and obtained additional funding to accelerate the development of the Vienna device. The next section discusses details regarding the development of the Vienna device.

Second-Generation (Vienna) Device

R&D

In June 1981, 3M entered into a collaborative relationship with the Hochmairs of Vienna, Austria. The initial plan in July 1981 was to sequentially introduce three different versions of the Hochmair devices soon after the commercial introduction of the House device. In order of planned market introduction, these products were (1) the single-channel "selectable" electrodes for adults, (2) the extracochlear (EC) stimulator for children, and (3) the multichannel system.

These plans changed somewhat when 3M personnel heard in August 1981 of impressive results that the Hochmairs had recorded with the EC device. Reviewing these results, the technical manager from the biosciences laboratory wrote to the Hochmairs: "The original hypotheses and dogmas which led to the development of complex multichannel implants have to be reconsidered. Without adequate knowledge whether single or multichannel systems are required for improved speech communication, a basic single-channel system may be the choice for initial commercialization."

3M researchers had also been to an European conference, where otologists had spoken favorably of the performance of the noninvasive EC device. Impressed with these arguments, 3M program members became convinced that they should offer an EC device immediately after the market introduction of the House device.

In February 1982, 3M formed a team to develop and commercialize the Vienna EC device, which incorporated an "epoxy" design. Intensive developmental work was begun by mid-1983 to develop a "ceramic" design. Developmental work to convert the internal receiver to a ceramic package was begun in October 1984, and the first prototypes were received in August 1985. Some changes were made to the processor as well.

While 3M engineers were making design changes in the original Hochmair device, the Hochmairs were also making technological advancements in several areas, including (1) speech processing, (2) the development of an interim intracochlear device, (3) incorporation of an additional channel to explore performance enhancement, and (4) an eight-channel cochlear device.

In the United States, significant design changes were required during the middle of 1985 when the U.S.-redesigned Vienna device was found not to perform as well as the original Vienna device had in Europe. After unsuccessfully attempting to identify the cause of this performance discrepancy between the two devices, 3M program members made a decision to change to an intracochlear (IC) electrode orientation to improve the efficacy of the device.

Another major design change was undertaken at 3M laboratories in September 1985 to achieve several objectives, including (1) improved reliability, (2) greater ease in manufacturing, (3) improved aesthetic appeal, and (4) greater ease with which the device could be fitted into patients. This "enhanced" system was eventually ready by March 1987.

Clinical Trials

Clinical trials of the Vienna device were initiated in Europe by the Hochmairs and other clinicians. Clinical trials were also begun in the United States under an IDE from the FDA in April 1984. The IDE provided 3M and its clinical associates permission to implant up to fifty patients initially with the Vienna EC device. While these clinical studies were under way, 3M received information from the Hochmairs in November 1984 that six European EC patients had demonstrated remarkable open set speech performance with the EC device. By February 1985, twelve patients in the United States had been implanted with the Vienna EC device, with encouraging performance data received from eight patients who had been implanted for three months. A 3M clinician went to Vienna in April 1985 and reported that the Hochmairs indeed had recorded promising performance results.

On the basis of this preliminary information, the performance of the 3M Vienna EC device was promoted at the Thirteenth International Otologic Conference at Miami. This device could, 3M claimed, provide the same benefits as did other multielectrode devices but was much safer as it did not invade the cochlea. Nucleus and Symbion accused 3M of exaggerating the safety and performance of the device. This skepticism arose due to 3M's inability to duplicate the results recorded by the Hochmairs in Vienna. In particular, comparative tests conducted at the University of Iowa, a neutral and self-proclaimed testing institute, had demonstrated very poor results with a Vienna device that had been manufactured by the Hochmairs.

Scientists began speculating about the possible reasons for the Hochmairs's outstanding results. One theory was that the Hochmairs had administered the speech-tracking test a number of times to the patients; as a result, the Hochmairs could be recording learning that patients had displayed rather than improvements in speech-hearing abilities. Another theory was that Vienna patients had performed well because the German language was phonetically easier than the English language to recognize. At a conference held at New York in the summer of 1985, the scientific community openly attacked and questioned the Hochmairs's results. The FDA, too, was asking 3M to substantiate its claims with the Vienna EC device. In May 1985, the FDA judged an informal PMAA of the Vienna device to be unacceptable. Further clinical work would be required to document the claims of safety and efficacy.

By late 1985 it was clear that the U.S.-Vienna EC clinical data were not supporting original performance expectations. Moreover, rumors had begun spreading that the "inappropriate" electrode placement and the additional electrical power required for the extracochlear electrode could cause facial twitching. 3M researchers began efforts to try and understand the reasons for the lack of clinical performance and to also begin work on the IC device. Data collected by the Hochmairs suggested that the IC device would outperform the EC device because of the ease of electrode placement, lower power requirements, and greater dynamic range. In September 1985, program members realized that the realistic time schedule for filing a PMAA the for the Vienna EC device would be the fall of 1987 and not the fall of 1985.

Both 3M and the Hochmairs offered several reasons for the discrepancy between the performance reported in Vienna and that reported in the United States. 3M had allowed patients with a wide band of hearing deafness to benefit from the Vienna device; the Hochmairs, by contrast, suggested that only patients with a high potential for improvement be chosen, at least initially, in order to establish the legitimacy of the device.

While deciding to shift to an IC electrode orientation, 3M program members also made a decision that appears contradictory to the decision to proceed with the IC route when viewed acontextually. In May 1985, 3M executives decided to pursue partially hearing-impaired patients, as this segment offered 3M a much bigger market than did the market for just the profoundly deaf. The EC implant was the most suitable for such patients with some residual hearing as the EC device did not invade the cochlea and therefore would not damage residual hearing cells in the hearing-impaired person.

After a preliminary clinical exploration, 3M decided to postpone entry into the residual hearing market for several reasons. First, several changes would be required to make the device suitable for patients with residual hearing. Second, 3M was not yet clear what criteria to use to select patients or what audiological tests should be employed to record improvements in hearing.

3M obtained an IDE clearance from the FDA in October 1985 to initiate clinical studies with the IC electrode orientation. In early 1986, 3M salesmen reported that audiologists and surgeons were not convinced of the potential performance of the Vienna IC device when the EC device had failed to live up to its expectations. In early 1986, 3M decided that it would sell its EC device to patients with residual hearing. Program members also decided to initiate clinical studies of children with the Vienna EC device. A number of clinics were eager to try out the Vienna EC device on children, especially because of its electrode orientation. 3M decided to seek an IDE for the Vienna device for children. Reviewing this additional charge to the clinical group, one program member likened the substantial number of regulatory issues that the group was currently handling to a "boa-constrictor digesting a watermelon." However, 3M did put an IDE application for the Vienna EC for on hold as the House children's device PMAA was at that time being reviewed by the FDA.

Manufacturing

With mounting operating income losses, management focused on manufacturing costs (which at that time were 200% of the retail price). One action was to consolidate manufacturing operations located in Santa Barbara, Michigan, and St. Paul. This action reduced overhead costs, but the manufacturing manager said that there was little else the program could do to drastically reduce manufacturing costs. Economies of scale had not set in as yet, he argued, and there was a minimum overhead cost to be incurred to ensure that the small volume being manufactured was of high quality and reliability. However, there was one operation that could reduce direct material cost. This was a welding operation that was being performed by a vendor at a cost of $230 per weld. However, the yield of this operation was very low, with a 60% acceptance rate. Direct material costs could be reduced if the program was to invest in a laser welder costing $400,000. This would increase not only the yield but also the overall reliability of the product. After discussing the pros and cons of purchasing a laser welder, program members decided to continue to contract out the operation until such time as they had more positive information about the market size and about the performance of the Vienna device.

Marketing

By March 1985, the Nucleus multichannel device had been able to achieve a perceived "FDA approved" status even though the FDA had yet to officially approve the Nucleus device. The Nucleus PMA panel meeting was scheduled for July 1985. With this perception and imminent threat of actual approval, the challenge from the Nucleus device to the recently approved House device was great. To counter this threat, 3M executives decided to promote the Vienna EC device at the Thirteenth International Otologic Conference. 3M claimed that this "multifrequency" device was safer and yields performance comparable to multichannel systems. This performance claim was based on the favorable results that some patients in Vienna demonstrated with devices manufactured and fitted by the Hochmairs. To promote its device, 3M made the following claim at the conference: "The human ear is single-channel and so are 3M's devices making them more compatible with the human ear than multichannel devices. 3M's devices provide more meaningful signals, not more channels, that maximize information and minimize miss-information."

Confronting these claims, competitors accused 3M of exaggerating the benefits of the Vienna system and asked for clinical data to support these claims. 3M had a policy of promoting its products only on the basis of documented performance. However, despite several efforts, 3M was unable to replicate performance results of the Vienna EC device with U.S. patients.

The promotion of the Vienna EC device at the international conference also had an inadvertent negative effect on sales of the HEI device. In the months following the conference, salespeople reported that instead of implanting the House device, physicians and patients were awaiting the commercial release of the Vienna EC device, which promised better performance with lower risk. But the Vienna device was not commercially available. The FDA imposed a fifty-patient limit while granting an IDE to the Vienna EC device—a limit imposed to monitor the possibility of electrode displacement before allowing further clinical trials. 3M did plan to file a PMAA for the Vienna EC device in the fall of 1985, but did not when it was unable to corroborate in the United States the exceptional performance that had·been recorded in Europe.

By the beginning of 1985, sales figures indicated that profoundly deaf people were not embracing the House device as anticipated. 3M program members decided that offering a device to patients with some residual hearing could provide 3M with a much larger market—more precisely, the inclusion of the residual-hearing category of patients could increase the market potential by about 900,000. This number provided the program members a basis to sell the overall potential of the cochlear implant program to top management at 3M, who were questioning the dismal sales of the House device. Program members argued that 3M was the only manufacturer that possessed a noninvasive EC electrode device that could be used to access this potential market.

In June 1987, 3M program members made an important decision to discontinue the promotion and sales of Vienna devices. The program manager stated that exploration of the residual hearing market had not been successful because patients had been difficult to attract. Patients with residual hearing represented a "critical zone of deafness that was difficult to identify, attract, and motivate," stated the program manager. Clinical protocols for the Vienna IC device had not been successful because of a lack of patients. Furthermore, the Vienna device did not bridge the performance gap between the House device and 3M's own multichannel efforts. As one audiologist, interviewed in 1986, stated, the Vienna device had "fallen through the cracks of time."

Overall Program-Level Strategy Update

A new set of objectives had emerged by 1986. While working to get the House product back to the market after the voluntary recall, program members said that their prime objective had shifted to establishing reliability and quality. Among the steps it took to accomplish this, 3M established a separate manufacturing technologies group to interface with the laboratory and the manufacturing group to ensure better product quality.

A second important objective was regaining lost technological leadership. In November 1985, soon after Nucleus had been granted PMA by the FDA, 3M program members for the first time acknowledged they were no longer the technological leaders. Whereas safety was the dominant criterion in the past, performance had become the major performance criterion in the market. Fears of IC electrodes invading the cochlea had declined. Industry participants believed that multielectrode devices had a greater performance potential than single-channel devices. The idea that "more channels were better" had gained market acceptance. Many of 3M's key physicians had started implanting the Nucleus multichannel device. 3M, therefore, had to establish its presence with a multichannel device.

A 1986 estimate of the allocation of resources among various products showed that 62% of developmental resources was spent on the Vienna device, 29% on developing a multielectrode device, and 9% on developing the House device. Program members planned to finish redesigning the House device by June 1986 and developing the Vienna device by the end of the year. In the meantime, the plan was for researchers in the biosciences laboratory to complete basic research activities connected with the multielectrode device, which, then, would form the main thrust of the program.

Another major shift in program objectives was to enter the hearing-aids market. In February 1986, the program manager said: "The business mission is to be able to solve any problem in the hearing-health area, not cochlear implants only. However, we have to first win in cochlear implants." Top management at the sector level overseeing the program concurred with this strategy and in June 1986 agreed to continue funding the program on the condition that the program expand its focus to the hearing-aids market. In late 1985, a separate group began preliminary work developing hearing aids. But commitment to cochlear implants had not waned completely. Unclear about the market potential for cochlear implants, the program manager wanted to keep his options open between hearing aids and cochlear implants. The plan was to develop a multichannel device; if improved performance did not result, 3M would shift completely toward a hearing-aids program.

A change in the promotional objectives was also under way. A content analysis of articles that had appeared in the mass media during a ten-month period beginning in September 1985 showed that 50% of the articles were negative about the 3M-House device and described the superiority of multichannel devices. Only 18% of the media stories were positive about the House device. Program members decided to emphasize the advantages, not the limitations, of cochlear implants. It was also decided to publicize the 3M multichannel device.

Third-Generation (Multichannel) Devices

3M's initial contact with the multichannel device dates back to the inception of the program in 1977 when program members evaluated the University of Melbourne twenty-two-channel cochlear implant. While 3M proceeded to enter into a relationship with House and the Hochmairs, the University of Melbourne had entered into a relationship with Nucleus. 3M had planned to commercialize the Hochmairs's multichannel device soon after it had introduced the House and the Hochmairs' single-channel devices.

3M researchers had also worked with scientists at the UCSF to develop a multichannel device. Together they developed and implanted a multichannel cochlear implant device during 1980 and 1981. The relationship with UCSF terminated, and UCSF entered into a relationship with Storz.

Subsequently, 3M made several efforts to either develop or acquire the multichannel technology. They initiated one effort to acquire a multichannel technology in 1983. Even at this early stage of industry emergence, several researchers within 3M and in the otological community had started viewing the single-channel device as a "gross approximation of what was needed to provide speech discrimination." The biosciences research manger identified the development of a multichannel, multielectrode system as important for the overall development of the program. 3M's inaccessibility to patients implanted with multielectrode devices precluded the in-depth development of a novel multichannel processing scheme. Considering the rapid technological changes, the biosciences manager identified acquisition rather than internal development as the most appropriate strategy to access the multichannel technology.

Program members explored a relationship with Nucleus in October 1983 for several reasons. First, Nucleus had the longest experience with the multichannel device, and there was a possibility that Richards Medical would join Nucleus, making the Nucleus-Richards team a formidable competitor. Second, Nucleus and 3M possessed complementary skills. Nucleus had strong manufacturing expertise from its experience in pacemaker technology, and 3M had a strong distribution advantage in the United States. Third, 3M and Nucleus had taken contrasting but complementary approaches to speech processing. 3M devices transmitted an "analog" signal; the Nucleus device transmitted a "pulsatile" signal.

One key 3M program member, however, argued that a collaborative relationship with Nucleus did not serve 3M's interests. First, there was no evidence that Nucleus had a processing scheme that would allow true speech discrimination. Second, from a sales point of view, the multichannel device would not be a significant for the next five years. This time frame would allow 3M to develop internally the technological and manufacturing skills required to match or better Nucleus competencies. Rather than offer to enter into a joint venture with Nucleus, 3M offered to market the Nucleus multichannel devices in the United States. Nuclear, however, did not agree. Nucleus executives believed that a simple Nucleus-3M distribution agreement would leave Nucleus vulnerable in the future. Nucleus proposed that a 50:50 joint venture would benefit both parties. In December 1983, 3M program members rejected this counterproposal as the multichannel concept had not yet been sufficiently clinically proven. 3M had invested heavily in cochlear implant R&D and was unwilling to forego future opportunities by entering into a joint venture with Nucleus.

3M efforts to develop a multichannel device were initiated in 1984 in collaboration with the Hochmairs. One scientist said that this initiative soon "degenerated" into an effort at developing a device with two single channels. Efforts to develop a true multielectrode, multichannel system were shelved as the group at 3M became more involved in developing and manufacturing single-channel devices. When competitors claimed that single-channel devices would not provide speech discrimination, 3M countered that the claims were exaggerated and downplayed the risks of the multichannel device. When the FDA also supported the potential superiority of the multichannel device in its status reports, 3M tried to convince FDA staff members that the single-channel device was indeed safer and more effective than the multichannel devices.

In February 1985, an opportunity to acquire rights to the Stanford-developed multichannel device presented itself. Biostim, Stanford's industrial partner, had exited from the cochlear implant industry after lawsuits by its shareholders, and Stanford was searching for a suitable industrial partner to commercially develop its eight-channel device. 3M researchers considered Stanford's technology to be sophisticated and upgradable because of the wide latitude of stimulation paradigms that could be employed with the receiver. The 3M technical manager said that 3M could save two years in its multichannel efforts by joining Stanford, but that considerable developmental work was required with the Stanford device. Moreover, Stanford was only willing to enter into a five-year exclusive relationship with 3M, a time frame that 3M executives felt was too short. There was also a risk that Biostim would sue 3M because Biostim executives thought they owned the Stanford technology. After weighing the pros and cons, 3M eventually decided not to proceed with the Stanford opportunity.

In April 1985, CIP members stated that resource constraints hampered developmental progress on multichannel systems. In August 1985, the new program manager questioned the superiority of the single-channel device over multichannel devices. In September 1985, another technical person working on cochlear implants, a recipient of the 3M citation for technical excellence, also said the multichannel device would eventually prove to be superior in performance to the single-channel device. In January 1986, independent tests conducted by the University of Iowa showed that the multichannel device performed better than the single-channel device.

These events motivated CIP personnel to reemphasize its multichannel devices. The plan was to develop sequentially different aspects of the multielectrode, multichannel device. First, a processor would be developed by December 1986, which would be tried with the Vienna internal receiver. Second, a four-electrode device would be developed by August 1986 and a ten-electrode device by July 1987. Third, a multichannel processor, transmission system and hermetic package would be developed by December 1987. The biosciences laboratory manager was confident that the advanced multichannel device would leapfrog Nucleus's technology. Appropriately called the "Sprint" project, the 3M device would be based on clinical physiology, whereas the Nucleus device was based on speech physics.

However, 3M experienced mixed results from its efforts to develop a multichannel device. In July 1986, the program was granted an IDE by the FDA and clinical trials began. In October 1986, the 3M biosciences and the otological products laboratories were merged into one laboratory. According to the program manager, the purpose of the reorganization was to increase the effectiveness and efficiency of the laboratories' operations. By February 1987, scientists working on the multichannel device reported that the Sprint processor with the Vienna transmitter had not demonstrated results superior to those obtained by the Vienna device and that the Sprint program was two to three months behind in its patient-testing schedule. Earlier, the team had estimated that it would be able to file a PMAA for the multichannel device by 1989; it was revised to 1990. 3M experienced difficulties attracting appropriate postlingually deaf adults for clinical trials because the patients had trouble getting insurance payments for the "experimental" Sprint device. Even though 3M agreed to cover the cost of the device, patients were reluctant to be implanted with the Sprint device, reasoning that they would rather not risk trying an unproved device when the Nucleus FDA-approved device was available.

In September 1987, 3M reduced resources in CIP and in the Sprint project, from thirteen to eight people. In efforts to expand access to patients and reduce development costs, 3M biosciences lab scientists explored collaborative arrangements with Massachusetts Institute of Technology (MIT) to develop its multichannel device. MIT scientists agreed to initiate work on the Sprint device if it was compatible with the Symbion device that had earlier been developed by MIT researchers. In December 1987, the CIP program manager officially announced that 3M would orchestrate an "organized retreat" from cochlear implants. The House and Vienna devices would be kept on a maintenance mode. A low-profile attempt would be undertaken to obtain FDA approval for the 3M/House children's device during the first quarter of 1988. Eighty percent of the personnel in the program shifted to developing hearing aids. In January 1988, group members in the biosciences laboratory also terminated developmental activities of the Sprint device. Project members were experiencing difficulties finding patients to implant with the Sprint device. Moreover, 3M decided not to incur the liability supporting patients that it would assume by implanting the Sprint device.

Children's Devices

Although a decision had been made at the program level not to continue with cochlear implants, efforts to obtain PMA for the 3M-House cochlear implant for children persisted. To understand reasons for this persistence, a historical perspective on the development of a children's cochlear device follows.

Between 1981 and 1983, while 3M was commercially developing the House device for adults, House had been accumulating clinical experience with children under an IDE from the FDA. Consequently, even though 3M had initially planned to commercialize the Vienna EC device for children, it decided to seek PMAs for the House device for children.

By early 1984, 3M implanted almost 80 children and House planned to implant 250 more by the end of 1984. 3M and House planned to submit a PMAA to the FDA as soon as the application for the adult device had been approved. An early PMA for the children's device would again provide 3M with a two-year lead, which would allow it to corner a dominant share in the children's market. Other competitors had yet to start clinical trials with children, partly because the FDA had limited research on children. FDA staff members were concerned that cochlear implantation could damage a child's small cochlea, precluding future cochlear implantation (Simmons, 1985). Consistent with this philosophy, the FDA had also restricted the number of devices 3M could implant in children to 100 in the first instance.

In April 1985, 3M asked the FDA to remove the restriction on the number of children it could implant under the IDE. 3M also informed FDA staff members about the exceptional performance that the Hochmairs had observed with the Vienna EC device while posing lower risks to patients. FDA staff members impressed with the risk and benefits of the Vienna device suggested to 3M that waiting for an EC device for children might be desirable.

The potential of the EC device also caught the attention of customers. Several key implanting centers reported that they preferred the Vienna EC device for children. But 3M had not as yet sought an IDE for beginning clinical trials with the Vienna EC device. The unavailability of the Vienna EC device for children raised dilemmas for parents who wanted their children to have cochlear implants. Although the House device could be implanted immediately, there seemed to be great benefits in waiting for a Vienna EC device. This dilemma was reflected in a response that a 3M marketing manager provided to a parent who inquired whether her child should wait for the Vienna EC device or go ahead with the implantation of the House device. The marketing manager replied, "I am moved by the difficulty of your dilemma and the seriousness of your decision. But I cannot predict early availability of the 3M EC device for children. Until any cochlear implant device has seen extended use in sanctioned clinical studies with adults, I would recommend caution in pursuing its use in children."

A PMAA for the House children's device was submitted in September 1985. After reviewing this document, FDA staff members suggested changes in the study design and statistical analysis. Before 3M could address these requirements, it voluntarily recalled its House device for adults in November 1985 and initiated a redesign. Because the children's device was based on the adult version, the FDA asked 3M to resubmit the PMAA after the adult version had been redesigned.

Data collection and analysis efforts were soon resumed for the House children's device. By November 1986, program members said they were a couple of months away from making a PMAA for the House children's device. In the meantime, clinicians were showing great interest in a Vienna EC children's device. 3M program members debated the benefits of submitting a PMAA for the House device or initiating clinical trials with the Vienna EC device and abandoning the House children's PMAA. 3M members were concerned that by pursuing a PMAA for the House device, they would pave the way for a Nucleus PMAA for children while their own device would fall prey to the anticipated superior Vienna device, as had been the case with the House adult device. But because so much work had already been done in collecting and analyzing the House children's clinical data, 3M members decided to proceed with the PMAA for the House children's device. 3M would seek an IDE to begin clinical trials with the Vienna device soon after the House children's PMAA had been approved. Also, 3M would file a lawsuit against Nucleus for infringing a magnetic coupling patent that 3M had licensed from Baptist Medical. Nucleus had employed such a connecting system in its mini-twenty-two-channel device designed for children.

The PMAA for the House children's device was submitted in January 1987. In April 1987, FDA panel members recommended conditional approval for the PMAA contingent upon the resolution of major deficiencies but then rejected it. In its letter to 3M in July 1985, the FDA asked 3M to rearrange the clinical data to reflect a single-subjects, repeated-measures design for each age group to show progress over time with the implant. A mere comparison of pre- and post-implant performance was not enough. Analyzing the situation, 3M's regulatory manager said, "Even though it may not make financial sense to pursue the House children's device PMA application given our current program status, we may want to pursue this to its conclusion if we consider our credibility with the FDA to be a critical factor."

Besides the need to maintain credibility with the FDA, there was one other reason to persist with the PMAA. Clinicians at a children's implanting center at Central Institute for the Deaf (CID) at St. Louis, Missouri, had recorded very encouraging findings with the House children's device. As a result, 3M program members decided in October 1987 to proceed with the PMAA.

After considerable efforts, 3M once again reanalyzed the data and was ready to make the PMAA by early 1988. At that time, the FDA, and the NIH had organized a consensus development conference for cochlear implants. When 3M regulatory manager contacted the FDA, FDA staff members suggested that 3M wait until after the conference to submit the PMAA. FDA staff members hoped to get some direction from the scientific community at this conference about safety and efficacy related to implanting cochlear devices in children. The FDA was also in the process of drafting PMAA guidelines for implanting and testing in children. One part of the guidelines required investigators to conduct a minimum two-year follow-up of patients after the implant. The guidelines also suggested that the performance of at least 25% of all the patients be followed for three years. These guidelines, 3M's regulatory manager explained, would have more of an adverse impact on Nucleus than on 3M because the requirements would considerably delay Nucleus's PMAA for children.

At the NIH-FDA consensus program in May 1988, resistance to implantation in children was considerably less than it had been earlier. Soon after the conference, the FDA held an open meeting to seek guideline suggestions for PMAAs for children. At this meeting, Nucleus successfully argued that a minimum follow-up length should not be imposed and that the clinical protocols should reflect the claims made by each organization. Nucleus also supported the inclusion of language as a part of the testing protocol but argued that it should not be part of the performance specifications. Nucleus had collected data on language and was ready to provide it to panel members. 3M, on the other hand, did not possess complete data on language abilities of children who had been implanted with the House device. Nucleus managers also informed 3M that they would like 3M to go through with the House children's PMA so that Nucleus could learn from 3M's experience.

By mid-1988, any possible financial justification for pursuing the House children's PMA had disappeared. The group at 3M had shifted its attention to developing hearing aids and had decided to close its efforts in cochlear implants. When asked why program members persisted with the PMAA, the program manager said that the continued efforts to seek a PMA represented one last attempt to benefit profoundly deaf children. 3M's affiliations with House also led to this persistence because House was very keen that his device be the first to receive FDA approval. The regulatory manager said that it would be a shame if Nucleus's children's device were to get PMA before the House device considering that House had pioneered the children's market.

3M decided to discontinue its efforts in August 1988. When informed of 3M's intentions, House requested 3M to make one last PMA effort, as otherwise the children's House device would languish for the lack of incremental efforts on 3M's part. 3M agreed to pursue the PMAA one last time.

The FDA panel that met on September 22, 1988, unanimously agreed the device was safe and effective to implant in children. However, the panel advised 3M to modify three claims related to patients' ability to hear and discriminate sound and speech and rejected a fourth claim that the device improved speech production. The FDA sent 3M a letter saying that 3M would receive PMA if it incorporated some changes in the original PMAA. Having decided not to continue with its CIP, 3M left it up to House to make these changes.

Diversification

An earlier section described the events that led the CIP manager to expand program scope from cochlear implants to hearing health. The hearing health idea was influenced by the possibility that cochlear implants might solve a debilitating ringing sound in the ear, called tinnitus, that afflicts many deaf people. 3M researched tinnitus from 1981 until 1986. In June 1986, the CIP research head said that work on tinnitus would be discontinued because researchers learned that none of 3M's approaches could solve the problem. In February 1985, the first program manager reported that the division vice president had encouraged him to look at a broader vision of the hearing-health industry. To explore this avenue, in April 1985, the program manager arranged for a special discussion to examine whether the CIP should diversify into the market of less profoundly impaired deaf people with cochlear implants and hearing aids or to continue serving the market of profoundly deaf people with cochlear implants alone. The program manager said that the CIP did not have adequate resources to pursue both efforts and that he preferred to follow the former route. Other program members unanimously voted to continue with their cochlear implant efforts for the profoundly deaf patients and rejected the program manager's proposal to pursue placing the cochlear implant in the residual-hearing market. CIP members wanted to win in cochlear implants first. With the reassignment of the program manager in August 1985, the idea was tabled.

In March 1985, as a part of another acquisition, 3M acquired a firm that manufactured devices that measured patients' hearing loss. Because this device appeared to fit well with cochlear implant activities, 3M offered the CIP an opportunity to sell the product as a part of the business. After evaluating the opportunity, CIP members decided to sell diagnostic devices in May 1985. In the same month, CIP members promoted the diagnostic device at the Thirteenth International Otologic Conference. Immediately after this, the international marketing manager reported that efforts to promote the diagnostic device at the conference had been premature and abortive because the CIP was unable to supply the device to customers immediately on demand.

The October 1985 realization that the second device was not demonstrating acceptable performance results and the November 1985 market recall of the first device implied that the CIP had no cochlear devices to sell in the market for the first half of 1986. As a result, at year-end 1985, CIP management decided to focus sales efforts on promoting and selling diagnostics devices. The reported objective was to generate revenues from diagnostic devices to sustain the program.

Later, in June 1986, the CIP sales manager reported that the resources required to sell and service the diagnostic devices far exceeded the revenues they could generate. As a result, in July 1986, top management and program members decided to divest from diagnostic activities. By January 1987, the CIP had ended its diagnostics business.

As discussed earlier, in October 1985, Nucleus was granted a PMA by the FDA for commercial release of its twenty-two-channel device. In February 1986, the CIP finance manager said this would enable 3M to determine how big the market for cochlear implants really was. By mid-1986, the CIP marketing manager said evidence suggested that the cochlear implant market was not growing fast enough for the CIP to sustain a program solely on cochlear implants. He observed that Nucleus's sales failed to grow as expected. In addition, as reported earlier, two other competing firms, Storz and Symbion, were seeking alliances, reportedly because they expected the cochlear implant market to grow at a much slower pace than they had anticipated.

Consequently, in February 1986, a special programwide meeting was held to discuss possible product ideas for diversification that could sustain the program while the cochlear implant market emerged over time. One idea was hearing aids, suggested by the personnel founding the CIP in 1980. After this meeting, program members gathered information about the hearing-aids industry and possible organizations that the CIP could join to develop and manufacture technically advanced hearing aids.

In May 1986, a plan presented to the sector committee by program members to continue work on cochlear implants and to expand into other unspecified products was tabled. Sector committee members asked the group to present more details of the alternate products that the CIP could pursue. One of the sector committee's main concerns was that the cochlear implant market was not increasing fast enough;

therefore, cochlear implant activities should not be the immediate thrust of the program. Later, in July 1986, the program presented a revised plan in which the CIP would enter the hearing-aids industry by acquiring a company manufacturing advanced hearing aids. This time, the sector committee approved the plan. In October 1986, the sector vice president granted permission to acquire a hearing-aids company. In January 1987, the CIP acquired Diaphone of Sweden to manufacture hearing aids.

Termination

The release of a statement by the cochlear implant research community at the NIH-FDA consensus development conference held in May 1988 endorsing multichannel over single-channel devices further dissipated momentum that remained in the program. By early 1988, most program members had exited from cochlear implant activities. Eighty percent of program members' time and resources had been directed toward developing a hearing aid. Decisions had also been made to discontinue most of the individual cochlear programs. But a decision to exit formally from the cochlear implant program had not yet been made. Sales of the House device for adults were still under way, and efforts at obtaining a PMA for the House children's device also continued.

A decision to exit formally from cochlear implants was made in September 1988 because maintaining even minimal cochlear implant operations required substantial resources and was distracting program members' attention from hearing aid–related activities.

However, efforts to exit from the cochlear implant business proved much more difficult than anticipated. "There are some things that are easy to get into but difficult to get out of," one program member said. "The cochlear implant program is one of them. Initially, the momentum and excitement had been great. Later, when we had decided to get out, everything and everyone seemed to hold us from getting out." The program member was alluding to difficulties in formally ending activities with (1) the Hochmairs, (2) House, (3) a randomized cochlear implant study under way at the Veterans Administration (VA) hospitals throughout the United States, and (4) the FDA. In May 1988, 3M made the decision to continue contractual relationships with the Hochmairs for an additional year because of several ties between 3M and the Hochmairs, including joint patent rights.

In August 1988, program members decided to continue pursuing FDA panel approval for the House children's device despite the lack of financial justification to continue. Encouraged by Dr. House, program members reasoned that not pursuing a PMA at this stage would rob profoundly deaf children of an opportunity to benefit from cochlear implants.

VA officials, when informed of 3M's decision to exit, expressed concerns about continued service of cochlear devices that had been implanted in patients. VA officials encouraged 3M to find another company that would take the responsibility of future service. 3M stated its intent to extend a three-year warranty and the supply of cochlear implant parts for five years. To fulfill this obligation, 3M built an inventory of cochlear implant parts during early 1988.

When 3M approached the FDA to formally discontinue its IDE and PMA, the FDA said 3M would have to maintain its IDE and PMA to continue providing warranty and future service activities. Maintaining this IDE and PMA would also require 3M to continue submitting periodic reports to the FDA, activities that 3M was reluctant to continue given its decision to exit the business. Considering the difficulties experienced in exiting the program, one program member said in February 1989: "We had made a decision to exit the program last September. But, cut one strand, and another grows in its place."

Efforts to sell the business were not immediately successful. Of the three firms operating in the industry, Nucleus, Pacesetter, and Symbion, only Nucleus and Pacesetter were potentially interested in buying 3M's technology. Symbion's program had encountered problems with the FDA's refusal to grant a PMA, partly because of the percutaneous plug. Moreover, the Symbion transmission system was not entirely compatible with the 3M cochlear implant components, making Symbion an unlikely candidate to buy the 3M cochlear implant business. Pacesetter expressed interest in the House device for children but not in other parts of 3M technology for further commercial development. Pacesetter was collaborating with UCSF scientists and believed that the UCSF-Pacesetter technology was superior to both Nucleus's and 3M's multichannel technologies. Moreover, Pacesetter was not willing to assume responsibilities of servicing the already implanted 3M cochlear devices.

Nucleus remained the only viable choice as a potential buyer of 3M's cochlear program. Nucleus had said that it intended to remain committed to cochlear implants despite "fewer than expected patients." Nucleus executives wanted to make Nucleus the leading company for cochlear implants. More important, 3M's Sprint technology was based on an analog stimulation approach that could become important in the future if UCSF's analog stimulation system demonstrated good performance. Nucleus's technology was based on a "pulsatile" stimulation design that the University of Melbourne scientists had steadfastly pursued.

The Hochmairs were keen that 3M not sell the analog Sprint technology to Nucleus because the sale would make Nucleus a direct competitor of the Hochmairs's own analog multielectrode technology in Europe. To remove potential confrontation between Nucleus and the Hochmairs, 3M submitted a proposal to Nucleus that would align the Hochmairs with Nucleus in Europe. Among other aspects, 3M proposed that Nucleus (1) have nonexclusive rights to certain 3M cochlear implant patents, and (2) be willing to service Vienna cochlear implants in Europe. Both conditions were acceptable to Nucleus, and on August 13, 1989, 3M sold its cochlear implant business to Nucleus.

Analysis of the CIP's Development

This section analyzes the development of the CIP in terms of (1) the temporal progressions in the CIP's development; (2) issues pertaining to resource acquisition and allocation; and (3) issues related to risk, persistence, and learning.

Temporal Progressions in the CIP's Development

Unitary Sequence between 1981 and 1984

The chronological list of events indicates that between 1981, when the CIP was formally initiated, and November 1984, when the FDA approved the first device, 63% of events were associated with developing the first device. This suggests that the development of the program followed a "unitary path" during this period.

One reason for this unitary development of the program between 1981 and 1984 can be linked to a key objective of the program manager in November 1984. The objective was to create and exploit a window of opportunity by being the first in the market with a cochlear device. Because the cochlear implant industry is regulated by the FDA, any device that first obtains FDA approval for commercial sale enjoys this head start until a competing firm's product also receives FDA approval.

According to a CIP research manager, program members made a tactical error in working toward an FDA PMAA for commercial sale of the first device despite the potential advantages of being the first to market. He pointed out that considerable resources were expended in creating this window of opportunity. He also said that by the time the FDA had granted its approval, the first device had become technologically obsolete compared to other devices available on an IDE basis. He suggested that it might have been wiser to have progressed only to the investigational stage for the first device and then to have moved on to develop the next generation of devices.

The unitary sequence of activities during this period also reflects an escalation of commitment. In March 1985, the group vice president suggested that the CIP should not expend more resources to develop the first device further. He suggested that the CIP should instead move ahead to commercialize the second device and initiate work on multi-channel devices. However, little progress was made in either direction. Offering a reason for this lack of progress, a program member reported in 1985 that lack of resources severely hindered progress on the multichannel device and that failure to develop a multichannel device was a critical omission for the program. In November 1986, the group vice president again expressed frustration that the program had not shifted focus from single-channel technology as he had suggested.

Divergent Sequence of Events between 1984 and 1989

After 1984, there was a proliferation of products in cochlear implants and in hearing-health. For instance, in the cochlear implant area, the development of a device for children and the second device for adults began during the end of 1984. In 1986, development of the multichannel device began. The overall concept of the business of hearing had evolved from tinnitus and diagnostics to hearing aids. These initiatives were unrelated because each specialty area required different specific skills and knowledge, although they used the same stock of basic knowledge about the science of hearing.

Iterative Sequence of Events

Each product had to progress through the FDA's iterative regulatory process of receiving approval for animals, then humans and finally achieving a minimum level of safety and effectiveness. The entire procedure of obtaining FDA approval took three to five years.

Partly because of these iterative steps, the development of functional competencies for each product generation emerged sequentially, as illustrated in figure 8.4. For example, in the case of the first device, R&D was followed by clinical engineering, which was followed by regulatory approvals, which were followed by manufacturing and sales. The sequence, characteristic of other product generations, was designed by the CIP program members to handle the increased scope of program activities without increasing resources.

Despite this sequential development of competencies for each product generation, we observed two instances of opportunistic "leapfrogging" in CIP's cochlear implant development. At the 1985 otolaryngology conference, 3M promoted the second single-channel device even though it had not yet (1) completed clinical trials, (2) obtained FDA regulatory approval, or (3) scaled up manufacturing. The marketing function began much before 3M completed the three other preceding

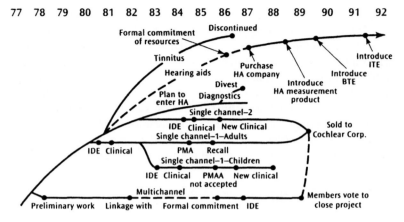

Figure 8.4 Temporal development of product and functions in the Cochlear Implant Program

value-creation functions. The second instance of leapfrogging occurred when 3M prematurely introduced its newly acquired diagnostic device. However, after generating customer interest for the diagnostic devices, 3M found it was unable to service the demand.

The case illustrates one of the problems associated with product transition management. According to the sales manager, promoting the second device in May 1985 at the Thirteenth International Otologic Conference caused audiologists and patients to want to wait for the second device rather than to use the first one. This premature promotion was one reason for poor sales of the first device in the second quarter of 1985.

Resource Acquisition, Allocation, and Regeneration

Resource acquisition, allocation, and subsequent regeneration are central to any business venture. The cochlear implant program provides unique insights in these processes. For example, the program began by tapping into corporate resources not specifically earmarked for the project. Different individuals "bootlegged" their time and organizational resources to explore a nebulous yet potentially important idea. Equally important, the emerging group found that other people in the company were already working in areas related to elements of the program, which made identifying and drafting them into a coherent program relatively easy. A budget was allocated formally only after a series of information-gathering steps that covered the technology, the market and competition, and the broader institutional environment. Financial resources and people involved in the program increased gradually.

Even after the formal inception of the program in 1981, the budget was "hidden" within the overall sector-level R&D budget, providing the program some degree of seclusion. However, the high profile of the product brought the program to the spotlight soon after the FDA approved the first device for large-scale commercial sale in November 1984. At that time, U.S. President Ronald Reagan congratulated 3M for its accomplishments.

This congratulatory note enhanced top management's expectations, which had already been elevated when CIP members sought "program status" with independent profit-center responsibilities. But expectations to generate revenues from the implantation of the FDA-approved cochlear devices did not match marketplace realities. While granting 3M's first device regulatory approvals, the FDA also released a statement that a more advanced device offered by competitors was being considered for approval. The FDA's announcement adversely effected the credibility of the CIP. Specifically, patients and surgeons choose to wait for the more advanced multichannel device rather than implant the approved single-channel device. As a result, the program could not generate revenues it had promised top management.

Internally, credibility problems flowed from the inability to meet milestones, especially financial ones. These credibility problems made it difficult to raise the internal resources required to perform the ever-expanding activities that addressed the lack of sales. More important, though, the revenues represented a new set of technical skills required to develop future generations of cochlear implants. Moreover, the regulated status of the product required that any new devices would have to undergo time- and resource-consumptive FDA approval processes. The recall of the first-generation device set into motion dynamics that drastically altered the program. Being the first mover turned out to be very costly.

Risk, Persistence, and Learning

Consistent with 3M's approach to fund projects that might eventually spawn a division-size business, the CIP also was funded with the expectation that it would provide 3M an entry into the hearing-health industry in ten years. Keeping this time frame in mind is important to understand the tensions between "action" persistence and "undue" persistence that seems to have been a key issue in the program toward its later stages.

In its early stages, the program was characterized by what we have labeled "action" persistence, the necessity to act and move forward

(Garud and Van de Ven, 1992; Brunsson, 1982). So powerful was the momentum to act and move that negative feedback from others did not dampen program members' enthusiasm. A failure to "explore" was considered an error more than a failure to "exploit" (March, 1992; Garud et al., 1996).

Such an attitude prevailed for several reasons. First, at this early stage of development, it was not clear which technical and strategic approach would be successful (Garud and Rappa, 1994). Second, top management had already allocated resources to the project with the expectation that milestones would be met much later. Third, conflicting and changing outcome criteria were being used across levels of management to measure the progress, as indicated in Table 8.1. Given these shifting outcome criteria among CIP managers and resource controllers, the program managers logically persisted with their course of action.

Another way to look at the dynamics at this stage was that "hurdle rates" were low, and program members' emphasis was on being the first in the market with a cochlear implant. Program members were encouraged to explore various avenues through which this objective could be accomplished and simultaneously to explore ways the program could support a family of hearing-health products at a later stage. This thinking led program members to pursue a variety of initiatives, and, eventually, as one manager said, the program became a bramble bush rather than an oak tree as they had hoped.

Pruning the bramble bush was forced on the program by a dramatic shift in the CIP's context. As members in the cochlear implant community began perceiving the superiority of multichannel over single-channel devices, ambiguity regarding the appropriate approach disappeared. In its place was left uncertainty about how improvements could be made along the multichannel trajectory and about the size of the market. At the same time, resources at 3M decreased because of the program's failure to generate revenues and increased difficulty getting additional funds from top management.

The absence of ambiguity and resource scarcity stopped action persistence. Program members became much more focused on modest, immediate, and measurable goals, resulting in a process in which actions and outcomes were more closely linked, a process we have described as representing "trial and error" learning (Garud and Van de Ven, 1992; Cheng and Van de Ven, 1996). CIP's lack of credibility with top management created an environment in which program members became increasingly cautious. They now felt "experimentation" could lead to outcomes that likely were considered "errors." Indeed, program members' perceptions about the transition of CIP program managers accentuated the risk they would bear if they committed these "mistakes." Consequently, program members began adopting a risk-averse attitude in which they were more inclined to reduce "errors of com-

Table 8.1. *Cochlear Implant Innovation*: Outcome criteria of resource controllers and innovation managers over time

Time	Resource controllers' criteria	Innovation managers' criteria
6/84	Build new business in new market with new technology.	Create new product for deaf.
	Become self-sustaining business in ten years.	Establish strong relationships with clinical research centers.
		Be first in market with FDA approval of first cochlear device.
2/85	Achieve operating income, expense and profit objectives. in market.	Take advantage of opportunity window with FDA-approved device
	Become number one player in new market in 10 years.	Meet sales targets.
	Accomplish technical objectives.	Develop otological distribution and training centers.
7/85	Implement marketing plan.	Correct internal organizational problems.
	Take advantage of window of market opportunity.	Develop production capacity for sales.
	Meet sales targets.	Improve quality control.
12/85	Competence of program managers.	Solve image problem of product recall.
	Can program make it?	Market and sell alternative products.
		Improve morale of program members.
8/86	Adequacy of market size for cochlear implant business.	Reorganize program.
	Shift from business to lab project - meet technical milestones and cost controls.	Develop children's cochlear device.
		Leap-frog competitors with new device.
		Expand program into hearing aids.
12/86	Competence of program management.	Build credibility for program.
	Overinvestment in single-channel device.	Manage new acquisitions.
	Misreading of market demand.	Start work on hearing aids device.
	Resources drain of product recall.	

(*continued*)

Table 8.1. (*continued*)

Time	Resource controllers' criteria	Innovation managers' criteria
9/87	Loss of market share. aids business quickly.	Transition from cochlear to hearing
	Technically inferior device.	Get cost credibility to buy time.
	Failure in cochlear devices, but hope in hearing aids.	Become fastest growing division in three years.
	Lack of matching people to jobs they are competent in.	

mission." Eventually, that perspective generated negative spirals that led to winnowing the program and eventually to a transition to another project—hearing aids.

These dynamics are revealed when we juxtapose plots of frequencies of action and outcome events in CIP's development in figure 8.5. The action plot shows the number of events that signaled continuation

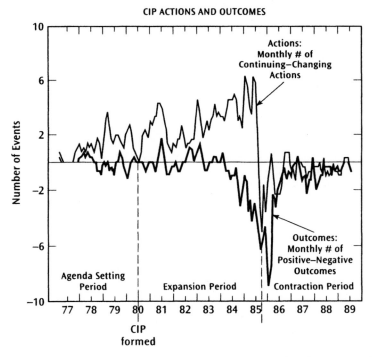

Figure 8.5 Action and outcome events in the development of CIP (plots are three-month moving averages)

and expansion minus the number of events that signaled change and contraction. The outcome plot tracks the number of events that were judged by CIP participants to result in positive outcomes minus the number of events that were negative. As the plots suggest, from the period 1980 to 1985, activities continued expanding in the CIP program despite signals, especially after 1983, that outcomes were not positive. Representing a process of exploration and learning by discovery, this period contrasted dramatically with the subsequent period of trial-and-error learning, in 1985 onward, when ambiguity about which type of device would be successful decreased.

An interesting fact is that the eventual termination of the cochlear implant program was a negotiated process between top management and program members. Top management controlled the flow of resources to the program and sought increasingly elaborate justifications and guarantees for additional funding. Program members continued seeking ways to make the program viable. Eventually they concluded that a fresh start with hearing aids was the best path to pursue.

Appendix: Dates and Events in the Development of the CIP

Initiation

01/01/77   University of Melbourne approaches 3M for a possible collaborative relationship to commercialize its cochlear implant technology.

12/15/77   3M preliminary evaluation suggests that the cochlear implant technology could be a promising project.

01/05/78   3M initiates search activities of cochlear implant activities in the United States.

12/15/78   3M and University of Melbourne fail to reach a mutually acceptable agreement.

02/01/79   The Australian Department of Productivity extends funding to the University of Melbourne under the condition that efforts would be made to indigenously develop and manufacture the cochlear device.

02/02/79   3M decides overall approach to conduct its search activities —buy rights to Audiotronics California Corporation (ACC), retain Michelson and Bartz as consultants, establish vendor relationship with University of California San Francisco, and further evaluate the House Ear Institute (HEI).

06/19/79   3M initiates discussions with the Hochmairs of Vienna.

07/26/79   3M engineer argues that 3M is losing a golden opportunity in single-channel systems by not finalizing an agreement with HEI.

07/27/79   3M becomes vendor to HEI for cochlear implant parts.

10/08/79   3M and UCSF enter into contractual agreement.

12/03/79   3M and Michelson and Bartz enter into contractual agreement.

12/11/79   3M faces difficulties in providing cochlear implant parts to UCSF.

03/31/80   Stanford enters into relationship with Biostim.

08/15/80   Key 3M program members caution that there is a danger of losing House because of 3M's ability to deliver contracted products.

09/22/80   House starts looking around for another company to manufacture its parts as 3M confronts difficulties in supplying cochlear implant parts to HEI.

09/23/80   University of Melbourne enters into a relationship with Nucleus Ltd.

02/19/81   Merzenich upset with 3M for various reasons and denies access to research activities under way at Coleman laboratories.

02/19/81   3M retains Don Eddington of the University of Utah as a consultant.

04/17/81   3M articulates plan to first take up the development of the House device to be followed by the Hochmairs's devices, and then a multichannel device.

04/20/81   3M and the Hochmairs enter into an exclusive relationship.

04/29/81   3M engineers find it difficult to fabricate the complex UCSF electrodes.

05/29/81   UCSF researchers demonstrate outstanding results with their multichannel device.

07/21/81   3M program members formally articulate overall strategy of wanting to be first in the market.

08/12/81   The Hochmairs present a paper at a West Coast conferences where they demonstrate open set speech with their single-channel devices.

12/08/81   3M finds that resources for developing the House and Hochmair devices compete directly with resources required to develop multichannel devices with UCSF.

12/18/81   3M and HEI enter into an exclusive relationship.

12/21/81   Eddington lets contractual agreement with 3M lapse.

12/07/82   3M does not renew contractual agreement with Michelson of UCSF.

01/02/83   Eddington enters into relationship with Symbion.

07/30/83   UCSF and Michelson enter into contractual agreement with Storz.

Initial Strategy Formulation

01/01/81   3M consolidates three separate cochlear implant efforts into a stand-alone entrepreneurial program.

01/01/81   Program members working on cochlear implant realize that they are involved in something of a much bigger magnitude than just cochlear implants—the whole area of hearing health.

07/21/81   3M cochlear implant group develops first formal business plan. Some essential elements of the plan are (1) be first in the market, (2) introduce a number of generations of product, (3) initiate chronic safety studies in animals, and (4) begin international activities.

01/01/83   3M researchers feel that Nucleus twenty-two-channel device is too sophisticated and that Nucleus is research rather than market oriented.

05/27/83   Paul Trainor of Nucleus advises 3M not to commercialize too fast.

08/18/83   3M mission statement is to be first multinational corporation to successfully enter the market and maintain a dominant market share in cochlear implants.

04/06/84   3M program members state: "As AT&T is to communication and IBM is to computer, 3M will be to hearing health."

First-Generation (House) Device

07/27/79   3M becomes vendor to HEI for cochlear implant parts.

02/01/80   HEI obtains investigational device exemption (IDE) approval from the Food and Drug Administration for the
House device.

07/21/81   Preliminary plan details following decisions: (1) make
minimal design changes in order to expedite commercial
introduction, (2) initiate chronic animal studies in order
to safeguard against questions from the FDA, (3) render
device safer by reducing length of electrode, (4) make
minimum capital investment to achieve high early return
on investment, (5) take early international action because
of long, drawn-out U.S. regulatory process.

12/18/81   3M and HEI enter into an exclusive relationship.

06/01/82   Marketing manager states that being first in the market
would provide strong opportunity to shape the distribution system.

08/10/82   Manufacturing manager confirms high-flexibility low-
investment manufacturing strategy.

01/01/83   Insurance agents agree to cover the House device.

04/15/83   Decision made to interface with a wide variety and large
number of clinics across the nation in order to gain dominance.

07/30/83   Manufacturing manager states philosophy of selective vertical integration leading to minimum capital investment.

10/01/83   3M submits premarket approval (PMA) to the FDA for the
House device.

02/17/84   FDA panel meeting for the House device.

02/24/84   Manufacturing manager confirms strategy of minimum
capital investment because of low sales volumes projected
for several years.

04/09/84   FDA asks 3M to stop implanting the House device while
the PMA is under review.

04/20/84   Manufacturing manager confirms strategy to be respon-
sive and flexible, realizing the fast-moving technology
evolution.

06/01/84   The FDA says that it will not accept clinical data that have
been recorded with the original House device as claims of
efficacy.

06/26/84   Sales of the House device lower than anticipated.

06/27/84   FDA advisory panel approves the House PMAA.

07/02/84	Redesign of electrodes and internal receiver identified as most urgent product developmental objective.
07/05/84	3M initiates focused distribution effort and novel marketing approach to field of otology.
10/12/84	Decision to seek only quantum jumps in House design and avoid incremental improvements; decision to seek quantum jump in processing scheme by focusing on Vienna processor design.
11/01/84	Formal FDA PMA approval for the House device.
11/26/84	FDA status report supporting the potential superiority of the multichannel device over the single-channel device.
12/01/84	3M establishes pilot manufacturing facilities at St. Paul and manufacturing facilities at Sarns.
01/01/85	3M establishes titanium vendor for the House device.
02/05/85	3M enters into a relationship with a local hospital and forms CISM to conduct rehabilitation.
06/12/85	Shift to titanium electrode becomes imperative because of warranty costs and future lawsuit liabilities.

Overall Program Level Strategy Update

11/17/83	FDA drafting clinical guidelines for cochlear implants.
01/09/84	FDA imposes restrictions on number of children that can be implanted with the House device.
04/01/84	FDA IDE granted for the Hochmairs's Vienna extracochlear (EC) device. The FDA imposes a fifty-patient limit.
06/01/84	Nucleus submits PMAA.
06/18/84	3M provides inputs to shape FDA guidelines.
07/25/84	Nucleus PMAA accepted for filing.
06/26/84	Program manager states that it is important to capture window of opportunity by promoting the 3M/House cochlear implant.
09/18/84	Nucleus president states that it will be easier for Nucleus to downgrade its device than it will be for 3M to upgrade.
10/11/84	FDA requests more clinical data from Nucleus.
11/01/84	3M article in *Hearing Journal* emphasizes safety and upgradability by preserving the future.
11/01/84	Typical testimonial in *Wall Street Journal* where Nucleus consultant states: "Single-channel devices are better than nothing."
12/05/84	3M asks FDA to police claims being made by competing firms even without FDA approvals.
12/18/84	3M informs FDA about the remarkable results achieved with the Vienna EC device.

01/01/85	3M organizes a seminar for FDA staff to share knowledge about cochlear implant safety.
01/01/85	Program members identify that key factor in achieving dominant market share will be to rapidly train physicians and facilities, which requires accelerated marketing resources.
01/05/85	Program members consider developing a hybrid design consisting of the House internal receiver and the Vienna processor in order to expedite the availability of a device that demonstrates performance.
02/01/85	Loeb of NIH supports superiority of the multichannel device over the single-channel device in an article in *Scientific American*.
03/06/85	Lack of sales leads to credibility problems with top management.
03/01/85	Cochlear implant positioning study completed by Marketing Services Inc. of Pennsylvania provides some of the reasons for poor sales of cochlear devices.
03/26/85	3M salespeople report that the Nucleus multichannel device has achieved perceived "FDA approved" status.
04/10/85	Sales for the first quarter were 5% ahead of forecast. Program members use this sales performance to requisition for five additional salespeople.
05/01/85	3M states in an American Speech Hearing Association (ASHA) article that it is concerned about competitors' raising unrealistic expectations among patients.
05/07/85	3M suggests to the FDA that a minimum of 100 patients be clinically tried to establish claims of safety and efficacy.
05/26/85	Each firm in the industry claims that the other is making exaggerated claims and express the need for industry standards.
06/01/84	3M article in *Hearing Instruments* that states that multichannel proponents with deep insertion electrodes are irresponsible.
06/01/85	Epoxy failure identified with the House device.
07/01/85	Unfavorable 3M internal survey findings.
07/15/85	FDA panel members ask Nucleus for additional clinical data.
08/08/85	Decision taken to downplay investments in 3M/House and position it in a maintenance mode.
07/01/85	3M evaluates linkage with Richards and decides not to enter into a relationship.
07/22/85	FDA draft guidelines will not specify number of patients required for PMA and sets maximum and minimum limits for cochlear implantation under an IDE.
08/13/85	Marketing manager states that the biggest problems confronting the program are perceptions of obsolescence of

the House device, the promise but inaccessibility of the Vienna device, and the misconception that the multiple channel devices are inherently more sophisticated.

09/01/85	3M sends out newsletter reinforcing concept of catalogue of products.
09/01/85	Program members acknowledge that they no longer are the technological leaders.
09/23/85	3M submits PMA for children's device.
05/31/85	3M provides FDA with inputs about the Hochmair Vienna EC device.
06/24/85	FDA ENT head says that it would be desirable for 3M to wait for an EC device for children.
11/20/85	3M voluntarily recalls its House device from the market.
02/06/86	Shift in program focus from getting product out to reliability.

3M Second-Generation (Hochmair Vienna) Device

04/20/81	3M and the Hochmairs enter into agreement.
07/21/81	3M plans to introduce three versions of the Hochmair Vienna device, starting with the selectable electrodes.
02/01/82	3M plans change to introduce EC device first.
02/01/82	Team formed to commercially develop Vienna EC device.
08/27/82	Burian requests for funding; 3M declines.
03/24/83	Burian not forthcoming with data.
12/04/83	3M retains Burian as a consultant
03/01/84	FDA IDE for the Hochmair Vienna EC device; limit of fifty patients initially.
04/20/84	Program members request top management for additional resources in order to accelerate time line for development of the Hochmair Vienna device.
11/05/84	3M obtains encouraging results from Europe of the Hochmair Vienna EC performance.
03/08/85	3M clinician confirms positive results with the Hochmair Vienna EC device.
03/26/85	Nucleus multichannel device has achieved perceived FDA-approved status.
04/12/85	Program members deliberate whether to pursue the profoundly deaf or the patients with residual hearing as program does not have adequate resources to pursue both segments of the market.
05/01/85	FDA judges 3M's informal PMAA of the Hochmair Vienna EC device to be unacceptable.
05/07/85	Program manager states intention to extend reach with cochlear implants into the residual hearing population to expand market potential.

05/07/85   3M researchers initiate development of ceramic 3M-Hochmair Vienna receiver which will set standards for industry reliability and longevity of cochlear implants.

05/26/85   3M promotes Vienna device performance at the Thirteenth International Otologic Conference as a multifrequency device.

05/26/85   Competitors accuse 3M of making exaggerated claims.

08/01/85   Program members find that the premature promotion of the Vienna device cramps sales of the House device.

09/01/85   Inadequate clinical support for U.S.-Vienna EC device performance; consequently, program members change thrust from an EC electrode to an intracochlear (IC) electrode.

09/04/85   Development efforts under way to build an enhanced processor which could be used for children and patients with residual hearing.

09/11/85   Program members discuss that the realistic time schedule for filing the PMA for the Hochmair Vienna device was the fall of 1987 and not the fall of 1985.

10/01/85   FDA grants 3M IDE for Vienna IC.

01/01/86   Program members scramble to get patients to begin clinical trials with the IC electrode.

01/22/86   Nucleus accuses 3M of making exaggerated claims.

09/03/86   Program members decide to postpone clinical trials with partially hearing impaired until beginning of year.

11/01/86   University of Minnesota clinician states that the Hochmair device has lost its place in time.

12/01/86   Enhanced processor ready.

12/17/86   Decision to postpone purchasing of welding machine until cochlear implant market and performance of the Vienna device become clearer.

01/01/87   Clinical efforts with patients with residual hearing begun.

01/23/87   Program members consolidate manufacturing operations.

06/01/87   Decision taken not to promote or sell the Hochmair device.

01/13/88   Richard Tyler of the University of Iowa corroborates the good results that the Hochmairs had achieved with their device in Vienna.

Overall Program-Level Strategy Update

07/17/85   Separate group working on hearing-aids program.

10/01/85   FDA grants Nucleus PMA approval.

09/01/85   Program members acknowledge that they are no longer technological leaders.

02/01/86   Move to enter into the hearing-aids market.

02/06/86   Program manager states that the business mission is to be able to solve any problem in the hearing-health area, not necessarily only in cochlear implants.

03/01/86   Program members state that the business strategy is to improve quality and regain technological leadership. Whereas safety had been a significant factor in the past, performance now was.

04/03/86   The idea that more is better is gaining ground in the industry now that fears are receding of IC electrodes invading cochlear.

05/21/86   3M sector planning committee accepts program's plans only when they propose to diversify into hearing aids.

06/01/86   Change in promotional objective—not be negative and introduce 3M multichannel device.

11/18/86   Many physicians who implanted 3M-House device have shifted to implanting Nucleus device.

Third-Generation (Multichannel) Device

01/01/77   3M evaluates the University of Melbourne's twenty-two-channel technology.

12/15/78   3M and University of Melbourne are not able to enter into a mutually acceptable collaborative relationship.

10/08/79   3M establishes vendor relationship with UCSF.

12/03/79   3M retains Michelson and Bartz of ACC as consultants.

12/07/82   Consulting agreement with Michelson terminated.

07/30/83   Program members decide to seek collaborative relationship with Nucleus in order to accelerate developmental efforts in multichannel device.

12/06/83   3M and Nucleus are not able to enter into a mutually acceptable collaborative relationship.

06/29/84   3M internal efforts to develop a multichannel device degenerate into an effort to develop two single-channel devices.

02/07/85   3M has the opportunity to acquire Stanford technology; 3M decides not to pursue this option.

04/01/85   3M program member states that resource constraint has prevented work on multichannel devices.

09/01/85   Symbion approaches 3M to explore possibility of entering into a collaborative relationship.

09/11/85   Technical manager states that the program has continually been defending single-channel implants and paying lip service to multichannel implants.

01/01/86   Security analyst report references tests conducted by the University of Iowa that show the clear superiority of the multichannel device.

01/01/86   Storz approaches 3M to explore possibility of entering into a collaborative relationship.

02/05/86   Biosciences laboratory formally commits resources to begin work on Sprint multichannel device.

02/26/86   3M explores possibility of linking up with pacemaker companies—Medtronics Inc. or Pacesetter, Inc.

03/11/86   C. R. Bard and Symbion sign tentative letter of intent.

05/01/86   Symbion once again approaches 3M for collaborative relationship after terminating discussions with C. R. Bard.

07/01/86   Storz acquired by American Cynamide

07/01/86   IDE granted for Sprint device by the FDA.

09/23/86   3M's proposal to market the Symbion multichannel device is not acceptable to Symbion.

10/06/86   Biosciences and otological laboratories merged for improved effectiveness.

10/06/86   American Cynamide turns down Storz funding proposal.

10/15/86   3M technical audit of multichannel laboratory program reported to be very successful.

10/15/86   OHTA report suggests that multichannel devices were superior to single-channel devices.

10/21/86   UCSF is organizing an R&D team to reassume control and responsibility for the development of an eight-channel device.

02/18/87   Sprint processor and Vienna transmitter do not perform well.

03/01/87   Business strategy is to provide products which improve hearing for impaired individuals. This will be done by regaining technical leadership with cochlear implant by focusing on versatile digital signal multichannel device.

05/22/87   Rejection of children PMAA by the FDA.

07/01/87   Symbion and Richards enter into a multimillion-dollar collaborative agreement.

07/10/87   The Hochmairs want to renegotiate contract with 3M to allow them to pursue other sources of funding for their multichannel device.

07/14/87   The Hochmairs and 3M discuss plans for the Hochmairs to develop receiver transmitter for the Sprint multichannel device.

09/01/87   Stanford University contacts 3M to inquire if 3M would be interested in taking up the Stanford multichannel device for development; 3M declines.

09/10/87   Sprint program confronting problems in attracting patients.

09/14/87   Program members adopt a "regroup" strategy.

09/16/87   Further reduction of resources to Sprint: manpower reduction from thirteen to eight.

12/01/87   Program manager announces organized retreat from
            cochlear implants.
12/16/87   3M enters into a research relationship with MIT scientists.
01/08/88   Decision taken to terminate Sprint development.

Children's Device

07/21/81   Program members plan to develop the Vienna EC device
            for children as the third product.
01/09/84   FDA imposes restrictions on number of children implants
            at 100.
10/01/84   Decision to submit children's device to FDA review of
            clinical investigation. It was ultimately approved.
11/26/84   FDA status report states that the FDA has limited the re-
            search on children because of concerns that the procedure
            may damage the cochlea, thereby eliminating the patient
            from future cochlear implants
01/01/85   Program members say that they will capture two-year
            competitive advantage in establishing dominant share in
            children's market population. Contingency plans: If
            Vienna device does not demonstrate performance, efforts
            will be refocused to capitalize on safety issues in the chil-
            dren's market and concurrently to expand involvement in
            multichannel and speech processing research.
02/02/85   Blair Simmons identifies dilemmas in the implantation of
            cochlear device in young children in an article in *Ear and
            Hearing*.
04/08/85   Application to seek extension for children's IDE submitted
            to the FDA.
06/24/85   FDA suggests that 3M wait for EC device for children.
09/23/85   Children PMAA submitted to the FDA.
11/06/85   FDA ENT head concerned about the study design adopted
            for the children's PMAA.
11/20/85   3M voluntarily recalls its House device.
12/03/85   FDA announces its decision to send back children's
            PMAA because of recall and questions about study design.
12/04/85   House expresses its concern about 3M's general support
            for children's program.
07/11/86   Nucleus announces commencement of its children's program.
09/25/86   3M withdraws children's PMAA.
10/16/86   3M requests the FDA to require that Nucleus use its own
            single-channel device for children.
11/25/86   Program members deliberate whether to offer a Vienna or
            House device for children. Group decides to continue
            with the House children's PMAA.

01/01/87   Children's PMAA submitted by 3M.

02/18/87   Salespeople report that there is great interest in the Vienna children's program.

05/22/87   FDA panel suggests that the children's PMA is approvable upon resolution of deficiencies.

07/07/87   FDA does not approve the children's PMAA and asks 3M to rearrange and reanalyze its clinical data.

09/16/87   Clinicians from CID report good results with House device in children.

09/16/87   FDA points out fourteen deficiencies with the Vienna children's IDE submission. 3M decides to make this IDE submission one more time.

09/29/87   House publishes results of a research with Nucleus implant in one ear and House implant in the other.

12/16/87   Letter sent to FDA to withdraw IDE for Vienna children.

02/17/88   FDA circulates draft guidelines for children. The minimum length of follow-up suggested is two years post-implant and at least 25% of the patients to be followed for three years.

03/03/88   FDA asks 3M to wait after the May NIH consensus meeting before submitting a PMAA for the House children's device.

03/16/88   Clinician at House compares Nucleus and 3M devices on a child and finds that the Nucleus device performs better.

05/02/88   Scientists at the NIH/FDA consensus development conference are no longer upset about implanting into children.

07/29/88   FDA open meeting to draft guidelines for children 2–18 years of age. Nucleus convinces FDA that long follow-up period should not be stipulated.

06/15/88   House children's PMAA submitted to the FDA.

08/23/88   3M decides not to go ahead with the panel meeting for the children's PMAA.

09/14/88   Dr. House convinces 3M to make one last effort.

09/23/88   FDA panel recommends conditional PMA.

Divestiture

10/15/86   Group decides to expand during the next six to nine months into hearing aids development.

06/01/87   Decision not to promote or sell the Vienna device. None of the Vienna initiatives had demonstrated encouraging results.

09/14/87   3M adopts strategy to focus on development of a multi-channel device.

12/01/87   Program manager announces reduced commitment to cochlear implants.

01/08/88	Decision made to wind down Sprint project.
05/01/88	Decision made to extend contract with the Hochmairs for one more year because of interlinked patents.
09/01/88	Decision made to exit from cochlear implant business.
09/14/88	Dr. House persuades 3M to attempt the children's PMA one last time.
02/02/89	Veterans Administration raises issue of continued service and warranty after 3M has exited.
01/12/89	3M offers technology to Nucleus and Pacesetter.
01/30/89	FDA informs 3M it will not permit 3M to terminate IDE and PMA approval process if 3M intends to continue to service and provide warranties for its devices.
02/02/89	VA raises questions continued service and warranties after 3M exits from the market.
05/30/89	Nucleus considers whether to acquire 3M's cochlear implant assets and engages in negotiations with 3M.
08/03/89	3M hearing health program manager is replaced.
08/15/89	Negotiations with Nucleus are completed to transfer 3M cochlear implant technology to Nucleus.

The Innovation Journey in an Interorganizational Joint Venture

The Therapeutic Apheresis Case

This case describes the Therapeutic Apheresis Program (TAP), a joint venture by three corporations to create a new business based on a new medical technology that removes disease-causing components from patients' blood. TAP involved the novel use of filtration technology and an unusual cooperative effort among three major organizations. The Minnesota Innovation Research Program (MIRP) observed and monitored the innovation for most of its life, providing a unique opportunity to understand the problems associated with cooperative innovation development.

The idea of using blood removal to treat diseases dates back to the use of leeches to remove blood. In the time of George Washington, bloodletting was still common. The idea of removing specific parts of the blood originated in 1914 but did not gain popularity until World War II, when it was used to obtain needed plasma. The first therapeutic uses of apheresis, specific blood component removal, appeared in the late 1950s. The first continuous-flow separator was introduced by IBM (now COBE Laboratories, Inc.) in 1966 and was followed by other continuous-flow machines. The dominant technology used by these manufacturers was a centrifuge device, which separates blood components by centrifugal force in a spinning cylinder. Three companies dominated the domestic marketplace for this technology: Baxter-Travenol, Haemonetics, and COBE. By the early 1980s, it was quite common to use apheresis to extract platelets and blood plasma for

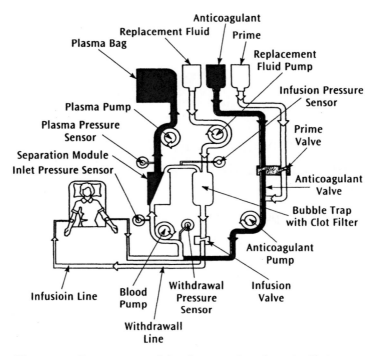

Figure 9.1 Components of the therapeutic apheresis device

transfusion to other patients. Therapeutic uses of apheresis were much less frequent.

More recently, filtration and adsorption technologies were introduced. The filtration devices, introduced in 1978, pass the blood through a membrane that rejects certain blood components. The adsorption technology is even more recent. Adsorption uses the capabilities of certain materials to bind blood components to remove them from the system. TAP represents one of the first efforts to commercialize apheresis filtration technologies for treatment of specific diseases. Figure 9.1 provides a diagram of the major components in the apheresis process.

All medical devices in the United States must have approval from the Food and Drug Administration (FDA). The FDA requires a variety of testing to ensure that the devices are safe and that they do what the manufacturers claim. The FDA requires testing with animals before testing with humans can begin. Approval to begin human testing (investigational device exemption, or IDE) allows a limited number of hospitals and clinics to test the safety and effectiveness of the devices. These initial human tests lead to the premarket approval (PMA). With the PMA, devices may be sold in the United States. PMA does not

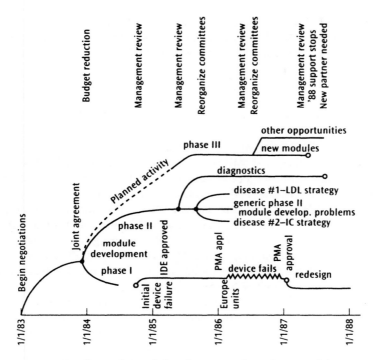

Figure 9.2 Chronological development of products and functions in the therapeutic apheresis program

allow the manufacturer to make claims about the therapeutic benefits of the device. Such claims can be made only after additional testing demonstrates the accuracy of these claims. The FDA testing process represents a major commitment of time and money by medical product developers.

Observation of TAP began shortly after the formal inception of the innovation in 1983 and continued until its conclusion in 1988. Data collection included nonparticipant observation at bimonthly management meetings and at periodic briefings presented to senior management. Semiannual interviews with key TAP managers and questionnaire surveys of all key TAP personnel provided additional data. Company records, industry trade publications, and medical research journals provided supporting information.

Changes in people, ideas, transactions, and context were coded into events and the events were classified into categories (initiation and start-up, product development, management, and related business opportunities). Figure 9.2 provides a brief chronological diagram of how these activities took place and the appendix to this chapter provides a more detailed list of events. The remainder of this case develops more details about the events that transpired during the innovation development.

Initiation and Organization of the Joint Venture

The official initiation of TAP began in late 1983 with a joint-venture agreement among 3M, Millipore Corporation, and a 3M subsidiary, Sarns, Inc. Millipore, headquartered in Bedford, Massachusetts, develops, manufactures, and markets products for analysis and purification of fluids with total 1985 sales of $367 million and 4,450 employees. 3M is a diversified manufacturer and sponsored TAP activities through the Health Care Products and Services group of 3M's Life Sciences Sector headquartered in St. Paul, Minnesota. The Sarns subsidiary is also a part of the Health Care Products and Services group and is located in Ann Arbor, Michigan.

The interest in apheresis at both 3M and Millipore predated the cooperative effort. Events from early 1980 until November 1983 were grouped into the initiation period that led to the cooperative agreement. At the beginning of this period, 3M, Millipore, and Sarns were independently exploring technological developments related to apheresis. From 1980 to 1982, 3M researchers were working a new technology for the removal of noxious blood components. Although this effort was discontinued because of technical and marketing difficulties, interest in apheresis remained.

Millipore was interested in medical applications of its filtration expertise and had developed a prototype blood-filtration module. In 1980, the Millipore chief executive officer (CEO) approached the president of Sarns to discuss the possibility of a joint venture. As a leading developer and manufacturer of heart-lung equipment, Sarns was perceived as having the expertise to develop the blood pumps and tube sets necessary for the filtration module.

Soon after the initial approach by Millipore, Sarns became engaged in discussions with 3M regarding a possible merger, and Sarns discontinued its discussions with Millipore. Negotiations to execute a Sarns acquisition by 3M occurred throughout the first half of 1981 and were completed in June 1981. Subsequent to the merger, executives learned that personnel at 3M and Sarns were still interested in developing apheresis business opportunities, and a new round of negotiations began in March 1983. These negotiations resulted in the announcement of a joint agreement among Millipore, 3M, and its Sarns subsidiary in November 1983. This marked the formal beginning of the blood-treatment program (TAP) examined here. Observations by MIRP began in December 1983.

The joint-venture agreement identified a division of labor between 3M and Millipore as well as a sequence of products and a mechanism for sharing revenues. Millipore's filtration technology would be combined with Sarns's manufacturing expertise and 3M's research and worldwide marketing capabilities. Millipore was responsible for developing the filtration modules, and 3M-Sarns was responsible for conducting clinical trials, FDA regulatory review procedures, manufacturing the hardware, and marketing the devices worldwide. 3M and Millipore agreed to cover their respective developmental costs and share revenue from unit sales when the product was finally approved for sale.

The joint-venture agreement also specified three phases of product development: phases I, II, and III. The phase I product was designed to compete with current apheresis products on the market, which were based on a centrifuge technology rather than filtration. The existing apheresis market focused on plasma removal and did not involve extensive treatment of diseases. Because Millipore had already developed a phase I filtration device, development of a phase I product was initially expected to require relatively minor resources. Although the phase I product was not perceived by TAP managers to be a significant product innovation, its commercial introduction was judged to be important for gaining a market presence.

The product envisioned for phase II was an enhancement of the phase I device that would return additional albumin to the donor during apheresis. Albumin is a valuable blood component lost during the centrifugal apheresis process and being able to return more to patients would provide a substantial economic advantage to the TAP device.

Phase III in the TAP was to develop future apheresis technologies jointly. The joint-venture agreement was intentionally vague in this area because part of the innovation process was to determine how to match technology with diseases to create an effective product market. The intention was to structure an agreement sufficiently broad to incorporate a wide array of potential technological developments and related business opportunities as they arose.

Organizationally, a strategic business unit (SBU) operations committee met bimonthly and was responsible for the strategic direction of the joint venture. The members of the SBU were managers in their respective organizations and, except for two TAP staff members from 3M, had other responsibilities within their own organizations. TAP, therefore, was highly dependent on staff members in each organization who were only involved in TAP efforts on a part-time basis. As a result of this initial structure the specific TAP activities were located in three geographic areas with several reporting chains for the SBU members. Figure 9.3 illustrates the initial reporting structure associated with the TAP SBU. TAP is shown with indirect connections to these organizations based on the current SBU membership. 3M estab-

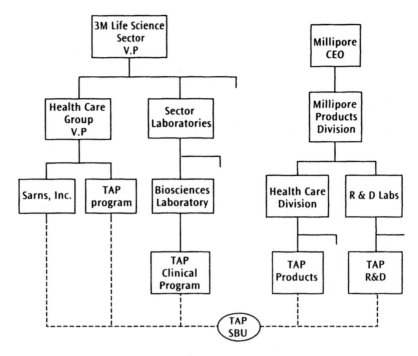

Figure 9.3 TAP organization chart, January, 1984

lished a full-time project manager for TAP, but this individual still needed to work through the SBU to direct activities within partner locations. Thus no individual had sole responsibility for the entire TAP activity.

Charter members of the SBU involved three managers from Millipore and three from 3M. They included a program manager from 3M, a Sarns development director, and a research and development (R&D) manager from the 3M biosciences laboratory. The Millipore members included the marketing manager, a research scientist, and the director of apheresis development activities. When a full-time marketing manager was hired for TAP at 3M, this individual was added to the SBU. Over time, a variety of changes took place within the composition of the SBU. Table 9.1 highlights events related to the SBU itself.

The next four sections describe the developments of TAP over the years from 1984 through 1988. The delineation of years seems a natural division of this time despite the asynchronous occurrence of events. After this description, the case concludes with a review of key themes that will help readers understand the innovation progression.

Table 9.1. Internal organization events in TAP SBU

Date	TAP organization and managerial turnover events
1983	SBU formed with three members from 3M and three from Millipore.
10/83	Clinical development manager hired for TAP.
1/84	Millipore marketing manager leaves and is replaced.
4/84	3M hires marketing manager for TAP—adds him to SBU.
4/84	Marketing manager hired by 3M-TAP.
12/84	Two new SBU members from Millipore.
12/84	3M marketing person leaves the program as result of budget reductions.
01/85	Millipore marketing manager leaves the SBU. New Millipore individuals become permanent SBU members.
07/85	New vice president of marketing at Millipore replace Millipore SBU member.
12/85	President of Sarns retires and is replaced by 3M executive.
12/85	Millipore development director appointed vice president of Millipore Products and general manager of Health Care Products. This individual remains on the SBU. The Millipore vice president who joined in July resigns from Millipore.
12/85	Millipore vice president of research and development returns to SBU to replace vice president of marketing.
01/86	Millipore vice president of research and development returns to SBU.
02/86	Marketing staff person added to Sarns TAP staff.
05/86	Domestic sales representative added at Sarns.
05/86	New Sarns lab director replaces previous director on SBU.
10/86	Marketing manager for TAP promoted to Sarns marketing manager.
12/86	New committee structure for TAP consists of a business team, market development team, and a Sarns-3M core team.
12/86	3M program manager for TAP agrees to become direct coordinator of a three-person team (one member from each organization) to monitor progress on problems and development.
04/87	3M hire marketing development manager.
08/87	Lead engineer for TAP at Millipore resigns.
08/87	TAP begins seeking additional outside investors.
12/87	3M gives official notification of program termination.
04/87	3M lab manager resigns.
06/87	3M TAP program manager assumes new position in 3M Health Care.
06/87	Final agreement is reached on transfer of TAP proprietary rights to Millipore.

Year One

The first year of the TAP venture began with the formalization of the joint venture in late 1983 and ended with 3M budget cuts about one year later. This period was one of considerable growth of innovation activity and elaboration of a detailed research and development program. The major outcomes of this period were organization and plans rather than finished products.

The unit supplied by Millipore as the initial phase I device had been examined at focus group sessions in late 1983. At these sessions, nurses and technicians identified difficulties with the operator interface and tube sets that required changes before the final unit could be put into production. Two outside vendors were chosen to complete these design changes. One would work on the tube sets; the second would work on the operator interface. Outside staff members allowed 3M to "have as few permanent full-time employees as possible until we make the final decision that the market expansion and technology development warrant the permanent commitment," according to an executive interviewed in 1984.

3M and Sarns SBU members also developed a business plan and reviewed it with management in late 1983. This plan represented both a general strategic outline of the competitive situation for the innovators and a statement to 3M and Sarns management about the program's expected direction. The plan included a list of key issues and assumptions.

Issues:

- Reimbursement
- Timeliness and market acceptance
- Plan to market before PMA
- Selection of target clinical conditions
- Definition of program for specific apheresis
- Establish effective treatments for specific diseases
- FDA approval
- Project coordination

Assumptions:

- Apheresis will be cost-effective.
- Proven clinical efficacy will increase demand.
- International market will grow as fast as U.S. market.
- Albumin recovery is feasible and practical.
- Additional compatible products and services will be acquired.

Clinical testing of the TAP technology represented another major program component. Initial efforts focused on development of clinical tests using animals. These animal studies were needed to support application to the FDA for approval of human studies. Along with the development of the animal tests the team began planning for the FDA approval process for the phase I device including in vitro testing, application for IDE and human trials, followed by a PMA application (PMAA). Additional testing to identify therapeutic claims would follow PMA.

The work on phase II almost immediately changed the underlying product definitions contained in the initial agreement. The major reason for the changes for phase II was that Millipore research showed current membranes could remove specific molecular weights. TAP researchers also recognized that they might be able to associate certain specific molecular weight particles with diseases. Thus, the concept of disease treatment was effectively moved forward to phase II of the plan. Subsequent to this observation the SBU dropped efforts to recover albumin and used the phase II label to refer to the initial therapeutic devices. Phase III became the products envisioned beyond the initial phase II products.

During the first year, various advisory boards and internal study groups were formed. These included a medical advisory board, intended to obtain feedback from physicians, and what was called the real-world advisory board. The SBU included a variety of Ph.D. scientists but no physicians. In addition, the plan was to identify medical researchers who could aid in testing phase II. The real-world advisory board would provide more broad-based feedback on market-related issues. An internal Clinical Indications Task Force (CITF) was also formed. The purpose of this task force was to study the available research and determine which diseases were the most likely viable candidates for treatment using apheresis. The primary disease criteria used by the CITF included the following:

Phase II:

- Measurable patient disease status using accepted diagnostics
- Ability to test apheresis results
- Reasonable population of treatable patients
- Medical community interest in treating the disease
- Reasonable expectation that apheresis is an efficient, effective form of therapy

Phase III:

- Must know what factors to remove
- Method must be found to remove fractions (filtration or adsorption).

By mid-1984, a variety of minor obstacles had been reported and were resolved. Problems with module leakage and software delayed the phase I program by two and a half months. In addition, by June, the CITF had narrowed the disease list to three. From this list, the SBU eventually selected high cholesterol-related conditions and autoimmune diseases as the two major disease categories for phase II.

A management review in June presented a schedule for phases I and II. The phase I IDE was to be submitted in November 1984 and the PMA submitted in July 1985. FDA approval of the PMA was anticipated in April 1986. International sales of the phase I device were planned for July 1985 concurrent with the submission of the PMAA. Sales in the United States, of course, could not start until PMA. The international sales efforts were a key part of the early marketing plans for TAP. 3M managers indicated that they would be able to begin limited sales of the product in Europe using the data from the PMA tests submitted to the FDA. International sales would allow for early revenues to help support continuing research and development. Phase II plans indicated the first phase II module prototype (medium-weight molecules) for August 1984 and initial laboratory studies for January 1985. These dates were the first formal presentation of schedules to Millipore and 3M-Sarns management.

Also at a July phase II development review, clear responsibilities for individual phase II tasks were further reinforced. Millipore was responsible for the membrane and module development, initial module testing, and manufacturing. Sarns was responsible for instrument development and manufacturing. 3M was responsible for regulatory, safety, and effectiveness testing and medical and biochemical support. All three partners retained primary responsibility for system integrity and planning. Structurally, each organization implemented organizational entities needed to carry out their respective tasks. By midyear a TAP steering committee was meeting at 3M-Sarns to discuss its portion of the program. At Millipore, a phase II operating committee was formed to monitor Millipore efforts.

A major change in the SBU discussions started in August 1984. At this meeting, 3M managers noted a probable one-third cut in the 1985 3M funding for TAP. The SBU discussions focused on the impact of these cuts. 3M SBU members recommended about a one-year delay in phase I. Phase II would receive fewer reductions because this was the key focus of the TAP venture. Discussion included how to pass this information on to Millipore senior management. The SBU decided to delay telling Millipore management until further details about the reductions were available and a meeting could be set up. The August meeting otherwise seemed relatively uneventful. Progress on the CITF was noted and progress was also reported on development and planning.

The decisions about budgeting at 3M were reflected in the 3M sector planning committee recommendations dated November 7, 1984. This 3M executive team was responsible for evaluating a variety of projects that made claims for scarce funding and resources. The planning committee saw considerable potential for the program but was concerned with the extensive clinical testing needed to verify disease therapies. They "strongly recommended that the project consider an alternate strategy involving . . . modules which are effective for different molecular weight cutoffs." This would eliminate considerable clinical expense, on 3M's part, and would lead to earlier market entry. In addition, the committee suggested that this approach would lead to increased clinic use, which would "find other beneficial effects."

While the sector planning committee provided strategic reasoning to support their recommendations, observers noted that the SBU members from all organizations viewed the changes as a "budget reduction" rather than a "strategic change." Not only did the changes appear to aim at modifying the initial agreement, but they also seemed to violate the sense of the social contract between 3M and Millipore to "work together" to complete the planned effort.

By November 1984, the budget cut had become a part of the TAP culture. Millipore members looked at the cut as a reduction in commitment by 3M. Millipore interviews indicated problems with 3M commitment and the disparity of investment. Millipore perceived that 3M invested only a small part of its R&D money in TAP while they put about one-third of R&D efforts into TAP. The satisfaction level of Millipore was reported at an intermediate level.

The 3M vice president who sponsored the TAP effort saw the budget changes as a redirection rather than a reduction in commitment. The sector planning committee continued to support TAP but felt objectives could be achieved for less than the budget request of $3.3 million for 1985. The vice president then picked the $2 million amount and a new strategy. He also noted in year-end interviews that 3M's initial plan was to invest for one year and then reevaluate. He acknowledged that the entry fee was small ($2 million) and that Millipore was not aware that 3M had such a viewpoint.

At the end of 1984, the 3M health care group was reorganized. At this point, the reporting chain for the 3M TAP program manager changed. Previously, the 3M TAP effort had reported directly to the vice president of the Medical Products division. Now the program would report to the president of Sarns and only indirectly to the Medical Products vice president. The TAP program manager would remain in St. Paul rather than relocating to Ann Arbor. This change represented a formal recognition of the link between TAP devices and Sarns manufacturing. The net effect of these changes was to remove the direct reporting of TAP to the vice president of Medical Products and substituted a longer reporting path. These changes are reflected in the organizational charts shown in figures 9.3 and 9.4.

Year Two

The second year involved continued progress on both phases of the development. The year began with IDE approval and ended with PMA filing and a variety of organizational changes related to TAP.

Phase I human trials began in February. Early reports from Sarns about phase I were favorable. Initial plans for 1985 included six specific goals:

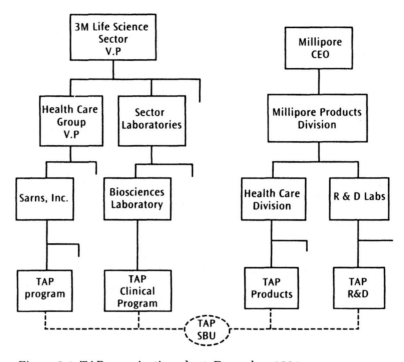

Figure 9.4 TAP organization chart, December, 1984

1. File phase I PMA by fourth-quarter 1985.
2. Deliver four or five phase I systems internationally.
3. Complete first phase II separator.
4. Complete engineering design for phase II hardware.
5. Complete global phase II market study.
6. Establish global systemic lupus erythematosus (SLE) clinical protocol.

Clinical efforts to develop protocols for product use remained an integral part of the program. The changes in financing at the end of 1984 resulted in some reduction in the final amount of clinical testing but did not eliminate the need for protocols. The revised strategy would introduce phase II without making any claims about how effective it was for disease treatment. This would eliminate the need to do the clinical trials associated with such claims. Nevertheless, it would be necessary to explain how doctors might use the product to treat patients, which would require clinical protocols.

As an adjunct to the clinical efforts the first serious discussion of new business opportunities associated with TAP diagnostics appeared early in 1985. Apheresis treatments were expected to cost up to $1,000 each. Therefore, it was important to identify patients in the target population who could actually be helped by apheresis and to measure the amount of improvement the apheresis treatment generated. In some cases, no diagnostics were commercially available to serve this purpose, and the clinical scientists had to develop new ones. Some diagnostic tests appeared to present legitimate business opportunities. The SBU recognized that diagnostics were not specifically mentioned in the joint-venture agreement and decided that further consultation with home organizations would be needed before the relationship of diagnostic business opportunities could be resolved.

Technical discussions about which diseases to target for phase II were also salient management issues. The disease choice was between LDL/HDL cholesterol and autoimmune diseases. Budget restrictions necessitated a choice of the one that would receive the most attention. The parameters of this choice represented a dilemma because the market could not be established until the technical characteristics of phase II were determined. The technical characteristics, however, depended on planning for a specific disease treatment.

By midyear, the TAP SBU had made progress but encountered additional problems. Initial reports of phase I trials were positive and provided some anecdotal evidence that the developers viewed as very strong. One of the first patients treated was critically ill, and the successful use of apheresis in this case was viewed very positively. Problems with the phase I were also noted. There were further delays in the redesign of the tube sets and some problems with pump motors. The field trials also generated a variety of problems that included mild toxicity to the anticoagulant used in the trials and questions about whether appropriate quantities of fluids were being returned to the patients. These issues were not threatening to the trials but needed to be investigated as part of the ongoing development. They appeared to be normal problems expected with implementation of new technology. Other problems with phase I trials were not due to the equipment or technology. In one case, a clinical researcher had stopped the trials to negotiate for more money. At a second location, there was a shortfall in expected patients, which caused a risk that the trials would not be completed on schedule. The TAP team still projected initial sales by year-end.

The Sarns SBU member also requested funds for an industrial redesign for the phase I unit that would accommodate human factors, modularity, building costs, and schedule. The minimal effort—repackaging—would cost from $50,000 to $70,000 and remain on schedule. More complete redesign could ultimately take $300,000 to $500,000 and extend up to a year. One SBU member suggested that the redesign should be delayed until a working model of phase II was completed. Sarns responded that this delay would be costly because initially manufacturing would have to tool up for a design that would be kept for only about six months.

The redesign issue was not resolved at this SBU meeting and the redesign never took place.

Phase II continued on schedule. Millipore reported minor delays in delivery of filtration modules and reported some problems with membranes under high blood flow. The phase II filtration module compared quite favorably with potential competitors for eliminating LDL cholesterol. Millipore also reported some initial problems with its manufacturing scale-up. The apparent success with phases I and II allowed the SBU to begin exploring additional product development by mid-1985. A task force was formed to look at separating additional blood components. It was specifically asked to look at both filtration and adsorption.

The SBU also discussed marketing and diffusion of innovation. Researchers were puzzled when they found that centrifuge apheresis was effective for treating Goodpasture's disease but was not widely used for that purpose. This meant that the market estimates of phase II apheresis use might be overstated or that the adoption process for new medical technology was more complex than anticipated, which led to discussions about how to diffuse the TAP innovation into the medical community. One set of developers preferred access through leading cardiologists for cholesterol treatment; another set of developers felt that accessing hematologists, who were more familiar with blood filtration, would be most effective.

Also by midyear, the SBU was informed that consultation between 3M and Millipore had determined that diagnostics were outside the joint-venture agreement. Each partner would pursue diagnostics independently. Where new diagnostics directly related to TAP efforts, they could be discussed again. Meanwhile, Millipore presented another new outside opportunity. The Navy asked Millipore to bid on a project to cleanse fresh frozen blood plasma. Millipore offered TAP the opportunity to take this as a TAP venture. Again the SBU members delayed a decision to consult with their respective organizations.

A new vice president of marketing at Millipore joined the SBU in September 1985. He became the senior Millipore staff person on the SBU, and his initial skepticism about the program led to discord within the SBU. At one point, this individual suggested that the agreement between Millipore and 3M was really just an original equipment manufacturer arrangement while the SBU seemed to be treating it as though it were a joint venture. A number of members of the SBU reported to researchers that they were "surprised" by some of these issues. Millipore SBU members thought this individual should have been given more respect whereas 3M members wondered why old issues needed to be covered again.

The future separation task force did not deliver its report at the SBU meeting in the fall as expected. There was some indication that the "troops" were not motivated to examine long-term possibilities they felt would never be funded. This was one of the few times that morale issues and the effects of earlier reductions in funding appeared on the SBU agenda.

Outside activity by 3M also concerned Millipore SBU members. The acquisition of Omnis by 3M and the possible acquisition of Haemonetics Corporation by 3M were discussed. The concern was that Omnis filtration products might conflict with Millipore interests or that the Haemonetics acquisition might conflict with the TAP effort. The 3M TAP project manager indicated that if 3M acquired Haemonetics, the operation would probably be placed under TAP jurisdiction and therefore would result in revenue sharing with Millipore, a big surprise to Millipore.

Other strategic issues were also evaluated at the SBU meeting in September. These included a report about possible revisions of the TAP mission that would include purification of tissue and fluids. This report suggested considering veterinary and cell-wash applications. The issue of diagnostics was reopened. The 3M laboratory manager reported that diagnostics for cholesterol were going well but immune complex diagnostics for the advanced phase III separator were not. The new lipids tests used some media from Millipore and a business opportunity was possible. Despite the previous agreement that diagnostics were outside the joint-venture agreement, 3M and Millipore SBU members agreed to reconsider the diagnostics business.

As a result of the diagnostics discussion, Millipore asked whether the advanced phase III separator was really important. Millipore SBU members had defended phase III to their management but now felt that 3M labs might not be able to test this module. The Millipore project leader requested SBU support before he continued. The SBU decided phase III was important. The 3M TAP project manager promised that 3M would test the module even if outside help was necessary.

The year 1985 ended with a variety of organizational changes related to TAP. Millipore appointed a new president and CEO, and another senior Millipore executive left. One of the original SBU members from Millipore became a vice president at Millipore, and the recent leader of the Millipore SBU members left Millipore, his position eliminated when Millipore reorganized along product lines. A third Millipore SBU member had emergency bypass surgery and was away from the office recovering. At Sarns, the founder retired in December 1985 and was replaced by an experienced 3M manager.

All these changes led to a cancellation of the December 1985 SBU meeting. Instead a smaller "mini-SBU" meeting was held. The mini-SBU was primarily to prepare for the phase II planning meeting in January 1986. A key desire was to identify five to six major program objectives that would be the foundation for the planning of phase II.

The PMAA was filed with the FDA in December 1985, which marked a transition and a major milestone for phase I of the program. The clinical trials were now complete, and efforts shifted to shepherding the PMA through the complex bureaucratic evaluation process. Several clinics kept their phase I units and continued testing.

At year-end, screening tests for phase II were going well. All targets were being met except for LDL rejection, which was 87% to 89% versus a target of 90%, which seemed acceptable. The current plans for the phase II filtration modules called for a stack of twenty-five levels of membrane, which might not be enough for some patients who needed higher flow rates, so new plans extended the number of layers to twenty-five to thirty-five.

During late 1985, SBU leaders from 3M and Millipore also negotiated an agreement regarding payments to Millipore. Some SBU members had recommended treating initial units shipped as test marketing, which would have avoided triggering minimum payments called for in the joint-venture agreement. The SBU leaders from Millipore and 3M decided that Millipore should begin receiving revenue when initial machines were sold. This moved the payment date from potentially late 1986 to early 1986. The minimum first-year payment of $300,000 should be contrasted to the projected 1986 sales revenue of $618,000.

Year Three

During the third year, the innovation encountered an increasing number of problems with both product phases. Thus, the initially high expectations at the outset of the year were not achieved. TAP survey responses show a variety of declines in the measures used to track the innovation (figure 9.5).

The PMA filing for the phase I product marked a major milestone for the program and provided a positive beginning for the year. Using the data TAP submitted to the FDA, 3M began efforts in Europe to sell phase I devices. Several TAP SBU members noted this change to researchers. One individual described this sales effort as the "end of the honeymoon": The program would find out how well phase I units sold. Sales would generate additional use of the phase I units and, finally, the initial sales would trigger payments from 3M to Millipore. Thus, there was a general sense that things had become more "real" with this transition.

In January 1986, the SBU was more upbeat and less controversial than the previous SBU. For example, the respective leaders from 3M and Millipore met before the SBU, which appeared to make the SBU meeting proceed more smoothly. The two leaders now sat together rather than across the table from each other. And although the senior Millipore SBU member's promotion at Millipore reduced his available

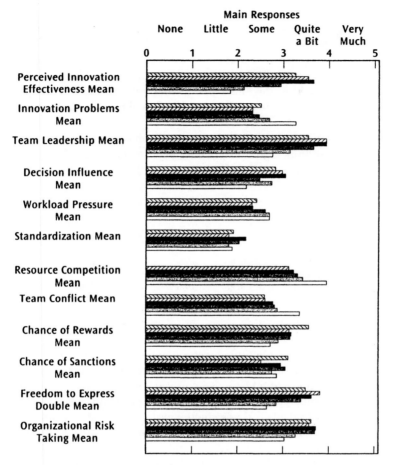

Figure 9.5 Average responses by TAP members to six repeated surveys at times: 1 (2/85, top bars), 2 (6/85), 3 (1/86), 4 (8/86), 5 (2/87), and 6 (9/87, bottom bars).

time for TAP, it also provided a TAP advocate at a higher level within Millipore.

Initial meetings in 1986 included discussing problems with regulatory approval in Europe. The 3M program manager accepted responsibility for these problems. 3M had originally thought the entire process would be easy but now realized that it could take up to two years to achieve full approval. Until fully approved, each shipment would require a separate letter from the importing country saying that it was okay to use the product. This process could be used for up to ten units per country per year. One SBU member noted that to achieve sales projections, these procedures would have to operate at or near this upper limit.

The SBU also continued to discuss diagnostics and blood recovery business alternatives. 3M was not interested in blood recovery, which meant that Millipore could continue alone. One Millipore SBU member asked, "How can we get to yes?" instead of getting to no. In the ensuing discussion, it was discovered that the senior Millipore SBU members thought a previous cell-washing opportunity had been rejected by the SBU while another member thought it had never come to the SBU.

Shortly after the January SBU meeting, a phase II planning meeting occurred involving a group of twenty-eight technical staff members, who designed a revised development schedule. Some dates provided at the January SBU were revised. For the phase II high molecular weight (HMW) separator the revised dates were:

	Now	1/86 SBU	4/85 SBU
Preclinical equipment ready	6/86	3/86	12/85
File IDE	8/86	6/86	2Q86
IDE approval	10/86	7/86	2-3Q86
File PMA	3/87	1–2Q87	1Q87

Critical issues at the planning meeting included the following: (1) resource availability and schedule tightness; (2) animal tests; (3) interdictive protocols; and (4) how to get physician adoption.

By mid-1986, pump motor problems surfaced in phase I units, which jeopardized all six preproduction units. When asked whether intervention was needed with the pump motor manufacturer, a key Sarns technician requested and received another two weeks to work with current processes. The 3M TAP marketing manager worried that delays would affect sales. Sarns also noted other problems with tube sets and modules. Because first users would have a strong influence on future adopters, solving problems with these initial units were very important. SBU members decided that someone needed to watch the entire product rather than having everyone watch just his or her own part.

Phase II also reported problems in early 1986. Modules were delayed because of low quality. Modules from the Millipore pilot plant had low flux (20–25 ml/min. versus target of 40 ml/min.). For clinical testing, a rate of 30 ml/min. was needed. Millipore indicated it had problems moving from prototype development to pilot production. A decision to delay to get better flow led to objections from 3M clinicians because of 3M's desire to get to market quickly.

External events also appeared to reflect problems. Recent information from Japan indicated that competitors, especially Kanegafuchi, had made more progress than the SBU previously thought. It also appeared that Millipore was aware of some of this work but did not bring it to the attention of the SBU.

At midyear, a management review was prepared for both Millipore and 3M-Sarns executives. TAP SBU management interpreted the outcome of this review as an affirmation of the program. Senior managers asked for more information about the next twelve to eighteen months and asked fewer questions about long-range strategy. TAP also would no longer need to report to management every six months. SBU managers took the latter change as a sign of acceptance by their management. The proverbial wolf was no longer at the door.

Problems with phase I continued during the second half of 1986. Sarns assigned an individual full time to service phase I units in the field. As a result of these problems, the October SBU meeting reported that 1986 revenues likely would be only 10% of the initial projections. MIRP data collection in August showed concern by the 3M program manager that Millipore might become discouraged and leave the venture. Survey data (figure 9.5) also showed the first drop in overall innovation effectiveness. These data seem to confirm further an increase in concern about persistent problems. Millipore interviewees noted that manufacturing scale-up at Millipore and Sarns had not gone well, and although some short-term progress on European regulatory issues did occur, the long-term problems remained. Something of a closet mentality also appeared. The senior Millipore SBU member was unhappy with Millipore communication to 3M. He noted that Millipore technical staff members were not surprised by Kanegafuchi information and should have shared it with 3M sooner. The Millipore manager also noted that he had freedom to move money around and could help fund "3M activities" but would want something in exchange.

In late 1986, phase I underwent a reliability review that showed thirty-five failure modes for the primary device. These findings resulted in a halt of sales until problems could be resolved. In addition, the reliability review found that the phase I units could not be manufactured reliably. Recommended changes would require additional funding of $300,000 to $400,000 to make changes and reestablish manufacturing. The proposed changes reduced the number of computer boards in the unit from nineteen to three and the number of electronic connections from eighty to less than twenty. In addition, the changes simplified the tube set design that contained 147 connections.

At the same time as the reliability review, the FDA approved the PMA for the phase I device with no postmarket surveillance. The latter indicated that the FDA needed no additional information, which was a positive sign that the FDA was satisfied with the phase I testing. Mayo Clinic staff members liked their upgraded system, but the problems overshadowed the good news.

By the fall of 1986, Millipore had reestablished its manufacturing process for the filtration modules, but managers encountered other problems. Testing the phase II units required phase I devices because the phase II filtration module was designed to work with blood that had already passed through a phase I separator. The problems with phase I began to affect the phase II activities during this period. By October, the SBU decided that advanced filtration modules beyond the cholesterol filtration device should be given a lower priority, which presented an additional long-term problem for the SBU. The absence of new technology would cause voids or long waits for new products.

At year-end the president of Sarns addressed the SBU. She explained that the Sarns strategy was to move to cardiovascular products, and it would be that company's first priority. TAP provided a diversification for Sarns beyond this. Sarns promised to continue to strengthen its organization to provide TAP a better home.

The SBU decided that the single most critical issue with regard to schedule slippage was program management. The 3M program manager agreed to become the overall program manager. He would supervise a small group whose goal would be to intensify individual ownership and accountability for deadlines. Two Millipore engineers were designated to report to the program manager. These changes involved the program manager more directly in activities at Millipore than before.

Year Four

During the early period of 1987, the SBU continued to struggle with problems associated with phase I units. One vignette illustrates some of the conflicts these problems engendered: At the February SBU meeting, the Millipore SBU leader challenged the Sarns SBU representative to take charge of the Sarns development effort related to the phase I instrument. The Sarns SBU member refused and the discussion became heated. The Sarns SBU member said that another Sarns staff member was in charge of design and building efforts at Sarns. The Millipore SBU member responded that he had earlier asked that individual about who was in charge at Sarns and had received the name of a third Sarns staff member. The Millipore SBU member asked: "Will the Sarns SBU member get fired if this doesn't work?" The answer was "no." The Millipore SBU member asked, "Does anybody [get fired]?" The Sarns SBU member responded, "There is a committee in charge." The Millipore SBU member observed, "Committees don't get results."

The 3M program manager passed the Millipore SBU member a note suggesting the Millipore individual keep this discussion going and that the program manager would act as a peacemaker later if necessary.

Another 3M SBU member suggested that he had become personally responsible for the entire program by virtue of SBU membership. The Sarns SBU member indicated he understood what the SBU was asking, but he was still unable to commit to what the members wanted. Eventually, the Millipore SBU member got up and took a fruit basket around and offered each SBU member a piece. The symbolism of this was quite clear: The discussion had heated up to the point that overt peacemaking was needed.

One Millipore SBU member reported that module performance was "not there." He indicated that things he had been told in September were not true and that "This will be corrected." Further, one Millipore SBU member said the flat plate tangential membrane technology used in the phase II filtration module might be at its performance limits. The issue was not whether the design would work but whether it could be manufactured.

New business approaches continued to be discussed. Marketing staff members from 3M suggested that there may be an opportunity for lipids management centers. These would be centers where patients with high cholesterol would go to receive treatment and diet to reduce cholesterol. The marketing concept was to work with one of the health care delivery companies to establish apheresis as a part of such a treatment concept.

The 3M clinical manager was the most upbeat of the SBU members at this point. He reported that one of the researchers had had some success in treating his dog, which had autoimmune disease. The dog was quite seriously debilitated but after several apheresis treatments appeared fully recovered, indicating, at least anecdotally, the potential value of the technology. The laboratory manager indicated in interviews that he had found it difficult to communicate his increased enthusiasm for the technology and was frustrated by the inability to get machines and modules for further testing. He suggested that being supportive in meetings simply gave people a reason to lay back while being assertive rubbed them the wrong way.

Phase I problems continued at midyear. Delays in manufacturing caused cancellation of some clinical studies. Additional problems with tube sets (kinking) were reported and these delayed phase I for an additional two months. By August, the phase I units received top SBU priority because of budgetary restrictions and the need to show tangible products for the market.

During 1987, several structural changes took place. Clinical work was completed in June and no further clinical work was scheduled. The clinical developments were the last of the activities needing St. Paul facilities, and the TAP efforts moved entirely to Sarns. A new agreement with Millipore was also under way that would no longer call for minimum royalties. Royalties now were applied only to products related to Millipore. Finally, some SBU members expressed concerns that the committee structure for monitoring the innovation was too cumbersome and further organizational changes were suggested.

Midyear reports on the secondary phase II system indicated that a new spacer manufacturer for modules was on line. The focus now turned to the problem of reducing to practice a process for making modules with sufficient membrane to deliver the desired flux and separation efficiency.

Additional difficulties for TAP surfaced when, in May 1987, 3M managers held an internal review of all sector projects. TAP had increased risk and decreased competitive effectiveness vis-à-vis other projects within 3M. At this point, the vice president of health care indicated that he would not fund TAP beyond 1988. The result was serious discussions about the likelihood of TAP's becoming self-sufficient and what the other implications of this decision would be.

The June 1987 SBU meeting was canceled at 3M's request. Reports to researchers indicated that 3M felt that its partner was spending significantly less on TAP than 3M was and that 3M had asked Millipore for additional contract concessions such as royalty deferment. In June, 3M and Millipore managers met for a project review, and at this time, the health care vice president suggested that an outside partner should be considered to assist with funding. Millipore reported major concern that its partner, 3M, was no longer committed but agreed that 3M could seek an outside partner. The 3M TAP program manager began contacting possible outside parties in October 1987.

In August 1987, the SBU members spent considerable time reviewing the overall viability of the program. This was one of the first times the team had confronted squarely the problem of whether the TAP effort should continue. SBU leaders asked SBU members a hypothetical question: If SBU members had $1 million to invest, would they invest it in TAP? The leaders from 3M and Millipore agreed before posing this question that they should not take part in the debate because they did not want SBU members to be swayed by their opinions. During the debate, however, SBU members angrily demanded that these individuals participate. At one point, one member said, "How can you ask us to make a decision on this product when you [the leaders] are not willing to actively participate in the discussion?" After considerable debate, the team reached a consensus that the program was viable and should continue.

In August 1987, one of the lead engineers on the Millipore filtration module resigned. By October, however, Millipore reported an improved module design with a larger number of membrane layers. Testing of this process and design began immediately.

Late in 1987, two outside events took place that reflected directly on the decisions made by the TAP phase II developers. In September,

Merck & Company, Inc. won FDA approval for Lovastatin, a drug used to reduce LDL. TAP researchers were not surprised because they had monitored the progress of the drug testing. Nevertheless, it represented a step forward for a potential alternative therapy for some patients with heightened cholesterol. In October, the National Heart, Lung, and Blood Institute's National Cholesterol Education Program produced a major report calling for cholesterol testing and cholesterol reduction to below 200 mg/dl. This report was a major statement by a major thought leader who emphasized the importance of monitoring and treatment of high cholesterol and validated the choice of cholesterol as a disease for the apheresis treatment.

In December, the vice president of 3M's health care division formally informed Millipore of 3M's intent to withdraw from the venture. Meetings between 3M and Millipore in January 1988 included corporate lawyers and focused on terms and conditions for project termination. The TAP manager continued to seek outside partners during the early portion of 1988 without success, and 3M and Millipore reached a final agreement in June 1988. According to this agreement, the residual rights to build apheresis units returned to Millipore and the units still in the field were to be withdrawn. At the time of final closure, field reports showed that the redesigned phase I units were working well.

Analysis of TAP Business Development Process

As noted, the TAP case has unique structural properties that helped to create its character. It was a joint effort by geographically remote and culturally diverse companies. It was organized under a committee governance structure that had multiple links to the respective parent organizations. In addition, it faced the full set of problems and opportunities that other new product innovations face.

The TAP outcomes are less clear than the actual project cancellation might suggest. The program was successful in developing and testing the phase I apheresis unit. Evidence for this success includes the FDA PMA with no postmarket surveillance and reports at the end of the project that there were indications of the successful operation of field units. In addition, the phase II module was developed and appeared ready for additional testing at the end of the project.

Environmental circumstances were mixed. At the end of the project in late 1987, the TAP decision to emphasize treatment of high cholesterol was bolstered by the attention directed toward this condition by the National Institute of Health (NIH). This attention appeared to validate the decision by TAP developers that this was a critical problem and that attention by the medical community would help develop the market for cholesterol treatments. Opposite this was the approval of the drug Lovastatin, which program members anticipated. While Lovastatin further validated the importance of cholesterol treatment, it also represented the threat that effective treatment by drugs might reduce the demand for apheresis cholesterol treatments.

Despite some positive outcomes, TAP encountered more problems, which cost more time and money than any of the developers anticipated. These surprises damaged the developers' reputations within their host organizations and called into question the initial estimates of profitability for the program.

The ultimate cancellation of the program focuses attention on outcomes and causes: Why did the cancellation take place, and could it have been avoided? Did the effort have the right resources, and were they managed effectively? To answer these questions we examine the temporal elements of the development process, the use of resources, issues of learning, stakeholder management, and leadership.

Temporal Progressions

Examination of temporal progressions emphasizes the process by which events unfold over time. Many components of the TAP effort illustrated in figure 9.2 appeared independent but later became interconnected in unexpected ways. Examining the interplay between product development efforts can highlight the transitions that affect innovations. In addition to looking at the internal flow of events, it is important to examine changes that occur in the external environment because these often-asynchronous changes can have a significant impact on the innovation direction.

For TAP, one major factor that paced the phase I development was the need to meet regulatory requirements. The emergence of alternate technology, adsorption, and the changing medical opinions regarding the importance of specific conditions were less predictable. TAP correctly anticipated the needs of the FDA review process, and this element of the external interface proceeded in good order. Regulatory requirements in Europe were less satisfactory because of the mistaken belief that initial U.S. testing would be directly applicable to European regulators. This error delayed sales of European products, but it ultimately was less important than the technical problems with the initial phase I units.

New technology contributed both substitutes for the membrane technology used by TAP and substitutes for the entire process of apheresis. The main alternative apheresis technology was the adsorption column, primarily developed by Kanegafuchi in Japan. The main alternative to apheresis was the development of the drug Lovastatin, to treat high cholesterol. At the outset of the innovation, neither of these was seen as a major threat, yet both became significant during the innovation de-

TAP ACTIONS AND OUTCOMES

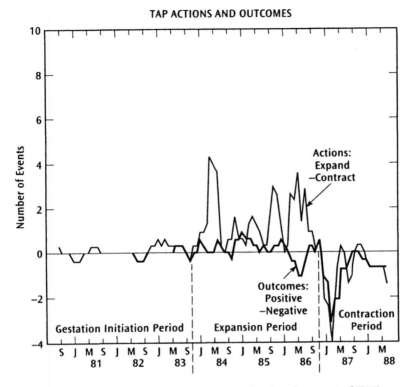

Figure 9.6 Action and outcome events in the development of TAP
(plots are three-month moving averages)

velopment. The drug was monitored regularly by TAP personnel and
held few surprises for the developers. The efforts by Kanagafuchi appeared to surprise some TAP managers but were better known to some
Millipore scientists. Thus, the discovery of this technology's capabilities led one SBU member to wonder whether TAP had chosen the right
technology. Despite the competitive threat of these technologies, both
targeted diseases were similar to those chosen by TAP, which validated
the market TAP chose to emphasize. Increased emphasis on cholesterol detection and treatment was also an asynchronous factor in the
changing environment that further supported the TAP approach. This
emphasis also helped validate the importance of the disease choices
made by the TAP developers.

Examining events within TAP can be categorized into three major
temporal periods: initiation, expansion, and contraction. Figure 9.6
provides a graphic representation of the actions and outcomes in these
three periods. The initiation is marked by sporadic and separate actions related to the separate activities of the three organizations before

the formal joint-venture agreement. During the expansion period, we observed an excess of expansion actions and mostly positive outcomes. At the end of the expansion period, outcomes became more negative, leading to the contraction period with increasingly negative outcomes and contracting actions.

Examining the innovation details makes apparent that the efforts to develop different phases of the innovation were mostly parallel at the start of development. Although the phase II filtration module was to be attached to the phase I hardware, it was not necessary for phase I to complete market entry before starting phase II development. Throughout 1984 and 1985, progress and problems in these areas were reported at SBU meetings, and solutions to problems were developed largely independently of problems in other areas. In addition, discussions of new TAP business opportunities proceeded independently of other developments.

Using van den Daele's (1969) distinction of conjunctive and disjunctive progressions, the development of the different phases, illustrated in figure 9.2, can be seen as disjunctive, and activities within each phase can be seen as conjunctive. For example, from the beginning of the observation period until late in 1986, the development activities of phases I and II remained mostly separated and proceeded independently of each other (disjunctive).

Within each phase, the efforts to develop modules, hardware, clinical protocols, and marketing required closer coordination. With the exception of marketing, the separate portions of the product were all required before moving from development to clinical trials or to sales. For example, the phase I effort entailed developing a prototype filtration module first, then pilot producing a few custom-designed devices for testing, and finally scaling up full production capabilities. In addition, the FDA regulatory process imposed sequential execution of animal tests to obtain an IDE approval followed by clinical trials on humans to obtain a FDA approval to manufacture and distribute the product in the U.S. market. Marketing was permitted in European sales before the FDA PMA but was required before approval from European regulatory bodies. All these characteristics suggest that within each product phase, the steps were conjunctive.

For phase I, the case shows that all but three key sequential activities in the development occurred smoothly. Difficulties with early tests on the phase I prototype were corrected quickly by an outside contractor. And the initially uninformed efforts to gain product approval from European regulatory bodies were eventually resolved with the help of 3M European subsidiaries and consultants, although the problem delayed sales for six months. The third and only major problem encountered was the scale-up of hardware manufacturing at Sarns for the phase I device and the problems associated with the phase I units initially manufactured. Technical manufacturing problems emerged incrementally, and the case shows they were reported in piecemeal fashion in SBU meetings over time. However, their cumulative effect did not become apparent until late in 1986.

A similar pattern was observed in developing the phase II product. A prototype filtration module was successfully developed, and a few modules were produced in pilot production to permit testing. However, problems were encountered in shifting from pilot to full-scale production of the phase II filtration module at Millipore.

During most of 1986, development work and problem resolution of the two product phases continued in parallel and primarily independently of each other. It was not until late 1986 that the SBU began to appreciate the lagged interdependency among the two product development efforts. By year-end 1986, the two phases of the program had ceased to be entirely parallel. The key underlying assumption that made the parallel activity feasible was that the phase I devices were ahead of the phase II devices in the development cycle. Thus, the phase I units could be used in the continued development for phase II. By 1986 year-end, this assumption was no longer true. Had it not been for the difficulties encountered in phase II module design, the phase I impact on phase II would have been even more severe. As it was, delays occurred in clinical tests of phase II modules because of manufacturing's inability to produce working phase I machines. This indicates how parallel activities that appear disjunctive can become conjunctive when lagged interdependencies become activated.

Budgeting and marketing provide related examples of difficulties in anticipating the timing of events necessary to build momentum in the start-up of a new business. Anticipating approval of the 1985 budget, TAP managers began program expansion in late 1984. When the 3M vice president approved a reduced budget in line with a revised strategy, TAP managers begrudgingly downsized the program. Similarly, marketing acquired resources in late 1985 and 1986 in anticipation of phase I product market entry, which was delayed by the manufacturing problems, and the resources were left idle.

This case turned out to be much like the baton passage at a relay race. However, it is a "just in time" relay race, where one runner starts before the others arrive at the track. At other times, the next runner begins running before the baton arrives to gain sufficient momentum to match the prior runner's pace. Although several handoffs occurred successfully within and between phase I and phase II component parts, it is clear that the race stops when the next component does not arrive on time for the baton handoff.

The final chapter in TAP included the search for an additional partner and the ultimate closure of the project. 3M's decision to seek outside funding sources dramatically changed the pattern of management attention. TAP managers from 3M focused on the search for new partners, and although efforts to solve problems with phases I and II continued, SBU managers became increasingly focused on finding a partner. In addition, the hint of failure became psychologically critical as individuals began to question the ultimate success of the venture and the relative costs and benefits on behalf of TAP.

Resource Acquisition and Allocation

3M, Millipore, and Sarns brought considerable resources to the TAP venture. In addition to the capital that each unit put into its portion of the effort, the organizations brought considerable tacit knowledge related to the various technologies associated with TAP. Despite this commitment of resources, the TAP effort made heavy use of outside vendors to correct its phase I unit and used part-time staff in most of the other activities. Using shared resources allowed TAP to call on a wider variety of individuals than might have been possible with dedicated staff. Balancing this was the conflict between the demands of TAP and the other work elements assigned to shared staff members. Although this resource allocation represented a major asset for TAP, it also represented an inherent liability. The low level of committed resources allowed the innovation to be canceled more easily.

Another critical resource was access to the host organizations and senior management. These resources were subject to frequent changes in reporting structures and frequent changes in personnel within TAP and the parent organizations. Over the course of the innovation, the president of Millipore was killed in a plane crash, a key leader in the Millipore TAP operation was promoted, and the management structure at Millipore was reorganized. At 3M, the TAP program initially reported to the health care vice president but was later moved to report directly to Sarns, which placed TAP in a more natural location for the long term, because Sarns was the planned manufacturer of the apheresit units, but removed the direct reporting to a lower level in the overall organization. In the short term, the changes at Sarns (departure of the founder, expansion, and even a product recall) focused management attention on issues unrelated to the TAP venture.

Despite program emphasis on expertise and functional responsibility, the parties were conscious of the relative weight of dollar expenditures even though the partners did not regularly exchange this information. Millipore viewed its dollar investment in research and development on TAP as relatively more significant than the amounts invested by 3M in TAP. Millipore managers remarked to researchers that Millipore was investing a major part of its overall R&D budget on TAP while TAP was only a small part of the overall R&D effort by 3M. Alternatively, 3M viewed the comparison more frequently in absolute terms. Thus each organization tended to see itself as the disadvantaged partner. Although these differences were present early in the program, they were less critical when things were going well. When more extensive problems appeared and partners began to question their involvement, they also questioned the inherent fairness of the venture.

Learning, Persistence, and Risk Management

The division of tasks based on functional expertise allowed TAP to access key expertise in each organization. This allocation also contributed to persistence when problems developed. When one organization was unable to resolve a problem in its area of responsibility it continued to maintain responsibility and other SBU members were unwilling to force the issue back to the level of the entire venture. This may have occurred because the project lacked resources, money, and expertise. An alternate explanation is similar to the "diffusion of blame" concept and occurs when one party is able to escape responsibility for a project delay because other parties have also generated problems that could account for the delay. Thus, each individual problem and component had a responsible party but overall responsibility for TAP's products and efforts was widely distributed, and hence the responsibility of no one.

Learning was made more difficult by the transfer of people and by the part-time nature of staffing. Because much of the learning was embodied in tacit knowledge gained by participants, it was diffused and difficult to reach. In addition, TAP tried to share knowledge among technicians by forming committees and having regular technical "exchanges" among the organizations. Nevertheless, it was difficult to share information among the widely differing technical disciplines. For example, 3M had little expertise on filtration, and Millipore depended on 3M for diagnostic and clinical evaluation. In addition, the geographic separation of staff members created an isolation that sometimes made communication difficult. As noted, the 3M laboratory had a major success treating a dog using apheresis. It was a visible and dramatic example of the ultimate value of the technology, but the 3M laboratory manager noted, "It is very difficult to communicate my enthusiasm across the other aspects of the project."

The individuals and the products that the organizations retain also represent learning for the organizations. Because of the TAP demise, little learning from the technical aspects of the program was retained. A lead researcher left Millipore, the laboratory manager at 3M left, and ultimately the project manager also left 3M. The management learning also was not codified. The approach was typified by one senior 3M executive who asked, "What can we learn from a failure?"

Managing Relationships and Contracts with Business Stakeholders

The SBU placed greater reliance on the nature of the joint-venture agreement than might have been expected given the opinions expressed by more senior managers. This might be related to the lack of role clarity of SBU managers and organizational representatives. It might also be related to the considerable uncertainty that surrounds any innovative activity and the need to find criteria that can be used to reduce this uncertainty. This reliance on the formal agreement appeared most frequently when opportunities for new business arose related to TAP.

The outside opportunities generally originated within individual organizational units such as 3M biosciences laboratories or Millipore research laboratories and were then brought to the SBU for discussion. A key issue for the SBU was the ownership of interests in items developed in conjunction with developing therapeutic products: Should these belong to TAP or to the host organization that found them? Could host organizations move forward unilaterally on these businesses, or did TAP have the right of first refusal? Who got to make these decisions, the SBU or individual managers within the host organizations?

Discussions of new TAP business opportunities appeared throughout the project and seemed to follow an iterative and preoccupied gestation process. For example, diagnostics business opportunities were repetitively proposed, rejected, and reproposed for TAP business expansion at the 1985 and 1986 SBU meetings. Outside opportunities for TAP business expansion were more asynchronous to the program's progress.

The diagnostic business opportunity appeared to be the most consistent outside business opportunity primarily because new tests were needed to evaluate the effectiveness of TAP phase II and phase III filtration. Because these tests were essential, the possibility that they could be commercialized was natural, and the SBU continued to consider the diagnostics business as late as April 1987.

Initially, diagnostics were viewed as outside the contractual joint-venture agreement. 3M and Millipore team leaders reached this decision after discussion at the SBU. Later the diagnostics reappeared as new information about needs and uses became available. At this later juncture, the SBU decided to pursue the diagnostics and asked for a formal business plan to be presented by 3M researchers.

Communication with outside stakeholders at Millipore, 3M, and Sarns occurred through periodic management reviews and normal internal discussions within each organization. The reviews provided an opportunity for TAP to assess its support and present its case for needed resources. A key element in these reports was the development of schedules for innovation milestones. Management was aware of projected schedules and seemed to acknowledge that slippage in these schedules would occur. In spite of this, management also expected the innovation to meet their projections.

TAP reviews with management took a proactive attitude in most cases. When successes were achieved, the team emphasized progress; when problems occurred, the presentations emphasized that resolution was under way and under control. These presentations were effective and deemed necessary by SBU members to handle the ongoing list of projects that competed with TAP for executive resources and attention, but it continued to create a series of expectations in executive ranks that TAP was ultimately unable to fulfill.

Relations between 3M and Millipore did change when the "honeymoon" ended. The transition occurred when the program delivered initial machines to the marketplace. This milestone triggered decisions about the royalties and minimum payments called for in the joint-venture agreement. Lack of effective sales caused 3M and Millipore TAP leaders outside the SBU to renegotiate the royalty portions of the agreement. They described these negotiations as "brutal" and "blunt." While the other SBU members were spared this negotiation, the SBU also realized that a major decision process related to TAP was taking place outside the SBU, which reinforced the emphasis in the SBU on technical and tactical issues in contrast to overall program direction.

Psychological contracts were even harder to renegotiate. As noted, the assignment of responsibility, both formal and informal, led to persistence. When one group was responsible for resolving a problem or designing a component, the other SBU members seemed willing to leave that responsibility unchanged even when problems continued. Another psychological contract was the sense of commitment that each partner held. Beginning with the budget cuts in 1984 and continuing through the end of the program, Millipore personnel often wondered how committed their partner really was.

Leading the Business Creation Journey

Leadership in the TAP development took many forms and occurred at many levels in the organizations. Early support within 3M came from the vice president of health care and executives at Millipore. Leadership at the SBU level came from the 3M project manager and leaders of the Millipore contingent. Also, all SBU members fulfilled a leadership role.

The relationship with external organizational leaders was initially strong but weakened over time. On the Millipore side, key leaders involved in the early period of TAP were lost in an airplane crash. At 3M,

Table 9.2. Time resource-controllers criteria innovation managers' criteria

	Insiders	Outsiders
11/84	Potential to build new business with new technology In 5–10 yrs.	Develop an effective and marketable filtration device.
	Build strong relationship with corporate partner and explore other opportunities with them.	Develop technological understanding.
	Undertake Innovation until program manager decides its time to quit.	Meet developmental schedule.
4/85	Accomplish technical objectives.	Accomplish product development schedule.
	Show reasonable progress.	Build Strategic Business Unit group.
	Meet timelines and budget.	
9/85	Is the market there for the apheresis?	Meet budget and technical schedules.
		Solve engineering-production problems.
		Solve coordination problems among co-venturing firms.
4/86	Competence and productivity of innovation personnel.	Survival: Keep program alive.
	Meet financial and technical targets.	Plan execution and implementation. Show financial and technical performance.
11/86	Demonstrate bottom line in market entry of Phase I product.	Get "bugs" out of apheresis system.
		Prediction accuracy of technology and market competition.
6/87	Two-year schedule slippage.	Maintain program credibility.
	Investment attractiveness of program relative to others.	Solve device quality problems.
	Find another investor.	Improve communication among firms.
		Demonstrate program success relative to others.
12/87	Resource drain of program.	Maintain commitment to program.
	Competence of program managers.	Demonstrate clinical need in market.
	Renegotiate program with partners.	Relocate program personnel.

the change in assignment of the 3M project manager to Sarns reduced the level of access to the 3M health care vice president, a key management supporter.

In addition, the views of managers inside the innovation often differed from the views held by the external managers. Table 9.2 contrasts the patterns of criteria held by insiders and outsiders. Initially, external managers looked for development of a new business while SBU members worked to create the initial devices. Subsequently, the SBU directed its efforts toward developing a major line of business, in April 1985, while outsiders moved to more concrete measures.

Leadership stability within the SBU eventually took place and worked to the benefit of TAP, but not until the Millipore SBU leadership had stabilized and only after leaders realized that organizational members were taking an increasingly proprietary perspective. For example, in 1986, the SBU leaders made a conscious effort at SBU meetings to sit next to each other at the conference table. Previously, the SBU members frequently grouped themselves either by company or by functional responsibility. This somewhat belated realization of the need for coherent leadership appears to have occurred as a result of the problems that the innovation was experiencing by this time.

Appendix: Dates and Events in the Development of the Therapeutic Apheresis Program

Organization and Evaluation of TAP

01/80   3M works on blood treatment systems from 1980 to 1982, when work discontinues but interest remains.

01/81   Millipore initiates talks with Sarns regarding plasma-pheresis.

01/81   Millipore contacts Sarns about treatment device. Discussion delayed by merger.

06/81   3M acquires Sarns.

03/83   Joint-venture negotiations begin between Millipore and 3M.

03/83   After Sarns merger, 3M reactivates its interest in pheresis.

11/83   3M-Millipore sign agreement to pursue apheresis, including specific disease treatment.

01/84   Initial business plan completed.

05/84   Management review.

10/84   3M sector planning committee supports TAP 1985 budget request but at a reduced level.

11/84   TAP progress presentation to Millipore management.

12/84   3M health care group reorganized; TAP now reports to Sarns.

02/85   3M program manager presents a business plan for 1985 that includes several goals for 1985.

04/85   Need for additional resources in marketing is agreed on. 3M offers money for research but no staff.

05/85   3M, Sarns, and Millipore top management review TAP.

05/85   Initial risk analysis meeting.

07/85   New Millipore vice president of marketing joins the SBU, replacing Millipore marketing person.

09/85   3M, Sarns, and Millipore top management review TAP.

11/85   Millipore reorganizes.

12/85   Sarns general manager resigns and is replaced by 3M executive.

12/85   TAP has met five of its six 1985 goals.

12/85   3M budget for TAP approved.

12/85   Millipore development director appointed vice president of Millipore products and general manager of health care products. This individual remains on the SBU. The Millipore vice president who joined in July resigns from Millipore.

01/86   Millipore vice president of R&D returns to SBU.

02/86   Marketing person joins TAP marketing group. European sales representative added in October 1985.

03/86   Marketing manager and 3M program manager visit Japan and assess competition.

04/86   Risk analysis review with risk consultant.

05/86   Effective May 12, 3M-TAP domestic sales representative appointed.

05/86   Report of new Millipore organizational chart. New Millipore products president appointed after death of previous president of the corporation.

05/86   New Sarns laboratory director replaces previous director on SBU.

06/86   3M and Millipore top management review TAP.

08/86   A new organization for TAP activities is proposed based on Detroit meeting.

10/86   Considerable debate among SBU members about planned reorganization.

10/86   TAP marketing manager is promoted to marketing manager at Sarns.

10/86   Report on 1986 goals. Sales at only 10% of projections. Credibility is in question.

12/86   SBU meeting. Sarns general manager reports on the future of TAP at Sarns. Problems at Sarns indicated in areas of nonassertive culture, first sterile product recall in March 1986, management changes and ideas for new business. The Sarns general manager committed to necessary changes. TAP is funded from health care division to reduce impact on Sarns mainstream, which is president's first priority. Sarns had revenues $15M–$18M in 1983. Revenues now about $30M, primarily because of Omnis acquisition.

12/86   New committee structure: business team, marketing development team, and Sarns-3M core team.

12/86   No effort for advanced separations in 1987 because of need for resources on current problems.

12/86   Millipore vice president on SBU agrees to forgo half of royalties in 1987. He takes criticism from management for this.

12/86   3M program manager agrees to become direct coordinator of three individuals, one from each company, to monitor progress on problems and development in response to agreed need for a program manager. Considerable discussion involving how the current problem situation evolved. At one point an informal survey indicates that there is little agreement with regard to who is in charge of various program aspects.

12/86   Millipore funding for 1987 to be about $500K compared with $700K in 1986, a result of a move into manufacturing engineering and a cut in R&D. Millipore has profitability problem on modules and now no longer needs automation for manufacturing.

01/87   Money will be moved from marketing and clinical areas into problems so additional money from life sciences sector vice president is not needed. Vice president still supportive despite problems.

02/87   SBU meeting: Issues are management responsibility at Sarns, further problems with secondary module, problems making sales projections for 1987. New business discussion about diagnostics and lipid centers.

02/87   Some staff complain about too many meetings due to recent reorganization. After discussion, it is decided to wait a while longer before making any changes to see whether situation gets better with experience.

03/87   Risk consultant meeting with Sarns-3M only. Still over 80% of the risk is on phase II. Efficacy reduced 30 points, quality increased 35 points, and availability of product in 1990 increased 30 points.

04/87   New individual hired to be marketing development manager for TAP, reporting to Sarns marketing director.

04/87   3M program manager to work on eliminating TOT (Therapore operating committee). Problems arise because of too many committees, including primary operations committee and secondary operations committee.

04/87   Competitive assessment task force report indicates competitive activity by Kanegafuchi (columns), Haemonetics (primary only), Cobe (precipitation), and Rogesin (Imminoadsorption). Haemonetics and Kuraray Chemicals Company are no longer working together.

05/87   TAP internal management review places TAP more favorably than CIP. The evaluation shows negative change in attractiveness and competitive assessment, and a slight increase in risk. 3M health care vice president indicates unwillingness to fund TAP beyond 1988.

06/87   3M health care vice president will not support TAP beyond 1988. 3M now spends about $4M per year, and it learns Millipore is spending $1M to $1.5M. 3M thinks Millipore should contribute more. 3M program manager meets with Millipore vice president (SBU member) and offers several options such as donating modules, writing a check for $1M, or taking less royalties. Millipore vice president will see whether Millipore is still interested. New contract not pushed. Millipore gets proposal and is not pleased. Issues are fairness of expenditures, profitability or viability for 3M and Millipore, and possibility of belt tightening or other cuts to keep program running. Rumors say the project is doomed.

06/87   June SBU canceled.

06/87   Emergency meeting of 3M core team to discuss restructuring finances as a result of recent internal management review.

Items for discussion included 10% to 15% across-the-board budget reductions, omission of diagnostics, assumption of improved electronics by 1/1/88, 70% of sales by 1995 will come from tube sets manufactured outside Sarns, and no significant research beyond LDL and immune complex.

06/87   Joint 3M-Millipore review. 3M health care vice president suggests bringing in third partner because 3M desires reduced financial burden. Phase II animal tests set for 1/88, and FDA approval scheduled 4/89. Primary system time lines shifted from 1/86 to 9/87. LDL apheresis shift from 6/87 to 6/89. 3M suggests a spin-off joint venture with a third partner in executive session. No substantive results. Millipore asks if 3M is really committed. 3M suggests that it is just an issue of financing and additional opportunities for investment.

08/87   3M program manager begins contacting outside firms in search of investment partner.

08/87   Nine types of investors identified. Three types inside 3M. 3M program manager has already begun contacts with outside investors in five of six classes.

08/87   Leading engineer-scientist on Millipore membrane efforts resigns.

08/87   SBU review sets priorities as (1) find new investor, (2) implement phase, (3) phase II cholesterol, (4) phase II immune complex schedule to be determined, (5) other clinical indications (to be determined). Only the first three will receive current effort. Primary now assumes clear priority over secondary. This list results from discussion of what program should be doing to move ahead. Separate lists developed in working groups and includes generic items such as need for dedicated personnel, stronger leadership, more resources. What can be done in a timely manner, specifically done by year-end? Conflict over whether phase I is higher priority than phase II. Issue of what kind of day-to-day leadership SBU needs. 3M program manager recommends five priorities. Everyone agrees.

08/87   Outside sources contacted for new investment: R&D Funding Corp., VHA venture fund, Hoffman-LaRoche, Medtronic, Smith-Kline-Beckman. Other possibilities include apheresis competitors or hospital chains.

08/87   Extensive discussion about whether program should go on even if financing can be found outside. Debate about whether it would be worthwhile to invest $10M more in TAP. Answer is generally yes, but Sarns staff members suggest that business is good for 3M but not for Sarns. Other reservations as well. Summary statement is: "Focus the program on the major opportunity(s) in a dedicated more well managed environment with spending tied to demonstrated results and market emergence." Program warrants investment and should go on. Many concerns are raised: Credibility based on track record, size of cholesterol market, need for clinical effort, appropriateness of structure, long time to provide proof of investment, and better uses for the month.

09/87   Merck wins approval of LDL reducing drug, Lovastatin.

09/87   Sarns general manager asks 3M program manager to cancel October SBU.

10/87   Initial report of National Cholesterol Education Program calls for all adults to achieve a desirable cholesterol level of below 200 milligrams per decaliter of blood. Calls for additional testing and lower acceptable cholesterol levels.

12/87   3M officially notifies all that program is terminated via phone between 3M health care vice president and Millipore CEO on 12/20/87 and in a letter to Millipore vice president on 12/29.

01/88   3M, Sarns, and Millipore staff meet with legal council from 3M and Millipore. TAP is dead, and the two companies have a frank exchange of views regarding residual rights. 3M legal department will make offer in letter by 1/27 and the group will meet again on 2/3/88. Millipore vice president now believes the program belongs to Millipore and has begun to contact possible new partners.

03/88   Hoffman-LaRoche partnership has fallen through. Attorneys are still working on turning over TAP to Millipore. 3M program manager will start looking for a new job next week.

04/88   3M clinical lab manager (SBU member) resigns to take position with small firm in Connecticut doing cancer diagnostics research. New position is director R&D.

06/88   3M program manager assumes new job in health care specialties area as marketing manager at same salary but at one job grade lower.

06/88   Final agreement tentatively reached on transfer to Millipore. Proprietary rights are licensed to Millipore. Assets and knowledge go to Millipore for pump part of system. Joint rights control algorithm. Devices in the field will be withdrawn.

Phase I   Product Developments

10/83   Focus panel shows need for changes in initial prototype system.

06/84   A redesign of the apheresis system is performed by an outside consultant. Animal tests begin in June 1984.

02/85   FDA approves phase I IDE.

04/85   Initial deliveries of units are delayed due to technical manufacturing difficulties.

12/85   TAP files phase I PMA with FDA.

01/86   Five instruments shipped to 3M France. In-service planned for 2/10/86, a delay from 1/6/86.

05/86   Difficulties encountered in pump motors. Distribution of other units held up.

08/86   Three problems noted with European machines.

11/86   FDA gives final PMA for phase I device. No postmarket information required.

12/86   Report of reliability review results in hold on sales until 9/87.

12/86   Sarns SBU representative reports that reliability design evaluation indicates that machines cannot be consistently built in a reliable fashion. Repackaging by outside vendor, pump head work, and production debugging consultant recommended for 1987. Units to be built two at a time in pilot production. Considerable discussion is involved. It is noted that a redesigned product would not guarantee resolution of all problems. It is also noted that this might mean that it would be 1988 before a quality manufacturable unit would be available. Three to four people are needed for six to twelve months to pursue changes to phase 1, which translates to an additional $300K–$400K.

12/86   3M marketing manager on SBU projects $38K sales for 1986 and projects $1M for 1987.

02/87   Software Electronic Research Co. (SERC) and HTC are internal 3M consultants retained to help with redesign of primary system. The outside vendor's redesign prototype due in April 1987.

02/87   Major debate over individual ownership of Sarns's part of program. This debate was primarily the SBU against Sarns SBU representative in an attempt to get this individual to take ownership of entire program at Sarns. He did not do this and professed ownership of laboratory effort only. The 3M program manager agrees to assume direct control of one Sarns engineer and Sarns TAP activity as compromise. There is need for greater responsibility for program activities. Some SBU members feel they have limited roles in host organizations. Sarns SBU member is uncertain he can satisfy SBU.

02/87   Sales projection for 1987 is now $300K.

02/87   3M program manager suggests sales goal of twenty primary systems by 12/15/87 based on 9/15 availability from manufacturing. This is reduced from recent sales plan. 3M marketing manager objects to sales and notes slip from 7/15 availability. General discussion about dates deteriorates with no final schedule agreed on at meeting. This is part of overall discussion about accountability.

03/87 Society of Hemopheresis specialists conference. TAP has booth.

04/87 American Society for Apheresis conference. TAP has booth.

04/87 The team is now working together. A breakthrough on system errors. It is in the computer.

04/87 Problems with tube set kinking. Lack of quality assurance. Will take about two months to resolve.

04/87 Written report of control consultant due in two weeks. New algorithm will be forthcoming. Final recommendations for phase I problems due 7/15 based on experiments in June. New phase II filtration module spacer manufacturer now on line. Phase II filtration modules for animal tests scheduled for 5/22. Some additional problems can be dealt with although it may entail more FDA work. Filing of IDE now estimated for May 1988.

04/87 Two 3M staff now working on international regulation. German testing scheduled for September through November at Sarns.

04/87 Marketing forecast and machine schedule. Schedule for phase I units: July 4, September 4, October 6, November 10, December 4. Eighteen to twenty units will be placed. Three of these will be sold. Total of twenty-eight to be built. Total sales including machines and tube sets is $216K.

08/87 Old-style unit in the field with upgrades has not had problems. Production schedule now calls for three units in October and four in November and December. Production schedule is October 3, November/December 4, January 6, February 8. Parallel work on pump head redesign, ITMP, and quality assurance/reliability testing.

Phase II Products and Advanced Developments

02/85 Discussion of diseases to treat. Short list developed.

04/85 Discussion on the next system to be developed. This activity will proceed despite difficulties in the laboratory.

04/85 Discussion of marketing strategy to leaders or a broad base of prescribers.

04/85 Lab manager reports on research into diseases. He recommends that the list be reduced to two diseases.

06/85 Difficulties encountered in phase II module construction.

09/85 Prototype advanced separator to be built despite concerns about ability to match with disease states.

01/86   Millipore development manager replaced by 3M regulatory
         manager for phase II program manager.

03/86   Phase II module encounters additional technical difficulties.

03/86   Diagnostics will be ready for clinical trials in November
         1986. More resources requested.

05/86   Delays reported in phase II modules due to performance.

08/86   Phase II modules still have some problems. Schedule slips by
         four months.

08/86   Priorities will be to finish current products. Advanced separa-
         tions priority reduced.

10/86   Production process for modules reestablished. Continued
         problems may cause schedule delay.

10/86   Problems with phase I instrument; conflicts over phase II
         testing.

12/86   Phase II milestones: Clinical (in vitro) studies start 1/87, IDE
         filing 6/87, FDA trials start 8/87, clinical trials done 2/88,
         PMA filing 4/88, FDA approval 9/88. The start dates for these
         activities are at risk due to secondary availability.

01/87   First meeting of Competitive Assessment Task Force (CATF)
         on 1/29/87.

02/87   New recovery plan for modules has been established.
         Progress reported on module operation. Still losing 50% of
         flux and problem may be in control algorithm, which is
         Millipore responsibility for design. Millipore management
         not pleased with delays and will reexamine profitability.

02/87   Millipore lab director and others have emergency meeting to
         determine what to do about module problems. Report due
         within a week. Problems include flow rate and wettability.
         Until report comes back, it is an open question whether
         problems can be solved. Considerable debate ensues on
         alternatives.

03/87   Millipore retains process control consultant to assist under-
         standing module problems. Data will be reviewed by 4/15/87
         and recommendations made by 7/15/87.

03/87   Rabbit studies end because of machine problems at Mayo.
         Lupus studies in Europe are also lost because of machine
         problems and changing interests of clinicians.

04/87   Agreement is to continue to emphasize phase II separator for
         cholesterol. Other alternatives were to emphasize LDL in
         other ways or to emphasize immune complexes. One possibil-
         ity was to stop phase II and do adsorption. Initial voting was
         split between phase II cholesterol and generic phase II ap-
         proach. Consensus emerged after discussion.

08/87   Still encountering some problems with pyrogen-free modules
         and with need to use bottled saline to wet modules. Goal is to

make wettable with bagged saline by market introduction. Delays in screening studies by two weeks (end of August to 9/15) and maybe more with emphasis on primary. Schedules may slip by up to three months given emphasis on primary.

Related TAP Business Opportunities

02/85 Issue of whether diagnostics belongs in the basic agreement is raised in SBU meeting.

04/85 SBU decides not to fold diagnostics into the current joint agreement.

04/85 Millipore offers TAP the right of first refusal for spin-off product.

05/85 Sarns will not participate with Millipore on spin-off because of resource limits.

09/85 A list of possible new mission statements for use beyond phase III is presented at SBU meeting.

09/85 Progress reported in diagnostic area. Decision not to include diagnostics in TAP affirmed, but it could be brought in later.

01/86 Additional discussion is held on new products in SBU meeting.

03/86 Millipore vice president reports on new business opportunities. TAP has right of first refusal.

05/86 SBU meeting continues discussion on the next big product idea for TAP.

10/86 $69K instead of planned revenue of $618K for 1986. Credibility of TAP is being questioned. Concern over general slippage across goals.

11/86 Kanegafuchi gets U.S. IDE for column separator.

11/86 FDA approves phase I PMA with no postmarket surveillance.

12/86 New committee structure: business team, market development team, and Sarns-3M core team.

12/86 3M TAP manager assumes role of overall project manager for both 3M and Millipore efforts.

12/86 More information needed on problems—Sarns SBU representative to report in January.

01/87 First meeting of Competitive Assessment Task Force (CATF).

02/87 Agreement to ask management to support diagnostics business. 3M clinical manager and 3M program manager to present business plan at next SBU.

02/87 3M marketing manager presents possibility of involvement with free-standing lipids centers. A clinic proposed a joint venture with 3M to franchise lipids centers. The SBU does not agree to this.

03/87 Risk analysis consultant meets with 3M-Sarns. Still over 80% of points are on secondary.

03/87	Rabbit studies and European Lupus studies discontinue because of machine problems at Mayo and shifting interests in Europe.
04/87	New person hired to be TAP marketing development manager.
04/87	SBU meeting: clinical diagnostic business plan draft presented. Continued market development: 1987 placements at eighteen to twenty (three sold), hardware sales $80K and disposables $136K. CATF progress. Reoganize by dropping one coordinating committee. Phase I: Upgrade going well and on schedule, ITMP task force continues, international registrations being pursued, time line for phase I is on schedule. Phase II module: Focus is on reduction to practice for module with sufficient membrane to deliver desired flux and separation; July 1 is target date for demo. Strategic discussion on cholesterol versus other diseases reaffirms current strategy.
04/21/87	Sarns marketing director will develop further analysis of lipids diagnostics based on report given at this SBU. Three panels of tests are proposed for three environments: research, lipids management clinics, and offices. Initial introduction of first research panel in 8/87 and extending until 1993. No revenue forecasts were presented and some questions were raised about market-size projections.
05/87	Management review at 3M places TAP more favorably than CIP. However, TAP has increased in risk while attractiveness and competitive assessment decline. 3M vice president will not fund TAP beyond 1988.
06/87	June SBU canceled. 3M believes Millipore spends about $1M to $1.5M to their $4M. 3M asks Millipore for more contributions to the program.
06/87	3M/Millipore review. 3M vice president suggests bringing in third partner to reduce financial burden. In executive session 3M suggests that the effort be spun off with a third partner. Millipore asks whether 3M is really committed.
08/87	3M TAP program manager begins contacting outside parties in search of investment.
08/87	Leading TAP engineer at Millipore resigns.
08/87	SBU meeting: considerable discussion about whether the program should go on or not. What are the priorities? Phase II problems seem improved and new modules are made. Testing continues.
09/87	Merck wins approval of Lovastatin to reduce LDL.
09/87	October SBU meeting is canceled.

10/87   Wall Street Journal report on cholesterol from National Heart, Lung, and Blood Institute's National Cholesterol Education Program. Report calls for testing and reduction of cholesterol to below 200 mg/dl.

12/87   3M vice president gives verbal notice of program cancellation to CEO at Millipore. Written notice on 12/29.

01/88   Sarns, Millipore, vice presidents and 3M TAP program manager meet with legal counsel to discuss residual rights. Millipore believes it will own the program.

03/88   Hoffman-LaRoche deal falls through. 3M TAP program manager starts looking for a new job.

04/88   3M lab manager responsible for TAP activities resigns from 3M.

06/88   3M and Millipore reach final agreement. Millipore asks that field units be withdrawn.

06/88   Primary was ready for production when program phased out. ITMP problems now at levels comparable to other membrane competitors. Reliability improved: One unit ran sixty-six procedures in one hospital last month.

10

The Innovation Journey in a New Company Start-Up

The Qnetics Case

This case describes the journey of creating a computer software business, Qnetics, established in September 1983 with the merger of two new start-up companies: Quality Computing Systems (QCS) and Medformatics. Located in Minneapolis, Minnesota, QCS was incorporated in April 1980, and Medformatics in December 1980. Qnetics grew to thirty-one employees in 1983, and then dropped to four employees in 1985. After a brief resurgence in 1986 and early 1987, Qnetics ceased operations on December 31, 1988.

In efforts to become a financially viable company, Qnetics and its predecessor firms pursued a variety of new business creation efforts in its short history. They include a computer distributorship and maintenance business, a custom-design computer software contractor primarily for electric power utilities, a line of medical software for patient records in hospitals and third-party payers, and a developer of software for a load-management system for the electric power utilities industry.

A longitudinal study of Qnetics began in May 1983 when the QCS and Medformatics founders became involved in discussions to merge their firms. Data collection involved quarterly interviews with company founders and top managers and two questionnaire surveys of all company personnel in 1983 and 1984. Because Qnetics had only two to seven employees between July 1985 and December 1988, no questionnaire surveys were administered after 1985. During this period, data collection involved observing and recording company board of directors meetings, repeated quarterly interviews with company principals, and obtaining information from company records and minutes from management meetings. From the data collected, we compiled a chronological list of nearly 350 events that occurred as Qnetics developed. To reduce the complexity of this list, the events were content-analyzed and grouped into five temporal periods. Figure 10.1 graphically illustrates events within each of these periods .

The first period, "Initiation," occurred from January 1980 to November 1983 and includes the founding of QCS and Medformatics and the events leading to their merger to create Qnetics effective September 1983. The second period, "Start-up," details the growth in the products, competencies, and resources within the firm from November 1983 to September 1984. A third period, "Survival and Retrenchment," occurred from about October 1984 to February 1986 and includes a tragic series of failed-take-off events that led the company to the brink of collapse. A "Restart-up" period, from March 1986 until February 1987 includes a financial restructuring of the company, new management, and efforts to position the firm as a viable growing business. Finally, a "Decline-and-Demise" period involves the phase of failed attempts at re-start-up and the final closure of operations in December 1989.

Table 10.1 provides a yearly summary of the financial and personnel status of Qnetics. As table 10.1 shows, Qnetics reached peak sales revenue and net income in 1983, the year of merger. After that, revenues and profits eroded primarily because of an aborted computer hardware sale and an inability to market medical records software. While operating costs steadily increased from 1983 to 1985, operating expenses were drastically cut in 1986 through large-scale personnel layoffs and operations retrenchment.

Based on these data, we describe the progression of events in each of the five periods of Qnetics's development.

Initiation Period

Quality Computing Systems (QCS) was incorporated by three investors in April 1980. They made personal investments and obtained a $25,000 line of credit from a local bank. One of the investors, Joe Doe, who became one of the two full-time principals of the firm, reported that he enjoyed the entrepreneurial atmosphere of his former employer, Dain Bosworth. But he said he foresaw limited advancement opportunities at Dain and had "a strong urge to start something on his own." He and his partner began QCS with three business ideas:

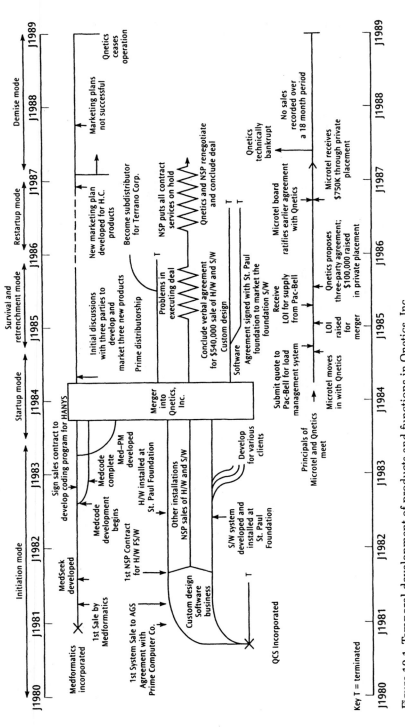

Figure 10.1 Temporal development of products and functions in Qnetics, Inc.

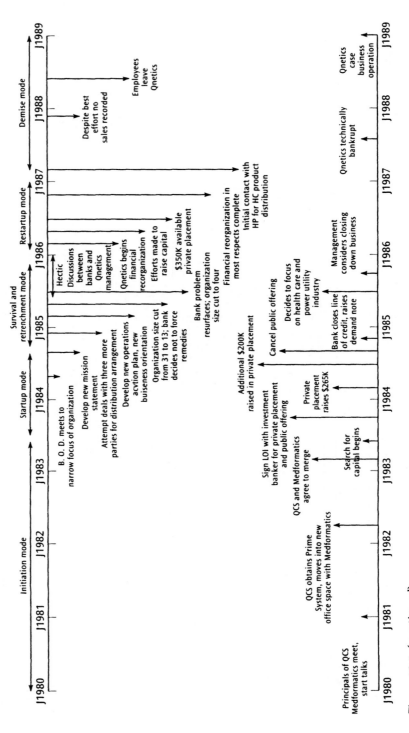

Figure 10.1 (*continued*)

Table 10.1. Financial summary of Qnetics for the fiscal years 1983 to 1986 (All figures in $000s)

	1983 (n=31)	1984 (n=31)	1985 (n=13)	1986 (n=5)
Revenues	2369	1727	990	938
Direct expenses	1866	1517	302	560
Operating costs	484	862	1399	676
Total expenses	2350	2379	1701	1236
Other income	3	2	1	0
Net income	22	(650)	(710)	(298)

n = no. of personnel. Figures in parentheses are losses.

computer maintenance pool, computer distributorship, and custom software development. The principals dropped the maintenance pool idea within a few months because it proved to be financially unfeasible. The idea for a distributorship came from the principal's fellow investor, who used his position at Prime Computer Company to obtain Prime hardware distribution rights for QCS. The first Prime computer sale occurred in May 1981. The first sale to Northern States Power (NSP), a major power utility, was in the fall of 1981. After that, NSP continued to buy hardware upgrades, new systems, and customized software from QCS and later from Qnetics. QCS added three key employees during 1981 and 1982.

Medformatics was incorporated in December 1980 by two principals, one who devoted his energy full time, without pay, to starting the firm from his home office. The two principals made personal investments totaling $1,000 and obtained a $37,000 line of credit from a local bank. One of the principals, Bob Smith, a technically creative person who could not gain acceptance of his business idea from his former employer, started Medformatics. The idea was to develop and market a system of computerized medical records that were required by hospitals to manage and maintain medical information in their medical records departments. Smith initially contracted another medical software expert to develop an automatic coding system. However, from the inception, Smith and the contractor held different opinions about how this service should be provided to hospitals. Medformatics dropped the contractor's services in December 1982 and then proceeded to develop the following line of medical products.

The first medical product developed in the summer of 1981 was MEDSEEK, designed as the database manager for the rest of the medical software line. MEDCODE, the second medical product was an automatic coding system, developed between July and December 1982 with the help of QCS. It used the data obtained from MEDSEEK database and automatically assigned the diagnostic codes for diseases according to international coding systems. These codes are then submitted by hospitals to agencies controlling reimbursements under Medi-care and Medicaid. In 1983, QCS developed a third system in the medical products software called MED-PM. The aim of this system was to improve the efficiency of hospital maintenance operations.

In addition to the principal and his part-time partner, one employee, experienced in medical information, joined Medformatics in 1981 as a marketing manager. Medformatics made its first sale to a group of hospitals in the Twin Cities in April 1981 and won a contract for $60,000 to develop a coding program for a hospital association in New York in December 1982.

The principals of QCS and Medformatics met each other through a common acquaintance in January 1981. They met several times in the next few months to discuss their common problems in business start-up. One year after start-up, both companies faced resource and competency constraints in developing their businesses into viable entities. Medformatics needed computer resources to develop its programs, programmers, and capital, while QCS needed proprietary products in software programming. In April 1982, when QCS obtained its Prime Computer contract and moved into new office space, Medformatics moved in with QCS. The requirements of the two companies complemented their resource endowments, thus prompting them to work closely together. After working together for more than a year, QCS formally acquired Medformatics, although the personnel in the two firms considered it a merger, effective September 1, 1983. The combined companies were renamed Qnetics, and they continued to pursue their three combined businesses in health care software, Prime equipment sales, and custom software development. QCS's principal became chairman and chief executive officer (CEO) of Qnetics. In July 1984, Medformatics's principal became president and chief operating officer (COO). The combined companies continued to recruit new employees in programming, design, and software services.

Start-Up Period

From August to November 1983, the principals of Qnetics undertook a strategic planning process to create a formal mission statement for the newly merged organization. This new mission statement was reviewed and approved by Qnetics's board of directors in June 1984 and indicated that Qnetics would focus on delivering information systems to the health care industry. Qnetics management said clients not in health care would continue to be supported and would be revenue generators for development work in the health care areas.

Products

During the start-up period Qnetics's management proposed developing six new products in the health care area, three of which were to be jointly developed and marketed with three other parties during 1984. The company was successful in developing only one of these products during 1984.

The first product was a hospital cost-accounting system to be developed jointly with McGladdery, Hendrickson, and Pullen. This product was completed in early 1985. The second product, a claims processor for third-party payer situations, was to be completed jointly with DCA Health Care Management Group, a firm specializing in claims processing and cost-containment systems for third-party administrators. Although development began in October 1984, Qnetics shelved the project in August 1985, when DCA stopped investing in the project. The third product was software for a memory-key device in which demographic and medical information about the key carrier can be stored. Qnetics entered into an agreement with Eltrax Inc. to develop software for the Eltrax memory key. Qnetics also entered into a distributor agreement with Eltrax to market the key, peripherals, and software. Distribution costs turned out to be prohibitive, and Qnetics did not proceed to develop this product.

No new products were developed outside the health care area during the start-up period. However, Qnetics concluded two key agreements, one in April 1984 and the other in November 1984. Qnetics reached an agreement with St. Paul Foundations to market the foundation software product Qnetics had developed for it earlier and concluded a verbal agreement with NSP for a $540,000 sale of hardware and software as a follow to earlier contracts.

In October 1984, the principals of Qnetics and Micro-Tel Inc., a Minnesota-based company, came into contact. Micro-Tel had designed an intelligent remote terminal for home and business use that could address load-management problems for electric utilities. Micro-Tel approached Qnetics to manage and raise capital for Micro-Tel. Qnetics's management saw this as a significant opportunity in Qnetics's utilities business and signed a letter of intent with Micro-Tel in February 1985 for merger between the two companies.

Organization

By June 1984, Qnetics employed thirty-one people involved in management, software development, marketing, technical support, finance, accounting, and staff support. Qnetics management reported organizational growth problems because of unclear divisions of labor and job assignments among its employees. In July 1984, Qnetics management undertook a reorganization. The new organization grouped technical functions under the president's direction. Salary studies, compensation changes, and job descriptions for all employees were completed by the end of 1984. In addition, management tried to improve personnel skills and communications by conducting companywide meetings and occasionally featuring guest speakers who lectured on various technical and management topics. According to Qnetics management, these activities helped reinforce the organizational changes.

In July 1984, the vice president of finance established the first operating and capital budgets for the firm. In addition Qnetics transferred its computerized accounting system to run on Altos, a newer system that allowed more integrated financial reporting than the old Prime system. The transfer to the new system was completed by January 1985.

The CEO concentrated on raising external financing and marketing activities. Developing a solid marketing program was a major concern to Qnetics management. The vice president of sales was judged not to be generating sufficient sales growth for the firm. In September, a vice president of marketing was hired, and by November 1984, he had created a marketing plan to sell the firm's health care software by obtaining leads through magazine advertising that would be followed up by four regional sales representatives.

External Financing

Obtaining additional external financing to support most of the firm's employees engaged in research and development was another pressing problem for Qnetics management immediately after the merger. Qnetics reached an agreement with an investment banking firm specializing in small companies to arrange for a private placement followed by a public offering. A private placement drive for $400,000 began in October 1983 and raised $265,000 by February 1984. The public offering to follow was to raise $1.8 million. The private placement drive, however, soon stalled, so the period of the drive was extended and the amount to be raised was increased to $600,000.

By late August 1984, Qnetics obtained an additional $200,000 through the private placement that totaled $465,000. However, it became apparent that the investment banker was having difficulty raising the remainder of the capital under the prevailing market conditions. Qnetics management and the investment banker canceled the planned $1.8 million public offering scheduled for March 1984. The investment banker said the financial market had become "very soft."

Survival and Retrenchment Period

In October 1984, after the aborted public offering, Qnetics's bankers expressed concern about the financial position of the company and, after a review of the situation, said that without changes in the organization, the bank would not renew Qnetics's line of credit. In fact, on December 31, 1984, the bank closed the line of credit Qnetics held. This action by the bank denied Qnetics the use of $30,000 remaining in the original working capital line of credit of $350,000. It also forced Qnetics to use cash flow to pay the $17,000 issued in checks before the line of credit was closed. Further, the bank raised a demand requiring full repayment on all of Qnetics's notes including interest, but it did not exercise its rights to take control of Qnetics's assets at that time by enforcing the remedies.

Qnetics's principals developed a plan in January 1985 in an attempt to overcome the serious financial crisis and took action on the basis of this plan. Qnetics's bankers were satisfied with the actions and changes taken by the management and agreed not to exercise the remedies at that time, on the condition that each of the seven owners make a joint personal note to cover a new loan in the amount of $20,000. However, the bank did not renew its line of credit to Qnetics at that time.

In the fiscal year ending June 30, 1984, Qnetics realized a loss of about $694,000 on sales of $1.7 million. The firm carried nearly $430,000 in long-term debt and $1 million in short-term debt and had a negative net worth of ($498,000). Qnetics management said the implementation of its operating plan helped reduce operating costs by $75,000 per month. Qnetics also realized $100,000 in revenues from sales for December 1984 and January 1985. In December 1984, the firm employed thirty-one full-time staff members, as illustrated by the organization chart in figure 10.2.

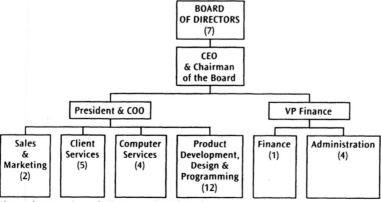

Figures in parentheses indicate number of employees

Figure 10.2 Qnetics Organization Chart, December, 1984.

Unrealized Marketing Efforts

By early 1985, management observed that the cost of direct marketing and distribution of health care products to hospitals was prohibitively expensive for Qnetics due to lack of capital and competencies in the area. In early 1984, the management tried to enter into joint-venture agreements with some exclusive or even nonexclusive distributors for distribution of health care products to hospitals. They approached as many as six parties between February 1984 and May 1985 but were not successful in coming to an agreement with any one of them. During 1985, faced with serious financial crisis and a lack of distribution resources, outlets, or capital to develop its own distribution outlets, Qnetics discontinued developing medical software and stopped selling and promoting most of it. In 1986, according to the president, the company dropped all its medical products except MEDCODE and MEDSEEK. The president observed that MEDCODE continued to provide the only "window of opportunity" in the health care field in 1987.

The NSP agreement for $540,000, which was verbally committed by NSP officials in October 1984 and was awaiting the signatures of NSP managers, did not materialize. On December 31, 1984, Qnetics had to withdraw as an authorized distributor for Prime Computer and move to become a subdistributor to Terrano Associates because Qnetics's bank had canceled its letter of credit worth $250,000 to Prime Computer. During the end of 1984, the local office of Prime Computer approached NSP and tried to sell a Prime computer system to NSP, that Qnetics was negotiating to sell to NSP. However, NSP remained loyal to Qnetics's proposal and thwarted the bid of Prime Computer to take the business away from Qnetics. Prime Computer did not have the software to deliver the services to NSP. In the process of renegotiating the deal, Qnetics's revenue margin from Prime Computer for the sale of the hardware was reduced from $180,000 to $60,000.

Strained financial circumstances led Qnetics to discontinue work on the St. Paul Foundation software in May 1985, and the agreement to market the software never materialized. Along with the foundation software, Qnetics dropped servicing two other contract software clients. NSP turned down a proposal in November 1984 to develop a long-term management system for Legislative Associates because Legislative Associates was fighting for its own survival.

In July 1986, NSP was involved in a scandal about hiring an employee from the regulatory body. The utility put all contract services in research activities on hold until management changed and the new group was able to develop new budgets. Several of Qnetics's software development contracts were put on hold. Between May 1985 and February 1986, the business was managed entirely on a cash basis. Much of the revenue accrued from the medical software and the NSP agreement. According to the CEO, Qnetics management succeeded in reducing costs and the company's cash flow break-even point by about $60,000 per month, a two-thirds reduction in cash requirements.

The only promising prospect for new business with significant revenue potential during 1985 occurred in May, when Pacific Bell issued a letter of intent to supply a load-management system to Qnetics and Micro-Tel. The potential contract was worth $56 million. However, at this time, Micro-Tel had difficulty commercializing the product. Micro-Tel had a cross-licensing joint-venture agreement with Applied Spectrum Technologies (AST), which gave AST joint proprietary rights to the technology. The CEO of AST refused to enter into an agreement with Micro-Tel that would permit Micro-Tel access to the technology to develop the software required to make the hardware run. Without an integrated product, Micro-Tel was having trouble raising the capital for further project development because no investor was willing to make an investment under the current arrangement.

On December 30, 1985, Micro-Tel made one more attempt to reach an agreement with AST that would give it access to the technology. This time, a new CEO of AST expressed willingness to enter into a relationship with Micro-Tel. A letter of intent was drawn on February 12, 1986, which gave Micro-Tel access to the technology. Qnetics's CEO said that on March 14, 1986, a letter of intent between Qnetics and Micro-Tel was signed, which permitted Qnetics to proceed with the software development.

Qnetics management considered creating a new company called Technetics, which would acquire Micro-Tel. Qnetics would then be a contractor to integrate the hardware and software. This approach was considered so that capital-raising measures for Micro-Tel would not be hampered by Qnetics's poor financial situation. However, no progress was made on this alternative.

In August 1985, Qnetics proposed a three-party agreement to private investors to fund and operate Micro-Tel. Under this agreement, Qnetics assigned the services of its CEO and COO, a facilities contract, and software development to Micro-Tel. This three-party agreement resulted in a commitment of $600,000 from private investors, of which $100,000 was funded for Micro-Tel.

Bank Confrontation

In July 1985, the bank again informed Qnetics's management of its intention to terminate its relationship with Qnetics by exercising the remedies. The ensuing discussion between the bank and the owners of Qnetics resulted in an intense face-to-face confrontation, and the bank gave Qnetics's owners until September 3, 1985, to restructure the business or the remedies would lead to Qnetics's closure.

According to the CEO, after long and agonizing discussions, the owners of Qnetics decided they would not be intimidated by this strategy and would not satisfy the bank at the expense of the other stakeholders. The owners of Qnetics returned to their bankers on August 27, 1985, with two alternatives: the bank should (1) support the plan Qnetics proposed in January 1985 or (2) exercise the remedies. If the bank chose the latter alternative, the owners would each file for personal bankruptcy and the company would file for Chapter 7 bankruptcy, which would not leave the bank with sufficient assets to cover its loan.

On September 3, 1985, the bank agreed not to exercise the remedies. This was the "first major battle" Qnetics's owners won in saving the business.

Revised Company Strategy

The strained financial circumstances and the emerging opportunity in the load-management system prompted Qnetics managers to revise their business strategy, which they articulated late in February 1985:

1. Qnetics is a product development company and not a marketing company.
2. Qnetics's business is information and communication and is not restricted to medical industry.
3. Qnetics would enter markets that are volume related (e.g., load-management system for power companies) rather than concentrate solely on markets with relatively few clients (e.g., health care industry).

Organizational Retrenchment

To deal with the serious financial crisis, Qnetics managers undertook several steps to reduce the size of the organization. First, the salaries of management employees were reduced. The owners went without pay for the last quarter of the 1984. Second, the organization size was reduced from thirty-one to twenty employees, which included the seven owners. The eleven employees who left the firm were mainly from marketing, administration, support, finance, and technical writing. During the summer of 1985, the size of the company was further reduced. Four of the owners were laid off, including the CEO and the president. However, the CEO and the president continued to work without pay for several months. That left only two employee owners who were producing enough direct revenue to pay for themselves.

According to the CEO, 1985 and early 1986 had been a big disappointment for the owners. But, he said they had accomplished something unique in the community. The knowledge, skill, and experience they had gained in weathering the various crises, he said, could only be acquired by experiencing it. According to the CEO, it cannot be taught in classrooms, nor can one write textbooks about them. He said, "We have become good street fighters and learned survival." He also strongly felt that "somewhere down the line Qnetics will make a lot of money." When asked to sum up the principal reason for this survival, the CEO said that tenacity had carried them through all the crises, while at the same time they had the will to draw the line beyond which they would not go, as in the case of the confrontation with the bank.

In the fiscal year 1985, Qnetics had sales revenue of $990,000 and a loss of $709,000. Although sales remained stagnant in 1986 at $938,000, Qnetics managed to reduce the loss to $245,000 through extensive cost cutting. From a high of thirty-one employees in December 1984, the company size had dropped to just four employees in mid-1986.

Restart-Up Period

The focus of Qnetics's management in early 1986 was to form a strategy to reorganize the business financially. The investment banker and a consultant, who was an experienced business person, helped Qnetics's management with the task. Further, the investment banker extended $20,000 on a no-commitment basis to provide Qnetics with "a little breathing room" during February and March. This, in addition to averting another closure threat from the bank, helped Qnetics's management concentrate on restructuring rather than fire fighting. Because the Micro-Tel project was moving ahead, investors were again interested in investing in Qnetics, the CEO said. Efforts were directed toward raising $350,000 through private placement. A number of existing debenture holders converted their holdings to fund the proposed private placement drive. This capital became available in July 1986.

With a new infusion of funds from the second private placement, Qnetics's financial problems eased somewhat by mid-1986. The CEO and the president were able to come back on the payroll, and Qnetics was able to hire three people to work on a custom-contract basis for software work in health care and power utility areas. By October 1986, the company also hired a general manager for health care software marketing to renew marketing efforts. By January 1987, Qnetics had eight employees.

During February 1987, the board was reconstituted and four new members were elected. The experienced businessperson, who helped reorganize the business, became the new president and CEO, while the previous CEO became the chairman of the board.

The company had developed no new products since the financial restructuring. The major focus of the company in late 1986 and early 1987 had been to renew marketing of the medical products and to continue contract software development for the Micro-Tel load-management device.

The board of Micro-Tel ratified the agreement with Qnetics in February 1987. Under this ratification Qnetics was to develop software for the load-management system and receive a 50% royalty split for past and future services. This royalty was expected to yield $3 million.

In the health care area, the general manager reported that he had begun making contacts with Minnesota's hospitals and had been following up on leads to generate revenues from the medical software. Management also reported that it had initiated a contact with Hewlett Packard Corporation (HP) and had received interest from them in the medical software business. HP had vertical market niche in health care. Qnetics's strategy was to build a strong partnership with an organization such as HP, for distribution of its products. Based on demonstration provided to a HP representative in early February 1987, Qnetics's management hoped to receive an invitation for further demonstration. If it received this invitation, the chairman said in February 1987 that there would be a 90% chance of entering negotiations for an alliance with HP. The invitation never came.

Termination Period

After reviewing its various business lines, the board decided to close the computer distribution business and devote all its attention to the medical and utility divisions. The management of the company began renewed efforts to market its products and explore possible unions with larger organizations, such as Unisys Corp., Melyx Corp., and Nelson Data Resources, that had the necessary marketing resources.

Despite the efforts of the sales personnel to send out forty-seven sales proposals to potential clients and arrange eighteen product demonstrations, Qnetics was successful in generating only $60,000 in revenues between March and May 1987. The CEO reported an asymmetry between the rate at which Qnetics was using cash to meet operating expenses and the decision cycle of the hospital industry. Typically, the software product buying cycle in the hospital industry was long, involving multiple approvals for closing a deal.

At the same time, the CEO noted that the market for products of smaller software suppliers was shrinking. The trends toward consolidation in the hospital industry and the tendency of small regional and community hospitals to form buying cooperatives meant that suppliers to hospitals also were larger organizations, which obviated the need to deal with small, independent software suppliers.

Faced with a continued cash crisis and the emerging trend toward greater consolidation in the hospital industry, Qnetics managers realized that they were better off leaving the selling function to a larger firm while concentrating on product development. Accordingly, the principals of Qnetics decided to search vigorously for licensees or buyers to the rights of Qnetics's software to the medical field. Meanwhile, one of the owner-directors made a personal investment of $20,000 to meet operating expenses. The board also decided, at this time, to look for prospects to whom to sell the medical division. However, the division would be put on the market after the new products were developed to enhance the value of the business.

Meanwhile on the utility division front, Micro-Tel and Qnetics did not meet milestones to demonstrate a deliverable product to Pac-Tel and under the terms of the letter of intent (LOI) issued earlier, the LOI to supply load-control devices expired by default. With no sales in the medical division or the utility division between June and September 1987, the board noted that Qnetics was technically bankrupt but decided to continue the business for a while longer in the hope of securing a buyer for the medical division.

All stakeholders were affected by the financial crisis facing Qnetics. The top managers and several employees of Qnetics went without pay for several months. Some of the owner-directors met the operating expenses of Qnetics with periodic infusions of personal funds. The lessor of the building occupied by Qnetics, who was also the largest creditor with $170,000 in past-due rent, converted the entire amount of the debt to stock in Qnetics. Further, the lessor invested $44,000 in additional debt in the hope of turning around the company.

Some of these sacrifices bore fruit briefly because Qnetics and Micro-Tel were successful in developing a prototype of a load-management device. On the strength of the prototype and initial demonstrations, Qnetics secured orders for nearly $75,000 from three utility companies. However, sales to utilities and hospitals did not pick up. Despite numerous efforts, Qnetics was unsuccessful in all its negotiations to secure licensees for its products, sell the medical division outright, or find corporate partners to handle sales and marketing. Two more employees left the firm, and another investor was called on to provide $20,000 to meet operating expenses.

Not seeing much success for the future, the CEO wrote a letter to the board informing its members of his intention to resign from Qnetics at the end of December 1988. On receipt of this letter, the board decided to close the business. On December 21, 1988, the board informed the bank of its decision to close. On December 23, 1988, the bank took possession of the company's assets and auctioned them on December 30, 1988. On December 31, 1988, Qnetics officially closed business and all existing liabilities were treated as null and void.

Looking back a couple of months later, the CEO reported that running Qnetics has been a "personal fiasco" because he had lost all of his savings. He reported that he was "personally devastated." In the future, he said, he would get signed contracts from previous owners and he would also "get a CPA to really investigate if a company like Qnetics would actually make a go of it." He planned to settle his personal and financial affairs shortly and look for alternative employment.

Analysis of Qnetics's Innovation Journey

We will now assess the new company start-up case along five themes: (1) temporal progression of the business creation; (2) acquisition and allocation of resources; (3) risk, persistence, and learning; (4) managing relationships and contracts; and (5) leadership and entrepreneurship.

Temporal Progression of the Qnetics Business Creation Journey

In this section, we try to interpret the different forms of progression that the overall business creation journey took. As figure 10.1 shows, the overall business creation process followed multiple paths. Although there was convergence or divergence within each business line, the company itself always followed multiple paths. Only one unitary path is evident, at the very early stages of the formation of Medformatics. It appears that the Qnetics entrepreneurs always emphasized multiple paths as a hedge against the failure of any one business line leading to the failure of the whole company. The trade-off for such hedging was divided attention to the various business lines. Within each business product line there was first an elaboration of the business ideas leading to proliferation of products. Three paths are discernible from the inception of QCS and Medformatics. These are the medical software business, the custom software business, and the Prime equipment sales business. To these three business paths Qnetics added a fourth path, the load-management software business.

The history of Qnetics revealed three cycles of start-up expansion and contraction. Each cycle began with an infusion of resources from external sources, followed by a "honeymoon" period of expanding business development activities that continued until resources were depleted. The cycle concluded with a contraction period of retrenchment in which the company restructured to satisfy stakeholder demands and obtain resources to initiate the next cycle of business development. Each structural arrangement facilitated or enabled the initiation of each cycle and became a liability to replace at the end of the cycle.

Cycle 1: The Birth of QCS and Medformatics, 1980–1983

Ironically, the seeds for the birth of both independent start-ups—QCS and Medformatics—were sown by the limiting conditions of the large corporate structure. The starting point for the cycle for John Doe was the idea of becoming an entrepreneur. In Smith's case, the corporate setting throttled his product development idea, and Smith had to strike out on his own to bring his idea to the commercial marketplace. In both cases, the expansion of the original ideas occurred only when the entrepreneurs abandoned the corporate structure and set out on their own. Thus, by replacing one structural form with another—corporate for independent start-up—the process of expansion was initiated.

The early expansion came in two forms. The first was the modifications of product ideas that each company tried to create; the second was the customer leads they were able to generate for their potential products.

In both cases, the company was successful in completing a small subset of its product ideas and bring them to market, but the limitations of the independent start-up structure soon began to assert itself. The trigger for stopping the expansion and initiating a contractionary cycle was the "liability of smallness." Both entrepreneurs reported that their ideas far outstripped their ability to execute them and bring the ideas to the market. Both felt the need to address the resource constraints but had limited and uncertain options to pursue. While they were exploring ways to overcome the resource constraints, the two entrepreneurs met through a mutual friend, and the merger of the two companies seemed an ideal way to solve their resource problems and provide the new fuel to initiate a new round of expansion. This restructuring of the independent start-ups into a new merged entity began the next cycle of expansion and contraction.

Cycle 2: Qnetics, Merged Company Start-Up, 1984–1985

The merger of QCS and Medformatics into Qnetics allowed fresh infusion of capital into the business. Qnetics was able to raise $465,000 through a private placement process, thus raising a sum seven times the total raised by QCS and Medformatics about three years earlier.

The infusion of capital combined with the synergies of the two companies allowed a new round of expansion. The expansion in this cycle was qualitatively different from that in cycle 1. Although there was no proliferation of ideas in this cycle, the merged companies were able to execute some of their ideas from the earlier cycle. The new structure allowed them to expand in the following order. The cycle began with an expansion in the number of people in the company. The size grew from about four in 1983 to 31 by December 1984. The growth in people and talent in the firm allowed the company to increase its customer base. In eighteen months, the total sales revenues of the company went from about $200,000 to $2.37 million.

The growth in the employee base and customer population put new demands on the organization of Qnetics. The solution to the organizational problems resulted in the expansion of the hierarchical levels in the organization.

The final area in which expansion took place was in the ambitions of the entrepreneurs. The success of Qnetics motivated the entrepreneurs to aim high for the company and plan an initial public offering to raise the capital to fuel the growth to the next stage of evolution. This, they hoped, would launch them from a small company start-up to a high-technology growth company.

The expansionary cycle was halted and then reversed by a combination of external shock and the "liability of adolescence" faced by the five-year-old Qnetics in 1984.

By the fourth quarter of 1984, Qnetics had launched several new projects and had realized a loss of $694,000 on sales of $1.7 million. In October 1989, the entrepreneurs were informed by their investment banker that the planned $1.8 million public offering had to be canceled because of very soft financial market conditions. The ensuing contractionary cycle unfolded in a sequence of domino effect that left the fledgling company devastated by the end of the cycle.

The contractionary cycle began with Qnetics's bank closing any further draws on the line of credit and requiring the company to repay in full the notes outstanding, including interest. Denied critical growth resources, the entrepreneurs took a series of steps, the order of which presents an interesting sequence.

The entrepreneurs first reacted by shifting their strategy from internal development of products and markets to one of collaborative development or a subcontractor arrangement for essential functions. When this proved inadequate, they shifted their strategy from raising investment capital to increasing revenues from products and services and cutting costs. When this step also failed to make a significant dent in the crisis, the entrepreneurs took drastic action by cutting back in all critical aspects of the business including the focus, products, projects, and people. (They had dropped several lines of business and scaled back employees from a high of thirty-one to five.) The whole contractionary cycle took a mere eighteen months.

The duration of the contractionary cycle was determined by the extent of coupling among the various aspects of business operations. First, the success of the medical software line depended on the success of the computer distributorship because of facilities and talent sharing. Second, the company was able to obtain bank credit with the promise of a public offering, thus making the continuous availability of credit contingent upon an uncertain event in the future. Finally, revenues had to be generated from one line of business (e.g., computer distributorship) to develop the product line for another business (e.g., medical software). When some of these contracts or relationships failed, the others failed in a domino effect. The light coupling between contracts, business lines, and stakeholders made the contractionary cycle swift and acute. The reemergence from this acute contraction required a fundamentally new business model approach.

Cycle 3: Qnetics Micro-Tel Load-Management Business, 1986–1988

The organizing force to carve out a fresh approach appeared in the form of a new business opportunity. The circumstances were quite similar to the ones surrounding the early meeting of QCS and Medformatics to solve their problem through merger. Qnetics and Micro-Tel, the company developing a load-management device, also planned to join because of many perceived synergies. However, in developing this new business opportunity, Qnetics abandoned the old failed strategy of simultaneously developing multiple lines and concentrated on developing one single opportunity, albeit with greater uncertainty but with obvious potential.

Qnetics and Micro-Tel created a new equity alliance, and the new structure allowed Qnetics to raise fresh capital: $370,000K. The new opportunity also allowed the company to restructure its balance sheet significantly. Many of the debtors converted their debt to equity stock in Qnetics. The company was thus able to shift a portion of the risk from the existing investors to the new investors and previous debt holders. Qnetics also restructured its board and executive leadership. Restructuring the governance body and the balance sheet again permitted a new expansionary cycle.

The number of employees grew from four to eight. New prospects for the load-management device and the two existing medical products were identified. The company began and ended a series of successful product demonstrations to prospective clients. However, Qnetics had a new problem this time. Although its ideas and products received favorable reviews, it was not able to close a single significant deal between 1987 and 1988. After repeated failures to close deals, the board finally ceased operation in December 31, 1988. The inability to close a deal arrested the expansionary cycle and triggered a new and final contractionary cycle in Qnetics and then in final closure of the company.

The underlying reason for the inability to close a deal seemed to reside again in a form of the liability of small size. There were significant asymmetries in the size and decision-making speeds between Qnetics and its prospective customers. The asymmetries in size and speed proved fatal in the context of a new, emerging, untested technology company.

The prospective clients of Qnetics included such larger and established companies as Pac-Tel and Hewlett Packard. Because of the novel technology involved in the Micro-Tel business, these companies could afford to take a wait-and-see attitude toward developing the new technology. However, this absence of decision proved fatal for Qnetics because its lifeline was cut off. Because no additional cash was generated for a whole year, the company had to operate on a bare-bones existence for an extended time, which proved fatal.

Eventually the company ran out of ideas, people, resources, and stamina. As the CEO of the company put it, "running Qnetics has been a personal fiasco" because he had lost all his savings. He reported that he was "personally devastated." He planned to settle his personal and financial affairs shortly and look for alternative employment.

Acquisition and Allocation of Resources

The consistent story at Qnetics, like most new business start-ups, is the ever-present resource problem. The ideas of management for product and market development always seemed to exceed the available resources. One interesting feature of this start-up is that both the founding entrepreneurs, John Doe and Bob Smith, managed to attract significant start-up capital while investing very little of their own money. The major resource commitments the principals made were their time, energies, and ideas. The significant risk exposure for them at start-up was the opportunity lost because both entrepreneurs gave up lucrative corporate careers to devote full attention to the start-up. This level of commitment from the founding principals was sufficient for them to leverage their social capital and raise significant start-up capital from family, friends, and business contacts. Indeed, Medformatics was able to raise $35,000 on the basis of a mere $1,000 investment by the founding principal. However, even with this early success in raising capital, the entrepreneurs never had enough to develop a strong portfolio of products or customers.

One way in which the principals tried to overcome subsequent resource scarcity problem was to pool or tightly couple resources of two different entities. Because the company was primarily engaged in computer software business, the very nature of the business required no tangible assets that could be used as collateral or used to signal credible commitment to the business development. Because the most valuable assets were creative employees, who were highly mobile, Qnetics had little collateral that could be pledged to obtain debt financing. Thus, the available capital was always less than the available portfolio of product and marketing ideas waiting to be developed.

Four distinct levels of resource pooling or coupling are evident in the case. The first is the coupling of two independent business entities to form a new one. Medformatics tried to solve its resource scarcity by first moving in and later merging with QCS to form Qnetics. Similarly, to overcome a subsequent financial crisis, Qnetics and Micro-Tel formed an equity sharing strategic alliance to develop, market, and distribute key lines of products. In both instances, the entrepreneurs expected resource constraints to be alleviated by the resulting efficiency of joint operations and by the increased effectiveness in product and market development possible from the synergy arising from complementary resource profiles of the different entities.

The second level is the coupling of two stakeholder relationships. For example, the first business line for QCS, the Prime distributorship, was obtained through the contacts of one of the key investors in QCS, who was a former executive in Prime Computer. Similarly, new investors were typically brought on board with the help of previous investors who used their network of relationships on behalf of the company.

The third level is the coupling of two contracts. A typical instance of this approach was the agreement with the investment banker to arrange a public offering to raise both a working capital loan from a bank and arrange a successful private placement, which eventually totaled $465,000. Similarly, a letter of intent from Pac-Tel to buy the load-management device was used as "collateral" to raise $600,000 in a fresh round of capital for product development efforts.

Finally, the fourth level is the coupling of two or more business lines. For example, Qnetics management decided to use the custom software business and the Prime distributor business to generate revenue and cash flow to develop a line of products in the health care business. Thus, the output of one business line became the resource generator for another business line. In a similar fashion, the programming resources of Qnetics were used to develop software programs required to run the load-management device of Micro-Tel, for a royalty arrangement. Managers hoped to generate revenue for the health care line from the load-management line, and the load-management line depended on the health care line for programming skills.

Risk, Persistence, and Learning

The strategy of coupling different levels of the business had its costs. Tight coupling made the different parts of the company highly dependent on each other, such that a crisis in one business affected the operations of another, often resulting in a domino effect for the overall firm. This is illustrated by the following vicious cycles in the case.

To market its health care products, the company pursued the "make and buy" strategies of creating its own marketing and sales branches and contracting with independent dealers and distributors. But Qnetics was unsuccessful in implementing both strategies. Qnetics had to abort the public offering because of poor market conditions. This paucity in finances restricted the company's ability to develop its own marketing and distribution outlets. Further, Qnetics could not consummate any contract with third-party distributors even though it explored relationships with as many as six parties. The poor capital situation led the bank to withdraw its line of credit, worsening an already resource-poor situation. Eliminating the bank's line of credit also led to Qnetics's losing its Prime Computer distributor status. Loss of this distributorship, in turn, stimulated Prime district sales representatives to take control of the large computer sale that Qnetics was negotiating with NSP over an extended period. Loss of this NSP sale would have occurred had it not been for the intercession by the customer in favor of Qnetics. Nevertheless, Qnetics received a substantially lower margin on the large sale than it would have if it had not lost its Prime distributorship.

Faced with lack of development capital and a marketing capability, the company dropped several products in the health care line, dropped current services in the custom-software line, stopped all development on new products, and laid off or terminated twenty-seven employees. Lack of new products and discontinued services further hampered revenue generation, thus creating a further cash crisis in the almost never-ending loop.

Interestingly, the major source of power to break this cycle came from external sources and never from within the organization during the first five to six years of its life. But when the "honeymoon" period wore off, the resources to break this cycle came only from inside the organization after 1986. The external support to survive the critical period of 1985 and 1986 came from several sources. The first was in the form of financial support from the company's bankers, its investment banker, and the experienced businessperson. The second was the unexpected new business opportunity with Micro-Tel that emerged in early 1986.

With the help of a survival loan from its investment banker, temporary working arrangements with the bank, and the expert's advice, the company was able to stave off bankruptcy. The new opportunity that emerged in the electric power utility business enabled Qnetics to raise a fresh round capital through private placement and helped the company rearticulate its business orientation and initiate its present second effort at company start-up.

When Qnetics continued to face crises in the second attempt at start-up, it had used up all the goodwill of these external supporters. Interestingly, the main source of support for this phase came primarily from those stakeholders who held the largest stake in Qnetics. It was obviously important for them to see Qnetics succeed and repay their investments. Thus, the main resource suppliers were the lessor of the office space, the largest individual investor, and the new CEO and investor, Dick Kraemer. Qnetics had virtually no success in obtaining fresh resources from any of the new parties it contacted, investors, marketers, or alliance partners.

It is also interesting to note how the downside risk of the company shifted gradually and cascaded down from the original founders, finally resting with the residual risk bearers, namely, the principal investors of the company. Bob Smith, one of the founders of Medformatics and Qnetics, left the company at the earliest signs of trouble. Bob had barely $1,000 invested in the company, and he managed to leave with his reputation mostly intact. John Doe was the second principal to leave the company. He too had only a fraction of his net worth in the company, and although his reputation was affected, John was able to find alternative employment fairly quickly because of his management skills, technical knowledge, and entrepreneurial experience. The person most affected by Qnetics's failure, ironically, was the person brought in to save the company, not the two original founders. Dick Kraemer seemed to be affected both economically and psychologically.

The founders, John Doe and Bob Smith, managed to shift the level of risk gradually to two other stakeholders. In retrospect, this seems to have come about by accident, but the process appears inexorable. Thus, the lessor was forced to choose between evicting Qnetics and losing the past-due rent or converting the outstanding liability to risky equity position in the company. He chose the latter. In the choice between cutting the losses and running versus escalating the risk, the lessor chose the latter again. Similarly, the largest individual investor and the new CEO, Dick Kraemer, continued to inject fresh rounds of working capital in the company, in $20,000 installments, thus escalating exposure in the company rather than walking away. It is also worth noting that no new investment was forthcoming after 1986 from the other previous investors, who had a much less stake in the company, or new investors. At one level, the existence of Qnetics was very fragile. It never had a strong portfolio of products or customers, but at another level Qnetics held tremendous promise because it had talented people and a plausible set of opportunities, which if successful would produce significant rewards. It is instructive to note that at the later stages only existing stakeholders were attracted to make further investments. In contrast, at the earlier stages of the company, the risk-return trade-off attracted many new stakeholders.

Management of Relationships and Contracts

As we have already discussed, a central feature of Qnetics's strategy in engaging in relationships was coupling contracts by leveraging one contract to obtain another. Often this strategy had negative consequences, especially during bad times. It is instructive to look at the behaviors of these relationships during both good times and bad as the firm evolved. Tables 10.2 and 10.3 show the number of entries and exits of relationships with stakeholders during the life of Qnetics. The entries and exits are shown for two kinds of periods: good times and bad times. The duration of each of these periods, it turns out, are about equal. The numbers in parentheses show the base on which the proportions are calculated and represent the total number of stakeholders dealt with during the relevant period.

The tables reveal two patterns: The exits during bad times are twice as large as exits during good times (table 10.2). Similarly, the entry of new stakeholders into the set are significantly less during bad times when compared with good times. Although we might expect these patterns, when we divide the stakeholders into different categories, the results reveal the following underlying patterns.

1. It is relatively easy to add new stakeholders during good times but extremely difficult to add new stakeholders during bad times.

2. Among the different stakeholder groups, Qnetics added very few new investors during bad times but was able to add proportionately more new customers. This suggests that even during the worst of crises, there are opportunities for a firm to save itself.

3. It is difficult for investors to exit the relationship with the firm even during bad times. In direct contrast, it is most difficult to keep employees during bad times. Sustaining employee contracts requires a continuous and predictable stream of cash flow to meet payroll. One of the first things affected during bad times is cash flow. However, uniform cash flow may not be necessary to maintain customer or even supplier relationships. In the various crises Qnetics encountered, employees were laid off first to reduce cash demands. Further, some of the displaced employees were replaced by supplier contracts to provide the same service the employees provided, a less costly proposition, at least in the short run. A second reason for the differences in the patterns observed in entries and exits among the various stakeholder groups is the information asymmetry among employees, customers, and suppliers. Typically, the employees of Qnetics had more and better information about the prospects and problems of the company than customers and suppliers because of their access to critical information.

Table 10.2. Comparison of proportion of entries and exits of stake-holders during good times and bad times

Entries during bad times	Exits during bad times	Entries during good times	Exit during good times
0.11 (178)	0.24 (178)	0.90 (100)	0.12 (100)

Figures in parentheses indicate the total number of partners during each period in consideration.

Fearing for their job security and salaries, some employees took quick action and left the company as soon as a crisis was evident.

Although the investors had the best information about the prospects and problems of the company, they could not easily exit from the relationship with Qnetics. When they invested the cash in the company, as debt or equity, it was quickly converted to nonliquid assets or spent on operating needs. Thus, the investors were locked into the deal. Even if they wished to exit the relationship, after the various crises, it was very difficult to do so, as the banker and the lessor discovered. The only way to do so was to take Qnetics through bankruptcy proceedings, which was an unattractive option because Qnetics did not have sufficient assets to cover the liabilities. Indeed, Qnetics was able to hold the largest investors "hostage" and force the bank to drop bankruptcy proceedings and arrange a favorable repayment schedule. The managers were also successful in getting the lessor to convert past-rent due to equity, thus altering the risk-return trade-off to Qnetics's advantage and inducing the largest investor and the CEO to inject more cash in a bid to salvage prior investments. Thus, the company was able to use its dire situation to its advantage by striking very favorable deals that may not have been feasible during better times.

Table 10.3. Comparison of proportion of entries and exits of various stakeholders during good times and bad times

Type of stakeholder	Entries during bad times	Exits during bad times	Entries during good times	Exits during good times
Customers	.49 (134)	.76 (91)	.51 (134)	.24 (91)
Investors	.07 (68)	.80 (5)	.93 (68)	.20 (5)
Employees	.27 (161)	.72 (120)	.73 (161)	.28 (120)
Suppliers	.38 (45)	.68 (22)	.62 (45)	.32 (22)

Figures in parentheses indicate the total number of partners in each category.

Table 10.4. Comparison of proportion of exits of founding stakeholders with exits of nonfounding stakeholders

Type of Stakeholder	Exits during bad times	Exits during good times	Total survived
Founding	.36	.64	0
Non-founding	.51	.08	.41

4. Finally, as shown in table 10.4, by the end of the firm's life, none of
the stakeholder relationships struck during the founding stage of QCS
and Medformatics remained. All the stakeholders at the company's
closing were later additions. Thus, the founding members had managed
to exit the company and leave it in the hands of others with the atten-
dant risks and losses. It is also interesting to note that most of the founding members left the company during good times, but most of the nonfounding members exited during the bad times. It is likely that because
the founding principals were different from those who eventually took
over the company, the stakeholders associated with the previous principals left the company along with the principals. But it is still noteworthy that they managed to exit during good times, while the later
stakeholders were left holding the residual risk.

Leadership and Entrepreneurship

The circumstances under which John Doe, Bob Smith, and Dick Kraemer
launched their respective entrepreneurial careers were fundamentally
different: Each took a completely different route to the same end point.
In Doe's case, he was bitten by the entrepreneurial bug, and finding his
current job at a dead end, he made the decision to become an entrepreneur and only then decided to look for opportunities. Thus, Doe's
case is similar to a "garbage can" approach: a solution looking for a
problem. In contrast, Smith's case was a problem looking for a structural solution. Smith was forced to become an entrepreneur when his
organization would not support a passionate idea and an insight he
had about a possible market opportunity. Smith was, thus, a "reluctant" entrepreneur who had no other recourse but to start his own
company to pursue an idea. Finally, Kraemer may be termed a "turn-
around" entrepreneur. He was brought in specifically for his skills in
turning around difficult business situations, his knowledge of accounting and managing balance sheets, and his ability to negotiate and deal
with creditors.Thus, in a single firm we see represented three different
types of entrepreneurs, who were valuable at different stages of the
company's evolution.

In the early days of the firm, the organization was driven more by entrepreneurial vision of the opportunity, by the needs that could be fulfilled by the firm, and by the euphoria of the realization that the principals could control their own destiny. Doe brought selling skills, important business, and financial contacts; Smith brought software and product development skills. The skills and competencies available within the firm provided much of the direction for the growth of the firm. However, after the crises of 1984 and 1985, the locus of control shifted, slowly at first but more rapidly later, to external stakeholders. The investors took charge and put an outsider in control of the organization. From this point on, the firm was directed more by the need to survive another day than by some vision or insight about business or the marketplace. Similarly, the skill set had gradually shifted from product development and selling to accounting, creditor relations, and deal making.

These patterns in the evolution of managerial control of Qnetics can be generalized with a model developed by Venkataraman and Van de Ven (1998) of how the relative influence of managerial choice and environmental determinism directs the evolution of a firm. The model is illustrated in Figure 10.3. Entrepreneurial choice and adaptability may be a function of both firm age and luck. The fact that adaptability is a function of age and experience may be justified because the entrepreneurs start with an initial stock of capital and resources that are used to build the factors of production and competencies required to start and carry on a business. Many early transaction partners are prior social and business contacts who become actively involved in the start-up and early development of the organization, as indeed happened at Qnetics. This initial stock of assets and close-knit group of transaction partners insulate the organization from the environment. Further, at the early stages, the organization is sufficiently small and its resource requirements fairly negligible so that it does not pose a threat to other organizations and institutions in its economic niche. It also takes some time for other organizations and institutions in the niche to become aware of the new organization. Given this initial stock of capital and goodwill of network members and a relatively benign economic niche at the start-up stage, entrepreneurial managers can have a dominant effect on developing a firm's transaction set while environmental selection pressures may be nonexistent or more easily overcome.

However, a firm's initial endowment of assets is soon depleted with start-up activities, and the firm must meet the "acid test" of the market to replenish and grow its assets by establishing business transactions with a new and expanding set of customers, suppliers, investors, and employees. As the firm grows, more organizations and institutions in the environment become aware of it. As the new organization grows larger, it places greater demands on the resource base of its economic

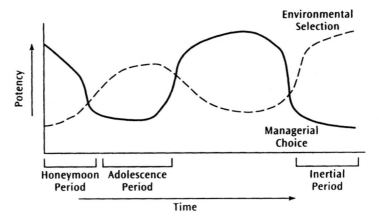

Figure 10.3 Relative influence of environmental selection and managerial choice in business development and change

niche, posing a threat to the constituent members and incumbents of that niche. The organization crosses a critical threshold where the environment, in terms of other organizations and institutions, is no longer ignorant of or indifferent to its presence and demands. Because the organization has existed long enough and has grown large enough to be a significant presence in its economic niche, selection pressures gradually begin to ascend. Organizations are particularly vulnerable at this stage to disturbances in the environment because of their relative inexperience in handling crisis at this growth stage.

With the experience of repeated jolts, one of two things can happen. Either the firm becomes increasingly emaciated with each succeeding hostile jolt and finally succumbs, as happened with Qnetics, or it becomes "fit" through the accumulated experience of successfully surviving such jolts. But, as the firm's managers gain experience in handling repeated crises emanating from environmental disturbances, through trial and error, hiring other competencies, and mimetic and other strategies, responses to different kinds of crises gradually become standard operating procedures. With the routinization of responses, selection pressures recede in influence and managerial choices begin to dominate again. Managerial choices may continue to dominate until organizational inertia becomes a major factor and the managers of the firm are unable to respond to novel and discontinuous changes in the environment. Indeed, although Qnetics managers had numerous ideas, they were never able to implement any of them fully because they could not convince customers, alliance partners, and new investors that Qnetics had significant prospects. Hence, managerial choices again receded in importance and selection pressures began dominating. This discussion of the relative influence of managerial choice and environmental selection on the behavior and performance of the firm during its life is summarized in figure 10.3.

The shifting potency of managerial choice and environmental selection shown in figure 10.3 has an important public policy implication for new, small companies. Conventional wisdom holds that given liabilities of newness, new businesses are appropriately started and encouraged in an incubator environment, ostensibly to provide the new company with start-up resources and protection from environmental disturbances to enhance its probability of survival. Such new, small firms are expected to leave the incubator after a few years and after having achieved a certain level of growth. The findings of this study would recommend precisely the opposite. Incubator environments are best provided not at start-up stage to new businesses but to companies that have exhibited a potential for survival, demonstrated that their ideas and products have merit, and shown some level of growth. It is during the adolescent stage that the firms are most vulnerable to environmental disturbances.

Finally, figure 10.3 emphasizes the role that chance plays in early survival and growth. Firms "lucky" to avoid or escape hostile environmental jolts after their "honeymoon" period (i.e., during their adolescent period) are better placed to grow rapidly, other things being equal. This fact emphasizes the idea that new, small business success, or failure, is only partly within the control of an entrepreneur and partly a random process beyond the entrepreneur's control. Despite sound management and superior exercise of enterprise, bad times appear in the lives of firms in a stochastic, often unpredictable, fashion. Although it is not clear that firms that have superior enterprise, ability, and slack are more likely to succeed than those that do not, it is clear that the ability to survive and grow is seriously affected with each succeeding jolt, ability aside.

Appendix: Dates and Events in the Development of Qnetics, Inc.

01/01/68   Commission on Professional and Hospital begins to computerize information on patient records in eight hospitals.

01/01/68   Joint commission on hospital accreditation requires all accredited hospitals to provide periodic information in standard abstractions of patient records, opening opportunities for providing computer-based abstraction services to hospitals.

01/01/68   Professional Standards Review Organization (PSRO) requires same information for all Medicare and Medicaid patients.

01/01/68   Smith introduced to Dr. Elmer Gabrieli (Buffalo, NY pathologist) by Dr. Mike Jenkins, a surgeon, Centers for Disease Control (CDC) consultant, and founder of Society of Computer Medicine. Smith convinces Gabrieli to apply his specialized computer program to develop an automatic ICD 9 coding program.

01/01/68   Smith writes and tests automatic coding programs for Mercy Hospital.

01/01/68   Smith tries to interest Foundation for Health Care Evaluation (FHCE) in developing business out of abstracting and automatic coding services for hospitals. FHCE declines the proposal.

01/01/74   Smith is director of data systems and analysis at FHCE, evaluating adequacy and cost of care provided by Twin Cities' hospitals using ICD 9 diagnostic codes. Poor data prevented evaluation.

01/01/74   Robert Smith is study director in U.S. Air Force.

12/01/78   John Doe employed at Dain Bosworth, responsible for computers and communications. Wheelock Whitney is CEO.

10/01/79   Faced with shrinking advancement opportunities at Dain Bosworth, Doe begins search for other business opportunities in discussion with Stan Blarek (Prime Computer employee) and Lars Carlson.

10/07/79   Blarek recognizes opportunity to undercut Prime's maintenance prices. Doe and Blarek submit proposal for Prime maintenance pool of six systems.

01/01/80   Other abstracting services enter the market: McAudo and hospital associations.

01/04/80   Doe draws up an informal business plan for QCS with three business ideas: distribution of Prime computers, maintenance, and software development.

01/08/80   Doe shares business plan with two Dain Bosworth people and is told "he was crazy to leave Dain."

01/12/80	QCS members now feel confident that they could survive in a competitive environment.
04/01/80	QCS is incorporated.
04/07/80	The personal banker for QCS's principal becomes banker for QCS and supplies working capital.
05/01/80	QCS begins discussions and negotiations with NSP, Minnesota Power, and several other companies for computer maintenance.
10/01/80	Only four of six Prime Computer Company users could be found to agree to maintenance pool, and Doe abandons the idea.
10/07/80	A Prime system distributor and builder agreement is signed by QCS with Prime Computer.
11/01/80	FHCE repeatedly refusing to fund his ICD 9 coding project. Smith leaves employment with the foundation.
11/07/80	Smith founds Medformatics with idea to provide hospitals with software to enter patient records data and be intermediary with Gabrieli's ICD 9 coding service.
11/15/80	Gary Appel and Smith negotiate with Gabrieli to provide communication links to the system Gabrieli was developing. Gabrieli does not follow through on his commitment.
11/21/80	From the beginning, Smith and Gabrieli have differences of opinion on how the ICD 9 system should be developed.
12/01/80	Smith and Appel incorporate Medformatics in Smith's home. When Medformatics becomes financially viable, Appel will leave his position as president of Council of Community Hospitals to join Medformatics.
12/11/80	Medformatics terminates relationship with Gabrieli.
12/15/80	Personal banker of Medformatics's principal becomes company's banker.
12/21/80	Medformatics begins development of its first product, a data entry system for an automatic coding system to be developed later.
01/01/81	Through common acquaintance, Appel, Doe, and Smith meet and begin monthly discussions to explore joint-venture opportunities.
03/01/81	Cynthia Gorshe, marketing executive and company director, joins Medformatics.
03/01/81	QCS obtains its first customer contract from AGS for supply of a Prime system.
04/01/81	David Lund, previously with a financial firm, joins QCS as vice president of marketing and company director. Lund had known Doe through professional associations.
04/07/81	Principal of Medformatics completes data entry system for the automatic coding system.
04/11/81	Medformatics makes first sale of coding system.

06/01/81	A vice president and company director joins QCS.
07/01/81	Medformatics completes development of medical records information system.
09/01/81	QCS wins contract from NSP for a Prime hardware and software system.
11/01/81	Darvin Bauer, former director of computer operations for Mid Continent Power Tool, begins implementing the NSP system.
01/01/82	Gabrieli and Smith provide joint services but develop different business strategies on services.
04/01/82	Minnesota Power offers to acquire 80% of QCS for $1.5 million.
04/01/82	When QCS obtains its Prime computer and moves into its offices at 14170 23rd Ave., Medformatics moves into the same office space. Companies develop informal arrangements for sharing resources, computing time on the Prime and joint consultations. The activities and needs of the two companies complement each other well. Medformatics needed computers, programmers, and capital, which QCS could provide. In turn, QCS needed expertise in the medical computers field, which Medformatics could provide.
05/01/82	When Smith and Appel hear of Gabrieli's attempt to sell his coding program to McGraw-Hill, they decide to develop their own coding program.
07/01/82	Smith writes a program to assign codes and generate patient record reports.
08/01/82	Jon Otto, formerly a senior accountant with a consulting firm, joins QCS as vice president of finance, company director, and treasurer.
09/01/82	QCS initiates discussions with Minnesota Power for joint ventures.
12/01/82	Medformatics completes development of MEDCODE.
12/10/82	Medformatics accepts $60,000 contract to develop customized text entry and coding program for Hospital Association of New York State. Development costs are greater than anticipated, and company breaks even with hardware and maintenance revenues.
12/15/82	With close proximity and daily interactions, over time personnel from the two companies acted as though they were a "single company." Trust between the two companies is high. Considerations for a permanent joint arrangement evolved.
12/21/82	Although program is superior, Medformatics charges $0.85 per record and loses money on each transaction.

01/01/83   Medformatics begins work on development of a case-mix analysis product.

03/01/83   Enhanced patient medical information system developed for consortium of three hospitals in Twin Cities, each contributing $15,000. This is the first customer for the new company, Qnetics.

04/01/83   QCS principal Doe denies an offer from Minnesota Power to acquire 80% of QCS for $1.5 Million.

04/07/83   QCS and Medformatics principals begin discussions to merge the two companies.

04/10/83   QCS develops and sells foundation software and installs the hardware and software system at St. Paul Foundations to do foundation management.

05/01/83   QCS and Medformatics agree, tentatively, to merge.

06/01/83   Company principals begin search for capital and begin search for venture capitalists, banks, and investment bankers to handle capital raising efforts and begin discussions, negotiations with, and evaluations of more than ten companies.

10/01/83   Qnetics signs LOI with M.H. Novick and Co. for private placement. Initially the private placement was planned for $400K and later expanded to $600K.

10/07/83   An employee of Medformatics leaves the company.

11/01/83   QCS acquires Medformatics effective September 1, 1983. Businesses include contracts with utility companies, Prime computer distributorship, medical information systems, and nonprofit foundation systems. Combined companies renamed Qnetics.

11/07/83   Cleo Kalonick becomes director of information systems at Qnetics; formerly with Hospital Association of New York State.

11/11/83   Qnetics principals decide to recruit employees at programmer and lower levels in the organization to meet expanding needs of the company.

11/30/83   Qnetics hires eleven employees for various technical and administrative requirements of the company.

12/01/83   Qnetics hires eleven more people at various levels.

12/07/83   Principals of Qnetics consult with the investment banker and decide to raise $450K through private placement and $1.8M through public offering.

12/29/83   Qnetics employs about thirty-five people involved in management, software development, marketing, technical support, finance, and staff support. An entrepreneurial atmosphere prevailed.

12/30/83	During the first half of fiscal 1983, Qnetics has revenues of $1M: 35% health care software, 50% hardware sales, and 15% time sharing.
12/31/83	Private placement initiated by M.H. Novick and Co. to generate $600K followed by a public offering of $1.8 M depending on market prices at the time of the offer.
01/01/84	Qnetics principals begin search for software companies with which they can develop and distribute software products for the hospital industry.
02/01/84	Private placement drive raises $265K through convertible debentures from twenty-six parties.
03/01/84	Qnetics moves into expanded office space at 14260 23rd Ave. N. from 14170, 23rd Ave. N., and enters into lease with the external party.
03/10/84	A public offering memorandum is prepared for filing with Securities and Exchange Commission (SEC) by venture capitalist but is not submitted at this time.
04/01/84	Qnetics establishes an agreement with McGladry, Hendrickson and Co. to develop and market MEDLINK, a software module for standard costs and revenues for hospitals. Work begins in June.
04/04/84	Qnetics currently negotiating agreements with four hospitals to develop other products: quality assurance systems, operating room tracking system, long-term tracking system.
04/07/84	Qnetics initiates negotiations with DCA Health Care Management Group to develop and market medical software for third-party payers.
04/12/84	Qnetics initiates negotiations with Health Incentives Inc., an intermediary between health providers and insurers, to develop and market software for third-party payers. Management hopes to enter other cooperative joint ventures, similar to the McGladry relationship.
04/15/84	Qnetics initiates development of a patient information system, which includes a data key, hardware, and software. Qnetics negotiates an agreement with Eltrax Inc. to distribute data key peripheral devices.
04/21/84	Qnetics has four sales representatives calling on Twin Cities-area hospitals.
04/24/84	Qnetics repurchases the 10% stock owned by Minnesota Power for a note value of $75K.
04/28/84	Qnetics reaches agreement with St. Paul Foundation to market the foundation package. Also starts a consulting project with Wilder on some specialized data processing job.

05/01/84	Qnetics advertises medical software products nationwide and receives 500 responses and requests for 200 demonstrations. Responses highlight need for marketing staff.
06/01/84	Qnetics offers a MEDSEEK family of products (MEDEASE, MEDCODE, DRG Assignment and Reporting System, Grouper, and DRG cost-analysis package). Management believes the product family is one and a half years ahead of nearest competitor, and further improvements are being developed.
06/01/84	Board of directors of Qnetics meet to clarify and narrow the focus of the organization. New organizational missions and focus are developed.
06/29/84	Qnetics is faced with technically unsophisticated customers in the health care industry. This becomes a handicap for penetrating and boosting sales in the health care industry. Internally the firm experiences rapid growth and fluctuations in the job content, responsibilities, and relationships, leaving the employees highly confused.
06/30/84	In fiscal year ending June 30, 1984, Qnetics realizes a loss of about $649K on sales of $1.7M. The firm carries nearly $430K in long-term debt and $1M in short-term debt. It has a negative net worth of ($498K).
07/10/84	Qnetics establishes first operating budget; also working capital budget and improving its financial reporting and accounting systems to run on Altos.
07/11/84	Internal organizational changes include grouping technical and operating responsibilities under Smith as COO. Doe continues as CEO and concentrates more on sales and external activities. Company holds companywide meetings featuring outside speakers on various management topics. The firm currently employs thirty-one full-time staff.
07/15/84	Qnetics develops employee philosophy and principles document.
07/21/84	Principals report that Qnetics has no coherent marketing/selling plans or philosophies for Qnetics sales force.
07/31/84	Three people have left the firm, including an original owner of Medformatics who moved to Florida.
08/02/84	Qnetics obtains $200K in private placement. Private placement totals $465K, leaving a shortfall of $135K from the planned offering of $600K. Sluggish market delays plans of the $1.8M public offering proposed earlier. Qnetics management experiences constant pressure of having inadequate funds to meet monthly business expenses plus a slowdown in growth and expansion plans.

08/07/84	Principals of Qnetics decide to postpone the public offering on the advice of the venture capitalist.
09/01/84	Qnetics hires a new vice president of marketing.
09/07/84	Qnetics obtains a contract to develop a preventive maintenance system and develop and install the system at United Hospitals, St. Paul, Minnesota.
09/15/84	Qnetics reaches distributor agreement with Nelson Data Resources, an accounting software firm, for mutual marketing and distribution of each other's products to hospitals.
10/01/84	Qnetics enters joint-venture agreement with DCA group to sell medical; the joint venture is named Health Incentives Inc.
10/01/84	Micro-Tel, a Twin Cities–based hardware company, and Qnetics begins to explore mutual working arrangement. Micro-Tel moves into same office space as Qnetics.
10/04/84	Qnetics develops new mission statement and marketing plans, which are needed to attract outside capital. Primary focus of Qnetics will be to provide health care products. Other products are viewed as revenue sources to meet immediate cash flow needs.
10/07/84	Qnetics has commitment from NSP for $540K sale of hardware and software as a follow-on to earlier contracts. Only signatures from NSP managers are needed. The agreement is subsequently signed in September 1985 and executed in November 1985.
10/11/84	Translated existing products to run on Altos and IBM computers in addition to Prime by translating all systems in "C" language. This increases the marketability of products and makes them less hardware dependent.
10/15/84	Canceled the $1.8M public offering scheduled for fall of 1984 as market conditions were not seen as conducive for the offering.
10/21/84	Qnetics negotiating to be software facilities manager for Legislative Associates, mostly owned by NSP.
10/24/84	Marketing plan focuses attention on an integrated set of hospital products, previously viewed as separate products, in a limited geographic area, using a team of three or four salespeople.
12/01/84	Qnetics discontinues Prime Computer distributorship.
12/07/84	Qnetics begins subdistributorship for Prime Computer with Terrano Associates.
12/11/84	Qnetics principals develop new mission statement and marketing plans.

12/15/84	Wayzata Bank, Qnetics's bankers, closed the line of credit and raised a demand note on Qnetics requiring full payment, including interest, of the loan. Thus, Qnetics was denied $30K of the line of credit, which was not drawn from the working capital loan of $350K. Reason was cancellation of public offering and lack of collateral or capital.
12/21/84	Qnetics principals meet and decide to lay off employees.
01/01/85	Started discussions with CDC, Honeywell Inc., and CPT for distribution arrangement of clinical software.
01/01/85	Three employees leave the firm and the organization size is cut to twenty-five from twenty-eight.
01/01/85	Doe and Smith develop an operating action plan to overcome financial crisis. They also develop a new business orientation.
01/04/85	Smith takes on direct operational responsibility. Smith becomes president and COO and assumes responsibility for developing and implementing the business operating plan, while Doe, as chairman and CEO, takes on responsibility for raising resources.
02/01/85	Qnetics lays off six more employees, and size is reduced to nineteen employees.
02/15/85	Employee owners operate without pay during January and February, and pay to other management employees is reduced.
03/01/85	Based on actions taken in the organization, Wayzata Bank refrains from executing the demand note and allowed Qnetics to operate and use cash coming in as receivables. However, any capital coming through sale of capital goods had to be paid to the bank.
03/15/85	Operating costs were reduced by $75K per month, and Qnetics was left with a positive cash flow of $3K to $4K per month.
03/21/85	Qnetics principals decide to pursue load-management business as they foresee tremendous growth potential in this area.
03/31/85	Doe sends out a communication to all debenture holders explaining the business situation and the progress made since December 1984.
04/01/85	Qnetics, based on the letter of intent to merge with Micro-Tel, submits a price quotation to Pacific Bell for the load-management device.
04/07/85	Principals of Qnetics and Micro-Tel verbally present the load-management system proposal to Pacific Bell.

04/11/85	A letter of intent is prepared to merge Micro-Tel with Qnetics.
04/20/85	Discontinuation of Foundation Software (the agreement to market the software remains unexecuted).
04/25/85	Qnetics management enters into negotiations with CPT, Lanier, Harris Computer System, and Trinity Computing systems to supply integrated systems to health care industry. Qnetics would supply the hardware and the above companies would do the distribution.
04/28/85	A draft business plan for the period 1986 to 1989 is completed. The plan highlights the load-management device, the market for the device, the marketing plan for the product, and the financial analysis and projections for the whole company from 1986 to 1989.
04/30/85	Qnetics proposal to develop upgrades and supply computer systems for Legislative Associates is turned down by NSP.
05/01/85	Pacific Bell awards the LOI for supplying load-management device to Qnetics and Micro-Tel.
05/04/85	Qnetics's management decides to focus mainly on areas operating in expanding markets (health care and public utilities).
05/10/85	Legislative Associates support contract discontinued. Also discontinued third-party distributing of general products MUSE and INFO.
07/01/85	To reduce rent costs, Qnetics physically relocates to a smaller office space. Agreement to terminate lease on former property is not reached with landlord, and Qnetics accumulates rented debt on vacated property for remainder of lease.
07/07/85	Wayzata Bank again wants to terminate relationships with Qnetics. The bank gives Qnetics management until September 3, 1985, to close the business.
07/11/85	Organization size is further reduced, leaving only four full-time employees plus four individuals on part-time contract work. Four owners are laid off, including Doe and Smith, who, however, continue to work without pay.
07/15/85	Qnetics owners meet several times to decide the actions to be taken in the light of closure threat from the bank.
08/01/85	Qnetics principals obtain studies done by independent research organizations on power utilities industry, which predicted tremendous market potential between 1986 and 2000 for load-management and control devices.

08/01/85	Qnetics signs the services of Doe, Smith, space, and software to Micro-Tel. Major activities during July through October period have been on Micro-Tel's operations.
08/04/85	Qnetics stopped development on DCA-Qnetics joint-venture project because DCA stopped investing in the development. Federal Cartridge Co., a much larger company, acquires DCA in early 1985, and the DCA-Qnetics joint venture does not receive the required level of attention from FCC management.
08/27/85	The owners presented the bank with two alternatives: Continue the relationship with Qnetics and follow the operating plan and financing options drawn up by Qnetics or to close Qnetics and take rights to the assets.
08/31/85	Micro-Tel is funded $100K by Alpha Group in late August. Qnetics proposes a three-part agreement under which (1) Qnetics will assign rights to Pacific Bell, (2) Qnetics will assist in managing and supervising software development, (3) Qnetics will receive $3M royalties for any sales in the California area for these services. Qnetics shareholders will receive 10% of stock in Micro-Tel.
09/03/85	Bank agrees not to exercise the option of closing the business.
09/30/85	The city of Fairmont, Minnesota, is interested in the utility load-management device and placed a LOI on Qnetics-Micro-Tel for the product.
10/01/85	Maintenance services vice president leaves Qnetics.
10/07/85	Qnetics sells the remaining contract in maintenance business.
11/01/85	Faced with acute problems on the finance front, Qnetics's management considers two alternatives of closing down the business or selling the business under best possible conditions. Doe and Smith meet with University of Minnesota professors to discuss these alternatives.
11/07/85	Qnetics reaches agreement with NSP to provide $540K worth of hardware.
01/01/86	Micro-Tel informs AST that it would go to court in an attempt to obtain commercialization from AST for the load-management device.
02/01/86	Efforts are made to raise $350K for Qnetics. Dick Kraemer and a number of existing debenture holders convert their debenture holdings to fund the proposed $350K. This capital had been available since July 1986. Venture capitalist assists in fund raising but himself does not convert his own debenture.

02/01/86	Financial reorganization of Qnetics begins with the help of Dick Kraemer and M.H. Novick and Co.
02/04/86	Negotiations continue with Trinity Computing Systems to enter into joint venture to develop and distribute products to the health care industry.
03/01/86	Doe, Smith, and representatives from Alpha complete Micro-Tel business plan.
04/01/86	Based on joint venture agreement between Qnetics and Micro-Tel, the draft plan of April 1985 is revised.
04/04/86	Under joint venture, Micro-Tel will supply the hardware and Qnetics will supply the software. Doe will continue to serve on the board of Micro-Tel.
05/03/86	Qnetics physically relocates its office to lower cost property.
06/01/86	Micro-Tel presents the completed agreement with AST and the business plan to potential investors in an attempt to raise $500K through private placement. The private placement drive raised $750K.
06/04/86	New CEO of AST expresses willingness to negotiate a new agreement with Micro-Tel regarding the commercialization of load-management device. Micro-Tel and AST in signed the three-part agreement in June 1986 and (1) eliminated joint-venture cross-licensing, (2) gave Micro-Tel commercial OEM arrangements, and (3) gave Micro-Tel rights to manufacture in energy management areas where AST chose not to pursue activities.
07/01/86	Private placement drive raises $450K from existing investors and one new investor.
07/31/86	NSP puts all contract services in the area of research activities on hold until new budget is drawn up. This is due to a change in research directorship in NSP.
10/01/86	Qnetics hires a general manager of medical products.
10/05/86	Qnetics sends a letter to creditors committee informing them that if the creditors take no action on the earlier proposal, Qnetics will file for Chapter 11 in an attempt to get the judge to mandate the creditors to settle the issues with Qnetics. This move is believed to be desirable to protect subsequent investors.
10/11/86	Contract services held up by NSP now begin to open up and may even yield more expanded services. However, this has not materialized yet.
10/20/86	Doe explores proposal by Qnetics to Micro-Tel expressing a willingness to sell the utilities portion of Qnetics to Micro-Tel while keeping the medical products portion of

the business and the rights to royalties from sale of utilities software in Qnetics.

10/21/86   Much effort is being placed into Micro-Tel operations regarding budget preparations, marketing plan, and product plan. Doe is responsible for marketing plan, while Smith is responsible for project development.

10/26/86   A proposal is submitted by Doe to Micro-Tel that Qnetics would fund software development for the load-management project and then would receive exclusive relationship on ongoing services business, royalties on the sales of software, revenues from any required customization of software, and any maintenance revenues from software already sold.

10/27/86   The test project being carried out by Pacific Bell in California on the load-management device is six months behind schedule.

10/31/86   A new marketing plan is developed for the medical products business and is hoped to be completed by the end of the calendar year.

10/31/86   Smith is able to sell his house and is starting plans to move to Hawaii, after which he will serve Qnetics in a consulting capacity, not in any managerial capacity. The move is expected to take effect on November 1, 1986.

12/19/86   Qnetics revises design of medical- software to enhance marketing sales.

01/01/87   Dick Kraemer becomes CEO and president of Qnetics. John Doe becomes a director on the board of Micro-Tel and takes over as general manager of Micro-Tel.

01/04/87   Qnetics completes creditor agreement. Five of the largest creditors convert their debt to stock in the company.

01/11/87   Smith ceases permanent employment with Qnetics but continues on the board and to serve as a consultant in the medical division.

02/01/87   Qnetics explores contact with Hewlett Packard resulting in a demonstration of the medical software line.

02/04/87   The board size is increased from two to five. Three members are brought from outside the company: a surgeon, a banker, and a professor.

02/09/87   Qnetics receives a call from HP for a demonstration of the medical software line.

02/15/87   Micro-Tel board ratifies agreement with Qnetics whereby Qnetics will develop software for the load-management device and receive a 50% royalty split on all sales made by Micro-Tel.

03/01/87	Qnetics develops new marketing objectives and marketing procedures for the health care software business.
03/04/87	Sales department sends out forty-seven sales proposals to potential customers.
03/07/87	Qnetics loses its last time-sharing customer and closes down the Prime Computer business.
03/11/87	Qnetics submits a proposal to Health Care Finance Administration (HCFA) for small business innovations grant.
03/15/87	Qnetics projects sales of $35K in March 1987 and $60K in April.
03/21/87	60% of the creditors approve agreement proposed earlier by Qnetics. Three of the largest creditors agree to take stock options. However, agreement with the largest customer remains unsettled.
03/24/87	One employee is transferred from Qnetics to Micro-Tel payroll.
03/27/87	Qnetics initiates contact with Unisys Corp., Melyx Corp., and Nelson Data Resources Corp., for possible joint ventures to distribute Qnetics health-care products.
03/31/87	Only $60K of second private offering of $350K is remaining for expenditure. Projected revenues from Micro-Tel are expected to slip by a quarter.
04/01/87	Qnetics begins or carries on discussions and product demonstrations with eighteen hospitals in the upper Midwest for possible future relationships.
04/04/87	Qnetics receives order from Montevideo Corp., for its medical software.
04/11/87	Qnetics sends several sales proposals jointly with Melyx Corp. to potential customers.
04/11/87	Qnetics enters a joint marketing arrangement relationship with Melyx.
04/14/87	HP sets a tentative date of May 7, 1987, to visit Qnetics for demonstration of medical software, while CPT sets a tentative date for May 12, 1987, for a demonstration.
04/15/87	Qnetics marketing staff members note the environmental trend among hospitals to put off automation and retain status quo.
04/16/87	Qnetics's management notes the environmental trend that software buying cycle in the hospital industry is very long, involving lengthy decision-making processes and multiple approvals for closing deals.
04/17/87	A significant new medical software opportunity, AVG (Ambulatory Visiting Group), is reported as emerging in the health care industry.

04/26/87	Principals of Qnetics note that environmental trends have begun shrinking the potential customer population for the products of medical software companies. Small, community hospitals and regional hospitals have begun developing relationships with larger hospitals for administrative and data processing support, thus obviating the need to deal with independent software companies. Similarly, multihospital management corporations provide a variety of support services to wholly managed affiliates.
05/01/87	Qnetics signs distributorship agreements with NDR Corp to jointly distribute each other's products.
05/04/87	Qnetics calls a special board meeting to discuss financial situation of the company.
05/07/87	HP executives visit Qnetics for a demonstration. They encourage Qnetics to complete development of coding systems on UNIX operating system environment. HP promises to revisit in the fall of 1987 to discuss joint-venture marketing arrangements.
05/11/87	CPT exhibits strong interest in Qnetics medical software and the potential to use Qnetics as value-added to its computer line.
05/12/87	Qnetics sees a marketing opportunity in the NCR Corp. contract and attempts to have ongoing relationship with NCR for subcontracting. NCR promises a visit to Qnetics in the fall of 1987 to see Qnetics's products.
05/14/87	Qnetics begins development of the outpatient records system for NCR's client.
05/15/87	Qnetics signs an agreement with NCR, to develop an outpatient-records system worth $28K for one of NCR's clients, St. Alexis Hospital.
06/01/87	One of the directors makes a personal investment of $20K to keep the company afloat.
06/11/87	Unisys representative contacts Qnetics about a sale of Unisys system to one of Qnetics clients. Qnetics sees opportunity for possible marketing relations and schedules a demonstration for Unisys representative in late June.
06/14/87	Principals begin search for possible licensees or buyer of medical division.
06/23/87	Qnetics marketing manager develops a business development program and strategic document for the medical software division.
07/01/87	The board discusses the inability of Qnetics to close any sales deals with potential customers.
07/04/87	Principals of Winson Corp., a Minnesota company, express interest in purchasing Qnetics's medical business.

07/07/87	A special meeting of the board is called during the first week of July 1987 to discuss alternative consequences of selling the medical business to keep Qnetics a viable company. The board does not come to any final conclusion.
07/15/87	Another special meeting is called in mid-July to discuss specifics of Qnetics-Micro-Tel agreement. Several options are discussed, including sale of both medical and utility divisions of Qnetics. No final conclusions are reached.
07/20/87	HCFA rejects Qnetics's proposal.
07/28/87	Qnetics employees go without pay during the month.
07/30/87	Qnetics does not have sufficient cash or assets to cover current liabilities.
09/01/87	Micro-Tel carries on discussions with six test sites in six states to demonstrate load-management device.
09/04/87	The Pacific Bell LOI for the delivery of load-management device expires as Micro-Tel and Qnetics did not meet milestones for demonstrating a deliverable product.
09/15/87	Qnetics management reports no sales in the medical division between June and September 1987.
09/16/87	Of the eighteen active prospects in April 1987, only ten remain.
09/17/87	Four new customer prospects have been identified with which Qnetics has begun discussions for possible relationships.
09/18/87	Qnetics's medical team identifies twenty-two new prospects and sends out proposals.
09/19/87	Qnetics employees express concern about lack of salary reviews and benefits.
09/20/87	One of Qnetic's directors writes out a check for Qnetics to meet operational expenses.
10/13/87	The board notes that Qnetics is bankrupt and discusses options open to the principals and directors.
10/14/87	The board decides to continue the business at least until December 31, 1987.
10/15/87	Several options are discussed including selling utilities division to Micro-Tel and the sale of medical division.
01/01/88	Qnetics relocates to different office space, though in the same building. New space is reportedly better than the old one and is cheaper.
03/01/88	Qnetics signs final agreement with NCR and Unisys to be value-added reseller to these two companies.
03/04/88	The prototype software for the load-management device is completed by Qnetics and is available for demonstrations to power utilities.

03/07/88 The HP agreement proposal is shelved by Qnetics due to lack of development resources and time.

03/11/88 Qnetics completes the outpatient software, and the product is ready for commercialization.

03/14/88 Unisys provides a computer with three terminals free to Qnetics for product development.

03/15/88 Qnetics receives its first royalty payment, $6K, under the royalty agreement with Micro-Tel, on a sale made by Micro-Tel to a utility in Maryland.

03/16/88 An employee in the medical division resigns.

03/17/88 Micro-Tel begins negotiations for the sale of the load-management device to a utility in Palo Alto, California.

04/01/88 A private consultant is retained by Qnetics to sell medical software on a 40% commission basis on all sales made by him.

04/21/88 The CEO expresses dissatisfaction with his situation in the company and says he is not being paid adequately.

05/13/88 A programmer is hired for the medical division.

05/21/88 A director invests $20K in return for stock options. The investment was required to meet daily cash needs.

05/22/88 The board authorizes the CEO to negotiate sale of medical division with the consultant to the medical division and a brokerage firm to find possible buyers for the medical division.

06/01/88 Qnetics principals begin discussion and negotiation with Strategic Case, a hospital management company specializing in clinical environment, to market products to hospitals.

06/07/88 Qnetics principals begin discussions and negotiations with Mayfield Corp., a company that does corporate partnering and investing to find a corporate partner or investor to bring capital into Qnetics.

07/01/88 A new programmer is hired in the area of power utility business.

07/07/88 A programmer resigns from Qnetics.

07/11/88 Qnetics and Micro-Tel install a load-management test system at a utility in Illinois and begin negotiation with the utility.

07/15/88 Qnetics and Micro-Tel install a load-management test system at an Elk River utility and begin negotiations with the utility.

08/01/88 Qnetics and Micro-Tel sell a load-management device to the utility at Palo Alto, California, and Qnetics gets $55K in royalties.

08/07/88 Qnetics begins software development on the Palo Alto installation.

08/14/88	Qnetics and its marketing partners observe the trend in hospitals market where hospitals are coming back into the software market as customers and are beginning to invest money in MIS development.
09/01/88	Qnetics and Strategic Case sign an agreement to jointly market to hospitals.
09/07/88	Qnetics and Mayfield Corp. sign an agreement for Mayfield Corp. to find a corporate partner or investor for Qnetics.
09/14/88	Qnetics renews contact with M. H. Novick and Co., its first investment banker, to find a corporate partner for Qnetics.
10/01/88	Kraemer continues dialogues with PDP, Unisys, and NCR to sell software or rights to the products in the health care software area. However, these dialogues produce no result, and Qnetics continues to be unsuccessful in generating sales or sales of rights to products.
11/01/88	Doe and Kraemer decide that if Qnetics could not sell software, there was no alternative but to close the business.
12/01/88	Qnetics continues to maintain existing hospital systems and draw minimal revenues.
12/05/88	The board develops plan and authorizes CEO and board members to enter negotiation with Micro-Tel to terminate and transfer contract to Micro-Tel for 10% to15% Micro-Tel stock.
12/12/88	Kraemer writes letter to board, resigning from Qnetics board but says he will continue as employee to close company by December 31, 1988.
12/15/88	Qnetics CEO, authorized by board, writes letters to Internal Revenue Service, bank, lawyer, Micro-Tel (now named Vusa Link), and landlord, notifying them of plan to close the company and requesting settlement or proposing terms of termination.
12/15/88	Kraemer calls a meeting of the employees of Qnetics and informs them that the company is closing, pays their salaries, and terminates all the employees.
12/16/88	Qnetics informs Vusa Link (Micro-Tel) CEO in letter of board decision to discontinue load-software development because Vusa Link has discontinued marketing of load-management system, after investing $400K investment and is forced to close the business. Qnetics proposes relinquishing royalties and contract to Vusa Link and in exchange, requests settlement-closing costs of $200K in Vusa Link stock.

12/21/88   Board decides to terminate business, closes Qnetics.

12/23/88   Kraemer goes to the bankers and reports that the company is closing and that it is bankrupt. He hands over the keys of the company to the bank.

12/30/88   The bank takes possession of all the assets of Qnetics, auctions off the assets, and uses the proceeds to pay the remaining portion of the bank loan taken by Qnetics.

12/31/88   Qnetics is officially closed for business, and all existing contracts or liabilities are treated as null and void as of this date as Qnetics has no assets.

02/27/89   Kraemer reports that running Qnetics has been a "personal fiasco" as he lost all his savings. He says he is personally devastated. In the future, he reports, he would get signed contracts from "the Does and Smiths of this world" and get a CPA to investigate whether a company like Qnetics could actually make a go of it. He plans to settle his personal and financial affairs and look for alternative employment.

Bibliography

Abernathy, W. J. (1978). *The productivity dilemma: Roadblock to innovations in the automobile industry.* Baltimore: John Hopkins University Press.

Abernathy, W. J., & Clark, K. B. (1985). Innovation: Mapping the winds of creative destruction. *Research Policy, 14,* 3–22.

Abraham, F. D., Abraham, R. H., & Shaw, C. D. (1990). *A visual introduction to dynamical systems theory for psychology.* Santa Cruz, CA: Aerial Press.

Akerlof, G. A. (1970). The market for "lemons": Quality, uncertainty and the market mechanism. *Quarterly Journal of Economics, 84,* 488–500.

Albert, S. (1984). A delete design model for successful transitions. In J. Kimberly & R. Quinn (Eds.), *Managing organizational transitions* (pp. 169–191). Homewood, IL: Irwin.

Aldrich, H. (1979). *Organizations and environments.* Englewood Cliffs, NJ: Prentice Hall.

Aldrich H., & Auster, E. (1986). Even dwarfs started small: Liabilities of age and size and their strategic implications. In L. L. Cummings & B. M. Staw (Eds.), *Research in organizational behavior* (pp. 165–198). San Francisco: JAI Press.

Aldrich, H. E., & Fiol, C. M. (1994). Fools rush in? The institutional context of industry creation. *Academy of Management Review,* 19(4), 645–670.

Aldrich, H., & Whetten, D. (1981). Organization sets, action sets, and networks: Making the most of simplicity. In P. C. Nystrom & W. H.

Starbuck (Eds.), *Handbook of organizational design* (pp. 385–407). Oxford: Oxford University Press.

Allen, R. C. (1983, March). Collective invention. *Journal of Economic Behavior and Organization*, 4 (1), 1–24.

Allen, T J. (1977). *Managing the flow of technology*. Cambridge: MIT Press.

Amabile, T. M. (1983). *The social psychology of creativity*. New York: Springer-Verlag.

Amabile, T. M. (1988). A model of creativity and innovation in organizations. In B. M. Staw & L. L. Cummings (Eds.), *Research in organizational behavior* (vol. 10). Greenwhich, CT: JAI Press.

Anderson, P. A. (1983). Decision making by objection and the Cuban Missile Crisis. *Administrative Science Quarterly*, 28, 201–222.

Anderson, P., & Tushman, M. L. (1990). Technological discontinuities and dominant designs: A cyclical model of technological change. *Administrative Science Quarterly*, 35, 604–633.

Angle, H. L. (1989). Psychology and organizational innovation. In A. H. Van de Ven, H. L. Angle & M. S. Poole (Eds.), *Research on the management of innovation: The Minnesota studies* (pp. 135–170). New York: Ballinger/Harper & Row.

Angle, H. L., & Van de Ven, A. H. (1989). Suggestions for managing the innovation journey. In A. Van de Ven, H. L. Angle & M. S. Poole (Eds.), *Research on the management of innovation: The Minnesota studies* (pp. 663–698). New York: Ballinger/Harper & Row.

Argyris, C., & Schon, D. (1978). *Organizational learning: A theory of action perspective*. Reading, MA: Addison-Wesley.

Aronson, E. (1973). The rationalizing animal. *Psychology Today*, 6(5), 46–50, 52.

Arrow, K. J. (1962). Economic welfare and the allocation of resources for innovative activity. In R. R. Nelson (Ed.), *The rate and direction of inventive activity* (pp. 609–626). Princeton, NJ: Princeton University Press.

Astley, W. G. (1985). The two ecologies: Population and community perspectives on organizational evolution. *Administrative Sciences Quarterly*, 30, 224–241.

Astley, W. G., & Van de Ven, A. H. (1983). Central perspectives and debates in organization theory. *Administrative Science Quarterly*, 28, 245–273.

Awan, A. A. (1986). Marshallian and Schumpeterian theories of economic evolution: Gradualism versus punctualism. *Atlantic Economic Journal*, 14(4), 37–49.

Barnett, C. K. (1994). *Organizational learning and continuous quality improvement in an automotive manufacturing organization*. Unpublished doctoral dissertation, University of Michigan, Ann Arbor.

Barney, J., & Ouchi, W. (1986). *Organizational economics*. San Francisco: Jossey-Bass.

Bartunek, J. M. (1993). Multiple cognitions and conflicts associated with second order organizational change. In J. K. Murningham

(Ed.), *Social psychology in organizations* (pp. 343, 337). Englewood Cliffs, NJ: Prentice Hall.

Bastien, D. T. (1993). *Toward a progressive theory of social acts.* Paper presented at the 1993 Annual Conference of the Midwest Sociological Association, Chicago, IL.

Baveles, A. (1960). Leadership: Man and function. *Administrative Science Quarterly, 4,* 491–498.

Bazerman, M. H. (1995). Biases. In B. M. Staw (Ed.), *Psychological dimensions of organizational behavior* (2nd ed., pp. 199–223). Englewood Cliffs, NJ: Prentice Hall.

Ben-Ner, A. (1993). Cooperation, conflict, and control in organizations. In S. Bowles, H. Gintis, & B. Gustafson (Eds.), *Democracy and markets: Participation, accountability, and efficiency.* Cambridge: Cambridge University Press.

Besen, S. M., & Saloner, G. (1989). The economics of telecommunications standards. In R. W. Crandall & K. Flamm, *Changing the rules: Technological change, international competition, and regulation in communication.* Washington, DC: The Brookings Institution.

Bijker, W. E., Hughes, T. P. & Pinch, T. J. (Eds.). (1987). *The social construction of technological systems: New directions in the sociology and history of technology.* Cambridge, MA: MIT Press.

Binswanger, H. P., & Ruttan, V. W. (1978). *Induced innovation.* Baltimore: Johns Hopkins University Press.

Bottomore, T. (Ed.). (1983). *A dictionary of Marxist thought.* Cambridge, MA: Harvard University Press.

Brinkman, P. (1987). *Commitment, conflict and caring.* Englewood Cliffs, NJ: Prentice Hall.

Brock, W. A., Hsieh, D. A., & LeBaron, B. (1989). *Nonlinear dynamics, chaos, and instability: Statistical theory and economic evidence.* Cambridge: MIT Press.

Brown, S., & Eisenhardt, K. (1998). *Competing on the edge: Strategy as structured chaos.* Boston: Harvard Business Review.

Bruderer, E., & Singh, J. V. (1995). Organizational evolution, learning and selection: A genetic algorithm based model. *Academy of Management Journal, 39*(5), 1322–1349.

Brunsson, N. (1982). The irrationality of action and action rationality: Decisions, ideologies, and organizational actions. *Journal of Management Studies, 19,* 29–34.

Brunsson, N. (1985). *The irrational organization: Irrationality as a basis for organizational action and change.* New York: Wiley.

Bryson, J., & Roering, W. (1989). Mobilizing innovation efforts: The case of government strategic planning. In A. H. Van de Ven, H. L. Angle, & M. S. Poole (Eds.), *Research on the management of innovation: The Minnesota studies* (pp. 583–610). New York: Ballinger/Harper & Row.

Bunderson, J. S., Dirks, K. T., Garud, R., & Van de Ven, A. H. (1998). *Spinning a web of relationships between organizations.* Strategic Management Research Center Discussion Paper, University of Minnesota.

Burgelman, R. A., & Sayles, I. A. (1986). *Inside corporate innovation: Strategy, structure, and managerial skills.* New York: Free Press.

Burgelman, R. (1983). Corporate entrepreneurship and strategic management: Insights from a process study. *Management Science, 29*(12), 245–273.

Burt, R. S. (1992). The social structure of competition. In N. Nohria & R.G. Eccles (Eds.), *Networks and organizations* (pp. 57–91). Cambridge, MA: Harvard Business School Press.

Cameron, K. (1980). Critical questions in assessing organizational effectiveness. *Organizational Dynamics, 9,* 66–80.

Cameron K. S., Freeman, S. J., & Mishra, A. K. (1993). Organizational downsizing. In G.P. Huber & W.H. Glick (Eds.), *Changing and redesigning organizations* (pp. 19–65). New York: Oxford University Press.

Cameron, K. S. & Quinn, R. E. (1988). Organizational paradox and transformation. In R.E. Quinn & K.S. Cameron (Eds.), *Paradox and transformation: Toward a theory of change in organization and management* (pp. 1–18). Cambridge, MA: Ballinger.

Campbell, D. T. (1974). Evolutionary epistemology. In P. A. Schilpp (Ed.), *The philosophy of Carl Popper. The library of living philosophers* (pp. 413–463). LaSalle, IL: Open Court.

Carley, K., & Svoboda, D. (1996). Modeling organizational adaptation as a simulated annealing process. *Sociological Methods and Research, 25*(1), 138–168.

Chakravarthy, B. S. (1984). Strategic self renewal: A planning framework for today. *Academy of Management Review, 9*(3).

Chandler, A. D., Jr. (1990). *Scale and scope: The dynamics of industrial capitalism.* Cambridge, MA: Harvard University Press.

Charpie, R. (1967). *Technological innovation: Its environment and management.* Report no. 0-242-736. Washington, DC: U.S. Department of Commerce.

Cheng, Y., & Van de Ven, A. H. (1996). Learning the innovation journey: Order out of chaos? *Organization Science, 7*(6) 593–614.

Cialdini, R. B. (1996). *Influence: Science and practice.* Glenview, IL: Scott, Foresman.

Clark, K. B. (1985). The interaction of design hierarchies and market concepts in technological evolution. *Research Policy, 14,* 235–251.

Cohen, M. D., & Levinthal, D. (1990). Absorptive capacity: A new perspective on learning and innovation. *Administrative Science Quarterly, 35,* 128–152.

Cohen, M. D., March, J. G., & Olsen, J. P. (1972). A garbage can model of organizational choice. *Administrative Science Quarterly, 17,* 1–25.

Cohen, M. D., & Sproull, L. S. (1991). Editor's introduction. *Organization Science, 2*(1), 1–13.

Commons, J. R. (1950). *The economics of collective action.* Madison, WI: University of Wisconsin Press.

Conant, R. C., & Ashby, W. R. (1970). Every good regulator of a system must be a model of that system. *International Journal of Systems Science, 1,* 89–97.

Conlisk, J. (1996). Why bounded rationality? *Journal of Economic Literature, 34*(2), 669–700.

Constant, E. W. (1980). *The origins of the turbojet revolution.* Baltimore: John Hopkins University Press.

Cooper, R. (1993). *Winning at new products.* Reading, MA: Addison-Wesley.

Cottrell , T. J. (1993, August). *Nonlinear dynamics in the emergence of new industries.* Paper presented at Academy of Management Conference, Miami, FL.

Couch, C. J. (1986). Elementary forms of social activity. In C. J. Couch, S. L. Saxton, & M. A. Katovich (Eds.), *Studies in symbolic interaction: The Iowa school.* Greenwich, CT: JAI Press.

Coyne, W. E. (1996, March). *Building a tradition of innovation* (pp. 1–16). The Fifth UK Innovation Lecture, Department of Trade and Industry, London.

Cyert, R. M., & March, J. G. (1963). *A behavioral theory of the firm.* Englewood Cliffs, NJ: Prentice Hall.

Daft, R. L., & Becker, S. (1978). *Innovation in organization.* New York: Elsevier.

Daft, R. L., & MacIntosh, N. B. (1981). A tentative exploration into the amount and equivocality of information processing in organizational work units. *Administrative Science Quarterly, 26,* 207–224.

Dalton, D. R., & Todor, W. D. (1979). Turnover turned over: An expanded and positive perspective. *Academy of Management Review, 7,* 212–218.

Damanpour, F., & Evan, W. M. (1984). Organizational innovation and performance: The problem of organizational lag. *Administrative Science Quarterly, 29,* 392–402.

David, P. (1987). Some new standards for the economics of standardization in the information age. In P. Dasgupta & P. Stoneman (Eds.), *Economic policy and technological performance* (pp. 206–239). Cambridge: Cambridge University Press.

Davis, S. M., & Lawrence, P. R. (1977). *Matrix.* Reading, MA: Addison-Wesley.

DiMaggio, P. J., & Powell, W. (1983). The iron cage revisited: Institutional isomorphism and collective rationality in organizational fields. *American Sociological Review, 48,* 147–161.

Dooley, K. (1997). A complex adaptive systems model of organizational change. *Nonlinear Dynamics, Psychology, and the Life Sciences, 1*(1), 69–97.

Dooley, K., & Van de Ven, A. H. (1997). The nonlinear dynamics of innovation. *Society for Chaos Theory in Psychology and the Life Sciences, 4*(1), 3–4.

Dooley, K., & Van de Ven, A. H. (1998*). A primer on diagnosing dynamic organizational processes* [Discussion paper]. Minneapolis, MN: Strategic Management Research Center.

Dooley, K., & Van de Ven, A. H. (1999a). *Explaining complex organizational dynamics. Organization Science* (in press).

Dooley, K., & Van de Ven, A. H. (1999b). *Organization change and innovation as cycles of divergence and convergence* [Discussion paper]. Minneapolis, MN: Strategic Management Research Center.

Dornblaser, B. M., Lin, T., & Van de Ven, A. H. (1989). Innovation outcomes, learning, and action loops. In A. H. Van de Ven, H. L. Angle, & M. S. Poole (Eds.), *Research on the management of innovation: The Minnesota studies* (pp. 193–218). New York: Ballinger/Harper & Row.

Dosi, G. (1982). Technological paradigms and technological trajectories. *Research Policy, 11,* 147–162.

Dosi, G. (1988). Sources, procedures, and microeconomic effects of innovation. *Journal of Economic Literature, 26,* 1120–1171.

Duncan, R., & Weiss A. (1979). Organizational learning: implications for organizational design. In B. M. Staw (Ed.), *Research in Organizational Behavior, 1.* Greenwich, CT: JAI Press.

Eisenhardt, K. (1989). Making Fast Strategic Decisions in High Velocity Environments. *Academy of Management Journal, 32,* 543–576.

Elliot J. E. (1983). Schumpeter and Marx on capitalist transformation: A reply. *Quarterly Journal of Economics, 98*(2), 333–336.

Etzioni, A. (1963). The epigenesis of political communities at the international level. *American Journal of Sociology, 68,* 407–421.

Evan, W. M. (1966). The organization set: Toward a theory of interorganizational relations. In J. D. Thompson (Ed.), *Approaches to organizational design* (pp. 175–191). Pittsburgh, PA: University of Pittsburgh Press.

Feldman, J. (1986). On the difficulty of learning from experience. In H. P. Sims, Jr. & D. A. Gioia (Eds.), *The thinking organization* pp. 263–291. San Francisco: Jossey-Bass.

Festinger, L., & Carlsmith, J. M. (1959). Cognitive consequences of forced compliance. *Journal of Abnormal Social Psychology, 58,* 203–210.

Fichman, M., & Leventhal, D. A. (1988). *Honeymoons and the liability of adolescence: A new perspective on duration dependence in social and organizational relationships.* Unpublished paper, Graduate School of Industrial Administration, Carnegie Mellon University, Pittsburgh, PA.

Freeman, C. (1986). *The economics of industrial innovation.* Cambridge, MA: MIT Press.

Friedman, R. A. (1991). *Trust, understanding, and control: Factors affecting support for mutual gains bargaining in labor negotiations.* Paper presented at the annual meeting of the Academy of Management, Miami, FL.

Galaskiewicz, J. (1985). Interorganizational relations. *Annual Review of Sociology, 11,* 281–304.

Galbraith, J. (1973). *Designing complex organizations.* Reading, MA: Addison-Wesley.

Garud, R. (1990). *Roles of researcher sub-communities in the development of a new technology: The case of cochlear implants* [Working paper draft]. Stern School of Business, New York University.

Garud, R. (1994). Cooperative and competitive behaviors during the process of creative destruction. *Research Policy, 23*(4), 385–394.

Garud, R. (1997). On the distinction between know-how, know-why and know-what in technological systems. In J. Walsh & A. Huff (Eds.), *Advances in strategic management* (pp. 81–101). Greenwich, CT: JAI Press.

Garud, R., & Ahlstorm, D. (1997a). Researchers = roles in negotiating the institutional fabric of technologies. *American Behavioral Scientist, 40*(4), 523–538.

Garud, R., & Ahlstrom, D. (1997b). Technology assessment: A socio-cognitive perspective. *Journal of Engineering and Technology Management, 14,* 25–48.

Garud, R., & Kumaraswamy, A. (1994). Coupling the technical and institutional faces of Janus in network industries. In R. Scott & S. Christensen (Eds.), *Advances in the institutional analysis of organizations: International and longitudinal studies* (pp. 226–242). Thousand Oaks, CA: Sage.

Garud, R., & Lampel, J. (1997). Product announcements and corporate reputations. *Corporate Reputation Review, 1*(1, 2) 114–118.

Garud, R., Nayyar, P., & Shapira, Z. (1997). Technological choices and the inevitability of errors. In R. Garud, P. Nayyar, & Z. Shapira (Eds.), *Technological innovation: oversights and foresights* (pp. 345–354). Cambridge, UK: Cambridge University Press.

Garud, R., & Rappa, M. (1994). A socio-cognitive model of technology evolution. *Organization Science, 5*(3), 344–362.

Garud, R., & Rappa, M. (1995). On the persistence of researchers in technology development. *Industrial and Corporate Change, 4*(3), 527–550.

Garud, R., & Van de Ven, A. H. (1987). *Innovation and the emergence of industries.* Best Paper Proceedings, Academy of Management National Meeting.

Garud, R., & Van de Ven, A. H. (1989a). Technological innovation and industry emergence: The case of cochlear implants. In A. H. Van de Ven, H. L. Angle, & M. S. Poole (Eds.), *Research on the management of innovation: The Minnesota studies* (pp. 489–535). New York: Ballinger/Harper & Row.

Garud, R., & Van de Ven, A. H. (1992). An empirical evaluation of the internal corporate venturing process. *Strategic Management Journal, 13,* 93–109.

Gellman Research Associates, Inc. (1976). Indicators of international trends in technological innovation.

Gell-Mann, M. (1994). *The quark and the jaguar.* New York: Freeman.

Gersick, C. (1988). Time and transition in work teams, *Academy of Management Journal, 31*(1), 9–41.

Gerth, H., & Mills, C. W. (1946). *Max Weber: Essays in sociology.* New York: Oxford University Press.

Gilfillan, S. G. (1935). *The sociology of invention.* Cambridge, MA: MIT Press.

Gleick, J. (1987). *Chaos: Making a new science.* New York: Penguin.

Goldman, J. E. (1985). Innovation in large firms. *Research on Technological Innovation, Management and Policy, 2,* 1–10.

Gordon, T. J., & Greenspan, D. (1988, August). Chaos and fractals: New tools for technological social forecasting. *Technological Forecasting and Social Change, 34,* 1–25.

Gould, S. J. (1982, April). Punctuated equilibrium—A different way of seeing. *New Scientist, 15,*137–141.

Gould, S. J. (1989). Punctuated equilibrium in fact and theory. *Journal of Social and Biological Structures, 12,* 117–136.

Graen, G. (1976). Role-making processes within complex organizations. In M. D. Dunnette (Ed.), *Handbook of industrial and organizational psychology* (pp. 1201–1246). Chicago: Rand McNally.

Greiner, L. E. (1970). Patterns of organizational change. In G. Dalton, P. R. Lawrence, & L. E. Greiner (Eds.), *Organizational change and development* (pp. 213–229). Homewood, IL: Irwin-Dorsey Press.

Granovetter, M. (1985). Economic action and social structure: The problem of embeddedness. *American Journal of Sociology, 78,* 481–510.

Hage, J. (1980). *Theories of organizations: form, processes, and transformation.* New York: Wiley Interscience.

Hage, J., & Aiken, M. (1970). *Social change in complex organizations.* New York: Random House.

Hagedoorn, J. (1989). *The dynamic analysis of innovation and diffusion: A study of process control.* London and New York: Pinter.

Hakansson, H. (1988). *Industrial technological development: A network approach.* London: Croom Heim.

Halpern, D. F. (1996). *Thought and knowledge: an introduction to critical thinking* (3rd ed.). Mahwah, NJ: Erlbaum.

Hannan, M., & Freeman, J. (1989). *Organizational ecology.* Cambridge, MA: Harvard University Press.

Harrigan, K. R. (1985). *Strategies for joint ventures.* Lexington, Mass.: Heath.

Harrison, J. R., & March, J. G. (1984). Decision-making and postdecision surprises. *Administrative Science Quarterly, 29,* 26–42.

Hauptman, O., and E. B. Roberts (1985). *The impact of regulatory constraints on formation and growth of biomedical and pharmaceutical start-ups.* Working paper WP/1651–85. Cambridge: MIT Sloan School of Management.

Hearing Instruments. (1985). Why combine multichannel processing with a single electrode? *36*(6), 14–16.

Hedberg, B. L. T., Nystrom, P., & Starbuck, W. (1976). Camping on seesaws: Prescriptions for a self-designing organization. *Administrative Science Quarterly, 21,* 41–65.

Helson, H. (1948). Adaptation level as a basis for a quantitative theory of frames of references, *Psychological Review, 55,* 294–313.

Helson, H. (1964). Current trends and issues in adaptation-level theory. *American Psychologist, 19,* 23–68.

Henderson, R. M., & Clark, K. B. (1990). Architectural innovation: The reconfiguration of existing product technologies and the failure of established firms. *Administrative Science Quarterly, 35*(1), pp. 9–30.

Hibbert, B., & Wilkinson, I. F. (1994). Chaos theory and the dynamics of marketing systems. *Journal of the Academy of Marketing Science, 22*, 218–233.

Hirsch, P. M. (1975). Organizational effectiveness and the institutional environment. *Administrative Science Quarterly, 20*, 327–344.

Howell, J. M., & Higgins, C. A. (1990). Champions of technological innovation. *Administrative Science Quarterly, 35*, 317–341.

Huber, G. P. (1991). Organizational learning: The contributing processes and the literatures. *Organization Science, 2*(1), 88–115.

Huber, G. P., Sutcliffe, K. M., Miller, C. C., & Glick, W. H. (1993). Understanding and predicting organizational change. In G. P. Huber & W. H. Glick (Eds.), *Changing and redesigning organizations* (pp. 215–265). New York: Oxford University Press.

Hughes, T. P. (1983). *Networks of power: Electrification in western society, 1880–1930.* Baltimore: Johns Hopkins University Press.

Hull, D. L. (1988). *Science as a process: An evolutionary account of the social and conceptual development of science.* Chicago: University of Chicago Press.

Hurwicz, L. (1993). Institutional change: Endogenous evolution vs. design. *Journal of Comparative Economics, 17.*

Janis, I (1972). *Victims of Groupthink.* Boston: Houghton Mifflin.

Jantsch, E. (1980). *The self-organizing universe.* Elmsford, NY: Pergamon Press.

Jayanthi, S., & Sinha, K. K. (1998). Innovation implementation in high technology manufacturing: Chaos-theoretic empirical analysis. *Journal of Operations Management, 16*, 471–494.

Jelinek, M. (1997). Organizational entrepreneurship in mature industry firms: Foresight, oversight and invisibility. In R. Garud, P. Nayyar, & Z. Shapira (Eds.), *Technological innovation: oversights and foresights* (pp. 181–213). Cambridge, UK: Cambridge University Press.

Jelinek, M., & Schoonhoven, C. B. (1990). *The innovation marathon: Lessons from high technology firms.* Cambridge, MA: Basil Blackwell.

Jewkes, J., Sawers D., & Stillerman R. (1958). *The sources of invention.* New York: MacMillan.

Kanter, R. M. (1983). *The change masters.* New York: Simon & Schuster.

Kanter, R. M. (1988). When a thousand flowers bloom: Structural, collective and social conditions for innovation in organizations. In B. M. Staw & L. L. Cummings (Eds.), *Research in organizational behavior* (pp. 184–194). Greenwich, CT: JAI Press.

Katz, D., & Kahn, R. L. (1978). *The social psychology of organizations.* New York: Wiley.

Kauffman, S. (1989). *The origins of order.* New York: Oxford University Press.

Kauffman, S. (1995). *At home in the universe.* Oxford: Oxford University Press.

Kelly, H. H., & Theibault, J. W. (1959). *The social psychology of groups.* New York: Wiley.

Kerr, S. (1975). On the folly of rewarding *A*, while hoping for *B*. *Academy of Management Journal. 18*, 769–783.

Killing, R. (1982). How to make a global joint venture work. *Harvard Business Review, 60*(3), 120–127.

Kimberly, J. R. (1981). Managing innovation, in P. Nystrom & W. Starbuck (Eds.), *Handbook of organizational design* (vol. 1, pp. 84–104). Oxford: Oxford University Press.

Kirzner, I. (1973). *Competition and entrepreneurship.* Chicago: University of Chicago Press.

Knudson, M. K., & Ruttan, V. W. (1989). The management of research and development of a biological innovation. In A. H. Van de Ven, H. L. Angle, & M. S. Poole (Eds.), *Research on the management of innovation: The Minnesota studies* (pp. 465–488). New York: Ballinger/Harper & Row.

Koput, K. (1992). *Dynamics of innovative idea generation in organizations: Randomness and chaos in the development of a new medical device.* Unpublished Ph.D. dissertation, School of Business, University of California at Berkeley.

Koput, K. (in press). A chaotic model of innovative search: Some answers, many questions. *Organization Science.*

Kuhn, T. S. (1982). *The structure of scientific revolutions.* Homewood, IL: Richard Irwin.

Lant, T. K., & Mezias, S. J. (1990). Managing discontinuous change: A simulation study of organizational learning and entrepreneurial strategies. *Strategic Management Journal, 11*, 147–179.

Lave, C. A., & March, J. G. (1975). *An introduction to models in the social sciences.* New York: Harper & Row.

Lawler, E. E., & Rhode, J. G. (1976). *Information and control in organizations.* Pacific Palisades, CA: Goodyear.

Layton, E. (1986). Technology as knowledge. *Technology and Culture, 15*, 31–41.

Leavitt, H. J. (1965). Applied organizational change in industry: Structural, technological, and humanistic approaches. In J. March (Ed.), *Handbook of organizations* (pp. 1144–1170). Chicago: Rand McNally.

Leblebici, H., Salancik, G. R., Copay, A., & King, T. (1991). Institutional change and the transformation of interorganizational fields: An organizational history of the U.S. radio broadcasting industry. *Administrative Science Quarterly, 36*(3) 333–363.

Levinthal, D. (1997). Three faces of organizational learning: Wisdom, inertia, and discovery. In R. Garud, P. Nayyar, & Z. Shapira (Eds.), *Technological innovation: Oversights and foresights* (pp. 167–180). Cambridge, UK: Cambridge University Press.

Levinthal, D., & March, J. G. (1981). A model of adaptive organizational search. *Journal of Economic Behavior and Organization, 2*, 307–333.

Levinthal, D., & Warglien, M. (in press). Landscape design: Designing for local action in complex worlds. *Organization Science.*

Levitt, B., & March, J.G. (1988) Organizational learning. *Annual Review of Sociology, 14*, 319–340.

Lewin, K. (1945). The research center for group dynamics at Massachusetts Institute of Technology. *Sociometry, 8,* 126–135.

Lindquist, K., & Mauriel, J. (1989). Depth and breadth in innovation implementation: The case of school-based management. In A. H. Van de Ven, H. L. Angle, & M. S. Poole (Eds.), *Research on the management of innovation: The Minnesota studies* (pp. 561–582). New York: Ballinger/Harper & Row.

Loeb, G. E. 1985. The functional replacement of the ear. *Scientific American, 252*(2), 104–111.

Lowenstein, G. F., Thompson, L., & Bazerman, M. H. (1989). Social utility and decision making in interpersonal context. *Journal of Personality and Social Psychology,* 57, 426–441.

Maitland, I. (1982). Organizational structure and innovation: The Japanese case. In S. Lee & G. Schwendiman (Eds.), *Management by Japanese systems* (pp. 55–66). New York: Prager.

Mansfield, E. (1985, December). How rapidly does new industrial technology leak out? *Journal of Industrial Economics, 34*(2), 217–223.

Manz, C. C., Bastien, D. T., Hostager, T. J., & Shapiro, G. L. (1989). Leadership and innovaiton: A longitudinal process view. In A. H. Van de Ven, H. L. Angle, & M. S. Poole, *Research on the management of innovation: The Minnesota studies* (pp. 613–636). New York: Ballinger/Harper & Row.

March, J. G. (1976). The technology of foolishness. Reprinted in J. March & J. Olsen, *Ambiguity and choice in organizations* (pp. 69–81). Bergen: Universitetsforlaget. (Original work published 1972)

March, J. G. (1981). Footnotes to organizational change. *Administrative Science Quarterly, 26*(4) 563–577.

March, J. G. (1991). Exploration and exploitation in organizational learning. *Organization Science, 2*(1) 71–87.

March, J. G. (1994). *A primer on decision-making.* New York: Free Press.

March, J. G., & Olsen, J. P. (1975). The uncertainty of the past: Organizational learning under ambiguity. *European Journal of Political Research, 3,* 141–171.

March, J.G., & Olsen, J. P. (1976). *Ambiguity and choice in organizations.* Bergen: Universitetsforlaget.

March, J. G., & Olsen, J. P. (1989). *Rediscovering institutions: The organizational basis of politics.* New York: Free Press.

March, J. G., & Simon, H. A. (1958). *Organizations.* New York: Wiley.

March, J. G., Sproull, L. S., & Tamuz, M. (1991). Learning from fragments of experience. *Organization Science, 2*(1), 1–13.

Marcus, A., & Weber, M. (1989). Externally induced innovation. In A. H. Van de Ven, H. L. Angle, & M. S. Poole (Eds.), *Research on the management of Innovation: The Minnesota studies* (pp. 537–560). New York: Ballinger/Harper & Row.

Marx, K. (1906). *Capital. 1.* New York: Modern Library. (Original work published 1867)

Masuch, M. (1985). Vicious cycles in organizations. *Administrative Science Quarterly, 30,* 14–33.

Mattsson, L. G. (1987). Management of strategic change in a "markets-as-networks" perspective. In A. Pettigrew (Ed.), *The management of strategic change* (pp. 234–256). London: Basil Blackwell.

McKelvey, B. (1982). *Organizational systematics: Taxonomy, evolution, classification.* Berkeley: University of California Press.

Meindl, J. R., Ehrlich, S. B., & Dukerich, J. M. (1985). The romance of leadership. *Administrative Science Quarterly, 30,* 78–102.

Metcalfe, J. S., & Soete, L. (1983, April). *Notes on the evolution of technology and international competition.* Paper presented at Science and Technology Policy, University of Manchester.

Meyer, A. D., Goes, J. B., & Brooks, G. R. (1993). Organizations in hyper-turbulence: Environmental jolts and industry revolutions. In G. P. Huber & W. H. Glick (Eds.), *Changing and redesigning organizations* (pp. 66–111). New York: Oxford University Press.

Meyer, J. W., & Rowan, B. (1977). Institutionalized organizations: Formal structure as myth and ceremony. *American Journal of Sociology, 83*(2) 340–363.

Milliken, F. J., & Lant, T. K. (1991). *The role of managerial interpretations in determining strategic persistence and change.* Paper presented at Academy of Management conference in San Francisco.

Mintzberg, H., Raisinghani, D., & Theoret, A. (1976). The structure of "unstructured" decision processes. *Administrative Science Quarterly, 21,* 246–275.

Mitchell, T. R., Green, S. W., &Wood, R. (1981). An attributional model of leadership and the poor performing subordinate. In L. L. Cummings & B. M. Staw (Eds.), *Research in organizational behavior* (vol. 3.) (pp. 197–234). Greenwich, CT: JAI Press.

Mitnick, B. M. (1980). *The political economy of regulation: Creating, designing, and removing regulatory forms.* New York: Columbia University Press.

Morgan, G. (1986). *Images of organizations.* Beverly Hills, CA: Sage.

Morrison, F. (1991). *The art of modeling dynamic systems.* New York: Wiley.

Mowery, D. C. (1985). *Market structure and innovation: A critical survey.* Paper presented at conference on New Technology as Organizational Innovation at the Netherlands Institute for Advanced Studies in Humanities, Wassenaar.

Mowery, D. C., & Rosenberg, N. (1979, April). The influence of market demand upon innovation: A critical review of some recent empirical studies. *Research Policy 8,* 103–150.

Mueller, W. F. (1962). The origins of the basic inventions underlying DuPont's major product and process innovations, 1920–1950. In R. R. Nelson (Ed.), *The rate and direction of inventive activity.* Princeton, NJ: Princeton University Press.

Murmann, P., & Tushman, M. L. (1997). Impacts of executive team characteristics and organizational context on organization responsiveness to environmental shock. In R. Garud, P. Yayyar, & Z. Shaira (Eds.), *Technological innovation: Oversights and foresights* (pp. 220–243). Cambridge: Cambridge University Press.

Murtha, T. P., Spencer, J. W., & Lenway, S. A. (1996). Moving targets: National industrial strategies and embedded innovation in the global flat panel display industry. *Advances in Strategic Management, 13,* 247–281.

Nelson, R. N. (1982). *Government and technical progress: A cross-industry analysis.* New York: Pergamon Press.

Nelson, R. N., & Winter, S. G. (1977). In search of a useful theory of innovation. *Research Policy, 6,* 36–76.

Nisbett, R., & Ross, L. (1980). *Human inference: Strategies and short-comings of social judgment.* Englewood Cliffs, NJ: Prentice Hall.

Nohria, N., & Eccles, R. G. (1992). *Networks and organizations: Structure, form, and action.* Cambridge, MA: Harvard Business School Press.

Nonaka, I. (1994). A dynamic theory of organizational knowledge creation. *Organization Science, 5*(1), 14–37.

Nord, W. R., & Tucker, S. (1987). Implementing routine and radical innovations. Lexington, MA: Heath.

North, D. D. (1990). *Institutions, institutional change and economic performance.* Cambridge: Cambridge University Press.

North, D. C., & Thomas, R. P. (1973). *The rise of the Western world.* London: Cambridge University Press.

Nutt, P. C. (1984). Types of organizational decision processes. *Administrative Science Quarterly, 29,* 414–450.

Oliver, C. (1990). Determinants of interorganizational relationships: Integration and future directions. *Academy of Management Review, 15,* 241–265.

Olson, M. (1965). The logic of collective action: Public goods and the theory of groups. Cambridge, MA: Harvard University Press.

Organization Science. (1992). Special issue on Organization Learning, Vol. 2, No. 1.

Ouchi, W. G., & Bolton, M. K. (1987). *The logic of joint research and development* [Working paper]. Graduate School of Management, University of Southern California–Los Angeles.

Pelz, D. C. (1985). Innovation complexity and the sequence of innovating stages. *Knowledge, Creation, Diffusion, and Utilization, 6*(3), 261–291.

Perrow, C. A. (1961). The analysis of goals in complex organizations. *American Sociological Review, 26,* 854–866.

Peters, T. (1991). *Thriving on chaos.* New York: HarperCollins.

Peters, T. J., & Waterman, R. H., Jr. (1982). *In search of excellence: Lessons from America's best known companies.* New York: Harper & Row.

Pfeffer, J., & Salancik, G. (1978). *The external control of organizations.* New York: Harper & Row.

Pinch, T. F., & Bijker, W. E. (1987). The social construction of facts and artifacts: Or how the sociology of science and the sociology of technology might benefit each other. In W. E. Bijker, T. P. Hughes, & T. F. Pinch (Eds.), *The social construction of technological systems: New directions in the sociology and history of technology.* Cambridge, MA: MIT Press.

Polley, D., & Van de Ven, A. H. (1995). Learning by discovery during innovation development. *International Journal of Management, 11*(7/8), 871–882.

Polkinghorne, J. (1989). *Science and creation: The search for understanding.* Boston: Schambhala New Science Library.

Polyani, M. (1966). *The tacit dimension.* London: Routledge & Kegan Paul.

Poole, M. S., & Van de Ven, A. H. (1989). Toward a general theory of innovation processes. In A. H. Van de Ven, H. L. Angle, & M. S. Poole (Eds.), *Research on the management of innovation* (pp. 637–662). New York: Ballinger/Harper & Row.

Poole, M. S., & Van de Ven, A. H. (1995). Explaining development and change in organizations. *Academy of Management Review, 20*(3), 510–540.

Poole, M. S., Van de Ven, A. H., Dooley, K. J., & Holmes, M. (1999). *Studying processes of organizational change and development: Theory and methods.* New York: Oxford University Press.

Porter, M. E. (1980). *Competitive strategy: Techniques for analyzing industries and competitors.* New York: Free Press.

Porter, M. E. (1985). *Competitive advantage.* New York: Free Press.

Powell, W. W. (1990). Neither market nor hierarchy: Network forms of organization. In L. L. Cummings & B. Staw (Eds.) *Research in organizational behavior* (pp. 295–336). Greenwich, CT: JAI Press.

Powell, W. W., & DiMaggio, P. (1991). *The new institutionalism in organizational analysis.* Chicago: University of Chicago Press.

Powell, W. W., & Smith-Doerr, L. (1994). Networks and economic life. In N. J. Smelser & R. Swedberg (Eds.), *The handbook of economic sociology.* Princeton, NJ: Princeton University Press.

Pressman, J. L., & Wildavsky, A. B. (1973). *Implementation: How great expectations in washington are dashed in Oakland Or why it's amazing that federal programs work at all.* Berkeley: University of California Press.

Pruitt, D. G., & Rubin, J. Z. (1986). *Social conflict.* New York: Random House.

Quinn, J. B. (1985, May–June). Managing innovation: Controlled chaos. *Harvard Business Review,* 73–84.

Quinn, R. E. (1988). *Beyond rational management: Mastering the paradoxes and competing demands of high performance.* San Francisco: Jossey-Bass.

Quinn, R. E., & Cameron, K. S. (1988). *Paradox and transformation: Toward a theory of change in organization and management.* Cambridge, MA: Ballinger/Harper & Row.

Quinn, R. E., Dixit, N., & Faerman, R. (1987). *Some archetypes of managerial performance* [Working paper]. Institute for Government and Policy Studies, State University of New York, Albany.

Quinn, R. E., & Rohrbaugh, J. (1983). A spatial model of effectiveness criteria: Toward a competing values approach to organizational analysis. *Management Science, 29,* 362–377.

Radcliffe, E. 1984. The cochlear implant: Its time has come. *Hearing Journal, 37*(11), 9–10.

Rappa, M. (1987). *The structure of technological revolutions: An empirical study of the development of III-V compound semiconductor technology.* Unpublished dissertation, Carlson School of Management, University of Minnesota, Minneapolis.

Rappa, M. (1989). Assessing the emergence of new technologies: The case of compound semiconductors. In A. H. Van de Ven, H. L. Angle & M. S. Poole, *Research on the management of innovation: The Minnesota studies* (pp. 439–464). New York: Ballinger/Harper & Row.

Reynolds, P., & West, S. (1985). New firms in Minnesota: Explorations in economic change. *CURA Reporter* (Center for Urban and Regional Affairs, University of Minnesota). Presented at Academy of Management Conference, San Diego.

Rice, R., & Rogers, E. (1980). Reinvention in the innovation process. *Knowledge: Creation, Diffusion and Utilization, 1*(4), 499–514.

Ring, P. S., & Van de Ven, A. H. (1992). Structuring cooperative relationships between organizations. *Strategic Management Journal, 13,* 483–498.

Ring, P.S., & Van de Ven, A. H. (1994). Developmental processes of cooperative interorganizational relationships. *Academy of Management Review, 19*(1), 90–118.

Roberts, E. B., & Hauptman, O. (1986). The process of technology transfer to the new biomedical and pharmaceutical firm. *Research Policy, 15,*107–119.

Roberts, N. C. & King, P. J. (1989). The process of public policy innovation. In A. H. Van de Ven, H. L. Angle, and M. S. Poole (Eds.), *Research on the management of innovation: The Minnesota studies* (pp. 303–336). New York: Ballinger/Harper & Row.

Rogers, E. M. (1995). *The diffusion of innovations* (4th ed.). New York: Free Press.

Rosen, B., & Jerdee, T. H. (1974). Factors influencing disciplinary judgments. *Journal of Applied Psychology, 3,* 327–331.

Rosenberg, N. (1983). *Inside the black box. Technology and economics.* Cambridge: Cambridge University Press.

Rosenberg, N., & Birdzell, L. E., Jr. (1986). *How the West grew rich.* Berkeley: University of California Press.

Rosenbloom, R. S. (1966). Product innovation in a scientific age, new ideas for successful marketing (ch. 23). *Proceedings of the 1966 World Congress.*

Ross, J., & Staw, B. (1986). Expo 86: An escalation prototype. *Administrative Science Quarterly, 31,* 274–297.

Ruhla, C. (1992). *The physics of chance.* Oxford: Oxford University Press.

Ruttan, V. W. (1978). Induced institutional change. In H. P. Binswanger & V. W. Ruttan (Eds.), *Induced innovation: Technology, institutions and development* (pp. 327–357). Baltimore: Johns Hopkins University Press.

Ruttan, V. W., & Hayami, Y. (1984). Toward a theory of induced institutional innovation. *Journal of Development Studies, 20*(4), 203–223.

Salancik, G. R., & Meindl, J. R. (1984). Corporate attributions as strategic illusions of management control. *Administrative Science Quarterly, 29,* 238–254.

Schein, E. (1969). *Organizational psychology.* New York: Prentice Hall.

Schon, D. A. (1967). *Technology and change: The impact of invention and innovation on American social and economic development.* New York: Delacorte.

Schoonhoven, C. B., & Eisenhardt, K. (1985). *Influence of organizational, entrepreneurial, and environmental factors on the growth and development of technology-based startup firms: A research proposal.* Unpublished manuscript.

Schroeder, R. G., Van de Ven, A. H., Scudder, G. D., & Polley, D. (1986). Managing innovation and change processes: Findings from the Minnesota Innovation Research Program. *Agribusiness Management, 2*(4), 501–523.

Schroeder, R. G., Van de Ven, A. H., Scudder, G. D., & Polley, D. (1989). The development of innovation ideas. In A. H. Van de Ven, H. L. Angle, & M. S. Poole (Eds.), *Research on the management of innovation: The Minnesota studies* (pp. 107–134). New York: Ballinger/Harper & Row.

Schultz, T. W. (1968). Institutions and the rising economic value of man. *American Journal of Agricultural Economics, 50,* 1113–1122.

Schumpeter, J. A. (1942). *Capitalism, socialism, and democracy.* New York: Harper & Row.

Scott, W. R. (1987). The adolescence of institutional theory. *Administrative Science Quarterly, 32,* 493–511.

Scott, W. R. (1995). *Institutions and organizations: Attempting a theoretical synthesis.* Thousand Oaks, CA: Sage.

Scudder, G. D., Schroeder, R. G., Van de Ven, A. H., Seiler, G. R., & Wiseman, R. M. (1989). Managing complex innovations: The case of defense contracting. In A. H. Van de Ven, H. L. Angle, & M. S. Poole (Eds.), *Research on the management of innovation: The Minnesota studies* (pp. 401–438). New York: Ballinger/Harper & Row.

Selznick, P. (1957). *Leadership in administration.* New York: Harper & Row.

Senge, P. (1998). *Towards an ecology of leadership: An emerging systems theory of leadership and profound organizational change.* [Discussion Paper]. Cambridge, MA: MIT Sloan School.

Shapira, Z. (1995). *Risk taking: A managerial perspective.* New York: Russell Sage.

Sheridan, J. H. (1994, December 19). Lew Platt: Creating a culture for innovation. *Industry Week,* pp. 26–30.

Siegler, R. S. (1983). Five generalizations about cognitive development. *American Psychologist, 69,* 493–515.

Simmons, B. (1985). Cochlear implants in young children: Some dilemmas. *Ear and Hearing, 6*(1).

Simon, H. A. (1945). *Administrative behavior.* New York: Free Press.

Simon, H. A. (1962). The architecture of complexity. *Proceedings of the American Philosophical Society, 106*, 467–482.

Simon, H. A. (1991). Bounded rationality and organizational learning. *Organization Science, 2*(1) 125–134.

Singh, J. V., Tucker, D. J., & House, R. J. (1986). Organizational legitimacy and liability of newness. *Administrative Science Quarterly*, 31, 171–193.

Sitkin, S. (1992). Learning through failure: The strategy of small losses. In L. Cummings & B. Staw (Eds.), *Research in organizational behavior* (pp. 231–266). San Francisco: JAI Press.

Smith, A. (1937). *The wealth of nations*. New York: Modern Library. (Original work published 1776)

Starbuck, W. (1983). Organizations as action generators. *American Journal of Sociology, 48*(1) 91–115.

Starbuck, W. H. (1988). Surmounting our human limitations. In R. E. Quinn & K. S. Cameron (Eds.), *Paradox and transformation: Toward a theory of change in organization and management* (pp. 65–80). Cambridge, MA: Ballinger/Harper & Row.

Staw, B. (1980). The consequences of turnover. *Journal of Occupational Behavior, 1*, 253–273.

Staw, B. M., McKechnie, P. I., & Puffer, S. M. (1983). The justification of organizational performance. *Administrative Science Quarterly, 28*, 582–600.

Staw, B. M., & Ross, J. (1987). Behavior in escalation situations: Antecedents, prototypes and solutions. In L. L. Cummings & B. M. Staw (Eds.), *Research in organizational behavior*. Greenwich, CT: JAI Press.

Stern, N. & El-Ansery, A. I. (1982). *Marketing channels*. Englewood Cliffs, NJ: Prentice Hall.

Stigler, G. J. (1957). Perfect competition, historically contemplated. *Journal of Political Economy, 65*, 1–16.

Stinchcombe, A. L. (1965). Social structure and organizations. In J. G. March (Ed.), *Handbook of Organizations* (pp. 153–193). Chicago, Rand-McNally.

Stobaugh, R. (1985). Creating a monopoly: Product innovation in petrochemicals. In R. Rosenbloom (Ed.), *Research on technological innovation, management and policy* (pp. 81–112). New York: JAI Press.

Stryker, S. & Statham, A. (1985). Symbolic interaction and role theory. In G. Lindzay & E. Aronson (Eds.), *Handbook of social psychology* (3rd. ed., pp. 311–378). New York: Random House.

Sutcliffe, K. M. (in press). What executives notice: Accurate perceptions in top management teams. *Academy of Management Journal*.

Sutton, R. I. (1987, December). The process of organizational death: Disbanding and reconnecting. *Administrative Science Quarterly, 32*, 542–569.

Teece, D. (1987). Profiting from technological innovation: Implications for integration, collaboration, licensing, and public policy. In D. J. Teece (Ed.), *The competitive challenge* (pp. 185–220). New York: HarperCollins/Ballinger.

Thirtle C. G., & Ruttan, V. W. (1986). *The role of demand and supply in the generation and diffusion of technical change* [Bulletin No. 86–5]. University of Minnesota Economic Development Center, Minneapolis.

Thompson, J., & Tuden, A. (1959). Strategies, struct··· s, and processes of organizational decision. In J. D. Thompson et al. (Eds.), *Comparative studies in adminstration* (pp. 504). Pittsburgh, PA: University of Pittsburgh Press.

Tornatzky, L. G., & Fleischer, M. (1990). *The processes of technological innovation.* Lexington, MA: Heath.

Tuckman, B. W. (1965). Developmental sequences in small groups. *Psychological Bulletin, 63,* 384–399.

Tuma, N. B., & Hannan, M. T. (1984). *Social dynamics: Models and methods.* San Diego, CA: Academic Press.

Turner, J. H. (1987). Toward a sociological theory of motivation. *American Sociological Review, 52,* 15–27.

Tushman, M., & Anderson, A. (1986). Technological discontinuities and organizational environment. *Administrative Science Quarterly, 31,* 436–465.

Tushman, M., & O'Reilly III, C. A. (1997). *Winning through innovation: A practical guide to leading organizational change and renewal.* Boston: Harvard Business School Press.

Tushman, M., & Romanelli, E. (1985). Organizational evolution: A metamorphosis model of convergence and reorientation. In B. M. Staw & L. L. Cummings (Eds.), *Research in organizational behavior* (pp. 171–222). Greenwich, CT: JAI Press.

Tushman, M. L., & Rosenkopf, L. (1990). *On the organizational determinants of technological evolution: Towards a sociology of technology.* [Discussion paper]. Graduate School of Business, Columbia University, New York.

Tversky, A., & Kahneman, D. (1986). Rational choice in the framing of decisions. *Journal of Business, 59,* S251–S278.

Ury, W. L., Brett, J. M., & Goldberg, S. B. (1988). *Getting disputes resolved.* San Francisco: Jossey-Bass.

Usher, A. P. (1954). *A history of mechanical inventions.* Cambridge, MA: Harvard University Press.

Utterback, J. M. (1971). The process of technological innovation within the firm. *Academy of Management Journal, 14,* 75–88.

Utterback, J. M. (1974). Innovation in industry and the diffusion of technology. *Science, 183,* 620–626.

van den Daele, L. D. (1969). Qualitative models in developmental analysis. *Developmental Psychology, 1*(4) 303–130.

van den Daele, L. D. (1974). Infrastructure and transition in developmental analysis. *Human Development, 17,* 1–23.

Van de Ven, A. H. (1980). Problem solving, planning, and innovation. Part II. Speculations for theory and practice. *Human Relations, 33*(11) 757–779.

Van de Ven, A. H. (1985). Spinning on symbolism: The problem of ambivalence. *Journal of Management, 11*(2) 101–102.

Van de Ven, A .H. (1986). Central problems in the management of innovation. *Management Sciences, 32*(5), 590–607.

Van de Ven, A. H., Angle, H. L., & Poole, M. S. (Eds.). (1989). *Research on the management of innovation: The Minnesota studies.* New York: Ballinger/Harper & Row.

Van de Ven, A. H., Emmett, D., & Koenig, R., Jr. (1974). Frameworks for interorganizational analysis. *Organization and Administrative Sciences, 6*(1), 113–129.

Van de Ven, A. H., & Garud, R. (1989). A framework for understanding the emergence of new industries. *Research on technological innovation management and policy* (vol. 4, pp. 295–225). Greenwich, CT: JAI Press.

Van de Ven, A. H., & Garud, R. (1993). Innovation and industry development: The case of cochlear implants. In R. Burgelman & R. Rosenbloom (Eds.), *Research on technological innovation, management, and policy* (vol. 5, pp. 1–46). Greenwich, CT: JAI Press.

Van de Ven, A. H., & Grazman, D. (1997). Technological innovation, learning, and leadership. In R. Garud, P. Nayyar, and Z. Shapira (Eds.), *Technological innovation: Oversights and foresights* (pp. 279–305). New York: Cambridge University Press.

Van de Ven, A. H., & Lofstrom, S. M. (1997). *The diffusion and adoption of innovations in health care.* Public testimony before Subcommittee on Quality Improvement and Environment, President's Advisory Committee on Consumer Protection and Quality in Health Care Industry, Chicago.

Van de Ven, A. H., & Polley, D. (1992). Learning while innovating. *Organization Science, 3*(1), 92–116.

Van de Ven, A. H., & Poole, M. S. (1988). Paradoxical requirements for a theory of organizational change. In R. Quinn & K. Cameron (Eds.), *Paradox and transformation: Toward a theory of change in organization and management* (pp. 19–64). Cambridge, MA: Ballinger/Harper & Row.

Van de Ven, A. H., & Poole, M. S. (1995, July). Explaining development and change in organizations. *Academy of Management Review, 20*(3), 510–540.

Van de Ven, A. H., Venkataraman, S., Polley, D., & Garud, R. (1989). Processes of new business creation in different organizational settings. In A. H. Van de Ven, H. L. Angle, & M. S. Poole (Eds.), *Research on the management of innovation: The Minnesota studies* (pp. 221–298). New York: Ballinger/Harper & Row.

Van de Ven, A. H., & Walker, G. (1984). The dynamics of interorganizational coordination. *Administrative Science Quarterly, 29*(4), 598–621.

Venkataraman, S., & Van de Ven, A. H. (1998). Environmental jolts, transaction sets, and new business development. *Journal of Business Venturing, 13* (3), 231–255.

Virany, B., Tushman, M. L., & Romanelli, E. (1992). Executive succession and organizational outcomes in turbulent environments: An organizational learning approach. *Organization Science, 3,* 72–91.

von Hippel, E. (1988). The sources of innovation. New York: Oxford University Press.

von Hippel, E. (1990). The impact of sticky data on innovation and problem solving [Working paper 3147-90-BP]. MIT Sloan School of Management.

Weick, K. E. (1979). *The social psychology of organizing*, Reading, MA: Addison Wesley.

Weick, K. E. (1989). Theory construction as disciplined imagination. *Academy of Management Review, 14*(4), 516–531.

Weick, K. E. (1993). Sensemaking in organizations: Small structures with large consequences. In *J. K. Murningham (Ed.), Social psychology in organizations: Advances in theory and research* (pp. 10–37). Englewood Cliffs, NJ: Prentice Hall.

Weick, K. E. (1994). *Sensemaking in organizations.* Thousand Oaks, CA: Sage.

Williamson, O. E. (1975). *Markets and hierarchies.* New York: Free Press.

Williamson, O. E. (1985). *The economic institutions of capitalism.* New York: Macmillan.

Williamson, O. E. (1991). Comparative economic organization. *Administrative Science Quarterly, 36*, 269–296.

Zaltman, G., Duncan, R., & Holbek, J. (1973). *Innovations and organizations.* New York: Wiley.

Index

Lightning Source UK Ltd.
Milton Keynes UK
UKOW040831060912

198561UK00003B/12/P